Teaching Nineteenth-Century American Poetry

Modern Language Association of America
Options for Teaching

Joseph Gibaldi, series editor

For a complete listing of titles,
see the last pages of this book.

Teaching Nineteenth-Century American Poetry

Edited by

Paula Bernat Bennett,
Karen L. Kilcup, and
Philipp Schweighauser

The Modern Language Association of America
New York 2007

LIBRARY OF CONGRESS CATALOGING-IN-PUBLICATION DATA

Teaching nineteenth-century American poetry / edited by Paula Bernat Bennett, Karen L. Kilcup, and Philipp Schweighauser.
p. cm. — (Options for teaching ; 20)
Includes bibliographical references (p.) and index.
ISBN: 978-0-87352-821-4 (alk. paper)
ISBN: 978-0-87352-822-1 (pbk. : alk. paper)
1. American poetry—19th century—Study and teaching. I. Bennett, Paula. II. Kilcup, Karen L. III. Schweighauser, Philipp. IV. Modern Language Association of America.
PS306.T33 2007
811'.4071—dc22 2007009026
ISSN 1079-2562

Cover illustration of the paperback edition: *Flag Gate.* Artist unidentified. Jefferson County, New York, c. 1876. Paint on wood with iron and brass. Collection American Folk Art Museum, New York. Gift of Herbert Waide Hemphill, Jr. 1962.1.1. Photo by John Parnell, New York

Published by The Modern Language Association of America
26 Broadway, New York, New York 10004-1789
www.mla.org

For our students

Contents

Part IV: Resources

Paula Bernat Bennett and Karen L. Kilcup

Rethinking Nineteenth-Century American Poetry

With modernism's triumph in the twentieth century, no group of American writers suffered greater loss of prestige than did the preceding century's best-known poets. The beloved practitioners of a hugely popular art form, writers such as Lydia Huntley Sigourney, Frances Sargent Osgood, Henry Wadsworth Longfellow, and John Greenleaf Whittier seemed not only old-fashioned to those who supplanted them but also, in a profound sense, literarily naive: conventional, timid, excessively genteel. In schoolrooms and domestic settings, the names of the Fireside Poets—Longfellow, Whittier, William Cullen Bryant, Oliver Wendell Holmes, Sr., and James Russell Lowell—lingered; but their works, entombed in the tooled leather bindings of the Riverside Press's Household Editions, were without influence, the very accessibility of their writing at odds with the critical spirit of the new age. The rest, whatever the actual scope of their achievement, were simply forgotten, most of them as if they had never been. By 1970, the list of nineteenth-century American authors whose poetry was deemed worthy of teaching was winnowed down to three: Walt Whitman, Emily Dickinson, and Edgar Allan Poe.

Volumes devoted to Whitman and Dickinson have been part of the MLA's Approaches to Teaching list for many years. This volume, which marks a major milestone in nineteenth-century poetry's resurgence as an academic field, speaks to the long-neglected remainder: those poets, like Longfellow and Whittier, who were taken as canonical in their own period, and those who were not—principally women and minority poets. As the essays in this volume demonstrate, there are complex ways of understanding, teaching, and enjoying these other poets, but they are not, on the whole, those that the dominant formalist strains in modernism (be they high modernist or New Critical) valorized. In particular, these poets did not share modernism's fetishization of the word; instead, they privileged alternative means to evoke aesthetic pleasure and stimulate intellectual interest. In this introduction, we sketch the various cultural and critical contexts in which their poetry's specific kinds of literary complexity and value are best understood.

Poetry and the History of the Book

Although many United States literature departments still position American literature as a subset of a greater Anglo-American literary tradition, recovery work over the past four decades by Americanists specializing in popular and cultural studies and in the history of the book has seriously challenged this academic paradigm. Particularly salient here is our new understanding of the role that eighteenth-century newspapers and periodicals played in shaping how writers thought about and used their poetry during that century. Books were prohibitively expensive for the colonial press to manufacture; most, especially luxury items like poetry books, were imported from England. As a result, native-born poets had only local newspapers and magazines as publishing venues; and the ephemeral qualities attributed to these venues were attached to their content as well. By the beginning of the nineteenth century, this attachment ran so deep that, as Isabelle Lehuu observes in her study of antebellum popular literature, the American judiciary wrote it into law in 1829, refusing to extend to newspaper and periodical contents the same copyright protection that books enjoyed.

According to Lehuu, the unintended consequence of this judicial intervention was to free newspapers and periodicals to create a popular literary tradition outside "the constraints of copyright legislation" (8). But for poetry, this tradition was already well established by the time the court delivered its opinion. Appearing side by side with shipping news, advertisements for runaway slaves (or slaves for sale), foreign intelligence, and so forth, and unregulated by academics and reviewers, American poems had assumed the coloration of the largely occasional material surrounding them. Without abandoning the delivery of aesthetic pleasure entirely, they had become a free space where those with power, like Benjamin Franklin, and those without, like Phillis Wheatley, could voice with at least a modicum of equality their opinions on personal and social affairs. High-culture poets such as John Milton, Alexander Pope, and Thomas Gray remained the gold standard for "book poems" in America as in Britain. But for American writers, especially for those who, like Wheatley, were disenfranchised, poetry became one of the few ways that individuals, whoever they were, wherever they came from, could not only represent their interests in crucial public debates but could also circulate their opinions widely because of the venues in which they published.

Initially barred from the one venue that granted poetry uncontested status as high culture, American poetry thus made its way into the nineteenth century as a popular and quintessentially democratic form of social and political address. Sigourney, Bryant, Lowell, Whittier, Holmes, Julia Ward Howe, and the highly regarded black poet Frances Ellen Watkins Harper were among the many antebellum writers who followed eighteenth-century practice, taking advantage of newspaper and periodical publication to express their opinions on subjects ranging from Indian removal and the destruction of natural resources to abolition and the Civil War. As Lehuu observes of popular literature generally in the antebellum period, the ironic result of this pattern of publication was to give newspaper and periodical poetry its own kind of artistic clout:

> Quite different from the so-called great works of literature, yet not without creativity, popular media fostered change in the world of cultural goods. In essence the new print was as much an agent of [artistic] transformation as a result of concomitant changes in the economic and social conditions. (8)

Although those strongly commited to the traditional canon might not relish "the new print," what emerged was poetry of another kind. And the formal and thematic concerns of this other poetry would have every bit as much influence on the evolution of American verse as did its British models, if not more. By the time book publishing in the United States came into its own in the 1840s, this robust periodical tradition was so deeply rooted it could not be dislodged, and the popular character of nineteenth-century American poetry was established. It was a tradition in which what might otherwise have been the cultural power of a limited number of (high-culture) major figures was redistributed through a host of largely populist poets. Not just "the book-press" but "[t]he village journal—the fashionable periodical, the grave Review . . . are teeming with the effusions of thousands, who in number, if not in energy, may be called legion," wrote an 1848 reviewer for the *Southern Literary Messenger*, feeling "overburdened with the crowds of volumes" on his desk ("Hoffman's Poems" 98). Nineteenth-century anthologists such as Rufus W. Griswold, George B. Cheever, and Edmund C. Stedman (*American Anthology*) all tout the heterogeneous mix of newspaper, periodical, and book poets in their collections as a sign of American cultural fecundity, suggesting in the process that the line between popular and high culture had yet to be drawn. If Lawrence Levine is correct in *Highbrow/Lowbrow*, this line would not be drawn until the century's final decade. In the interim, reviewers—possibly faute de mieux, but possibly not—continued to insist that American poetry's popular or demotic base was its greatest asset, no matter how "overburdened" with the "teeming effusions of thousands" they may on occasion have felt.

How the Reviewers Saw It: Poetry as the Nation's Voice

Although nineteenth-century reviewers often seemed of two minds about the burden of poetry they were forced to bear, they were eager to facilitate the birth of a truly autonomous American cultural identity, which for them meant a democratic identity. Taking fecundity as a guarantor of democracy, they argued, in a way that would doubtless have appalled Henry James, that American readers were the best judge of what American writers should write. Indeed, until the century's last quarter, most reviewers affirmed the importance of popular taste even over their own judgment. Reviewing Goethe, the *North American Review* for October 1824 bluntly observes, "If the multitude and the critic are at variance, the latter is in the wrong" ("Life and Genius" 306). Similarly, in an April 1833 discussion of Hannah Gould's poetry, a reviewer for the *New-England Magazine* affirms:

> Popularity is, generally speaking, a sure test of merit; at least so much so, that a single critic, whose opinions differed from those of the public, should rather distrust his own judgment, than call in question the taste of the majority. ("Literary Portraits" 309)

Pondering William Wordsworth's relative unpopularity among American readers in 1839, the *Boston Quarterly Review* takes the same approach:

> The popular voice is the only authority to which we may appeal in matters of poetry. . . . The many approve only that which is common to human nature, which is general, adapted to the race. To say of a poet, that he is unpopular, is about the same as to say that he is no poet at all. (Rev. of Wordsworth's poems 150)

"Genius," this reviewer adds, "is essentially democratic; his voice is always music to the democracy" (151–52). "If . . . verse needs explanation or comment," the *North American Review* declares in 1847, "if one must be educated before he can understand it, or go through a particular training before he can appreciate it, the busy world will pass it by" (Rev. of Holmes 209). For all these reviewers, the demotic, the democratic, and the national were one. The common man was the best judge of his own reading matter; and the best reading matter was a direct reflection of the common man—as American democracy constructed him. This was the essence of their populist, nationalist aesthetic.

No more moving—or explicit—expression of this aesthetic occurs than in a review written by a Southerner in 1867, just after a war that had tested Americans' faith in democracy as it had never been tested before. Writing of Southern war poetry for the *Southern Review*, this reviewer sets aside his allegiance to the geopolitical boundaries in whose name the war was fought and speaks confidingly of the semianonymous ballads that were the war's single most distinctive literary product and one, significantly enough, whose production and enjoyment knew no boundaries at all. Addressing a set of texts a number of which had in fact been claimed by North and South alike, he declares:

> No man can, in a sense, write the ballads of a people. The people write their own ballads. . . . [T]he ballad poetry of a nation is the expression of its character and feelings, and only one who is thoroughly possessed with the national spirit can write the national ballads. (Rev. of *The Southern Poets* 273–74)

Holding to a view of the relation between poetry and its readers as interative, this reviewer, like others before him, echoes Whitman's populism:

> The poet, in this case, writes for contemporaries, not for posterity; he must follow, not lead; and he will be the most popular ballad writer

> through whom the spirit of his people and time finds its most vivid expression; who says for them what they feel, but cannot say for themselves; who translates into the rhythm of verse the pulses of the national feeling. (274)

The best poetry is that through which the people's voice is heard, not that of some remote figure elevated beyond their reach. Although by the end of the century a second poetic tradition had emerged (Levine 223–26), one for which British high culture was the unequivocal model, for most of the nineteenth century the great majority of American writers and readers understood poetry's role in these profoundly inclusive terms.

Poetry's Democratic Vistas

If on the writers' side nineteenth-century publishing and reviewing practices encouraged the democratization of poetry writing, on the readers' side the spread of literacy democratized poetry's audience. There was hardly a periodical or newspaper, no matter how unlikely, that did not publish some poetry—from agricultural magazines and law journals to those targeting minority readerships such as the Shakers and the Cherokee. "Poetry for the million will be the great characteristic, the land-mark of this age," concludes a reviewer in the 1848 *Southern Literary Messenger*. "The son of poverty," "the day-laborer and the retired scholar" have equal access to education. "Knowledge, then, has here become popular—universal—limitless and unceasing in its diffusion; furnished to the poor and rich, it has been—it shall be the principal 'factor' in American civilization" ("Hoffman's Poems" 98).

Having such a diverse audience, poets were encouraged to speak diversely. One only has to compare Dickinson's and Whitman's poetry to that of their British peers (e.g., Tennyson, the Brownings) to realize that the extensive and deliberate mixing of popular and high-culture poetic strategies was one of the most important ways that Americans radicalized their verse, doing so, moreover, with explicitly subversive intent. True, most mainstream writers made their reputations by writing elevated lyrics in the genteel style; but some—Lowell in "The Biglow Papers," Whittier in ballads like "Skipper Ireson's Ride" and "Barbara Frietchie"—wrote best when they wrote for and about the people. Conversely, committedly populist poets, from Longfellow and Sigourney to the Lowell mill girls, took high-culture forms (epics, odes, etc.) and revised them with popular audiences in mind. Herman Melville and the Southern poet Sarah Piatt can be viewed both ways: as elite writers who play with populist poetic strategies and draw material from everyday life and as popular writers whose formal concerns and challenging stylistics mark them as elite. Virtually all these poets seem to have felt free to appropriate whatever they found useful, decorums of genre and style notwithstanding. Nor did the emergence of modernism in the early twentieth century abolish expectations of poetic heterogeneity overnight. As Edward Brunner notes in the strategically placed final essay in this volume: "In the first half of the century, modernist and experimental poets appeared in anthologies alongside poets who employed traditional forms and cultivated popular and commercial success." Even T. S. Eliot had his popular moments, as witness *Cats*.

Poets mixed levels of subject matter as well. Dickinson, scholars now agree, wrote passionately on at least one occasional topic—the Civil War; but even her most seemingly transcendent poems are typically grounded one way or another in the material world, the world of the body and of social interchange. Across the century's broad spectrum, it would be difficult to find any poet of name, with the possible exception of Poe, who did not direct at least some of his or her verse to the real. Three of the century's most ardent advocates of idealist aesthetics—Lowell, Emerson, and Melville—all violate their own prescriptions, apparently incapable of or uninterested in actually maintaining a rigid barrier between art and life as it is actually lived. To Edmund Wilson's dismay, Melville drew directly from newspaper accounts for his Civil War poems in *Battle-Pieces* (479), most strikingly in "Donelson," where his chilling poetization of military and newspaper reports powerfully conveys the confusion and horror of the four-day battle. In "The Poet," Emerson, though no practitioner of realist poetics, called for a poet who would sing "[o]ur logrolling, our stumps and their politics, our fisheries, our Negroes, and Indians, our boasts and our repudiations" (*Works* [path: Centenary Ed.; vol. 3, essays 2]), giving Whitman's antitranscendental poetic all the legitimacy it needed.

Like Whitman, Emerson enjoyed vaunting his self-contradictions. From our perspective, however, these contradictions constitute the American (poetic) grain, and to teach nineteenth-century poetry, one must begin, as Gerald Graff might say, by teaching them. For they are the contradictions that American poetry's base in popular culture—not in British high culture—made inevitable. One must, that is, take seriously the Emersonian-Whitmanian vision of American poetry as central, not eccentric, to the writing that nineteenth-century America produced. In terms of current definitions of popular culture, this vision means presenting nineteenth-century poetry as democratic. As John Storey suggests in his discussion of the neo-Gramscian perspective on popular culture in *Cultural Theory and Popular Culture* (1998), popular culture is, effectively, democracy in action. Understood thus, Antonio Gramsci's definition is merely an update of Whitman's definition of democratic poetry, differences in framing notwithstanding:

> a contradictory mix of competing interests and values, neither middle nor working class, neither racist nor non-racist, neither sexist nor non-sexist, neither homophobic nor homophilic . . . but an always shifting balance between the two (what Gramsci calls "a compromise equilibrium"). (106)

One can argue whether or not Whitman ever succeeded in incorporating all these contradictions into his poetry. What matters is that he recognized that they were there and that their presence went to the heart of what nineteenth-century American poetry (like nineteenth-century American culture generally) was about. Although there are many other ways in which this poetry could be configured, the editors of this collection of essays have chosen to present it in this way.

How to Use This Book

While our volume's overall focus is on teaching nineteenth-century American poetry, we have broken the contents down into three distinct, if interrelated, categories, on the basis of shifts of emphasis among the essays themselves. These shifts pertain to whether an essayist was primarily interested in describing the parameters of a particular subset of poems (Native American poetry, Civil War poetry, erotic verse), in considering a particular poet in a particular context (Paul Lawrence Dunbar, Emma Lazarus, Lydia Sigourney), or in discussing specific strategies found to be useful when poets and poems were brought into the classroom. Philipp Schweighauser's resources section, part 4 of the book, offers a guide to the wealth of materials now available for those who want to pursue topics beyond the limits of our volume, whether in print or posted on the World Wide Web.

In part 1, "Teaching Various Kinds of Poems," essayists address some of the principal categories into which American poetry can be assigned.

To a far greater extent than poets today, nineteenth-century poets wrote in distinctive lyric subgenres whose conventions were laid out for them beforehand. Doing so, they subordinated individual expressivity to the expressivity available in and associated with the kind of poem they were writing or the kind of poet they wanted to be recognized as. These subgenres could and did evolve around occasional circumstances (the Civil War), the ethnicity or social status of the author (Native American poetry, sorrow songs, mill girl poetry), and the social or aesthetic function of the poem (schoolroom poetry, minstrel poetry, erotic poetry, realist poetry). With the exception of schoolroom poetry, where the status of the author is key to membership in the group, this kind of genre-based poetry is often either entirely or partially anonymous, dictating a classroom approach that treats each poem in terms of its kind rather than its author.

In the second part, "Teaching Poets in Context," essayists engage the oeuvres of well-known poets who in different ways used their individual positions outside the cultural mainstream as a basis for critique: Sigourney, Fuller, Harper, Lazarus, Crane, Dunbar, and Gilman. Unlike the writers in the first section, whose choice of genre or whose status as representative of a subgroup is the point of departure both for writing and analysis, those in this section are approached in ways that privilege their individual voices and the individual struggles that led them to incorporate their personal (and often adversarial) vision in their verse. As the essays in this section demonstrate, however, even with these writers too much emphasis on individual genius would be misleading. Rather the essayists look at how these poets situate themselves in relation to the particular context to which their text responds, be that context social, personal, religious, literary, or political.

In part 3, essayists offer readers a variety of strategies that they have found especially effective when teaching nineteenth-century American poetry in the classroom. Because these strategies were developed in the actual course of teaching, and were tailored for specific audiences, they are difficult to generalize about as a group—nor is it wise to, since each teacher finally must discover what works best for him or her. Suffice it to note here that the possibilities are limitless. Some teachers play poetry off against other genres, mixing narrative poems in with prose narrative, for example, or using paintings to help students explore the way in which literature encodes ideology. Other essayists frame their treatment of verse in relation to specific scholarly cruxes in their field—the parameters of the American Renaissance and the way in which sentimentality is defined—while still others give direct advice on how to organize syllabi to meet particular pedagogical ends.

In a coda to the volume, we include Edward Brunner's "In Newspapers, over Radio Waves, on Envelopes." Brunner surveys the survival of the nineteenth century's tradition of popular poetry into the twentieth century. He refers to twentieth-century poetry that appeared, as so much nineteenth-century poetry did, in a wide variety of ephemeral venues: not just newspapers and periodicals but also newer media, in particular the radio. In his concluding discussion of Archibald MacLeish's popular "The Young Dead Soldiers Do Not Speak," a poem that, written for radio performance in 1943, is still quoted by orators of all sorts today, Brunner concludes by suggesting that the nineteenth century's populist tradition in poetry is with us still, even if we have not yet discovered "the way to look for it."

Brunner's discussion, like the others in this book, reminds us of the continuing immediacy and value of the kind of popular verse that nineteenth-century poets produced. Attempting to foster new ways of evaluating this poetry, our volume, with its interlaced essays, presents an invitation and challenge to today's scholars and students to approach what they read from an aesthetic and pedagogical but also from a social and political perspective, even as those who wrote this poetry did. The conversations in this volume will, we hope, engender further conversations, assisting in the recovery of an invaluable set of voices whose continued loss would diminish us all.

Note

We would like to thank Mirjam Werndli and Cindy-Jane Armbruster from the University of Berne for their skilled proofreading assistance and give a special thank-you to Barbara McCaskill for her generous assistance.

Part I

Teaching Various Kinds of Poems

Betty Booth Donohue

Oktahutchee's Song: Reflections on Teaching Nineteenth-Century American Indian Poetry

Far, far, far are my silver waters drawn;
The hills embrace me, loth to let me go;
The maidens think me fair to look upon,
And trees lean over, glad to hear me flow.
Thro' field and valley, green because of me,
I wander, wander to the distant sea.

—Alexander Posey

American Indians began to learn English in the early seventeenth century, and as soon as they were fluent, they set their thoughts and imaginative constructs into print. Since American Indians had been contriving literary works and transmitting them either orally or in Native writing systems since the beginning of human time, writing in foreign languages presented no unusual challenges. By the late 1600s, Eastern Algonquian students at Harvard were writing sermons in Latin, and before the seventeenth century ended, American Indian writers began publishing autobiography and protest literature in English as soon as they realized that their political sovereignty was endangered and their population numbers were plummeting. The eighteenth century saw continued literary output by American Indians, and, by the nineteenth century, they had broadened their genre interests to include histories and journalistic pieces written in prose. During this period some Native writers began publishing poetry in English. Among the established poets are Jane Johnston Schoolcraft (Ojibwe), Pauline Johnson (Mohawk), Alexander Posey (Muskogee), Zitkala-Ša (Lakota), and John Rollin Ridge (Cherokee). For the most part, these writers enjoyed name recognition in the dominant society. In some circles they had followings, and Ridge was named California's first poet laureate.

There are many more nineteenth-century American Indian poets who were published regionally in small presses or in newspapers and then forgotten. The Cherokee poet Too-Qua-Stee, whose English name is De Witt Clinton Duncan, is one of these neglected writers. Undiscovered works of even more nineteenth-century American Indian poets have not yet come to light because much Native poetry still languishes in attics, state historical archives, tree trunks, and other neglected spots. Ho-Pah-Moie (1863–1938), an Osage eccentric known by English speakers as John Stink, often left his verse scattered in trees all over the town of Pawhuska, Oklahoma, where local journalists frequently gathered and printed it. Modern researchers can still find regional historians who have accumulated portions of similar unpublished material, and these archivists are usually willing to share their collections with literary scholars. Perhaps the most moving of the published nineteenth-century American Indian poetry is that written by young women attending the Cherokee Female Seminary in Tahlequah, Indian Territory. Portions of their work have been preserved, but much of it is difficult to access because it is often stored randomly with family records and papers. Because so much nineteenth-century American Indian poetry remains in obscurity, it is difficult to judge its scope.

That nineteenth-century American Indian poets indeed existed is not common academic knowledge, so when harried instructors teaching American survey courses find that they must include American Indian literature in their offerings, they may hesitate, given the marginality of the topic. Unfortunately there is a dearth of *Indian Cliffs Notes* available to scholars, and for that reason this essay is designed to give very general suggestions to those relatively unacquainted with the field.

Instructors teaching this genre may opt simply to present American Indian poems as objects complete in themselves and bring nothing extraneous to discussions. Such a New Critical decision is certainly allowable, for the poetry speaks for itself and can be appreciated on several aesthetic and interpretative levels. Other instructors will choose to contextualize the poetry either historically, anthropologically, or politically, and that approach can also be productive pedagogically because American Indians are inextricably linked to history and to their land bases, and their literature reflects those connections. Rarely are American Indian studies courses taught in our nation's secondary schools; consequently, undergraduates, who often "don't know much about geography," enter universities with little knowledge of American Indians or their histories. Having students research the Native poets and their tribal affiliations can give them entry into the field. Even though much American Indian writing contains references to tribal societies, the old gods, languages, and culture heroes, to insist that beginning scholars and instructors have a thorough grounding in tribal cosmologies and worldviews could put American Indian poetry out of the modern reader's reach. My advice is to approach the poetry and enjoy it. Students usually rise to a challenge, and professors are often open to new possibilities for research. From time to time, American Indian students enroll in literature classes, and they may enjoy opportunities to share their knowledge with others, although this supposition is certainly not a given. Some American Indian students can be quite reticent about their tribal groundings or personal backgrounds, and their reticence should be respected.

First-time scholars coming to American Indian literature should understand that this discipline has its own critical theory. American Indian literary works center on the notion that literature is logocentric. Word power is the basis of all power. In serious American Indian literary compositions, words are patterned in such a way that reality changes. American Indian literature past and present is not mimetic; it is generative. Nineteenth-century American Indian poetry derives from and furthers this tradition: when words are spoken, either something physical happens or the hearer learns a lesson that effects change. Power is set loose. Because change or intellectual growth is the expected outcome of most American Indian literary works, these pieces often demonstrate obvious didactic intent, ranging from the simple morals of fables (trickster tales) to the inspired teachings and healing capabilities of the sacred narratives. For the most part, the sacred narratives are remembered, not written. They are handed down from word keeper to word keeper, or from medicine man to medicine man, from century to century. These remembered works, or medicine texts, are usually referenced as the American Indian oral tradition. The compositional strategies of the ceremonial works are quite discernible in nineteenth-century American Indian poetry and in a significant measure inform it.

Certainly not all American Indian literature, however, qualifies as medicine texts. Less serious offerings are created for the same reasons any writer creates literature: a love of words, an exercise of leisure, an expression of sentiment, a flight of fancy, an assertion of intellect, or a determination to correct the record. Just as nineteenth-century American Indian poetry has ties to its roots in theme, function, and authorial intent, it also has close connections to the prevailing Euro-American literary standards of the nineteenth century in form, rhyme, and meter. Its kinship ties, therefore, present several options for reading and teaching. Although this essay deals largely with the period's more somber pieces, it must be noted that some nineteenth-century American Indian literature is frivolous, humorous, and occasionally suggestive. Posey's "When Molly Blows the Dinner Horn," "The Athlete and the Philosopher," and "Kate and Lou" provide examples.

According to American Indian critical theory, narrative originates in the land. The earth supplies the forms in which the gods and their stories reside, and everything begins with a story. The place where an event occurs is central to the interpretation of the piece because the earth is first text. (For more on this concept, see Scarberry-Garcia.) In American Indian literature, there are myriad references to land and nature, but they should not be treated with the same intellectual mind-set that one uses in approaching Romantic poets, nationalistic bards, or nature writers. Nature is neither background nor inspirational source. It is interpretative center. As a general rule, readers should give land and animals the same attention that they give human characters.

To teach nineteenth-century American Indian poetry with historical accuracy, modern scholars must realize that the century brought traumatic social changes to American Indian people. The official government programs designed to address the "Indian problem" were first extinction, then assimilation. Helen Hunt Jackson speaks of the century as "a century of dishonor," and her book by that title, issued in 1881, details many outrages perpetrated against American Natives. It was in the nineteenth century that most American Indians lost their homelands and were subjected to forced removals during which thousands died. Others were killed by indirect means, such as starvation occasioned by the destruction of Native food supplies or by the government's issue of blankets infected with smallpox.

General Philip Henry Sheridan is credited with saying, "The only good Indian is a dead Indian," and that sentiment, for a time, ruled the day. Entire nations were systematically decimated. Survivors were forced onto reservations in desolate regions where food was inadequate and housing deplorable. Wandering bands were occasionally destroyed for no pressing military reason. The massacres at Sand Creek and Wounded Knee are two examples of such unprovoked attacks. In California, bounties were paid for Indian scalps at least until 1870. In "Estimating Aboriginal American Population," the demographer Henry Dobyns posits that at Contact, roughly ten million American Indians lived in the area now known as the United States. By 1990, only two million American Indians remained. Despite these figures, American Indians have not disappeared, and the idea of the vanishing Indian, once a political concern and a reasonable fear, is a cultural myth.

The Medicine Lodge Treaty of 1867 settled the Southern Plains people on reservations, while the Fort Laramie Treaties of 1851 and 1868 relegated the Northern Plains nations to similar restricted areas. The 1868 Treaty with the Navajos confined the Dine to a small region in the Southwest. California and Nevada tribes were hunted to near extinction. All these treaties, as well as the various instruments exiling approximately fifty tribes to Indian Territory, allowed railroads passage through the reservations, with the result that non-Indians with their enterprises associated with interstate trade were given access to American Indian lands. The government, furthermore, encouraged missionaries to proselytize the Natives, and it set up schools for Native children that were staffed by non-Indians. The convergence of commerce and non-Native influence on reservations brought about inevitable changes in Native society, modifications that the federal policies intended.

After American Indians were subdued, the assimilation program began. Again, the killing metaphor prevailed. "Kill the Indian, Save the Man" was the personal motto of Richard Pratt, founder of Carlisle Indian School, which was one of the nation's first nineteenth-century off-reservation boarding schools. (Harvard was the first.) To civilize the so-called uncivilized, the United States removed children from their families; incarcerated them in boarding or missionary schools; forced them to speak English; and inculcated in them the notion that Native cultures were savage, brutal, inferior, and repugnant. At such schools children were taught basic academic competencies, the Christian faith, social graces, and menial job skills that would keep them at the bottom of the sociopolitical ladder for the rest of their lives. For more information on American Indian history, Dee Brown's *Bury My Heart at Wounded Knee*, Helen Hunt Jackson's *A Century of Dishonor*, Francis Jennings's *The Invasion of America*, and David Stannard's *American Holocaust: The Conquest of the New World* are excellent resources. Books on American Indian cultures are plentiful, and the serious researcher should look for tribally specific volumes. General reference tools dealing with several tribes are usually too vague to be helpful.

Nineteenth-century history was brutal to American Indians. It is not surprising that Native writers found themselves in intellectual and spiritual quandaries. They were living in two worlds at once but were fully accepted in neither. As they watched their traditional lifestyles slip away, they were often troubled and emotionally reluctant to embrace the dominant culture wholeheartedly. Educated enough to be somewhat ill at ease in their old homes and uncertain of their place in modern America, they hovered like John Milton's Michael, "[b]etwixt the world destroyed and the world restored" (*Paradise Lost* 12.3). Because American Indian youth had been restrained, either by force or ridicule, from using their Native languages, the authentic voice they would instinctively have used for poetic expression was muffled. Exacerbating that problem even further was the want of adequate tribal writing systems and Native readers. The education the poets had received, grounded on the premise that Native cultures were primitive and worthy of neither transmission nor preservation, centered on the beliefs and values of the dominant society. Young American Indian poets exposed to this thinking ultimately found themselves assuming intellectual stances that to them must have seemed unsound and to modern readers now seem artificial. What was not stifled or modified, however, was the desire to write, and to borrow the modern Muskogee poet Joy Harjo's phrase, nineteenth-century American Indian poets employed the "enemy's language" (Harjo and Bird). Composing in English, these early Native poets fashioned a body of work that is obviously American Indian in terms of theme, nuance, tension, and intent.

Nineteenth-century Native students, like their non-Indian counterparts, studied both canonical and popular English-speaking writers in school and were imbued with the patriotism, heroics, and sentimentality of the period. When they began to write, it is not surprising that they tended at first to replicate what they had been taught in terms of poetic forms, appropriate subjects, and rhyme schemes. What is important now is the fact that they often retained Native metaphors, themes, and allusions. Typically, as the Native poets matured into skilled craftspeople, they developed styles that accommodated their heritages and were easier on the ear, but their first attempts tended to be clumsy and showed evidence of heavy borrowing from established poets. Percy Bysshe Shelley, John Keats, Alfred Noyes, Henry Wadsworth Longfellow, Edgar Allan Poe, and John Greenleaf Whittier were frequently copied, as were the more melodramatic versifiers like Robert Service and Hugh D'Arcy. In an American Indian world, it is acceptable to learn by imitation. Discovery is not valued over other kinds of epistemological acquisition. For the early poets, emulation was not only culturally imposed but was also to some degree inherent.

An example of the Indian patterning of established poets can be seen in Posey's first published poem, written while he was a student living in a frigid dormitory at Bacone Indian University. The poem appears in his collected works, compiled by his wife after the poet's premature death.

Death of a Window Plant

The air was chill,
The leaves were hushed,
The moon in grandeur
Climbed the spangled
Walls of heaven,
When the angel came
That whispers death;
Unseen, unheard,
To lisp that word, and
Leave my window
Sad when night should
Blossom into day.
The moon had waned.
And each bright star,
Like visions of a
Dream. . . .
. . . .
I mourned, and all
Was dark and drear
Within my chamber,
Lorn and bare, where
Sweetness was and
Beauty for a day.
My window-friend,
I'll dig thy grave,
Inter thee grandly.
No sod shall lie,
Nor blossom there
Thy kindred flowers.
Within my soul's
Deep core is built
Thy tomb enduring.
Ah, morn shall never kiss
Thee nevermore
In purple of dawn;
And stars shall rise
And twinkle in
Vain and pass away.
Should all thy race
Thus disappear,
In death forsake the
Soil in which you
Grew, the world would
Then be sad as I. (190–92)

Here the Poe-esque allusions are frequent and unmistakable. The alternating iambic/trochaic dimeter and nineteenth-century phraseology suggest that the work is in standard American versification peculiar to the period. What distinguishes this poem from others contemporary with it is the theme: a lament for an apparently vanishing race, a sentiment with which the poet has a personal affinity ("Should all thy race / Thus disappear, / In death forsake the / Soil in which you / Grew, the world would / Then be sad as I"). In terms eloquent for a very young man, the Muskogee Creek attests to the integrity, uniqueness, and reclusion of his Indian core being ("My window-friend, / I'll dig thy grave, / Inter thee grandly. / No sod shall lie, / Nor blossom there / thy kindred flowers. / Within my soul's / Deep core is built / Thy tomb enduring").

Another example of nineteenth-century American Indian literature combining current versification tendencies and Native themes can be seen in the Canadian poet Pauline Johnson's "Cattle Thief," published in 1912. The excerpt below, as well as the selections that follow, appears in Karen Kilcup's *Native American Women's Writing.*

The Cattle Thief

They were coming across the prairie, they were galloping hard and
fast;
For the eyes of those desperate riders had sighted their man at last—
Sighted him off to Eastward, where the Cree Encampment lay,
Where the cotton woods fringed the river, miles and miles away.
Mistake him? Never! Mistake him? The famous Eagle Chief!
That terror to all the settlers, that desperate Cattle Thief—
That monstrous, fearless Indian, who lorded it over the plain,
Who thieved and raided, and scouted, who rode like a hurricane!
But they've tracked him across the prairie; they've followed him
hard and fast;
For those desperate English settlers have sighted their man at last. (209)

In this dramatic narrative, Johnson duplicates the anapestic hexameter of "The Highwayman," by Noyes, but she radically departs from that poem's characterizations and theme. In the Noyes piece, the lawbreaker is just a lawbreaker beautifully dressed: "He'd a French cocked hat on his forehead, and a bunch of lace at his chin; / He'd a coat of the claret velvet, and breeches of fine doe-skin" (342). In Johnson's poem, the hero has stolen meat in order to feed his starving people: "You have killed him, but you shall not dare to touch him now he's dead. / You have cursed and called him a Cattle Thief, though you robbed him first of bread . . ." (210). Unlike Noyes's poor Bess, the landlord's black-eyed daughter, the Cree woman does not meekly die draped over a massive phallic symbol in order to save her outlaw lover. Johnson's heroine valiantly lives to exonerate her renegade father and to castigate his killers for genocide: "What have you left to us of land, what have you left of game, / What have you brought but evil, and curses since you came?" (210). Departing from the typical non-Indian portrayals of American Indians of the time, Johnson's Indians, both male and female, are vocal and heroic. They are the central figures of her narrative, not subservient characters lending local flavor to American Wild West georgics. This poem likely references the well-documented starvation of First Nation people that occurred after the signing of Treaty 6 in 1876 and the resistance to that atrocity offered by Big Bear and Poundmaker.

Not to be overlooked in "The Cattle Thief" is the deliberate use of irony. Johnson's speakers ostensibly utter their sentiments in Cree, a language not understood by their tormentors. This convention underlines the actual plight of most American Indians of the period. Because Native languages and cultures were not understood by the dominant society, Natives lost the power that any language conveys. Politics and history had rendered them mute, starved for language as well as food in their own country. The poem insists, however, that history has not left American Natives unaware of their predicament or unwilling to express their outrage.

Loss of land and loss of Native people are topics that run through most nineteenth-century American Indian poetry. Johnson again picks up this subject in "The Corn Husker," a tightly composed elegiac quatrain that portrays a Native woman "rich in tawny colouring of her race" who remembers her dead and forgotten compatriots that have been "banished from their lands" (210). In American Indian ontology, land and people are synonymous. According to Betty Jacob, a Choctaw scholar and linguist, human beings emerge from the land and are connected to it. It is not uncommon, therefore, that metaphors conflating land and people abound in American Indian works. Not infrequently, metaphors linking corn and Native people also appear. Because corn is both sacramental and commonplace sustenance to American Indians, it often transforms into a dominant motif running through Native works. In "Joe: An Etching," by Johnson, a "patch of rustling, yellow, Indian corn" grounds the poem symbolically, thematically, and metaphorically.

Joe
An Etching

A meadow brown; across the yonder edge
A zigzag fence is ambling; here a wedge
Of underbrush has cleft its course in twain,
Till where beyond it staggers up again;
The long, grey rails stretch in a broken line
Their ragged length of rough, split forest pine,
And in their zigzag tottering have reeled
In drunken efforts to enclose the field,
Which carries on its breast, September born,
A patch of rustling, yellow, Indian corn.
Beyond its shriveled tassels, perched upon
The topmost rail, sits Joe, the settler's son,
A little semi-savage boy of nine.
Now dozing in the warmth of Nature's wine,
His face the sun has tampered with, and wrought,
By heated kisses, mischief, and has brought
Some vagrant freckles, while from here and there
A few wild locks of vagabond brown hair
Escape the old straw hat the sun looks through,
And blinks to meet his Irish eyes of blue.
Barefooted, innocent of coat or vest,
His grey checked shirt unbuttoned at this chest,
Both hardy hands within their usual nest—
His breeches pockets—so, he waits to rest
His little fingers, somewhat tired and worn,
That all day long were husking Indian corn.
His drowsy lids snap at some trivial sound,
With lazy yawns he slips towards the ground,
Then with an idle whistle lifts his load
And shambles home along the country road
That stretches on, fringed out with stumps and weeds,
And finally unto the backwoods leads,
Where forest wait with giant trunk and bough
The axe of pioneer, the settler's plough. (214–15)

Native people in Canada endured the same losses of land and food supplies that vanquished indigenous people in the United States. This poem foretells the decimation of First Nation people as increased numbers of European settlers advance through their lands. "Joe: An Etching" begins by setting up the problem. It is September, a time of endings. The Indian world, presented here as a "meadow brown," is suffering a foreign intrusion represented by the split rail fence. The field, "Which carries on its breast, September born, / A patch of rustling, yellow, Indian corn," creates a nexus of American Indians, corn, and the earth: they are one.

The fence, cutting through the meadow and stretching for miles, accurately mirrors American history: the American Indian world is being divided by endless waves of immigrants. As the colonization process intensifies, the Native response, in the form of the underbrush cutting the fence in half, resists the foreign attack but is powerless to overcome it. The rails, with their "drunken efforts" to surround the meadow, triumph. Sitting on the fence is yet another foreign intrusion: Joe, the settler's son. He sleepily watches the "shriveled tassels," or the dying Natives. Though only a child and presumably harmless, he is anything but innocent. The "semi-savage boy" has, at least symbolically, spent the day ravaging Native people. "His little fingers, somewhat tired and worn, / [have] all day long [been] husking Indian corn." Joe is the future. He prefigures the waves of incoming settlers and the destruction that will accompany them. Either unaware of or insensitive to the damage he will ultimately wreak, he basks in the sun, yawns, and idly returns home through a forest that will eventually be felled by the pioneer's ax and "settler's plough."

The grim import of this poem is disguised by its bucolic air and similarity to John Greenleaf Whittier's "Barefoot Boy" (1856). Johnson's non-Indian readers may respond nostalgically to Joe's sun-kissed face, "vagrant freckles," "vagabond brown hair," nested hands, and "Irish eyes of blue." They may be comforted by the "warmth of Nature's wine" and the familiarity of an "old straw hat the sun looks through." American Indian readers, on the other hand, will very likely see in the boy's "mischief" only sad irony, and it is a tragic double irony at that. The boy will never be a chief or American Indian leader. Instead he will be a *mis*chief, an impostor. Like his non-Indian readers, Joe is unaware of the damage his "shamble" through the wilderness will eventually cause; but in the "stumps and weeds" fringing the forest, American Indian readers can clearly visualize their reduction in numbers and their loss of natural resources.

Johnson's seemingly innocuous choice of words and phrases, constructions like "shamble," "mischief," "semi-savage," "drunken," "zigzag tottering," and "trivial sound" create an ironic doubling of meaning that allows the poem to assert divergent views and to speak to different audiences at the same time. For instance, the phrase "drunken efforts" could refer both to the colonists' introduction of alcohol to American Indians, an event that contributed to the demoralization of countless Native people, and to the possible condition of some of the new settlers, who may have carried strong spirits with them to the New World. Even Johnson's choice of title, "Joe: An Etching," conveys a sense of corrosive action as much as it denotes a gentle impression.

Cultural loss was not a theme limited to adults. Children also felt the loss of land and people. Student writings at the Cherokee Female Seminary indicate that half a century before Johnson, newly removed schoolchildren articulated the grief and defiance characteristic of later poets. In an essay published in 1857 entitled "View from our Seminary," a young girl known only as Edith writes:

> Our Seminary commands a most delightful and varied prospect of the surrounding country. On the north, stretching away as far as the eye can reach is a wood; and though within the few years past many demands have been made upon its wealth of noble trees, yet for years to come will an inexhaustible number continue to lift their lofty tops proudly to the blue sky in defiance of the devastating stroke of the woodman's axe. (403)

Edith recognizes that the forest will last not forever but only for "years," given its present usage, yet she asserts defiance in the face of devastation. As she continues her essay, she stays true to Native poetics, a subject that she certainly was not taught in school but one that she must have absorbed as a result of her participation in tribal culture. She orients her essay in good Cherokee fashion by moving it in a counterclockwise rotation from north to south and bringing it to rest in the east. She honors the earth—its forests, prairies, hills, valleys, and flowers—and the seasons. Even though she makes a concession to the dominant society, or the "enlightened inhabitants of the *east,*" she nevertheless grounds "taste" and "refinement" with the Cherokees, synonymous with the earth she beautifully describes (403–04).

In conformity with American Indian poetics, nineteenth-century American Indian poets occasionally include Native words in their works. Because of societal resistance to American Indian languages, Native word usage is usually limited to proper nouns—given names, place-names, and short phrases. Often the place-names and the names for people are the same. The words *Erie* and *Adirondack* refer to tribes as well as features of geography, and that fact is critical to interpretation. Although Native words appear only rarely in the early publications, their presence is important. Native words give power, substance, identity, and artistic integrity to a work. In American Indian thought, power resides in the word itself.

When the word is spoken, the power is released. When Jane Johnston Schoolcraft calls up Keewaydin, the North Wind, or Baimwawa, the Thunder, she purposefully invokes the power of those names and invests her characters with their strength. The names also infuse her poems with invincibility. We are still reading them, are we not? These names remind us, even today, that the old gods are still remembered and revered by certain American Indian people. More important, their names prod present memory and work as transformative, cultural agents bridging time and tradition. Schoolcraft's work resonates with notions of transformation, perhaps the central theme of the sacred narratives. In her essay entitled "The Forsaken Brother: A Chippewa Tale" we find:

> *Neesya, neesya, shyegwuh gushuh!*
> *Ween ne myeengunish!*
>   *ne myeengunish!*
> My brother, my brother
> I am now turning into a Wolf!—
> I am turning into a Wolf. (69)

In an American Indian world, everything is part of a circle, and nothing ever ends. Forms change, but essences do not.

American literature is polyphonic, and Native writers contribute to that defining quality. Nineteenth-century American Indian voices waft ever so softly through the pages of our anthologies, and they should be heard with some degree of awareness and sensitivity. Because these writers remembered and adhered to many of the poetic conventions of the oral tradition, they facilitated and advocated the continuance of the practice by the American Indian poets who followed them. They were lodestars who set the compositional direction for the truly brilliant American Indian poets of the coming centuries. The nineteenth-century poets also created for us poignant literary artifacts that attest to their unvanquished spirit, their pain, their joys, their homes, their ancestors, their beliefs, their humanity, and their ultimate survival. They also attest to ours. Johnson writes:

> O! wind so sweet and swift,
> O! danger-freighted gift
> Bestowed on Erie with her waves that foam and fall and lift,
> We laugh in your wild face,
> And break into a race
> With flying clouds and tossing gulls that weave and interlace. (211)

Barbara McCaskill

Teaching the Sorrow Songs

In the twenty-first-century American South, where I teach large literature classes predominantly composed of white students, any discussion of mine concerning post-Reconstruction African American authors often meets responses ranging from the coarse to the sublime. The reception might be rage, alienation, guilt, shame, curiosity, astonishment, chilly politeness, insight. Most of the preconceptions that my students have about these years in African American literature, tracing roughly from the end of Reconstruction (1877) through the first two decades of the twentieth century, are neither happy nor thrilling. "In the late nineteenth century, the South was a violent place," is the terse appraisal of *African Americans: A Concise History* (Hine, Hine, and Harrold 242). Modern historical discussions and literary anthologies reinforce this assessment, yet they regularly elicit chagrin or unease from college-aged Southern youth.

One of the many bright occurrences during this "bootless strife for colored people," as the antilynching activist Ida B. Wells-Barnett painted the era (59), is the spirituals, what W. E. B. DuBois in his *Souls of Black Folk* coined the "sorrow songs" (154). This indigenous Southern folk music cohered the African's "rhythmic cry" and "heathen melody" (155, 157) and the religious hymns and work songs from the "foster land" of

Europe (158) into expressions of life, death, exile, despair, endurance, tribulation, and resilience. We can ask of them many questions that we pose in conversations about written verse: What images carry symbolic weight? How does form follow function? Who is speaking, to whom, and under what circumstances—and does any kind of speaker respond? What artistic influences are apparent? How and why does the speaker address historical, social, and political issues? In this context, the spirituals can find renewed appreciation in students' eyes. Both poetry and polemic, they come to contemporary audiences as the expressive equivalent of the silent record of African American agency, protest, and institution building in the post-Reconstruction era, which too long remained ignored and buried by what Wells-Barnett called the "red record" of race riots and lynch mobs.

The spirituals took on double lives after the Reconstruction. They contributed to the race uplift movement as further evidence of an African American culture, and they gathered new energy and heightened urgency as powerful collective outbursts against the epidemic of racial violence—in particular the lynchings—that characterized Jim Crow. Ranking them alongside the works of Aeschylus and Shakespeare, using them to calibrate black America's civilization and imaginative proficiency, DuBois defined them as "real poetry and meaning [concealed] beneath conventional theology and unmeaning rhapsody" (162, 159). The form, he wrote, "remains . . . the singular spiritual heritage of the nation and the greatest gift of the Negro people," and he designated to "the sole American music" a very high artistic stature, adding to an already flowering and far-flung chorus (155).

In his essay on the use of spirituals in *Souls*, Christopher A. Brooks reminds us that the "trend to elevate the genre" was not DuBois's innovation (276). As an effective counter to blackface minstrelsy, Booker T. Washington strategically praised the mulatto composer Samuel Coleridge-Taylor's revival of the spirituals in his *Twenty-Four Negro Melodies* (1904). And compilations such as *Slave Songs of the United States* (1867), edited by William Allen, Charles P. Ware, and Lucy McKim Garrison, bestowed dignity even earlier (Brooks 274, 270). The veteran Union officer and abolitionist Colonel Thomas Wentworth Higginson, writing in his memoir *Army Life in a Black Regiment* (1869), defined the melodies less glowingly as "quaint" and "picturesque" accompaniments to the black soldiers' "rhythmical barbaric dance" (187, 189) that he observed around the campfires. Yet this commander of one of the first regiments of former slaves in the Union army, the First South Carolina Volunteers, also compared the spirituals with the ballads of Sir Walter Scott and declared them an "essentially poetic" genre (187).

The literary critics Cheryl Walker and Paula Bernat Bennett both caution against forcing African American poetry to conform to standards of high art merely by measuring it against European texts and aesthetics. As Walker has stated, narrative poetry such as Frances E. W. Harper's, which demonstrated the influence of the spirituals and other African American expressive practices, "was designed to be delivered orally and preserves a strong theatrical vibrancy" ("Nineteenth-Century American Women Poets" 240). Likewise, Bennett adds that "fixing" the spirituals in print, as many nineteenth-century songbooks did, "inevitably falsifies them":

> These poems were not meant to be read, let alone read in isolation. They grew out of a total group experience that involved the daily activities of the slaves' lives: their moaning and chanting, their work songs and mourning songs. (*Nineteenth-Century American Women Poets* 263)

Assessments that value the spirituals based only on European frames of reference, even if by well-intended activists and intellectuals such as DuBois, Washington, Allen, and others, or by Higginson, call for further discussion in our classes so that students may understand the complex array of personal and political motives that underpin them: lifting the race, humanizing black people, encouraging race and class tolerance, announcing an indigenous American art, demanding that we think of how environment and heredity both operate to underline difference.

As the editors of the *Norton Anthology of African American Literature* describe, "With slavery officially outlawed, the white South moved quickly to protect its interests by codifying the very white supremacist ideology that had undergirded the chattel slave system" (Gates and McKay 464). The editors of another valuable reference source, *The Oxford Companion to African American Literature*, write:

> After emancipation, despite the efforts of the Thirteenth, Fourteenth, and Fifteenth amendments and federal Reconstruction legislation, white Southerners sought ways, legal and extralegal, to assert a white supremacy so extreme as to justify meting out ritual death to black persons without any formal legal process. (Andrews, Foster, and Harris 465)

When students ask for a precise account of the impact of this violence, I quote the historian Leon F. Litwack: "How many black women and men were beaten, flogged, mutilated, and murdered during the first years of emancipation will never be known." He continues:

> Nor could any accurate body count or statistical breakdown reveal the barbaric savagery and depravity that so frequently characterized the assaults made on freedmen in the name of restraining their savagery and depravity—the severed ears and entrails, the mutilated sex organs, the burnings at the stake, the forced drownings, the open display of skulls and severed limbs as trophies. (276–77)

Statistics do tell the gruesome story in the monumental study by John Hope Franklin and Alfred A. Moss, Jr., *From Slavery to Freedom.* "In the last sixteen years of the nineteenth century," Franklin and Moss write, "there had been more than 2,500 lynchings, the great majority of which were African Americans, with Mississippi, Alabama, Georgia, and Louisiana leading the nation" (345).

At first, my students often assimilate these statements awkwardly, if at all. If white, they may resist them, influenced by utopian notions of racial harmony that falsify discussions of the post–Civil War South. If black, they may have difficulty balancing the victimization of newly freed slaves that these scholars document with individual stories of survival and achievement preserved between the pages of family bibles or passed down by word of mouth.

Although Harper exclaims in 1876, "We are rising, as a people / We are rising, to the light" (*Brighter Coming Day* 237), and almost twenty years later, in 1893, Paul Laurence Dunbar's "Ode to Ethiopia" exhorts the race to "Be proud . . . in mind and soul; / Thy name is writ on Glory's scroll / In characters of fire" (qtd. in Gates and McKay 887), such lines are too often neutralized by students' suspicions that these poets were privileged Romantics and their poems mere longings, futile and wistful, written on behalf of their beaten and downtrodden brethren. Bandanna-wearing women soaked in sweat and hefting hundred-pound cotton bales; hunching gangs of men swinging shovels, pile drivers, axes, chains; smiling, ragged children hugging watermelon rinds to crusted lips—these stark yet ubiquitous images of rural, functionally illiterate African Americans in the Jim Crow South dominate and distort my students' reception of black poetry from this period. Yet this group of poets articulated and disseminated antilynching rhetoric through the spirituals they innovated, providing a counternarrative to the stereotypes deployed against them in literature and popular culture.

The minister Gwendolin Sims Warren defines spirituals as songs inspired by God and composed of lyrics alluding to biblical stories, themes, and verses, often derived during slavery from the Old Testament (14). Although the creators of the spirituals are too often stereotyped in students' minds, the musical genre they invented gains ground in courses where canonical nineteenth-century poetry by black authors has been summarily demoted by students to whimsical flights of fancy. In contrast to their lack of familiarity with postbellum African American poets—Harper, Dunbar, Alice Dunbar-Nelson, James D. Corrothers, James Weldon Johnson, Mary Ashe Lee, Josephine Delphine Henderson Heard, Henrietta Cordelia Ray, and others—first- and second-year majors at my university often have had prior classroom discussions about how rebellious or escaping slaves sung the spirituals as surreptitious warnings and announcements or coded messages of resistance.

Warren uses the term "invisible church" to describe the origin of many spirituals in the slaves' secret worship services, quietly conducted "in praise houses and cabins called 'hush harbors' " and removed in both distance and discourse from the master, overseer, and "pateroller" who constituted a Southern panopticon. She writes:

> Drawn from the Bible, hymns, African styles of singing, and their creators' aspirations, experiences, and circumstances, the spirituals spoke of this world and the next. They addressed a passionate longing for freedom and justice, and also embraced the virtues of Christianity: patience, love, freedom, faith, and hope. The music's authors used the Old Testament extensively, feeling a real kinship with the enslaved Hebrews. They expressed their trials as well as their hope. . . . Their criticisms of American slavery were usually couched in such symbolic language. (15)

Andrew Ward notes that these forms of music—"alternating verses and choruses, call and response" (112)—originated in the confluence of African dance songs and white Protestant hymns and folk songs, and he divides them into grief-stricken sorrow songs and optimistic jubilees (113). Those who sang the spirituals invented a tradition whose very form symbolized the desperate yet hopeful circumstances that had given it birth. Like the private, unpublicized meeting places that ensured the practice and survival of the slaves' religion, these religious songs held special meanings that only select listeners could enter into and understand. As protean and synthetic works, originating from, combining, and remaking

European and African aesthetics, spirituals could both address the restrictions of slavery before the war and adjust to new concerns of freedom after emancipation.

Almost every American student I have encountered recognizes "Go Down, Moses," "Steal Away," "Swing Low, Sweet Chariot," or "Didn't My Lord Deliver Daniel?" from Black History Month stories about how these songs were covert signals among field hands, how Maryland's Harriet Tubman, Kentucky's Lewis Hayden, or other "conductors" lionized in William Still's *Underground Rail Road* (1872), lingering in the vicinity or waiting in the quarters, used them to lead fugitives to the northern Promised Land. Some students' confidence in talking about the spirituals may arise from singing and hearing them in religious and secular settings as members of choral groups, choirs, or gospel ensembles. To others, these are selections they routinely pause to listen to as they surf the radio's FM dial. In my own childhood and in those of many fellow baby boomer teachers, the spirituals were sound tracks to everyday activities: Sunday worship services, Wednesday Bible-study meetings, christenings and funerals, Christmas and Easter holidays, a civil rights march or sit-in or a similar gathering of activists.

Now the spirituals are a centerpiece of and influence on America's mainstream popular culture, and they possess a broad currency that transcends racial and ethnic differences among students, their loyalties to different sports teams and political parties, or their religious affiliations. Crossover R & B and Christian groups such as Mary Mary, TLC, Destiny's Child, and Kirk Franklin and the Family have refreshed the tradition with contemporary rhythms and harmonies. A spiritual such as "O Mary, Don't You Weep" at one time could not be found on the *Billboard* Top 40 charts; today its crossover appeal can stimulate students' interest in nineteenth-century black poetry when examined as both a subversive and artistic statement.

Where would a historical contextualization of the sorrow songs in a literature classroom begin? DuBois identifies ten "master songs" or canonical spirituals, based on their popularity and cachet among turn-of-the-century Southern black audiences and their stylistic, linguistic, and thematic elements. His list is "I'll Hear the Trumpet Sound," "Nobody Knows the Trouble I've Seen," "Swing Low, Sweet Chariot," "Roll, Jordan, Roll," "The Rocks and Mountains," "Been A-Listening," "My Lord, What a Mourning! (When the Stars Begin to Fall)," "My Way's Cloudy," "Wrestlin' Jacob," and "Steal Away" (157–58). I prefer to introduce a song DuBois does not mention, "Go Down, Moses," which is perhaps more famous than any in his top ten. It typifies the sorrow songs' traditional relation to the history of Southern slavery, and it contains multiple layers of meaning.

After reciting "Go Down, Moses" aloud with the class and inviting them to sing it with me, I begin by discussing structure, style, and meaning. Its verses are marked by the characteristic call-and-response pattern—short, direct, irregular—and balladic *abab* rhyme scheme. Spirituals from slavery and its aftermath take this form to enable illiterate listeners or congregations short on hymnals but strong in devotion to recite and remember them with ease. The structure also lends itself to the spontaneous oral improvisation of additional lines and stanzas, which was central to the performative and transcendental aspects of the genre in African American houses of worship. "Go Down, Moses" consists of many stanzas (G. Warren and Hollander [vol. 2] each transcribe over twenty), but its opening lines are the most identifiable and widely known:

> When Israel was in Egypt's land,
> Let my people go,
> Oppressed so hard they could not stand,
> Let my people go,
> Go down, Moses, 'Way down in Egypt's land,
> Tell old, Pharaoh,
> Let my people go. (G. Warren 40–41)

The award-winning journalist Juan Williams writes:

> The story of Exodus, with Pharaoh holding the Jewish people in slavery in Egypt—and Moses leading his people to freedom by invoking the power of God even to part the sea . . . , inspired black people's faith in God's love for them and their struggle. (Williams and Dixie 7)

In the lyrics of "Go Down, Moses," Israelites enthralled in Egyptian bondage emblematize African servitude in what one stanza designates an American "wilderness of woe."

Students with only a passing or casual knowledge of the song can easily overlook that its narrative discusses *two* figures—Moses the prophet, who humbled Pharaoh and guided Israel out of Egypt, and his successor, the warrior Joshua, who actually led the nations of Israel across the Jordan River into the Promised Land of Canaan and then became their leader in bloody battles to repossess this territory from enemy tribes. The newly freed slaves quickly used this sorrow song to articulate the new postwar challenges they optimistically faced as well as the punishments that loomed from defeated Southern whites who fancied that blacks were obtaining privileges at the expense of their own well-being. In 1866, for example, Fisk's Jubilee Singers included the song in their repertoire when they gave a command performance for President Ulysses S. Grant, who, "more pharaoh than Moses," had given priority to the reunification of North and South and to concessions for the former Confederates over the security and enfranchisement of the former slaves (A. Ward 177). "Go Down, Moses" thus clearly applied not only to enslavement but also to emancipation and the joys it brought; to the growing pains, uncertainties, and disappointments that marked the newly reconstructed South; and to the imminent transition of all Americans into a modern century.

To sing a spiritual meant to model self-help as well as to state one's faith in heavenly assistance. "Go Down, Moses" asserts confidently that liberty from the economic and social restrictions of post-Reconstruction life, from what the historian Rayford Logan infamously termed "the Dark Ages of Recent American History" (xx), will occur as it did in bondage through the interventions of African Americans themselves as much as through the support of Providence. This twofold idea reverberates in other stanzas:

> The devil thought he had me fast.
> Let my people go.
> But I thought I'd break his chain at last.
> Let my people go.
>
> O let us all from bondage flee
> Let my people go!
> And let us all in Christ be free
> Let my people go! (G. Warren 42)

During slavery and Reconstruction, African Americans bestowed the title "Moses" on Tubman and Lincoln because they represented on a national or collective level how the words, efforts, and prayers of individual Americans mattered just as much to the success of emancipation as God's divine intercession.

I suggest asking classes to read Exodus so that they can by comparison observe how "Go Down, Moses" took on new life in the years of racial violence and legal discrimination that plagued post-Reconstruction Southern black communities. "To free the slaves," Litwack states, "did not make them equal" (256). In the 1880s and 1890s, after the exit from captivity and exodus "out of the house of bondage" (Exod. 13.3) that

"Go Down, Moses" celebrates, it indeed seemed as if the ex-slaves wandering in the wilderness were without benefit of the manna or "bread from heaven" (16.4) that God at least rained down on the children of Israel during their forty-year odyssey. One section in the composition assures its singers:

Your foes shall not before you stand
Let my people go!
And you'll possess fair Canaan's land
Let my people go! (G. Warren 42)

In the context of bondage, this is a clarion call for defiance against slaveholders. With its allusion to the paradisiacal "land flowing with milk and honey" (Exod. 13.5) that God promised to restore to the weary Israelites, it assures eventual freedom for American chattel who cannot own the fields on which they labor; whose labor remains uncompensated; and who do not even possess the bodies and flesh whose blood, sweat, and tears have intermingled with the soil they till.

But the intentional ambiguity of who the "foes" represent and what "Canaan's land" portrays enabled postwar African Americans to reassign new meanings to these symbols. The federal government's notorious broken promise of forty acres and a mule to former slaves on the Sea Island plantations; the tenant farming system and specter of chain gangs; the officials of the law who looked the other way when a black man, woman, or child was accused of some heinous or trivial crime and murdered without due process—in other words, the same old servitude recast in the form of new oppressions—did not escape notice by later generations singing this stanza.

By this point in the conversation, students can also see how this musical work's affirmations—

You'll not get lost in the wilderness
Let my people go!
With a lighted candle in your breast
Let my people go!

O Moses, the cloud shall cleave the way
Let my people go!
A fire by night, a shade by day
Let my people go! (42)

—echoed the positivity that defined the moods of post-Reconstruction black Southerners. I call their attention to how the blazing candle and the nocturnal "pillar of fire" (Exod. 13.21) that guided the prophet and his people across the Red Sea must have reminded the enslaved of the North Star's literal radiance that could deliver fugitives to safety, and the religious faith that could embolden them to step out on such perilous journeys in the first place. On the other hand, post-Reconstruction singers could fluidly reposition these images to refer to the new goals of secular and sacred black communities: citizenship, respectability, educational attainment, legal enfranchisement. Inspired by biblical imagery, titles such as Harper's novel *Iola LeRoy; or, Shadows Uplifted* (1892) and Lucy Delaney's memoir *From the Darkness Cometh the Light* underscored those meanings.

Turn-of-the-century Southern states were literally aflame. The historian Philip Dray has documented how the mob's use of fire to burn its victims alive was crucial to its ritual murders of African Americans. Participants in the spectacle of lynching that gained momentum in the 1880s and 1890s looked forward to a barbaric "cookout" where "human beings were also butchered and roasted, often with members of the crowd offering suggestions on technique" (81). Wells-Barnett, DuBois, and other reformers pointed out that lynchings were often intended to demoralize and defeat African Americans who had gained economic success or political influence in their communities. Coverage in African American newspapers and official reports of civil rights organizations such as the NAACP described stores, homes, and businesses set alight by hooded night riders for that purpose. In such a climate of intimidation, where a flickering sighted in the distance at night could signal the hellish bonfire of a lynch mob, black singers of "Go Down, Moses" perhaps evoked positive connotations of light as a counter to the Dantean fires and broken, combusted bodies that symbolized the bellicose forces that threatened to keep them down.

I bring the World Wide Web into my classroom to supplement this discussion with visual and documentary material. The Library of Congress's *American Memory* site, the Schomburg Center for Research in Black Culture's gallery of nineteenth-century photographs (*Images*), the link to the Public Broadcasting System's television series *The Rise and Fall of Jim Crow* and the *Without Sanctuary* virtual museum exhibit provide reliable information and ideas for class discussions and assignments. I also find that students enjoy conducting online research to examine case studies of Southern African Americans whose lives and achievements epitomized both the obstacles and the accomplishments to which the sorrow songs allude. In the *Multicultural Archive of Georgia*, a computer resource I have codeveloped, the photographs taken by Robert Williams, a former slave working in Georgia and South Carolina, visually evoke the debates at stake. The themes of a song like "Go Down, Moses" also intersect with issues raised by the sermons of black Protestant ministers such as Emmanuel King Love and Henry McNeil Turner and by the travels of the Jubilee Singers, who toured America and Europe singing spirituals and gospel songs to raise money for the education of the freedmen back home.

In the introduction to *Standing in the Need of Prayer: A Celebration of Black Prayer* (2003), Howard Dodson explains the centrality of speaking with God in African American life by stating simply that "prayer changes things" (Schomburg Center 6). I am amazed by how quickly students across ethnic and class boundaries get this signal theme of transformation in relation to the sorrow songs and recognize it as only one of numerous purposes that such classics serve. Some students are attuned to how the sorrow songs, like the blues, can make direct and overt statements about gendered roles in rural white and African American Protestant societies. Or students comment on how, like quilt patterns, heirloom seeds, and canning recipes, particular lyrics and tunes are preserved, reproduced, improvised, and then passed down from generation to generation or from congregation to congregation by church mothers, grandmothers, and other women. My students also observe how the overarching characteristics of sorrow songs in the vein of "Go Down, Moses"—their protest against oppression, their affirmation of hope and resilience, their protean ability to maintain relevance across generations, their lyrical ambiguity—also inform a significant portion of contemporary rap music. Tupac Shakur's loving tribute to the sufferings and triumphs of his "Dear Mama" from the 1995 *Me against the World* album and DMX's admission that "I know real so I wipe away the tears with a song" in his "Prayer (Skit)" from *It's Dark and Hell Is Hot* (1999) are such examples.

The sorrow songs, our students know, are everybody's songs. The themes they underscore are both specific to moments in African American history—particularly the struggle against slavery and Jim Crow—and transcend them. What may first seem to students like just another stiff and stuffy lecture on nineteenth-century American literature thus can become a marvelous entry into post–Civil War literature and life and a lens into what matters to their own generation.

Karen L. Kilcup

"Wild Nights"? Approaches to Teaching Nineteenth-Century Erotic Poetry

"What erotic poetry?" students frequently respond when they hear the term in connection with "nineteenth-century." Most students whom I have encountered, whether at small private colleges, large state universities, or elite research universities, express skepticism at this pairing; they are accustomed to thinking of any period before the sexual revolution of the 1960s as hopelessly staid and repressed. The task, then, is to invite them to progress from disbelief to an acknowledgment of the presence of various forms of eroticism in some of the earlier poetry to the understanding that such eroticism was not unusual, that it assumed different forms over the course of the century, and that how it emerged often depended on the poet's status and on attitudes toward eroticism, sexuality, and gender at the historical moment. With the appearance of anthologies such as Paula Bennett's *Nineteenth-Century American Women Poets* and John Hollander's *American Poetry: The Nineteenth Century*—which contain most of the poems to which I refer below—students now have ready access to this strand of nineteenth-century American poetry.

To begin, I remind them of some lines with which many are familiar:

The beards of the young men glistened with wet, it ran from their
long hair,
Little streams passed all over their bodies.

An unseen hand also passed over their bodies,
It descended tremblingly from their temples and ribs.

Walt Whitman is usually the best, because most available and overt, example of erotic poetry. The "twenty-ninth bather" section of "Song of Myself" provides a vivid entry into a discussion of how to define *erotic*, with the concept of desire figuring centrally (*Walt Whitman Archive*; path: *Leaves of Grass* [1855], pp. 19–20). Students frequently assume that this section is heterosexual, pairing the lady viewer with one or more of the young men. Depending on the students and the context—in more conservative institutions, students may be resistant to interpreting desire in this passage as homoerotic—one or more students may identify Whitman as a "gay" poet (I use quotation marks here to indicate an issue that always needs discussion—the anachronistic use of terminology). Exploring the difference between eroticism and sexuality is an important approach to prepare students for the more indirect, sometimes coded representations of the body that appear in other poets.

Moving from "Song of Myself" to "A Woman Waits for Me" has been a productive transition. This poem frequently engenders heated debate, sometimes between female and male students, about the aims of the desire expressed in the poem. For example, when Whitman avers that "Without shame the man I like knows and avows the deliciousness of his sex, / Without shame the woman I like knows and avers hers," students usually acknowledge his liberating vision, especially for women. On the other hand, many women students frequently express considerable distaste for certain lines, in particular:

It is I, you women, I make my way,
I am stern, acrid, large, undissuadable, but I love you,
I do not hurt you any more than is necessary for you,
I pour the stuff to start sons and daughters for These States—I press
with slow rude muscle,
I brace myself effectually, I listen to no entreaties,
I dare not withdraw myself till I deposit what has so long accumulated
within me.

(*Walt Whitman Archive*; path: *Leaves of Grass* [1867],
stanzas 3 and 7 [pp. 108–09])

Some women readers angrily observe that these lines represent a rape scene. Other students usually provide the best counterargument: that Whitman clearly loves and respects athletic women (stanzas 3–5); that he is merely speaking rhetorically and metaphorically, in particular attempting to represent the genesis of a new and reinvigorated United States (stanza 8). In general, a discussion of the poem is most productive when teachers work to elicit this dynamic in the poem. In considering Whitman, teachers can (and should) provide students with insight into the history of critical views of the poet's sexuality and the ways in which literary criticism has colluded to conceal Whitman's and other gay poets' erotic perspectives. The indispensable volume in this endeavor is Robert K. Martin's *The Homosexual Tradition in American Poetry.* Understanding the history of how masculinity has been constructed in the United States complements this interpretive framework; Anthony Rotundo's *American Manhood* provides accessible and interesting background reading.

It is an easy jump from Whitman to Emily Dickinson; students readily appreciate the erotic quality of her "Wild nights—Wild nights!" (*Poems*, poem 269):

> Wild nights—Wild nights!
> Were I with thee
> Wild nights should be
> Our luxury!   (lines 1–4)

In addition to focusing on the metaphoric language here, students are frequently able to articulate common formal features of this stanza that underscore its erotic energy: the capitalization, the exclamation points and dash, the use of ecstatic sound; and they are usually capable of extrapolating the effects of these formal features to the work of other poets. They are less able, sometimes, to appreciate that Dickinson's imagination is energized by the absence rather than the presence of her beloved, by desire rather than consummation. To nudge them in this direction, it is helpful to pair this poem with some of Dickinson's letters, such as one of the "Master" letters, or one of her intense early letters to Susan Gilbert Dickinson:

> . . . Susie, will you indeed come home next Saturday, and be my own again, and kiss me as you used to? . . . I hope for you so much, and feel so eager for you, feel that I *cannot* wait, feel that *now* I must have you—that the expectation once more to see your face again makes me feel hot and feverish, and my heart beats so fast. . . . (letter 75)

This juxtaposition virtually always leads students to conclude that Dickinson was a lesbian. The moment is a fruitful one for the teacher to engage them in a discussion of what they mean by *lesbian*: Who decides? On what basis? I frequently refer here to Adrienne Rich's classic essay "Compulsory Heterosexuality and Lesbian Existence," citing her concept of a "lesbian continuum" (648). This resource enables them to explore the complicated problem of naming and labeling. It is often useful also to introduce students to concepts and questions emerging from Marjorie Garber's *Vice-Versa: Bisexuality and the Eroticism of Everyday Life*: How is desire best conceptualized? Does it change over time, over a person's life span? How can we (or should we) characterize a person with erotic partners of different sexes? How do social and gender power relations influence the expression of desire and self-identification? Another provocative set of questions for students can emerge from the notion of sexuality as performance. In her collection *Inside/Out, Lesbian Theories, Gay Theories*, Diana Fuss argues that "sexual identity may be less a function of knowledge than performance, or . . . less a matter of final discovery than perpetual reinvention" ("Inside/Out"), while Judith Butler underlines that "sexuality always exceeds any given performance, presentation or narrative" ("Imitation"). Gayle Rubin's classic essay in *The Lesbian and Gay Studies Reader*, "Thinking Sex," offers additional theoretical and historical background that can enable students to think more fully about the connections among sexuality, gender, and eroticism.

One important avenue of discussion to consider is the complicated and oblique ways in which eroticism and sexuality are represented in the nineteenth century, not always obvious to students accustomed to graphic contemporary television, magazine, and film representations of sexuality and intercourse. Paula Bennett's essay on Dickinson, "The Pea That Duty Locks," provides an invaluable introduction to the notion of coded eroticism in the images of small round objects, such as pearls and pebbles, that appear everywhere in the poet's oeuvre. For additional contextualization, Bennett's "Critical Clitoridectomy" is indispensable. She observes:

> The language of flowers has been Western culture's language of women. Most specifically, it has been the language through which woman's body, and even more particularly . . . women's genitals have been represented and inscribed. (242)

The existence of a language of gems and flowers in the nineteenth century shocks many of the students that I have taught, who have been trained to see nineteenth-century women, in particular, as sexless. Rachel Maines's *The Technology of Orgasm: "Hysteria," the Vibrator, and Women's Sexual Satisfaction*, disabuses us of this view. As Bennett underscores, "male and female Victorians, like ourselves, were obsessed with sex, wrote about it constantly, and engaged in it frequently" (*Poets* 160).

Here and elsewhere, teachers can introduce images from American, British, and Continental nineteenth-century painting and sculpture to underscore the ubiquity of eroticism in Western culture, both obliquely and overtly represented. Instructive examples are Edmonia Lewis's controversial sculpture *The Death of Cleopatra* (c. 1876); Anne Whitney's famously "feminine" public sculpture *Leif Ericsson* (1887); Thomas Eakins's homoerotic *The Swimming Hole* (various versions in several media, 1883–85), which has long been associated with Whitman's "twenty-ninth bather" section of "Song of Myself"; and Dante Gabriel Rossetti's *The Beloved* (1865–66). Teachers can invite students to compare these works with those by well-known twentieth-century artists, such as Georgia O'Keefe, who denied that her flowers represented female genitalia (but which nevertheless continue the discourse of the language of gems and flowers into the twentieth century), and Robert Mapplethorpe.

A large part of students' understanding about female sexuality comes from the fact that historical accounts often focus on the ideology for white, middle-class women. Such a focus leads students astray in a number of ways. For example, a working-class woman, regarded as less pure, might respond to the ideology of virtue by representing herself as hypervirtuous or by eliding eroticism altogether. As factory workers whose virtue was subject to question, many *Lowell Offering* poets demonstrate this strategy of elision. Alternatively, she might critique or complicate confining mainstream notions of virtue and celebrate her erotic potential, as Lucy Larcom does in "Flowers of the Fallow," where an older woman speaker underscores the wildness of nature's female embodiment.

Most problematically, perhaps, the historical emphasis on white middle-class women obscures the pernicious stereotypes promulgated in the nineteenth century about working women and women of color as lustful, erotically driven creatures who were thus conveniently available for exploitation by more powerful white men (P. Bennett, *Poets* 161). In this context, a poem that raises difficult and productive questions for discussion, including questions about miscegenation, is Emma Lazarus's "The South," which represents the post–Civil War South in highly eroticized terms as a woman of color, as the opening stanza underscores:

Night, and beneath star-blazoned summer skies
    Behold the Spirit of the musky South,
A creole with still-burning, languid eyes,
    Voluptuous limbs and incense-breathing mouth:
    Swathed in spun gauze is she,
From fibres of her own anana tree.

For today's readers, the poem both idealizes and objectifies the spirit of the South in troubling ways, including a depiction of the personification as "listless . . . Like some half-savage, dusky Indian queen" (P. Bennett, *Nineteenth-Century American Women Poets* 285; lines 49–50). Nineteenth-century African American poets such as Sarah Louisa Forten ("Ada") rejected such conceptions, more often writing poetry that, like that of Frances Ellen Watkins Harper, imagined themselves and their sisters in familial, political, or spiritual terms. Harper's "The Slave Auction" and "A Double Standard" suggest the dangers for black slave women of the cultural perception of them as hypererotic and of their vulnerability to white male power. One of her most famous poems, "A Double Standard," emphasizes the dangers of the erotic and offers an implicit response to Lazarus's portrait. The betrayed female beloved speaks in angry and politicized terms, harshly interrogating the hypocritical society that would blame the woman and spare the man:

Can you blame me that I did not see
    Beneath his burning kiss
The serpent's wiles, nor even hear
    The deadly adder hiss?
        (149–50; lines 9–12)

In this context, instructors should point out that white women could also be the victims of male sexual violence, as Rose Terry Cooke's "Blue-Beard's Closet" suggests, and hence that eroticism was not always a celebratory matter. Offering an intimate and painful view of female subjectivity, women poets of all races, classes, and ethnicities wrote similar poems (Frances Sargent Osgood's "The Daisy's Mistake" is an early example), but Harper provides an important example of an African American poet who energetically counters the myth of the hypererotic woman of color with a profound investment in moral virtue—for both women and men.

Another useful way to contextualize erotic poetry and to augment students' understanding of sexuality and the interconnections among sexuality, eroticism, and power is to introduce students to such nineteenth-century women prose writers as Fanny Fern, Harriet Jacobs, and Sarah Winnemucca. For example, Fern's "A Word on the Other Side" criticizes husbands for bringing home to their wives sexually transmitted diseases from prostitutes—revealing not only the sexual double standard but also the presence of working-class sex workers. Jacobs's *Incidents in the Life of a Slave Girl* and Winnemucca's *Life among the Piutes: Their Wrongs and Claims* underscore and critique the ways in which the notion of virtue for white middle-class women underwrites sexual violence toward African American and Native American women.

Students need to know, however, that marginalized women did not always envision sexuality in negative or threatening terms, although their positive perspective may have emerged somewhat later. Writing after the turn of the century, Henrietta Cordelia Ray offered a powerful affirmative vision of African American female eroticism in her quatrain "At the Cascade" (1910):

> The waters rippled, gleamed and fell;
> Sweet Jessie tripped adown the dell.
> She heard his voice, their fond lips met;
> The rocks with silver spray were wet. (290)

Teachers should consider pairing this delicate and restrained portrait with such poems as Ray's "My Spirit's Complement," which suggests a similar erotic encounter in such lines as "the edges of a life / Alone encolored with the rose" but concludes by transcending bodily experience, hoping that the lovers will

> meet in Paradise,
> After the mystery of life's sweet pain;
> And find the strange prismatic hues of earth
> Transmuted to the spotless light again. (292)

Even Alice Dunbar-Nelson's affirmative 1917 poem "Violets," while it conjures "wistful April days, when lovers mate / And wander through the fields in raptures sweet," concludes by turning away from the body toward "heaven-mounting dreams" and "my soul's forgotten gleam" (374–75; lines 3–4, 12, 14).

Students also need to understand that eroticism may function differently in different cultural contexts, as traditional love charm songs sung by American Indian women underscore. Affirmative female eroticism can also emerge indirectly, in the context of nature writing, such as "Marshlands" by Pauline Johnson; the opening of this poem provides an accessible example of coding that today's students, steeped in Sigmund Freud, will readily acknowledge to be laden with eroticism:

> A thin wet sky, that yellows at the rim,
> And meets with sun-lost lip the marsh's brim.
>
> The pools low-lying, dank with moss and mould,
> Glint through their mildews like large cups of gold.
> (Kilcup, *Native American Women's Writing* 216; lines 1–4)

With these various poems in mind, teachers may ask students if women writers and in particular women writers of color are more likely to code depictions of eroticism and, if so, why. Ultimately, it is important to remind students that the putative absence of eroticism in certain poets' work does not mean that the poets are repressed. Rather, such absence can result from their responding to social inequalities and differences in the way women of varying races, ethnicities, and classes are regarded by the dominant culture and from how these poets wish to represent themselves. The overall point that needs to be made is that during the nineteenth century different women experienced eroticism in many different ways.

Although students are usually willing to recognize the erotic content of the familiar poems by Whitman and Dickinson cited above, they often point out that these two poets were exceptions. With Edgar Allan Poe, they are the "good" poets of the nineteenth century and so were more likely to experiment with subject as well as with form. Other poets, students argue (even with little experience) would be more likely to adhere to conventional subjects and perspectives. At this point I often take them back to Anne Bradstreet's "A Letter to Her Husband, Absent upon Public Employment" (Lauter et al. [5th ed.] A: 407). Students will note that Bradstreet, like Dickinson, wrote privately, not for publication, and so might be more willing to be overt in expressing her desire. This argument suggests the indirection of many published poems by American women poets. Students are astonished to see such freedom of expression this early in American literary history. When they read poems such as Melville's

"After the Pleasure Party," Nathaniel Parker Willis's "The Lady in the White Dress, Whom I Helped into the Omnibus," William Wetmore Story's "Cleopatra," selections from George Henry Boker's *Sonnets: A Sequence on Profane Love* (Hollander 2: 66–70, 1: 360–61, 2: 129–31), or poems from Ella Wheeler Wilcox's *Poems of Passion* (1883), they can see that Whitman and Dickinson were far from alone in the overt and conscious depiction of passion, whether straight, homoerotic, bisexual, or autoerotic (P. Bennett, *Poets*, ch. 7).

Depending on whether or not I am teaching a general survey course or a specialized course in poetry, I either turn to a pairing between Poe and Alice Cary or introduce students to less familiar writers and poems, such as Harriet Prescott Spofford's Romantic, autoerotic "Pomegranate-Flowers" (P. Bennett, *Nineteenth-Century American Women Poets* 215–22) with Bennett's affiliated essay ("Pomegranate-Flowers"). For Poe and Cary, two poems that work well in tandem are "Annabel Lee" and "The Sea-Side Cave," both because of their adjacency in subject matter and because of their availability (Cary's poem is now regularly anthologized [Kilcup, *Nineteenth-Century American Women Writers: An Anthology* 154–55]). Poe's poem is one that virtually all the students I've taught admire, both for its formal qualities and Romantic perspective. Nevertheless, inviting (or pushing) them to see the poem from a feminist perspective—and in particular to investigate the relation between gender and power in the poem—may lead at least one student to question the content of the closing lines:

> And so, all the night-tide, I lie down by the side
> Of my darling—my darling—my life and my bride,
> In the sepulchre there by the sea—
> In her tomb by the sounding sea.
> (Lauter et al. [5th ed.] B: 2545–46)

Students frequently squirm but ask, "Is the narrator simply hanging around Annabel Lee's tomb? Isn't there an element of necrophilia here?"

These kinds of questions, which reflect on how sexuality, eroticism, and power—especially speaking power—are negotiated in American culture emerge quite differently in Cary's Poe-esque "The Sea-Side Cave." These poems work together well in large part because many of the formal and substantive elements are parallel: the repetition of the *e* sound (echoed in Dickinson's "Wild Nights"), the setting, the notion of an untimely death, the suggestion of obsession. The epigraph and opening stanza provide a particularly accessible moment for students familiar with biblical stories:

> The Sea-Side Cave
> *A bird of the air shall carry the voice, and that which hath wings tell the matter.*
> At the dead of night by the side of the Sea
> I met my gray-haired enemy,—
> The glittering light of his serpent eye
> Was all I had to see him by. (154)

The images here—the “enemy” and the “serpent” in particular—alert many students to the idea of evil; the stanzas that follow suggest the erotic or sexual ramifications of that evil:

> At the dead of the night, and stormy weather
> We went into a cave together,—
> Into a cave by the side of the Sea,
> And—he never came out with me!
>
> The flower that up through the April mould
> Comes like a miser dragging his gold,
> Never made spot of earth so bright
> As was the ground in the cave that night.
>
> Dead of night, and stormy weather!
> Who should see us going together
> Under the black and dripping stone
> Of the cave from whence I came alone! (154–55)

Students inevitably struggle with the third stanza: “What does the flower represent?” “What’s the significance of the miser?” “What happens in that cave?” “What does the cave represent?” With its “lips that never lie,” Dickinson’s “A still volcano life” (*Poems*, poem 517) offers productive connections here, because it underscores the affiliation between erotic power and speaking power, both of which have customarily been denied to women. It is possible, then, to read “The Sea-Side Cave” as a kind of oral sex, inasmuch as the narrator claims her erotically based power through a strong, even ecstatic voice.

One of the best ways to approach these questions and difficulties in “The Sea-Side Cave” is to ask students to identify the speaker’s gender. I have found that despite students' customary conflation of the poet's and speaker's gender, here some resist that connection. Others, however, point to the feminine images that follow in the closing stanzas:

> Next day as my boy sat on my knee
> He picked the gray hairs off from me,
> And told with eyes brimful of fear
> How a bird in the meadow near
>
> Over her clay-built nest had spread
> Sticks and leaves all bloody red,
> Brought from the cave by the side of the Sea
> Where some murdered man must be. (155)

At this point, the subject of students' resistance to imagining a female speaker provides a useful pedagogical and interpretive strategy: What is it that makes many readers unlikely or unwilling to see a female narrator as the murderer? How might we compare the speaker of Cary's poem with the one in Poe's? And again: What are the connections among eroticism, sexuality, voice, power, and violence?

If the teacher has not already introduced students to the idea of coded sexuality through Dickinson's poetry, this poem can lead readily into the subject. In the discussions that I have had on "The Sea-Side Cave," someone in virtually every class has raised the issue of the cave as a womb or vagina image—and the students agree that in this poem, the metaphor is both frightening and empowering. On the other hand, some students raise the possibility that Cary's poem is a subtle parody of Poe, humorously ironic in tone. Phoebe Cary's "Samuel Brown," a drop-dead funny parody of "Annabel Lee" that *promotes* illicit sex, could be introduced at this point (P. Bennett, *Nineteenth-Century American Women Poets* 97–98). Referring to prose as well as to poetry can enable students better to understand coded eroticism in the nineteenth century. Nathaniel Hawthorne's Pearl in *The Scarlet Letter* and Mary Wilkins Freeman's cherry trees in "Two Friends" (Kilcup, *Nineteenth-Century American Women Writers: An Anthology* 410–17) provide obvious touchstones. In poems, any number of Dickinson poems will serve, as well as James Matthews Legaré's "To a Lily," John Rollin Ridge's "A Cherokee Love Song," Sophie Jewett's "A Song of Summer," Julia Ward Howe's "My Last Dance," Sidney Lanier's "The Marshes of Glynn," or Constance Fenimore Woolson's "The Florida Beach."[1]

An essential part of introducing students to erotic poetry in the nineteenth century is providing them with a historicized context for understanding. In addition to those already mentioned, good resources are John D'Emilio and Estelle Freedman's *Intimate Matters: A History of Sexuality in America*; Martin Bauml Duberman, Martha Vicinus, and George Chauncey's *Hidden from History: Reclaiming the Gay and Lesbian Past*; Michel Foucault's *The History of Sexuality*; and Lillian Faderman's *Surpassing the Love of Men*, about erotic relationships between women. Among their other benefits, such texts alert students to the notion of gender, sexual identity, and eroticism as historicized, politicized, culture-specific, and evolving. One way in which I help make the point about cultural specificity more concrete, in discussions about poetry or prose, is to frame these conversations with a consideration of various creation stories. The Iroquois version of the Earth diver story ("The Woman Who Fell from the Sky"), for example, shows a woman playing an important positive role in the creation of the world and enables students to interrogate the Western notion of sexuality as fundamentally evil and dangerous (Kilcup, *Nineteenth-Century American Women Writers: An Anthology* 1–2). Similarly, placing discussions of homosexuality historically—for example, in the contexts of the developing field of sexology at the end of the nineteenth century, the subsequent articulation of lesbian and gay identity, and the consequence of increasing social marginalization—helps even very conservative students consider sensitive issues with a measure of detachment. Such conversations also help students understand how social changes can have aesthetic consequences, such as an increased necessity for coding erotic desire in metaphor.

These discussions can also elicit conversation about such matters as the political consequences (for the poet, the reader, or the critic) of articulating—or not—a sexual identity. What disadvantages might there be to such a project? What advantages? For example, how important is the notion of tradition in American literary history? Why might the lesbian community, for example, want to claim the existence of a lesbian literary tradition? To make the subject more immediate, I sometimes refer to more recent events, such as the Stonewall protest and certain moments in the sexual revolution of the 1960s. Instead of lecturing on historical contexts, I usually assign presentations to groups of students (or individuals in graduate seminars), offering suggestions if they wish or allowing them to explore their own interests and surprise us with their findings.

One important consequence of discussing erotic poetry, historical contexts, and the social and political ramifications of sexual identity is that students may self-identify in class. There is no general approach that can be offered in responding to such identification. In my experience, gay, lesbian, and bisexual students reveal themselves only in the context of a classroom environment that they already perceive to be open-minded and hospitable. It is rare, even in a conservative academic institution or region, that overt hazing emerges. Often, in fact, such self-identification leads to greater warmth, understanding, and learning in a community of students. But unpredictable responses can occur, and it is crucial for teachers to be alert to and prepared for such eventualities. Again, placing erotic poetry in the contexts of politics, history, and culture provides students with a language and intellectual framework for responding to personal reactions to the poetry in a more sophisticated and generous way. Geography, institutional history, political climate, student populations, instructor position, and departmental dynamics are among the other factors that will govern both students' responses and instructors' possibilities.

The remarks above have been aimed principally at an undergraduate audience, but much of what I've suggested can be adapted for graduate seminars as well. Graduate students are likely to be interested in the politics of canon formation and the emergence of sexuality as a legitimate field of literary study. Such matters as the emergence of queer readings of Whitman and Dickinson form an important part of that intellectual history. In a graduate seminar, one useful focus is to ask a student or group of students to investigate and give a presentation on the history of Dickinson criticism in the context of larger historical forces. At what moment does the interpretive transformation occur, and what intellectual, political, and cultural streams foster it? But I have learned that most undergraduates also find matters of canon formation fascinating, for it demystifies the processes by which professors choose certain texts and perspectives on which to focus discussion. An exciting project for graduate students, as well as advanced undergraduates, is to explore nineteenth-century poetry found in periodical literature. Some of the most interesting and experimental work remains hidden from view, and participating in rediscovery generates tremendous excitement. Such a recovery project can include an exploration of the general context in which a particular poem is situated—how does *The Atlantic*, for example, differ from *Twin Territories* or *The Colored American Magazine*? It can include a study of a specific context—what essays, stories, poems, and advertisements appear around the poem? How do these contexts influence readers' perceptions and interpretations? What representations of eroticism and sexuality, as well as gender roles, are encoded in both the poem and the context?

One way to conclude a segment or a course on nineteenth-century erotic poetry is to invite students to think about the similarities and differences between the representations of eroticism in the earlier period and those today. I frequently give a research assignment that asks students to take an earlier text as a starting point (and touchstone) for discussing a contemporary issue or problem. In this context I have had a lesbian student take as her problem the representation of lesbian eroticism in nineteenth-century periodical poetry and the marginalization (or exoticization) of lesbian desire in the contemporary mainstream media. Finally, as with any teaching, what often works best in relation to this subject matter is to enable students to understand the literature and its historical and cultural contexts in the framework of their own lived experiences. Such an approach enables students to read past the silence in Sophie Jewett's "Entre Nous" to comprehend "The sweet encircling thought that neither names" (P. Bennett, *Nineteenth-Century American Women Poets* 334–35).

Note

1. These poems are in Hollander 2: 133 (Legaré), 185–86 (Ridge), 394–95 (Woolson), 412–16 (Lanier); P. Bennett, *Nineteenth-Century American Women Poets* 84–85 (Howe), 340 (Jewett).

Paula Bernat Bennett

Mill Girls and Minstrels: Working-Class Poetry in the Nineteenth Century

When I first thought about teaching nineteenth-century working-class poetry, not one of the writers who came to mind—Lydia Sigourney, John Greenleaf Whittier, Walt Whitman, and Rebecca Harding Davis—belonged to the working class. Indeed, Davis, although she figures prominently in this essay, was not a poet. Rather, they were authors who called attention to their society's social and economic inequities by speaking for others who, they believed, could not speak for themselves. But real working-class poetry? Where was it, why was it, and to whom was it addressed? Familiar only with the Lowell mill girls, principally Lucy Larcom, I did not know enough to know.

In restricting this essay to working-class poets, I am not dismissing the importance of teaching these other writers as well. On the contrary, Sigourney, Whitman, Davis, and Whittier were some of the century's most powerful witnesses to their country's wrongs, those suffered by labor among them. Teaching these writers exclusively, however, also has drawbacks, the most important of which is that it denies working-class people agency and voice by positioning them as passive victims instead. Here, I describe two self-contained bodies of verse that preserve working-class voice and agency intact: one, poetry published by Lowell mill girls in their magazine, the *Lowell Offering*; the other, infinitely more controversial, minstrel show lyrics.

Both these bodies of verse are well suited for teaching, not only because students find them engaging but also because specialists in American studies and cultural studies, if not in literary studies, have deeply invested in them. They are consequently far easier for students to research than most noncanonical nineteenth-century verse. Indeed, one need only go to the World Wide Web for an abundance of material. Because mill girl poetry and minstrel songs, despite some crucial commonalties, emerged from very different cultural contexts and present radically different teaching problems, I treat them separately here.

The Poetry of the Lowell Mill Girls

A good way to begin an undergraduate unit on mill girl poetry is to have students take a virtual tour of the mills themselves. As part of the United States National Park system, the Lowell Mills have their own Web site, where neatly packaged information bytes can be downloaded ("*Mill Girls*"). These PDF brochures, complete with pictures of the girls' dormitories and the interiors of the rooms where they worked, sketch the growth of the mills and the cotton industry, tell who the girls were (young women from New England's economically pressed farms) and what they did. The brochures also recount the mills' after-history as successive waves of immigrant workers supplanted first the mill girls and then one another, until 1960, when the last mills closed and ownership moved south in quest of cheaper labor. For teachers who want students to push beyond the brochures' sanitized format, Catherine Lavender's *Liberty Rhetoric* Web site, the Norton Digital History site *City of Spindles: the Textile Mills of Lowell*, and Jim Zwick's *The Campaign to End Child Labor* and *Bread and Roses* Web sites are especially helpful, as is Thomas Dublin's *Women at Work: The Transformation of Work and Community in Lowell, Massachusetts, 1826–1860.*

Most undergraduates at state schools such as mine work part-time and tend to sympathize with the mill girls' story, the more so since conditions at the mills were, comparatively speaking, not that bad during the girls' tenure. Their work was physically exhausting, to be sure, requiring that they spend long hours on their feet tending up to four of the huge power looms. Before concessions, their workdays were fourteen hours long, and excessive noise and air thick with dust and lint made the workrooms unhealthy. Meals were hurried and, at least to begin with, the girls had only two leisure hours a day. Many began working, moreover, at appallingly young ages, some as young as seven. Nevertheless, these girls—among the nation's first female industrial laborers—could boast perks that later workers could only dream of. Their housing was sound; their meals, though rushed, adequate; their health and education attended to; and their "respectability" preserved. As skilled workers, moreover, they ranked in the upper echelons of industrial labor, as Harriet Hanson Robinson's memoir of her time in Lowell makes clear. Robinson identifies four classes in Lowell's factory population: the mill owners' agents; the overseers; the operatives, as the girls were called; and, on the bottom, the "lords of the spade and the shovel"—the shanty Irish, whose hovels clustered around Lowell's one Catholic church and whose jobs were menial, perkless, and ill paid (*Loom,* ch. 1).

Overall, the mill girls could take considerable satisfaction in their situation. Unlike the Irish, they were not doomed to shovel and spade or, rather, to their distaff equivalents, the broom and the mop. In addition, as both Robinson and Larcom insist in their respective memoirs, most viewed their time in the mills as temporary. Mill work was an opportunity to gain independence while supplementing the family income, not as it is, say, for Hugh Wolfe, the Welsh puddler in Davis's *Life in the Iron Mills,* a dead end. It did not dehumanize them as Wolfe is dehumanized. Indeed, Larcom, the one mill girl to become a professional poet, explicitly refuses to use the term *operative,* because it suggests dehumanization to her. An operative, she explains, "is not necessarily a person; it may mean a wheel or a shaft, as well; and it is not good for us to think of men and women merely as part of the machinery they tend" ("Among Lowell Mill-Girls" 610). How different from Wolfe, who carves his surrogate self (the statue called the Korl Woman) out of waste material, pathetically unaware he has a right to something better.

Precisely because, unlike the mill girls, Wolfe has no sense of agency, comparing his story with theirs helps students understand what agency is and why it matters. An uneducated immigrant's son, Davis's hero is without ownership in his society. The mill girls, on the other hand, were the educated offspring of victorious revolutionaries. Not only did they know they had rights; like their grandsires, they were ready to defend them, as their first extant poem, written for an 1834 job action over pay cuts, attests. According to the Boston *Transcript,* the outraged mill girls made a run on the bank, marched brazenly through town, and cheered a firebrand who gave, the paper said, a "flaming Mary Wollstonecraft speech on the rights of women and the inequities of the 'monied aristocracy.' " The mill girls, whose concerns were in fact economic and not, as the *Transcript* insinuates, feminist, concluded their "Petition to the Manufacturers" with the lyrics of one of their songs. In the lyrics—which, along with the *Transcript*'s account, can be found on Lavender's *Liberty Rhetoric* Web site—the mill girls apply the language of the Declaration of Independence to their situation as (economically) oppressed workers:

Let oppression shrug her shoulders,
And a haughty tyrant frown,
And little upstart Ignorance,
In mockery look down.
Yet I value not the feeble threats
Of Tories in disguise,
While the flag of Independence
O'er our noble nation flies.

When the mill girls agitated over pay cuts two years later, they again resorted to liberty rhetoric, this time with a witty parody of the Irish marching tune "I Won't Be a Nun":

Oh! Isn't it a pity, such a pretty girl as I
Should be sent to the factory to pine away and die?
Oh! I cannot be a slave, I will not be a slave,
For I'm so fond of liberty,
That I cannot be a slave.

Using liberty rhetoric as leverage, the mill girls capitalize on the Declaration of Independence's slippage between political and economic protest to effect a series of reversals, turning the mill owners into "Tories in disguise" and themselves into staunch supporters of the nation's first principles, defending their independence—their right to economic equality—against a monied aristocracy that treats them like slaves. Rhetorically speaking, these were shrewd moves, and in their explicit grounding of worker agency in rights, they could not stand in starker contrast to Wolfe's blind and confused pleas for help.

The mill girls' use of liberty rhetoric would never have been politically viable, however, had there not been solidarity behind it. No less than their grandsires, these women spoke as one, their "We the People" making Wolfe's difference once more instructive. For not only is Davis's protagonist ignorant of his individual rights, he also exists in structural isolation from his peers—an artist trapped in an ironworker's body. Davis probably made Wolfe this way in order to garner sympathy for him from her original readership, the *Atlantic Monthly's* middle-class subscribers. Wolfe's artistic sensibility—heavily romanticized by Davis in the figure of the Korl Woman—sets him apart from his ironworker peers, men whom Davis depicts as so brutish that the horrors of their workplace barely register on them. The downside of Davis's decision is that it leaves Wolfe with nothing on which to ground agency. Without any sense of rights as an individual or as a member of a group, he is a victim by default.

The mill girls are not victims. Because of their living arrangements, these women were all but forced to think communally. They slept, ate, and worked together, and because they shared so much, they shared their thoughts too. As Robinson puts it, "they discussed the books they read, debated religious and social questions, compared their thoughts and experiences, and advised and helped one another" (*Loom*, ch. 3). It was from these group activities that their idea for the *Lowell Offering* sprang. As a magazine by, for, and about mill girls, the *Offering* instantiated worker agency and subjectivity in ways that Wolfe's statue, no matter how powerfully moving in itself, could not.

Given that most students come to us trained to prize the kind of highly individualized Romantic sensibility that Wolfe's statue embodies, establishing the worth of the mill girls' group creativity may need some explaining. Robinson and Larcom both tout Harriet Martineau and Charles Dickens among the *Offering*'s readers, but the periodical was never more than a coterie magazine—that is, a magazine put together by a homogeneous group of writers, writing for themselves and others like them. The mill girls signed their pieces, to be sure, usually with pen names or initials, but their primary reason for writing was not the desire for personal recognition or even for individual expression—the motives students typically assign to writers. Rather, the mill girls sought to satisfy their group's need for self-expression by publicizing feelings, needs, and desires held in common.

By today's standards, this sharing looks like derivativeness, and our students are far more likely to view it as a sign of artistic failure than to see in it a source of political strength. As one student complained to me, it's "all clichés," and much mill girl poetry does seem to confirm this judgment, especially the poetry on domestic themes. Such poems were nineteenth-century poetry's stock in trade; and the mill girls' efforts on these topics are, superficially at any rate, indistinguishable from those found in most literary periodicals of the day. Here, for example, is the opening stanza of "Home" by A. M. S. (Mary Anne Spaulding?):

> I dream of home, and much rejoice,
> For then I hear my father's voice
>   Ascend again in prayer;
> I see again my mother's face,
> Return each sister's kind embrace,
>   And meet a brother there.

Although this poem appears to make interiority its subject, the interiority is mediated through a discourse the mill girls absorbed by reading—and imitating—middle-class verse. This is decidedly *not* Hugh Wolfe creating a Korl Woman of his own.

But while students may rightly identify nostalgia for home, praying fathers, visions of one's mother's face, and the grief of separated siblings as common coin, to stop here ignores venue and what it means that a mill girl signed this poem. Read in these terms, the derivative elements of "Home"—regular meter, clichéd imagery, refined diction and tone—are signposts establishing the author's claim to a middle-class sensibility as delicate as that of any well-bred miss. Dickens honored this fact when he compared the *Offering*'s contents "advantageously to a great many English annuals" (qtd. in H. Robinson, "Lowell Offering" 465). Dickens also observes that the very idea of mill girls producing such a magazine would "seem 'preposterous' to many of his English readers" (qtd. in Larcom, "Among Lowell Mill-Girls" 609). In this light, even a poem as gentle and unprepossessing as "Home" becomes subversive, an undermining of the settled assumptions subtending and rationalizing society's hierarchical distributions of power.

The poems in which the mill girls side with the oppressed of other lands—"The Heroine of Columbia," by Adelaide, for example—for all that they are overtly political, work in much the same way. Employing iambic pentameter couplets—a rare meter in nineteenth-century American women's poetry, possibly because of its association with heroic epic—Adelaide rehearses the story of Polycarpe La Salvarietta, an eighteen-year-old girl of good family who, the poem claims, suffered torture and execution at the hands of the Spanish general Pablo Morillo rather than betray her associates in the resistance:

> Condemned to die, before that host she stood.
> And eyed Morillo, thirsting for her blood;

And kindled now, with almost prophet-fire,
Her spirit quailed not neath his frowning ire—
For pledged was she, in all her beauteous youth,
To live or die for freedom and for truth—
And, nobly nerved, she shrunk not from the fate
Prepared by foemen, in their savage hate. (59)

For Adelaide, as for the strikers in the 1830s, the language of the Declaration of Independence really was what the founding fathers said it was: an assertion of universal human rights. As such, any high-minded young woman could adopt its principles, whoever she was, wherever she found herself, even in the mountains of Colombia.

Unlike the strikers, Adelaide is not addressing her own situation. On the contrary, she uses liberty rhetoric here in the same way that middle-class poets from Sigourney to Whittier do when they choose to defend the oppressed. From this perspective, there is nothing explicitly mill-girlish in this poem. Like the (middle-class) authors just cited, the author of "The Heroine of Columbia" stands outside the circle of oppression she describes. Or does she?

Again, what differentiates "The Heroine of Columbia" from its middle-class models is not content but venue. The implied audience for middle-class-authored protest literature was the middle class. As in Davis's *Life in the Iron Mills*, the author's goal was to create sympathy for those unable to help themselves. The people empowered by such writing were therefore not the disadvantaged but those who chose to act as agents on their behalf. As recent scholarship into places like Carlisle Indian School and Hull House suggests, this failure to empower working-class peoples themselves could and too often did become the ugly underbelly of middle-class social interventions. What Adelaide does instead is take these conventions and use them to assert solidarity among the oppressed, whether in Colombia or "Columbia"—an ambiguity students enjoy teasing out. For mill girl strikers, the message of Polycarpe's "give me liberty or give me death" rang loud and clear: it went straight to their own situation.

In both kinds of poems (the domestic and the political), the mill girls leave genteel rhetorical conventions intact, even though, when the poems are read in situ, their subtextual message overturns the social assumptions underpinning those conventions. In a third set of poems, the satiric or ironic, the girls go public with their critique, bringing politics and publicity together in poems whose working-class origins are, as in the strike songs, part of the text. In these poems, the mill girl authors wed Polycarpe's determination to "speak truth to power" with a firm assertion of their place as working-class people in their culture. Legitimating their right to speak neither by an appeal to a higher order of shared ideals (the political poems) nor by an imitation of bourgeois sensibility (the domestic ones), they stake themselves as their own ground, the everyday ground of hardworking young women who have no time for cant or for people with pretensions. Larcom's "Sorrows of Sensibility" illustrates this impatience at the expense of two of the nineteenth-century's most revered literary figures, William Wordsworth and Ralph Waldo Emerson:

A form ethereal crossed my path—
  A lovely cherub child;
Her lips were wreathed with sunny smiles;
  Her glance was brightly mild.
I said, "Fair child; come! view with me
  Yon glorious sunset sky!"
"*I can't: for mammy said she'd have
  At tea, some pumpkin pie!*"

I wandered where a stranger stood
  With earnest heavenward gaze;
As if some mystic vision lay
  Beneath the horizon's haze.
His eagle eye met mine; he spoke:
  I stood entranced and dumb;
*"It's gwine to rain like sixty, gal!
  You'd better dig for home!"* (Nymphea)

Read in its entirety—there are six stanzas—"Sorrows" is literary satire at its most piquant. It is also wickedly sharp evidence of Larcom's sophistication and that of her peers. Through their discussion groups and magazine reading, the mill girls educated their sensibility in the best bourgeois manner. But, as Robinson's class division of the mills' population indicates, their eagerness to acquire bourgeois literary and social tastes did not blind them to the gulf that lay, classwise and powerwise, between them and those who controlled the cultural capital they claimed. Romantic literature, for all its mystique, was the product of a well-entrenched, albeit largely unacknowledged, class-gender system. In identifying dialect and literary style as class markers, Larcom demystifies this system, not just the self-aggrandizing way some Romantic poets wrote.

As Harriet Farley makes clear in "Factory Blossoms for Queen Victoria," not even the Queen of England was safe from mill girl puncturing. Using strategies uncannily like those that Phillis Wheatley employed when giving unsolicited advice to persons infinitely more powerful than herself, Farley makes humility her stalking horse, under whose protection she safely shoots her admonitions at the queen. With insouciant disingenuousness, she calls them a "factory girl's boquet [sic]." This bouquet goes on for thirty-nine stanzas, all in common meter, and it would have given the young queen much to think about if she read it. Like Wheatley, Farley makes no apologies—neither for her poem's length nor for its cheekiness. She takes it as her right, the right of one who can speak truth to power precisely because, simple factory girl that she is, she stands on her own ground:

> Even thus the factory girl may say
> What others leave unsaid;
> And, lady, read for this, I pray,
> What, else, would not be read.
>
> Smile not, as at some maniac's word,
> Though speech like mine be strange;
> Advice, I know, is seldom heard
> Where supple courtiers range. (3)

As in the strike songs and Larcom's literary debunkings, the reversals in Farley's poem are serious and witty at once, the young poet using her very lack of status and power to assert just what, in the world's eyes, she lacks—the right to speak and act on her own behalf. This same kind of wit—a topsy-turvy wit of reversals—crops up everywhere in the mill girls' writings, making targets of the mills' managers, the world's high and mighty, and even the girls themselves and their sometimes dreamy pretensions. Turning to minstrel poetry, I examine at greater length the connection between this particular kind of wit and the working-class status of its authors, for if these two radically dissimilar groups of writers meet anywhere, it is in their satirical appraisal of the powers that be.

Minstrel Lyrics

While it is unlikely that teaching mill girl poetry would stir controversy, teaching lyrics by predominantly Irish, blackface performers in the antebellum period is another matter. In this vast hoard of dialect poetry scarcely a piece goes by in which the epithet *nigger* or its equivalent fails to appear or in which black speakers (or, better, fantasy surrogates thereof) are not ridiculed in appalling ways. Indeed, the mere title of the collection from which my examples come, *Christy's Nigga Songster*, is trouble. Entering the domain of blackface minstrelsy means immersing oneself in some of the ugliest elements in nineteenth-century culture, a culture over which the idealizing values of middle-class gentility lay like a very thin veneer.

Nonetheless, scholars, especially in popular culture and American studies, have entered this domain for some very good reasons. Despite minstrelsy's many liabilities, it is an incredibly rich source of information about nineteenth-century working-class lives and attitudes on class and race. Its study has greatly expanded our knowledge of the formative years of such preeminent popular art forms as musical comedy, vaudeville, and burlesque and enlarged our appreciation of the sizable contribution made by African American performers to them in music and dance. Rich chunks of this scholarship are scattered through the Web. Among the best are the Library of Congress's *American Memory* Web site, with its vast collection of song lyrics and genealogies; the *Jim Crow Museum of Racist Memorabilia* Web site, which explores the role caricatures have played in racism; and Stephen Railton's Uncle Tom's Cabin *and American Culture* Web site, where a selected edition of *Christy's Nigga Songster* and performances of minstrel songs can be downloaded.

But should minstrelsy be given a place in the literature classroom as well? Should I even raise the question, since one of the volume's external readers argued vehemently against it? This is not *Huckleberry Finn*, banned from classrooms for using "nigger." Minstrelsy's racism penetrates to the form's core, and its presence is as deeply offensive to blacks today as it was in the nineteenth century, even to those black writers—Paul Dunbar, for instance—who drew on it. If, to use Eric Lott's terms, there is "love" and "theft" in minstrelsy, there is contempt and a blatant need to degrade also, and there is no way to escape these elements except by not teaching minstrel poetry at all.

Informed by carnival's transgressive license, minstrelsy is the expression of nineteenth-century working-class culture at its rawest, its most self-consciously not genteel. As such, minstrelsy provides a direct window into the nineteenth-century's ethnically mixed and racially divided working-class culture in ways no other nineteenth-century writing does, presenting this culture from the bottom up—its energy, its savagery, its odd inclusiveness, the viciousness of its racial and gender biases, its love of life, and its ebullient, mocking humor. Teaching minstrelsy confronts students directly with the complex burdens of their artistic and social histories. Coping with its insensitivities can help make them more sensitive, as well as more knowledgeable, readers. Although these considerations do not lessen minstrelsy's negatives, they shape the approach to teaching minstrel poetry I take here.

Like today's rap, minstrelsy emerged spontaneously out of the need for collective expression on the part of an (oppressed) urban minority—in this instance, predominantly but not exclusively working-class men of Irish descent. Given how Irish immigrants were received in the United States, never mind their history under British rule, there's more than a little irony in this. As studies from Robinson's memoir of Lowell in the 1830s to Noel Ignatiev's *How the Irish Became White* (1995) suggest, experientially speaking, the two groups, black and Irish, had at least as much in common with each other as they had differences dividing them. Both occupied the bottom rungs in the United States social hierarchy, and both were valued for their physical labor alone, what W. T. Lhamon calls "rough labor" (62). Both were the butts of crude humor by those claiming cultural superiority over them. Both suffered deracination, hunger, exile, and family separation. And both, marvelously and ironically, found solace for their many miseries in music, laughter, and religion.

Teaching students the interethnic and interracial dynamics of the minstrel shows thus directly exposes them to the complex stew of cross-cultural identifications (as well as antagonisms) out of which American popular culture came. Equally important, it helps them grasp how energizing this synergistic interchange could be and how forcefully it speaks to the possibilities of communality between seemingly antagonistic groups. One need go no further than the first song on the Web version of *Christy's Nigga Songster*, " 'Tis Sad to Leabe Our Tater Land," to see what I mean. In this parody of a tune from Michael William Balfe's wildly popular *The Bohemian Girl*, " 'Tis Sad to Leave Our Father Land," one finds just the kind of cross-cultural crisscrossings of debts and thefts that were minstrelsy's lifeblood:

> 'Tis sad to leabe our tater land,
> An' gals we dar lobed well,
> To wander from each darkey band,
> Whar taters don't grow well;
> Yet hard as am dis loss to bear,
> An' deep all stomach smart,
> 'Tis worse to be no longer near,
> De wirgins ob our heart. (39)

Not just the title line's "Tater" points this poem in cross-cultural directions. Balfe, who was a highly popular composer of the day, was born in Dublin in 1808. His opera's libretto is based on a French ballet, which in turn was based on a story by the Spanish writer Miguel de Cervantes. The opera's setting (despite the title) is Austria; its hero is a Pole in exile (Balfe, note 1). Focusing only on the racism of " 'Tis Sad to Leabe" blinds one to these nuances and thus to the far more layered response to the song that its original audience would have had. Beneath the cork, what that audience would have heard was an Irish tune, dealing with an Irish experience (i.e., exile), bravely living up to the tattered ensign of its ethnicity in that single, charged word "Tater." More, the song's theme of exile, together with its tangled European genealogy, would have struck a chord in every displaced person in the theater, Irish or not. The Irish among the Christy minstrels were, on one level, singing of themselves, but the period's diasporic communities generally (not to mention blacks) shared the same losses. It was from these communities that, in the antebellum period, minstrelsy's core audience (as well as its materials and performers) came.

In the light of this history, it seems oversimple to insist that pandering to racial hatred was all that a song like " 'Tis Sad to Leabe" was about. Racist minstrelsy could be and was hateful, especially later in the century when, in the aftermath of the Civil War, racism both north and south greatly intensified. But what made minstrelsy initially so powerfully seductive was not its racism alone but, as Spike Lee's controversial *Bamboozled* perhaps too effectively demonstrates, its interweaving of racism with skillful displays of music and dance, with wit, and (as in " 'Tis Sad to Leabe") with that most powerful staple of popular culture—intense sentimental nostalgia. As Lott argues, minstrelsy seduced with love—and a deep-rooted sense of identification—as much as with hate, celebrating the gifts of those it victimized even in the act of stealing them. It could do so precisely because the minstrels and their victims had so much in common. A brief look at the handling of sentimentality in " 'Tis Sad to Leabe" will clarify this point.

Largely because of Ann Douglas's *The Feminization of American Culture*, discussions of nineteenth-century sentimentality have, until this last decade, focused overwhelmingly on texts by white middle-class women, and sentimentality has been constructed as a white, middle-class, usually female discourse. Yet it would be hard to find a more masculinist setting for sentimentality's display than the blackface minstrel show, where all roles, including women's, were played by men. So why did the Christy minstrels select, even if for parody, a song as deeply saturated in sentiment as Balfe's pathos-dripping " 'Tis Sad to Leave our Father Land"? Certainly, at one level, the performers used the song to mock blacks for their putatively inept pretensions to fine feeling, just as, I might add, they mocked the fine feelings themselves by placing them in the mouths of such crudely drawn blacks. But at the same time, by retaining both Balfe's original melody and his theme of loss and separation, they did something more.

As its title line makes clear, parody though " 'Tis Sad to Leabe" is, it is also a self-conscious displacement onto funhouse speakers of the minstrels' own vulnerabilities and longings, the consequence and sign of their own status as victims. Given how endemic sentimentality was in minstrelsy—especially, as in " 'Tis Sad to Leabe," in the form of plangent nostalgia—were such songs (even if racialized) simply opportunities for the performers and audience to compensate for their own injuries by injuring those less powerful than themselves? Or did some of the appeal of the songs lie in the opportunity they gave these passionate and angry men to indulge their sense of victimhood also? That is, did avoiding having to identify their pain for what it was allow these men to give expression to it at the same time? Although these latter possibilities do not excuse the racism in the Christy version, they do suggest a basis for communality between whites and blacks that explanations tied solely to the song's racism do not.

These are the ambiguities of mind and heart that, as Lott, Lhamon, and others have argued, make nineteenth-century minstrelsy worthy of multidimensional reading—and teaching. One can without difficulty find songs so repulsive they foil any attempt to recuperate them. There are also plenty of moments in the lyrics, as undoubtedly in performance, of mindlessly stupid joking that has no purpose except to degrade. But there are songs, among them some by black composers, such as James A. Bland's "Oh, Dem Golden Slippers," that, cleaned up and their ancestry forgotten, have entered the basic lexicon of popular American music: "Goodnight Ladies," "Buffalo Gals," and "Oh, Susanna," for example. And there are others, such as the "Happy Niggers," "De Ole Banjo," and "Come with the Darkey Band"—all available in *Christy's Nigga Songster*—that temporarily, at least, set cruelty aside in order to celebrate a shared passion for music well played, whoever did the playing:

Music's de first ting clasp,
An' hold you in his grasp,
Den lub is sure to be at hand,
An' all comes through de darky band;
Den wid love and music blest,
You needn't care for all de rest
("Come with the Darkey Band" 73)

As a number of scholars now insist, and content analysis supports, one cannot in fact say that antebellum minstrels were either uniformly racist or proslavery. They blew both ways, their humor revealing not just contempt but also shared humanity. Certainly much of the humor is as ugly as the language used to express it; but, as in "Shad Time ob Year Is Comin'," some is as warm as the life essentials described. Indeed, this poem's evocative rendering of the appetite stirred by the running of this plentiful fish cannot to my knowledge be matched by any middle-class verse of the period:

Oh, de gentle breeze am smellin, smellin,
Oh shad from out de cookin stove
Hucksters around am sellin sellin,
Dar shad from barrow and tub,
Shad make de jaw mid raptures meet,
Shad make de maw mid hunga trill,
Each darkey runs de boats to meet,
With lubly shad dar tubs to fill. (74)

Other songs, like "De Ole Stingy Man," exhibit all the sharp wit of working-class satire directed at "Massas" of whatever stripe who would swindle workers with "Norfolk curry"—literally, a nonnourishing but cheap British dish composed of spicy sauce with little, no, or bad meat:

Massa's such a free trade man,
Ebery day he worry
Me to leave off eating meat,
And live on Norfolk curry;
I tried a pailful 'tother day,
To save the grub expenses,
But was obliged to eat a leg o' pork,
To bring me to my senses. (61)

In such lines, the clever slave and the clever Irishman share one perspective, whatever the differences in diction and color between them.

Finally, and most important, one finds pervasively songs that are explicitly committed to the same kind of topsy-turvy perspective that the Lowell mill girls also adopt, albeit less flamboyantly. Sounding eerily like the fool in *King Lear*—Shakespeare's most socially committed tragedy—the oxymoronic speaker of "Larned Nigger," for example, tops off his description of an upside-down world with a thoroughly Irish in-joke, identifying Sir Robert Peel, Britain's ambivalently anti-Catholic prime minister, with the pope:

> Dare's Moses hunted de wild racoon,
> And Noah dat vent up in a balon;
> And Adam who played de lively tune
> Upon de old banjo.
> Sir Robert Peel he was de Pope
> and Charles de First invented soap;
> Cromwell, de man dat made de rope,
> To catch de buffalo. (54–55)

At this point, the many masks of the minstrel stage, from "Jim Crow" and "Zip Coon" to "Larned Nigger," merge with those stock oxymoronic figures, the wise fools of Europe's highest (and lowest) literary and performative traditions. Not just individuals are sent up here but the entire system. When in the postbellum period numbers of blacks joined minstrel crews, did some view "blacking up" as an opportunity not just to make money but also to exploit minstrelsy's ability (as in "De Ole Stingy Man" and "Larned Nigger") to undercut racist stereotypes even while seemingly reinforcing them? Certainly, Dunbar in "Accountability" and Charles Chesnutt in "The Goophered Grapevine" capitalize on minstrel conventions in this way. There was a path to agency and voice for black artists here as well as white, however "nested," as Lhamon puts it, in less savory matters (34, 234n35).

Although I understand why teachers might believe that minstrelsy's offensiveness makes it unfit for a literature classroom, I can't agree. The lyrics and sketches of minstrelsy represent the largest extant body of United States literature by nineteenth-century working-class authors. Along with constituting a mother lode of working-class social satire, this literature has from its inception helped shape racial attitudes in this country both for better and for worse. Minstrelsy's influence can be seen everywhere in

American art forms, also for better and for worse, including in texts by many of our major writers: not just Harriet Beecher Stowe, Nathaniel Hawthorne, and Mark Twain but also black writers like Dunbar and Chesnutt. This influence needs to be acknowledged, the more so since, like the working class itself, minstrelsy is not monolithic. This understanding does not mean, however, that teaching minstrelsy is risk-free. On the contrary, any teacher considering a unit on it would probably do well to consult first the Web responses to Lee's *Bamboozled.* I would suggest playing the movie in class also, not only to put the destructiveness of racial stereotyping up front but also because the best way to confront the problem that minstrelsy nonetheless presents may well be to watch Savion Glover dance while trying *not* to enjoy it at the same time. Like the bamboozling seductiveness of minstrelsy itself, that of Lee's movie, no matter how provocative in its crudeness and in its use of racist content, cannot simply be dismissed.

Tyler Hoffman

Reenacting American Civil War Poetry

The word *reenacting* in my title is meant to call attention to the war as a performed event, resonating as it does with the modern cultural practice of restaging Civil War battles, and to our own recuperation of texts and performances of them in class. It also alludes to the performance of personal identity that occurs in poems about the war and in the war itself, the ways in which people imagine and recite socially prescribed roles and modes of conduct, or seek to contest and transcend them. Reenacting the Civil War thus serves as a metaphor for our critical activity with respect to Civil War poetry, which must be reactivated for it to speak to us today. As teachers, we must recall the contexts that elicited that poetry and rehearse the postures taken in it, measuring them against those we take in our own lives, in order that our students fully understand and appreciate what this verse represents. In particular, by setting partisan and self-assured war poems against those that somehow call into question the underpinnings of the enterprise, we help our students see how contested both the war and the writing of it were and how poets who raised questions were led to create special rhetorical effects to stake out their positions.

In addition to the well-turned Civil War verse of Walt Whitman and Emily Dickinson, I would encourage instructors to spotlight four poets whose unique angles on the war mark their verse in telling ways and inform important ideological differences. Despite Herman Melville's canonical status, his Civil War volume, *Battle-Pieces and Aspects of the War* (1866), has yet to receive the attention it deserves. Writing as a Northerner who knows about the war largely through newspapers, Melville experiments with changing speakers and shifting perspectives that undercut conventional partisan postures toward the conflict. The noncanonical writer Sarah Piatt depicts war and the memory of it from a white woman's point of view, a woman excluded from the front but living close to it. Although Southern-born, Piatt was critical of both North and South, and her speakers reflect her wavering allegiances and her abhorrence of war itself. The sensibilities and techniques of these two poets can be brought into conversation with those of a pair of African American poets—Frances E. W. Harper and Paul Laurence Dunbar—whose treatments of the war and its attendant ironies are inflected by race and by their people's long struggle to survive under slavery. The points at which these four poets converge and diverge tell us a great deal about the performance of race and gender in the act and art of commemoration, giving students a multiperspectival view of the conflict and the writing of it that conventional historical reenactments of the war, whether in person or in print, elide.

This quartet of writers rises out of a background of Civil War poetry marked by rigid partisanship and Christian piety, both of which drive the war effort by annealing the moral purpose of both combatants and civilians and banishing all ambiguities. In many of these poems the slain soldier is apotheosized in elegy:

> They fought in freedom's fight,
> Dispelling treason's night,
> And in their manhood's might
> Their life-blood shed.
> (qtd. in Steinmetz 65 [W. T. Adams, "Ode"])

That masculine "might" is emphasized by both sides of the war, with expressions like "manly breast" and "manly strength" reenacted over and over (22, 123 [Mary Evelyn David, "Chickamauga"; A. J. H. Duganne, "The House of Bondage"]). The soldier's sacrifice is confirmed when in death he stands "at the right of God" (63 [Mary H. C. Booth, "I'm Dying, Comrade"]). On the home front, women bereft submit to the "holy power of prayer" and play their part when word of death arrives, as when "the sweet young wife droops like a flower" (26, 24 [Mary Evelyn

David, "The Soldier's Fireside, after a Battle"]). These poems maintain gender within its binary frame and powerfully represent social norms to be imitated in the service of war.

Not all Civil War poets wrote in this hyperpatriotic, rigidly masculinist vein. Some of the most widely circulated poems of the war were ballads of mourning and consolation, such as Ethel Lynn Beers's "All Quiet along the Potomac" and Francis Miles Finch's "The Blue and the Gray," whose appeal transcended the political boundaries dividing North from South and whose emphasis on male vulnerability, in particular, crossed gender boundaries as well. Albeit quietly, such poems destabilized the very social norms that the partisan poems affirmed. Other poets, most prominent among them the four writers I discuss here, explicitly sought to expose these norms and challenge thinking about the war and those cultural phenomena that shaped it by raising the hard questions of whether "our" side is indeed the right one and how we would really know if God was on our side. With the war in Iraq, these questions remain part of our landscape, and debates about the ethics of war again open questions of what justifies war and how war gets justified. I have found that one of the most effective strategies for teaching Civil War poetry is to place side by side the more and less orthodox representations of fighting and its legacies: as students become aware of the contrasts, they are able to begin to question their own understanding of war and its politics. Deprived of easy answers to the moral questions posed by war, they can act out their own identities—their learned values and beliefs—and, in doing so, come to see just how contingent those identities are.

In his influential 1962 study of Civil War literature, *Patriotic Gore,* Edmund Wilson, who viewed Walt Whitman as the war's only laureate, dismisses Melville's war poems as mere "versified journalism; a chronicle of the patriotic feelings of an anxious, middle-aged non-combatant as, day by day, he reads the bulletins from the front" (479). In fact, however, Melville revises those bulletins in important ways that ironically comment on the conditions of war to "undeceive" us about its true nature (*Battle-Pieces* 63). Like Whitman, Melville paints the full horror of fighting and its lingering presence, permitting readers to see the war's dark side from disparate points of view. Unlike Whitman, he interrogates his culture's ideals of suffering and sacrifice and their enactment in war. Melville's refusal of a heightened diction and the sentimental strain constitutes a rejection of the prevailing consolatory notion of the Civil War as a holy war, even if occasionally his antiwar sentiments are eclipsed by his Union partisanship. Most of the seventy-two poems in *Battle-Pieces* were written in the wake of the war, inspired, as Melville tells us, by the fall of Richmond. Without a stable or coherent lyric voice, these poems freely take up a range of perspectives and, at their most provocative, represent the uncertainties and doubts conjured by fratricidal warfare.

It is notable that Melville thinks through art—and the lineaments of art—as he ponders what we now refer to as "the fog of war." In his poem "The Armies of the Wilderness," he paints the gruesome scene of the fighting to come on that Virginia battlefield and comments on the proper approach art should adopt as a recorder of ultimately incomprehensible events:

> None can narrate that strife in the pines,
> A seal is on it—Sabaean lore!
> Obscure as the wood, the entangled rhyme
> But hints at the maze of war—
> Vivid glimpses or livid through peopled gloom,
> And fires which creep and char—
> A riddle of death, of which the slain
> Sole solvers are. (*Battle-Pieces* 103)

Here Melville sets the woven scheme of rhyme—its tortuousness and backward glances—as a figure for battle and the problem of representing battle, the problem of witness. (Conversely, Whitman took unrhymed verse as a fit emblem of the harshness of war.) Only the dead know the truth of war, he says, and at best art can enact only the distance noncombatants feel, keeping up our faint connections to the fighting.

It is especially useful for teachers to focus on the prosody of Civil War poetry, distinguishing between those lyrics that contend with the rules of metrical composition and those that, in their simplicity of elegiac expression, do not. Melville, for one, is always aware of the problem of turning violence into art, and this awareness is of a piece with his larger moral probings. In "Dupont's Round Fight" he again imagines poetic form in terms of the war:

> In time and measure perfect moves
> All Art whose aim is sure;
> Evolving rhyme and stars divine
> Have rules, and they endure. (30)

The geometries of versification and of combat are rendered here in regular ballad stanzas, as the poet points up the immutable laws of nature and of commemorative art sure in its resolve. However, in "A Utilitarian View of the Monitor's Fight" rhyme flags, as does passionate purpose:

> Plain be the phrase, yet apt the verse,
>   More ponderous than nimble;
> For since grimed War here laid aside
> His Orient pomp, 'twould ill befit
>   Overmuch to ply
> The rhyme's barbaric cymbal. (61)

In this poem Melville reveals just how unromantic the field of battle has become ("warriors / Are now but operatives"; "War's made / Less grand than Peace"). With "the gaud / Of glory" stripped away, sound effects are muted, the terminal rhyme *nimble:cymbal* barely audible.

When not taking sides (he sometimes refers to the Union forces as "the Right" and the Confederate cause as "the Wrong"), Melville confronts squarely the ironies and ideologies of war. In "Shiloh" he acknowledges the sameness of all the wounded, their differences fading before the gun's brutal blast: "foemen at morn, but friend at eve— / (What like a bullet can undeceive!)" (63). In the second poem of the book (dated 1860) he also attends to the grim fact of war, with the early pomp and bravura yielding to "misgivings" about the course the country is on: "Nature's dark side is heeded now— / (Ah! optimist-cheer disheartened flown)—" (13).

Indeed, in the early "Apathy and Enthusiasm" we do not get anything like Whitman's eager call-to-arms in "Beat! Beat! Drums!" (*Poetry* 419–20). Rather, Melville's speaker comments on the elation of "striplings" as misguided, a product of raw youth; these young men cannot know that the firing on Fort Sumter, while awakening patriotism, also will bring on misery unlike any before (*Battle-Pieces* 20). He continues this strain in "The March into Virginia," where he critiques the "glory" of war by contending that "All wars are boyish, and are fought by boys," a ringing reversal of the gender politics that frame war as manly (22). Lulled by the promise of fame, these boy-soldiers are blithe in the face of impending death, ignorant of human suffering (23). Melville's irony is especially sharp when he notes that the young soldiers will perish "enlightened by the vollied glare" of First Manassas, July 1861, where enlightenment is all too literal—and too late—in the flash of the muzzles. When other of his speakers note that "Nature is nobody's ally," and that "GOD HE KEEPS THE MIDDLE WAY," Melville recognizes the absence of a divine plan that would provide contentment in the rightness of any cause (32, 18).

Melville's unsentimental, unromantic views of war go against the grain of much popular Civil War verse by his contemporaries, who frequently emphasized consolation over critique. When he claims that "much of doubt in after days / Shall cling, as now, to the war," he expresses a failure of righteousness. The poem "Donelson" ends in a divine appeal: "Ah God! May Time with happy haste / Bring wail and triumph to a waste, / And war be done" (52). Such rhetoric stands in stark contrast to that in Civil War verse and hymns where the prayer to God is for swift military victory (e.g., "We raise to thee our just appeal / And ask for conquering might" [qtd. in Steinmetz 53 (Reverend Frederic Denison, "Army Hymn")]). In his prose supplement to *Battle-Pieces*, Melville states that "the glory of the war falls short of its pathos" (265), and his most affecting poems are those that enact this condition, that make students question their presuppositions about war and its cultural effects.

Piatt's deft manipulation of point of view and prosodic form, like that in Melville's war poetry, allows her to ironize popular conceptions of the fighting, as she details its impact on those both on the front lines and the home front. In recognition of the complexities and dissonances of experiences of the war, her lyrics, like Melville's, do not have the authority of a central personal voice; rather, we get splintered, conflicting aspects of war, with realistic portrayals of homes destroyed, families bereaved, and bodies broken. Her gendered poetry's unsentimental vision resembles Dickinson's, although she does not join with Dickinson in her heroic tributes to soldiers killed in battle. Nor does Piatt adopt the stance of Caroline Augusta Ball, a Southerner who wrote pro-Confederacy verse and whose elegy "The Jacket of Grey" is a Romantic partisan performance in archaic diction that reflects none of the war's moral ambiguities (Steinmetz 33–34). In her verse Piatt recuperates the experience of those marginalized in and by the war and interrogates the certainties about war that pervaded poetry in her day. Like Melville's, her Civil War poetry does a different kind of cultural work than most, aiming to "undeceive" us about the nature of war and its aftermath as well as about the ideologies that shape these events.

Piatt is especially effective enacting gendered distances from war, complicating through her tonal postures the relation between soldier and civilian, theater of war and domestic sphere. In her ballad "Hearing the Battle.—July 21, 1861," the speaker reports that "from afar" she "heard the solemn echoes / Of the first fierce words of war," thereby pointing up the fact that she is not fully incorporated into the world of war, positioned as she is on the home front and forced to wonder when fighting will end: the war is "dim" to her, as it is to Dickinson (and to our students) (2). Reflecting on the "passion and moan" of dying soldiers far away, in "worlds unknown" (the first Battle of Bull Run or First Manassas), she experiences an incongruous "delicate wind," one untouched by the horrors of the battlefield (4). In the final stanza the wife recalls her charge to her husband:

> And I gave you a spray of the blossoms,
> And said: "I shall never know
> How the hearts in the land are breaking,
> My dearest, unless you go." (4)

As Paula Bennett notes, readers in the nineteenth century did not hear the irony behind lines like these, because they were conditioned not to (163). Specifically, what they were used to hearing in genteel war poetry was a woman urging her beloved on for God and country, that is, a stereotyped performance of gender. It is that performance that Piatt subtly deconstructs here, with the husband's service for the wife's own curiosity only.

I have found it useful in the classroom to set "Hearing the Battle" against the backdrop of stock call-to-arms verse where a woman is the impelling agent. For instance, the speaker of John Daly's poem "Confederate Daughters" refers to the "Southern wife or mother" who with "tear-dimmed eyes and breaking heart" launches her man on to war: "Go, my all, and come / Back with your shield or 'pon it!" In another, anonymous, poem of the period, "The Southern Mother's Charge," it is again the woman's commandment that wakes men to their duty:

> You go, my son, to the battle-field
> To repel the invading foe;
> 'Mid its fiercest conflicts never yield
> Till death shall lay you low.

The female speaker in Alexander B. Meek's "Wouldst Thou Have Me Love Thee" directly ties her affections to her lover's patriotic performance:

> Should the God who smiles above thee
> Doom thee to a soldier's grave,

> Hearts will break, but fame will love thee,
> Canonized among the brave!
> Listen, then! thy country's calling
> On her sons to meet the foe!
> Rather would I view thee lying
> On the last red field of strife,
> 'Mid thy country's heroes dying,
> Than become a dastard's wife!
>
> (Capps 199–200)

And in Lucy Larcom's "A Loyal Woman's 'No,' " we again witness a woman who refuses her man for his refusal to go into battle, this time for the Union cause: "[I am] [n]ot yours,—because you are not man enough / To grasp your country's measure of a man" (*Poetical Works* 98). In "Hearing the Battle" Piatt measures the sentimentalism and shrill patriotism that some women perform to commit soldiers to their deaths, undercutting that ideology with a fierce and foreign irony.

Piatt also tropes the pervasive cultural figure of the female survivor (whether betrothed, wife, sister, or daughter). Typically in Civil War verse the bereaved finds consolation in the cause for which the beloved died, and the poem enacts a patriotic recuperation of him and his noble sacrifice. Piatt dismantles the political and religious ideologies that normally offer comfort; instead she focuses on the unremitting pain and suffering—and bitterness and doubt—of the civilian survivor. In "Giving Back the Flower" (1867), her speaker addresses her dead lover and questions God's presence, his divine plan. Mocking her lover's claim that God witnessed his expression of love to her when he gave her a flower to wear as a token of his affection before going off to war ("as God as my witness"), she says, "if He [God] was near us at all, do you think that He would sit listening there . . . / While, so close to us, down in another street, in the wet, unlighted air, / There were children crying for bread and fire, and mothers who questioned His Grace?" She goes on to deride the idea of God's protection, with an eye on the terrain where her beloved was killed: "Or perhaps He had gone to the ghastly field where the fight had been that day, / To number the bloody stabs that were there, to look at and judge the dead" (7). The hexameter and heptameter lines point toward epic, but those generic associations are undone by the speaker's suggestion that the glory of war is false, that the Civil War cannot be constructed by either side as a holy war.

Similarly shaken is the female speaker in Piatt's poem "A Hundred Years Ago" (1870), who gives back her ring to the dead lover in his coffin, remembering with nostalgia her own psychic wholeness and unwavering faith in God—a faith forever shattered by war: "I did not feel this dim, far-trembling doubt / Of Christ's love in the sky, or man's below" (13). Nearly fifty years later, the modernist poet Amy Lowell in "Patterns" also will express the silent suffering that goes on for women on the home front, staging both the gendered restraint imposed by social proprieties ("my passion / Wars against the stiff brocade" [58]) and, ultimately, the breaking through in a firm (and perhaps profane) questioning of the divine plan that would rob her of her betrothed "In a pattern called a war. / Christ! What are patterns for?" (61).

Mourning on the home front is a concern of many of Piatt's war poems, and her configuration of that space is congruent with her assault on romanticism and sentimentalism generally. "Army of Occupation" was written presumably to commemorate the tomb of the unknown soldiers in September 1866 in Arlington National Cemetery, formerly the plantation of the Confederate general Robert E. Lee. The "sleeping army" interred at Arlington answered the call ("They saw the dust, they joined the moving mass, / They answer'd the fierce music's cry for blood") and unceremoniously "straggled here and lay down in the grass" (5). The mourners who have come to the cemetery are women unsupported by faith: "The mothers, sisters, wives with faded eyes, / Who call still names amid their broken talk" (7). Their anguished cries make them appear as "dreadful phantoms of the living," an ironic reversal that points up the death in life that the survivor must endure. In "There Was a Rose" (1872), the speaker desires to recover a lover (figured as the rose) who has been killed in war, even if it means reliving the deaths of all soldiers and reactivating "the women's widowed cries" (42). There is no solace in transfiguration or compensation, only pain and anger and longing, as the speaker strips war of all of its romantic ideologies, with even victory appearing "ghastly" (28).

If one sets Piatt's elegiac poetry beside others of its kind from the period, one can see just how rhetorically and politically challenging—and astonishing—it is. For instance, in Ball's popular poem "The Jacket of Grey" we are presented with a dead soldier's jacket "spotted and tattered, and stained now with gore" that must sustain: "Tenderly touch it, look on it with pride / For dear must it be to our hearts evermore, / The jacket of grey our loved soldier boy wore!" (Steinmetz 34). In Piatt's poem "One from the Dead," "The coat . . . shot through / The breast . . . and fiercely stained" does not provide comfort; rather, it provokes censure:

Oh, coward-praise men give to dust,
Only when it lies motionless and mute
Beneath the shining slander, which it must
Not, till the Judgment-light, refute! (25)

Also at odds with Piatt is "The Soldier's Fireside, after a Battle" by the anonymous M. T. C. Here we encounter a triptych of "A sister, a wife, and a mother, / With hearts too heavy to pray" awaiting news from the front; ultimately, though, their faith grants them relief:

Each thought of the loving Father
Who makes the brave soldier His care,
And their doubt and despair were routed
By the holy power of prayer. (26)

Laura C. Redden's "Left on the Battle-Field" constitutes yet another performance of gender in the elegiac verse produced by the Civil War that is at an angle to Piatt's. In it the betrothed woman of a fallen soldier bewails her fate:

Oh, my darling! My darling! Never to feel
    Your hand going over my hair!
Never to lie in your arms again,—
    Never to know where you are!
Oh, the weary miles that stretch between
    My feet and the battle-ground,
Where all that is left of my dearest hope
    Lies under some yellow mound!

This woman is in agony, unrelieved even at the poem's end:

You are not dead! You are not dead!
    God never could will it so—
To craze my brain and break my heart
    And shatter my life—I know!

However, the similarities to Piatt stop there. Redden's speaker renounces the world:

I am left alone, and the world is changed,
So dress me in bridal white,
And lay me in some quiet place
Out of the hateful light. (28)

Piatt's women on the other hand voice their anger in the light of day, in poems that lay siege to normative gender roles and the consolations that governed rhetorical performance after the war.

Escaping the romanticism to which others succumb, Piatt dwells on civilian enactments of gender and the ideologies that support them. Coupled with her tonal indirections and ambiguous phrasings, this approach marks her as a protomodernist poet. Indeed, the resistance that she puts up to the fictions of war and remembrance that shape cultural practice in America at the time offers a strenuous counterexample for readers trying to come to terms with their roles both during and after that event. Her poems shed light on the instability of identity that is written into the war and remains one of its most potent legacies.

If Piatt challenges the gendered positions of war and war poetry, Frances Harper and Paul Dunbar chart their racial constellations, writing from the charged atmosphere of Reconstruction and the Jim Crow era. Harper was active in the antislavery movement before the outbreak of the war, and the oratorical flair of her poems, meant to be recited, offers a different style from those of Melville and Piatt, as students easily hear. For all their formal regularity, though, Harper's poems do not lead to a reinscription of dominant positions; they seek through their regularity to build a consensus around a different course for the nation, to secure the civil liberties of African American citizens. In "An Appeal to the American People," Harper uses thumping three-beat lines to underscore the fact that during the war black men were "faithful to the end," fighting "side by side" with white Americans in common cause to bring the Confederacy down:

With your soldiers, side by side,
Helped we turn the battle's tide,
Till o'er ocean, stream and shore,
Waved the rebel flag no more,
And above the rescued sod
Praises rose to freedom's God.
(*Complete Poems* 82)

Now that Southerners are seeking to deny rights to African Americans won "upon the field," Harper's speaker plays to the "manhood" of Union veterans, urging them to stand up to the new assault lest "the name of freedom be / Linked with bitter mockery" (83). Similarly, in the ballad stanzas of "Words for the Hour," Harper exhorts Northern men not to "quit the battle-field," invoking their sense of duty as she insists that the war is not over yet: "Secure the victories won by blood / When treason bit the dust" (102, 103)

Ask your students how they feel about the approach Harper takes, her strategy to effect political change. It can be useful to show how certain ideologies that Melville and Piatt undermine are left largely intact by Harper, whereas ideologies that do not even register or register less significantly for Melville and Piatt become of crucial significance for African Americans years beyond the war's official close. While there is moral rectitude to the war for Harper (with the Union on the side of right), other ambiguities and paradoxes seep in. These are pointed up most vividly, perhaps, by the feisty Aunt Chloe in "The Deliverance." Chloe watches as the only son of her mistress goes off to war, and while Chloe says that she "felt sorry" for her, when the two women pray, they do so at cross-purposes:

> Mistus prayed up in the parlor,
> That the Secesh all might win;
> We were praying in the cabins,
> Wanting freedom to begin.
> (*Brighter Coming Day* 200)

The poem ends in a recognition of the power of the vote, which, Chloe argues, must not be sold or "fool[ed] away" (204). She stands as an effective counter to the popular white stereotype of the passive and incompetent ex-slave, and students should be encouraged to explore the canniness of her racialized performance.

Dunbar, whose parents had been slaves and whose father served in a black regiment during the war, was born in the year Harper's *Sketches of Southern Life* (1872) first appeared. His historical remove from the war does not, however, keep him from seeking to recuperate—to reenact—the experiences of the war in his poetry, which is focused on racial injustice. In "The Colored Soldiers" in *Lyrics of Lowly Life* (1896), he impresses on his readers the solidarity forged in war, a bond that must not be broken in the aftermath of fighting: "They were comrades then and brothers, / Are they more or less today?" Like Harper's "An Appeal to the American People," Dunbar's poem insists on the shared sacrifice of whites and blacks and on the heroism of black soldiers: "[T]heir blood with yours commingling / Has enriched the southern soil" (51). Students might compare these attitudes and tones to those in Whitman's war poetry, where fraternity is imagined in a Southern soil "leaven'd" with the bodies of both Union and Confederate soldiers (*Walt Whitman Archive*; path: *Leaves of Grass* [1891–92]; "To the Leaven'd Soil They Trod").

"The Colored Soldiers" is written in standard English. Dunbar's dialect poem "When Dey 'Listed Colored Soldiers" represents a very different register and reading experience. In this poem, Dunbar exchanges an ironic probing of "de glory of de right" for a probing of the racial background of war, the "rights" of blacks to fight but not to live on equal footing after the war. Spoken by a newly emancipated African American woman whose beloved goes off to war in the Union ranks (and ultimately is killed), the poem expresses a certain ambivalence in its sympathies and is itself about that feeling of ambivalence:

> "Bofe my mastahs went in gray suits, an' I loved de Yankee blue,
> But I t'ought dat I could sorrer for de losin' of 'em too;
> But I couldn't, for I didn't know de ha'f o' whut I saw,
> 'Twell dey 'listed colo'ed sojers an' my 'Lias went to wah. (183)

The African American poet-critic Sterling Brown has suggested the problematic nature of this lyric, where he feels Dunbar gives way to "plantation sentimentalities," with a love for the master expressed alongside the fight for freedom (33). Teachers might raise the issue of dialect poetry and its effects, asking students to judge for themselves whether Dunbar is conceding anything in these poems (and, if so, why) or slyly voicing dissent.

Like Harper, Dunbar does not call into question the heroism that the war stages or the sanctity of sacrifice ("dat's whut Gawd had called him for"), and in "The Unsung Heroes" he lauds "The men who feared the master's whip, but did not fear the fight" (184, 197). But he does question the idea that the war is over, asserting instead the war's continuance, "Till the pride of face and the hate of race grow obsolete and cold"(197). In his sonnet, "Robert Gould Shaw," honoring the famous leader of the first all-black regiment recruited to fight for the Union army, Dunbar clearly announces that the fight was "in vain!" as "the Present teaches" (221). His poem is meant to wake white citizens up to the fact that in Jim Crow America, the promise of equality and freedom for African Americans has been breached. It is instructive to juxtapose Harper's and Dunbar's poems to the lyric "Ethiopia's Dead" by Sarah E. Shuften, where the speaker unambivalently honors the memory of black soldiers killed in the war. Writing in 1865, Shuften views the cause as sacred ("The land is holy where they fought, / And holy where they fell"), and her speaker is full of hope in what is now "Our *free* and happy land" (P. Bennett, *Nineteenth-Century American Women Poets* 443, 444). Writing years later, Harper and Dunbar call into question the racial harmony and justice that Shuften celebrates. For them, the word *free* rings with irony.

In an effort to place these poems into an even fuller context, I often discuss them with my students in the light of Bret Harte's "A Second Review of the Grand Army" (24 May, 1865), a poem in which Harte imagines in charged political terms the sight of

> the dusky martyrs of Pillow's fight,
> With limbs enfranchised and bearing bright:
> I thought—perhaps 'twas the pale moonlight—
> They looked as white as their brothers!
>
> (Marius et al. 26)

Harte's message here is that war assigns everyone the same status and that the bravery of African Americans in war brings out their essential humanity, confirming their citizenship. Teachers also might highlight passages from James Madison Bell's "A Poem Entitled the Day and the War," in which he sings the praises of the "Union Black Brigade" who were "Prejudged of slavish cowardice" but "proved they were men" through their valiant fighting (Marius et al. 190, 191). In these poems, the performance of gender is stereotyped, for a clear purpose, even as racial ideology and its performance are contested and transfigured. Perhaps most effective for use in the classroom is Ambrose Bierce's "The Hesitating Veteran," a satiric poem that questions the worth of the war in the light of the fact that freed black men are being deprived systematically of their political rights in its wake (Marius et al. 433–35). Together, these lyrics reveal how poetry focused on the issue of race, whether by black or white writers, led not long after the war was over to questions as to whether it could be justified, whether it was in the end worth the high price paid.

When we bring these poets into the same frame in our syllabi and present teaching, we can begin to see how disparate the experiences of war and the responses to them are. We are able to note how reenactments of the war in verse—some in partisan hues, others not; some enigmatic, others less so—give voice to a range of perspectives, many of which contest conventionally heroic ideals and strains. Just as contemporary Civil War reenactments on the battlefield seek to remember and honor, so too every time we read a poem produced by the war, we are put into the position of reenactor: we are called on to remember, to revive the past in terms of the present, to review that literature in the light of our own experience of war and the moral questions that war raises. Reactivating these poems points us to a deeper understanding of ourselves—of our relations to others; of the codes that guide our conduct; and of our capacity for bearing and relieving "great after-grief," as Piatt puts it in "One from the Dead" (25).

When a nation commits itself to war, every citizen of that nation is committed to war, is on a war footing. It is everybody's right—and duty—to seek answers to the questions prompted by that new footing: What led us to this point? What are we fighting for, and is it worth it? How do we best express our consent or dissent? What are we to do after the fighting is over? Melville and Piatt effectively shatter the romance of war through a fierce realism that peels back the veneer of glory and through a subtle irony that punctures sentimental creeds and conventions. Harper and Dunbar interrogate the grounds on which the war was fought and call into question whether it has in fact concluded, reminding white Americans of the service black soldiers provided during the war and of the rights for black Americans that still must be secured. When our students ask hard questions about war, as they inevitably do and as the situation in Iraq has them doing and will have them doing, poets like these demonstrate that attempts in the nineteenth century to comprehend war and its effects are not unique; rather, they predict our own.

Elizabeth Renker

"I Looked Again and Saw": Teaching Postbellum Realist Poetry

The revolution in the American literature canon presents significant new challenges to the teaching of poetry. At the large state university where I teach, undergraduates are more resistant to poetry than to any other genre. They fear it for its foreign diction, its lack of syntactic familiarity, and its essentially metaphoric nature. Teaching postbellum poetry by poets whose names they do not instantly recognize as great presents additional challenges. While literary criticism has long provided a range of teachable narratives about the poetry of Walt Whitman and Emily Dickinson, scholars are still in the early stages of assessing what the recovered poets of postbellum America mean to literary history. Those of us who want to teach those poets therefore must devise pedagogies in a field still very much in flux.

When I teach postbellum American literature to undergraduates, I teach a concept that I call realist poetry. I situate realist poetry as a part of American realism more broadly construed. If you are teaching American realism for the first time, you will find that both the scholarship on realism and the American literature anthologies that discuss it routinely cover fiction by a relatively standard group of authors—William Dean Howells, Mark Twain, Henry James, the local colorists, Theodore Dreiser, Stephen

Crane, and so on—but they do not cover poetry at all. Like the anthologies, conventional scholarly accounts of American realism also fail to engage poetry, as Cheryl Walker has pointed out ("Nineteenth-Century Women Poets" 25). Even recent articles about expanding the canon of American realism neglect the genre entirely. Walker notes that this neglect of poetry's place in American realism is a product of recent history, since as late as the 1930s poetry was still considered part of it (39).

The time is right for reassessing poetry's place in American realism, both in scholarship and in the classroom. The post-1940 construction of realism that excludes poetry is utterly belied by the exploding new canon of postbellum American poems, in which we can see a powerful realist drive. For purposes of this short essay, I define postbellum realist poetry by way of two primary features. Like the realist fiction of the era, realist poetry attempts to represent something it construes to be the real, with all the attendant complications, both literary and ontological, that such a project entails. Simultaneously, realist poets engage, invoke, and reject in aggressive ways the poetic conventions of the romantic and the sentimental.

I teach realist poetry in a brief unit in the American literature survey as well as more extensively in upper-division courses on postbellum American literature. I have also adapted the concept to special-topics courses on nineteenth-century American poetry and on individual authors such as Herman Melville and Sarah Piatt. Even from a merely practical standpoint, the pedagogy of realist poetry works for a variety of reasons. First, at many institutions, postbellum American literature has typically been taught as a fiction course; the concept of realist poetry provides a motivated way to integrate the fiction and poetry of the era. Second, my undergraduates' frequently automatic bias against poetry often stems from their assumption that it is an airy kind of writing that has nothing to do with real life. Their experience with realist poetry shakes up this assumption, often with force. Third, realist poetry has proved in the classroom to be a capacious rubric under which to explore the other, sometimes discordant, poetic impulses of the era. As Carlin T. Kindilien points out in his 1956 *American Poetry in the Eighteen Nineties*, the literary marketplace between 1880 and 1900 was one in which more books of verse were published in the United States than ever before (5). Romantic, realist, decadent, symbolist, and other poetic strains coexisted. Instructors can play other literary impulses against the realist theme. This conceptual structure has the virtue of maintaining the kind of teachable, big-picture narrative that undergraduates thrive on; at the same time, it leaves ample room to explore its complications. In sum, the heuristic device of realist poetry provides not only a much-needed correction to the standard accounts of American realism but also a productive, integrative springboard from which to examine the diverse literary impulses of the era more generally.

To make sense of the concept of realist poetry, my undergraduates need a clear, solid grounding in the concept of realism itself, in the specific incarnation of realism in postbellum America, and in the relation of realism to romance as an alternative literary mode. My introduction to the unit explains that the term *realism* is a complex one, having a variety of definitions in philosophy, art, and literary history. I sketch these, in a general way, as engagements with the questions of what constitutes the real, how our minds could recognize it, and how to represent it. As scholars of realism such as Michael Davitt Bell and Eric J. Sundquist have noted, the practice of realism contains tremendous variation, so I also alert my students early on to the fact that realist practice contains modes that are sometimes at odds with one another. Realism does not always look the same way just because it is realism. As the class discussion becomes more sophisticated, I introduce the concept that realism too is a form of representation; it can never be the real thing itself. If you are teaching a mixed-genre course, then James's tale "The Real Thing" will make this point for you beautifully.

Although my focus in this essay is teaching postbellum poetry, it is important to let students know that recent scholarship has pushed the origins of realism well back into the antebellum period. A genealogy of earlier realist writing now includes fiction by Caroline Kirkland (*A New Home: Who'll Follow?* [1839]) and Rebecca Harding Davis (*Life in the Iron Mills* [1861]) as well as the poetry of Alice Cary, Phoebe Cary, and Maria White Lowell at mid-century (see Sharon Harris, *Rebecca Harding Davis*; C. Walker, "Nineteenth-Century Women Poets"). Classes centered in the postbellum era can note the new antebellum genealogy of realism, then point out that realism as a literary cause gains striking prominence after the war. At that time, the term *realism* becomes newly central to debates about the nature of the literary (Glazener 38, 43). Addressing shifts in the cultural role of realism can help students see that the postbellum United States did not invent realism but did afford it a new sphere of cultural work as a mark of literary distinction.

Noting that realism gathered increasing momentum in the United States after the Civil War for both social and literary reasons, I review the cataclysmic changes that characterized the period following the war. For example, I address the transition from a primarily rural, farm-based economy to an increasingly urban, industrial order and the shift from what the historian Robert H. Wiebe wonderfully calls a nation of "loosely connected islands" prior to the war to a newly unified nation linked by systems of communication and transportation (4). These vast social changes, I explain, are related to major shifts in American literary culture. Here I draw on the extensive body of secondary work on American realism. Although, as I've already noted, they contain no discussion of poetry, sources like Donald Pizer's *The Cambridge Companion to American Realism and Naturalism* provide useful critical overviews for instructors new to the topic, and Pizer's *Documents of American Realism and Naturalism* provides a useful collection of critical essays dating from the late nineteenth century (by James, Howells, Frank Norris, Dreiser, and the like) to the work of contemporary academics. From a more theoretical standpoint, Bell's *The Problem of American Realism* and Nancy Glazener's tour de force *Reading for Realism* provide instructors with an invaluable education about the genealogy of American realism, one that greatly enriches classroom teaching of the subject.

I then move from the larger conceptual frame to actual voices from postbellum literary culture. Howells, long considered the dean of American realism, proves very useful for setting up the major issues. I use his definition of realism as "nothing more or less than the truthful treatment of material" (Baym et al. 240 ["W. D. Howells"]) as a touchstone to which I return throughout the unit: students remember it, and it plays very well against both compatible and competing visions in the work of other realists (e.g., Sarah Orne Jewett and Hamlin Garland in the former camp; James, Melville, and Piatt in the latter). If your class has only a short time to spend on setting up the concept of realism, one economical way to cover Howellsian realism is either to summarize or to assign Howells's essay "Novel-Writing and Novel-Reading: An Impersonal Explanation." In it, Howells sets out a basic realist ethos and juxtaposes the realist to romancers both good (Hawthorne) and bad (almost everyone else).

Whether you assign it or summarize it, "Novel-Writing and Novel-Reading" gives your students the opportunity to see how actively and passionately realists like Howells opposed romance. It also gives you an opportunity to provide a brief but necessary lecture about romance as an orientation toward subject matter dramatically distinct from that of realism. Judicious quotation from Nathaniel Hawthorne's prefaces provides fruitful counterpoints to Howells's realist ethos in a way that quickly and clearly makes the distinctions my students need to learn.

I also explain that, while our class is concerned with a particular moment in literary history, the fundamentally opposed realist and romantic orientations toward subject matter extend far beyond the American postbellum period. We spend some class time talking about recent examples from popular culture that fall into each category, often from current films and television programs. My students observe that *In the Bedroom* is realism, while *Spiderman* and *Revenge of the Sith* are romance. We also have a lively exchange about reality TV, about why soap operas are romances, and about Mike Myers's parodies of James Bond–style romance in the Austin Powers series. We continue to draw current examples of realist versus romantic modes into our discussions of American literary culture throughout the term. I have found these contemporary anchors for the postbellum debate to be inspiring to my students; they make current and pertinent what could otherwise seem an antiquated literary problem. One student thanked me on an evaluation form for giving her what she felt to be just the intellectual ammunition she had long needed to defend her love of soap operas.

The opposition between the romantic and the realist has long animated assessments of postbellum fiction. It is an equally useful paradigm for reading realist poetry, another indication of the integrated rather than separate concerns of these genres. I have found it to be clarifying for students if I begin the unit by juxtaposing poems that are emblematic of both traditions, ideally ones that engage similar tropes from opposite standpoints. As Kindilien notes, romantic poetry was alive and flourishing in the postbellum era (34–56). If you are new to this topic, you will find that perusing any of the myriad poetry anthologies of the period (see, e.g., Bates; Stedman, *American Anthology*), as well as American periodicals such as *Scribner's Monthly*, *The Atlantic Monthly*, *Overland Monthly*, *The Galaxy*, and so on, will yield many gems for classroom use.

If your class is using a current anthology as a textbook, stray from it into the nineteenth-century archive, where you will find an abundance of poems that are not included in textbooks today—particularly the romantic poems that have disappeared from literary history as hopelessly conventional. If your institutional library has solid holdings, you will find many nineteenth-century poetry anthologies and periodicals on your shelves. Nineteenth-century periodicals are increasingly available online as well. Asking your students to locate and assess poems in these sources can provide the backbone of a terrific research assignment. A complete finding list for all Piatt's poems, for example, is available on the Web (*Finding List*), while the Ohio State University's Rare Books and Manuscripts Library holds a complete set of Piatt materials (see *Paula Bernat Bennett's Research Materials*). My undergraduates in a special-topics course on Piatt found it fascinating to look at her poems in their periodical and anthology contexts and to compare them with other poems of the era. Paula Bernat Bennett's 2001 selected edition of Piatt also records where each poem was published.

One romance-realist juxtaposition that I teach is Edmund Clarence Stedman's maudlin medieval poem "The Test," in which a series of pale maidens vie over who loved best an idealized dead man (*Poetical Works* 152–54), against Stephen Crane's "A youth in apparel that glittered" in which an "assassin / Attired in garb of old days" kills a youth who is "enchanted" by these "legends" (*Complete Poems* 29). My students enjoy teasing out the consequences of each perspective. The dead male figure that Stedman idealizes is set up by Crane as a fool. One of my students pointed out that Crane's youth cannot see the grimness of the "grim forest" in which he walks, because he is living in romantic illusion; that illusion results not only in his literal death but also in his artistic death. His vision cannot come to terms with the actual world that snuffs him out. In addition to the contrast in how these poets use the stock romantic tropes of courtly England, Stedman's conventional Victorian poetic form (trochaic pentameter terza rima) and diction work in illuminating contrast with Crane's spare lines of free verse, helping students see the ideological content of changes in poetic form, an element of poetry on which they otherwise tend to stumble. Formally speaking, the realist Crane strips away the poetic "apparel that glittered," then asks what poetry will become in its wake. Or, as he puts it in "If I should cast off this tattered coat":

> If I should cast off this tattered coat,
> And go free into the mighty sky;
> If I should find nothing there
> But a vast blue,
> Echoless, ignorant,—
> What then? (70)

As my class explores such juxtapositions, we also begin to compile a working vocabulary derived from the poems we discuss. We draw on this vocabulary throughout the unit. For example, my students noted, when we read Edwin Arlington Robinson's realist poem "Richard Cory"

(1897), the resurgence of Crane's metaphor of glitter. Robinson's realist critique of romantic illusion is similar to Crane's. The townspeople in the poem read Richard Cory romantically, interpreting him as if a figure of courtly England, "imperial" and like a "king" who "glittered when he walked" (Spengemann and Roberts 435–36). The well-known conclusion of the poem of course eviscerates this perspective. In our ongoing compilation of a working vocabulary, we concluded that "glitter" functions as a sign, for both Crane and Robinson, of false romantic veneer. We then became alert to similar tropes in other poems, words that might function like "glitter" elsewhere in the vocabulary of American realist poetry. Piatt's repeated trope of "moon-shine" was one we eventually added to that category.

Another, perhaps surprising, realist poet of the 1890s is the dean of realism himself, Howells. Although he is known today primarily for his realist fiction and his editorial crusade on behalf of realism, "in the estimation of his contemporaries, Howells the poet lagged only a step or two behind Howells the novelist," as Julie Bates Dock points out (224). He published an extensive body of poems throughout his life. Scholars of his poetry agree that his early poems are mostly sentimental, romantic treatments of conventional subjects such as death, passion, love, nostalgia, and what Dock calls "the poet's cruel alienation from the mass of men" (226). According to Bernard F. Engel, Howells's poetry "indulges in the practices which he excluded from his prose" (47). But, as Edwin H. Cady points out, after the tragic death of his daughter in 1889, Howells "joined poetry now to his realistic positions" (Introd. xxvii). The poems that followed, particularly in his dark 1895 volume *Stops of Various Quills*, express personal and social despair in an ironic, doubting voice.

Howells's poem "Society" works beautifully in the realist poetry unit, even while giving realism a phantasmagoric twist ("*Pebbles*" 60–61). The double-edged title, a synonym for upper-class company and a dispassionate scientific term for the mass of human beings, plays out in the two parts of the poem. In the first part, we find the trappings of a classic scene—"beautiful women and lordly men, / Taking their pleasure in a flowery plain," dancing and sporting in silken garments—that, had the poem ended there, might have featured in any number of romantic poems from a postbellum periodical. But Howells carefully allows the nightmarish to seep into his portrait. His figures are playing in a field of red flowers, and as they move about, the redness begins to stain their heels and hems. "In their delight; and all so high and proud / They seemed scarce of the earth whereupon they trod," the narrator tells us of these unearthly beings. In keeping with the premise in our realist poetry unit that realist poems themselves often imagine their own romantic antithesis, we note carefully the narrative frame. Part 1 begins, "I looked and saw"; part 2 begins, "I looked again and saw. . . ." The second time, the speaker sees "that flowery space / Stirring, as if alive" and goes on to recount an old man's head, a "baby's gasping face," a mother's bosom, a girl's throat: they are the field on which "society" is trampling, and "what had seemed the red / Of flowers was blood, in gouts and gushes," he reports. "Society" also provides a good opportunity to discuss with students the variations in realism: clearly Howells is pitting romantic and realistic visions of society against each other, but the realist critique in the second half is phantasmagoric rather than photographic.

Piatt is one of our most profound realist poets, increasingly recognized as a major American poetic voice, although her name was unknown just a few years ago. Born in Kentucky as Sarah Morgan Bryan, she married into the Ohio Piatt family. She published prolifically in periodicals and books during a career that lasted from 1854 until her death in 1919. Her poems work deftly with multilayered and discrepant perspectives, gaps in conversation, off-camera dialogue, and the speaker's own sometimes limited self-knowledge. My English majors are often familiar with modernist poems; Piatt's extensive experiments with perspective stun them, because they have been taught to see as modernist inventions poetic techniques that Piatt is already exploring in the 1870s. As one of my students commented, "I do think the concept of realist poetry in the postbellum US is very helpful . . . it allows me to understand the shift from sentimentalism to modernism more completely." Many students are uneasy with the perceived gap between nineteenth- and twentieth-century writers and appreciate having it filled.

Piatt frequently writes dramatic poems that Bennett calls "dialogue-based realist lyrics" (*Palace-Burner* xxxv). These dialogues are conversations between two parties (often lovers, husband and wife, or mother and child), but Piatt characteristically presents only one primary speaking voice, leaving other voices partial in a way that requires the reader's imaginative reconstruction. At first my students are baffled by these dramatic dialogues, but once I explain the conceit to them and show them how it works, they come to find their necessary participation in constructing the missing perspective to be an exciting puzzle. Then we come to the more complex question: In what does Piatt's realism inhere? Surely, her realism is in part about representing with accuracy the phenomena of American postbellum culture, the concentric circles of the public social world, the private domestic realm, and the interior workings of consciousness. Indeed, her poems are often simultaneously about all three and their necessary imbrications.

In "The Palace-Burner (A Picture in a Newspaper)" (1872), for example, the primary speaker of the poem, a mother addressing her young son, is propelled into crisis as his questions increasingly trouble her self-understanding (39–40). In the course of the poem, we see the concentric circles of public, private, and interior close in on one another. The historical context for the poem is the Paris Commune of 1871, an insurrection in the course of which rebels burned the Tuileries Palace (167n28). Her son has found an illustration of one of the arsonists on her way to execution. I circulate the illustration from *Harper's Weekly* (8 July 1871: 628), which Bennett identifies as likely the one to which the poem refers. The speaker judges this geographically and politically distant woman's life to be remote from her domestic scene ("But this is old, so old that everything / Is ashes here"). The faraway political crisis looms closer to home when the son says not only that he wishes he lived in Paris and burned the palace but also that he wonders if his mother would have done the same. By this point the speaker is worrying about her mothering skills and, in a time-honored gesture, sends him off to play so she can think. I always get a laugh here when I talk about my own son, of roughly the same age as the boy in the poem, and my occasional gratitude for his Game Boy.

The final, most intimate crisis staged in the poem is the speaker's dawning realization that she is estranged from whatever her soul "really" is. Her son, she acknowledges, might indeed know something about her that she doesn't understand: "Can he have seen my soul more near than I?" she asks in anguish. The maternal and domestic trappings of her life are revealed to be only so many romantic accounts—"lips to kiss away a baby's cry, / Hands fit for flowers, and eyes for tears and dreams"—leaving her consciousness, at the end of the poem, in a state of ongoing and very real "fear."

"The Palace-Burner" is, even on its surface, a poem that engages the prospect of burning down the social order. But many of Piatt's poems at first glance resemble the conventional domestic sentimental poems of the era instead. One of the ways that her realism looks different from Crane's and Robinson's—and herein lies the key to the obscurity into which she fell after her death—is that it often realistically mimics what it ironizes. This is a complex idea, and most undergraduates will need patient help with it. At the level of representation, Piatt's realism portrays what we might call the real world. But at the level of metarepresentation, she mimics the sentimental, genteel, romantic poems that she is in fact undermining. Thus poems having the typical subject matter of genteel and sentimental verses—romantic love, courtship and marriage, roses, beauty, and dead children, for example—are actually Piatt's caustic mirror images of their genteel counterparts. The ongoing resistance Piatt's poetry may continue to meet among readers today often hinges on just this misunderstanding. Exhaustive close readings, necessarily progressing line by line with care, enable students to see her irony.

My students are in fact consistently amazed at how Piatt manages to write surfaces and depths at active odds with each other. In the simultaneously witty and moving "The First Party" (1882), the surface tells a tale of a chattering, excited daughter recounting to her mother the story of her first party and her newly awakened feelings for boys (111–12). This poem constitutes an interesting reversal of Piatt's usual dialogue, in which the mother does most of the talking. The girl's energetic babble holds just at its edge the mother's own tale of maturity, loss, and the death of romance. Just as the daughter fails to comprehend her mother's few careful remarks, so Piatt's readers clearly break into two camps: those who enjoy the surface tale and those who also see its darker, ironic depths. Piatt's style pulls off both with astonishing brilliance. One of the most delightful experiences I had as a teacher of "The First Party" was that, after we discussed in detail the ironic intricacies of the mother's subdued presence, I got an incredulous laugh out of my students when I pointed out in what periodical the poem had been published: *Youth's Companion.*

Realist poetry offers a pedagogically effective framework not only for grappling with postbellum poetry itself but also for helping students understand what happened in American poetic history between Whitman and Dickinson and the modernists. Piatt stands as a major figure in this history, and she teaches beautifully. The number of students who tell me on evaluations that she has become their "favorite poet" is remarkable. As one wrote at the conclusion of our course:

> The class opened my eyes to the concept of the realist poet. Prior to this I would have seen the surface of Piatt's poems, glanced at the titles . . . and mistakenly dismissed her as a sentimental woman. Even as a female myself I would have been inclined to disregard her because I was unaware that such poetry, realist poetry, was a missing link in the canon.

I have no doubt that, from the standpoint of reception, Piatt and the postbellum realist poets have found their age at last.

Note

I wish to thank my students Eliza Rotterman and Shannon Dilman for permission to share their remarks.

Angela Sorby

Teaching the Schoolroom Poets

I use the schoolroom poets (William Cullen Bryant, Oliver Wendell Holmes, James Russell Lowell, John Greenleaf Whittier, and Henry Wadsworth Longfellow) to teach my students that many popular nineteenth-century American poems functioned as performance texts. These poems became well known because their rhymes and meters were easy to memorize, because their strong—albeit conventional—images were strikingly theatrical, and because nineteenth-century educators thought they taught important lessons. In the classroom, I reconstruct the material culture and the ideological assumptions of the nineteenth-century schoolroom setting, so that students can ask what a poem such as Whittier's "Barefoot Boy" or Longfellow's "Village Blacksmith" accomplished and why it became so familiar. My approach raises questions about oral performance, pedagogical power relations, individual and collective memory, and the politics of canon formation.

Who were the schoolroom poets? The core members of this group are Holmes, Lowell, Whittier, and Longfellow. These poets, while they differ in significant ways, were lumped together as the New England schoolroom poets by the end of the nineteenth century, when newly established school districts began naming schools after them. Bryant, as a New

Yorker, was a little less iconic, but his name too was chiseled over the doors of many schools. I often begin my discussion by asking if anyone attended a schoolroom poets school. In Milwaukee, Wisconsin, where I teach, there are Whittier and Lowell elementary schools as well as a Longfellow Middle School. These names continue to circulate, then—at least as names. One poem in particular remains in circulation, so another question that I ask, early on, is whether students can finish this sentence: "Listen, my children, and you shall hear . . ." Even today, many know that what "you shall hear" is Longfellow's tale of "the midnight ride of Paul Revere."

The schoolroom poets are no longer generally studied as a group, precisely because their group identity masked serious differences among them. Longfellow and Whittier, clearly the best known, are also the only two to have received much recent critical attention. Longfellow's work has been reclassified as "male sentimentalism" by critics like Eric Haralson ("Mars"), Matthew Gartner, and Mary Louise Kete. Certainly, Longfellow is sentimental: he celebrates home scenes, elevates feelings over thoughts, and performs as what Haralson calls "Mars in Petticoats," taming and recasting the terms of his male power. Whittier, on the other hand, has come to be appreciated mainly for his protest poems, several of which are reprinted in the *Heath Anthology of American Literature* (Lauter et al.). But while the term "schoolroom poets" is archaic, in the classroom it suggests a historical use value for these writers. This use value can, in turn, help structure our contemporary readings. The schoolroom poets are most significant (I would argue) not because they are Romantic or sentimental but because they were so very—indeed remarkably—widely read. American educators (and teachers and students) needed a usable American past, and so they invented a tradition—the tradition of the schoolroom poets.

To read Longfellow, Whittier, Lowell, and Holmes as schoolroom poets, it is first necessary to outline for students how nineteenth-century schoolrooms operated. Obviously, my description must be reductive, since a Boston dame school around 1800 bore no resemblance to a graded urban elementary school around 1899. Because the schoolroom poets circulated mainly in the latter half of the nineteenth century (and well into the twentieth century), I describe a schoolroom from the 1890s. The school's exterior architecture reflects a certain Arnoldian idealism: there are cornices, arches, and perhaps even a few faux marble columns. The classrooms are orderly and hierarchical, with rows of desks facing the teacher. The desks are bolted to the floor, the flag is prominent, and the walls are decorated with pictures of George Washington and Longfellow. The teacher is, in all likelihood, an unmarried woman: badly paid but a self-identified member of the middle class. The children are segregated by race, even in the North, but otherwise come from a variety of ethnic backgrounds. Not all are native speakers of English. If the school is in the West, the Midwest, or the South, their reading texts are probably *McGuffey's Readers.* Corporal punishment is going out of fashion, but humiliation (dunce caps, public shaming) remains a common disciplinary practice. And every Friday is recitation day, when children perform, aloud and in public, what they have learned.

American school systems—and in these systems, the American schoolroom poets—became compulsory state by state, mostly in the decades following the Civil War. Michael Apple's *Ideology and Curriculum* provides a good introduction to educational history. As Apple argues, the schools' exact social role was subject to constant debate, but most educators and politicians agreed that their main mandate was to turn children into good American citizens. Horace Mann saw schools as among the engines of democracy, and from the beginning there was a discourse of social control in American education. At the same time, precisely because they were engines of democracy, schools were also seen as gateways to success, offering merit-based upward mobility to new immigrants who could be taught American values. I often draw a line on the chalkboard to illustrate the tension:

social control ← school → social empowerment

By leaving this line up as we begin to discuss the act of reading, I help students remember the links between how schools were run and how schoolroom poets were read.

In my imaginary nineteenth-century classroom, I picture the children with *McGuffey's Readers* before them. This is more than a random guess. The *McGuffey's* series, first produced in 1839 and still in print today, slowly overtook competing schoolbooks in popularity, until, by the time of its final major revision in 1879, it was by far the most common series in American schoolrooms. Indeed, besides the Bible, *McGuffey's* was probably the most common title in nineteenth-century households. In my view, the best study of the *McGuffey's* phenomenon remains Richard Mosier's *Making the American Mind* (1947); readers seeking a more biographical approach might also consult Dolores Sullivan's *William*

Holmes McGuffey, Schoolmaster to the Nation. While the *McGuffey's* series did not actively promote the cults of personality that developed around the schoolroom poets, it did reprint many of their poems. By using *McGuffey's* as an introduction to the schoolroom poets, I give my students access to a concrete, textual culture—a way to read the poems in concert with rhetorical rules, prose selections, and illustrations.

Copies of *McGuffey's Fourth*, *Fifth*, and *Sixth Readers* (all from 1879) have been digitized and are accessible online (*Nineteenth-Century Schoolbooks*; path: Full-Text Collection, Browse Books, M–O). But I always begin with a brief look (through photocopies) at the first few pages of the most basic *McGuffey's* text, the *McGuffey's Eclectic Primer* (1879). To read schoolroom poets (or any nineteenth-century poets) it is useful to know, from the outset, how nineteenth-century children learned to read. As I share the primer, I point out to my students how reading is consistently linked, from square 1, to reading aloud. Already by 1879, the method used in this primer (which dates all the way back to the *New England Primer* [before 1690]) was being called "phonics." The idea is that students will first learn alphabet sounds, then combinations of sounds, then short words. Finally, these words are combined into absurd little sentences: "I see the ox." Meaning is secondary; sound (and "sounding-out") is paramount. This way of learning turns reading into an intersubjective activity: there is a speaker, and there is an auditor.

This sense of texts working as scripts for social exchange, or social performance, carries over into the more advanced *McGuffey's* volumes, which include numerous selections from poets, both English and American. Since our focus is the schoolroom poets, I invite students to read Longfellow's "Village Blacksmith" in its full context in the *Fifth Reader*. Copies of the *Fifth Reader* are widely available, since the series is still popular (for reasons that students might want to consider) among conservative Christian homeschoolers. Practically speaking, though, most instructors without classroom Internet access will want to assign it as homework, as I do: Go home, I tell my students, browse *McGuffey's Fifth* in the Nietz Old Textbook Collection (*Nineteenth-Century Schoolbooks*), and see if the surrounding text(s) illuminate or raise questions about Longfellow's poem.

When we discuss the poem, I begin the class by leading students through a close reading, noting first the spreading chestnut tree, Longfellow's strongly theatrical frame:

Under a spreading chestnut-tree
    The village smithy stands;
The smith, a mighty man is he,
    With large and sinewy hands;
And the muscles of his brawny arms
    Are strong as iron bands. (154; lines 1–6)

In case the child readers have not caught that they are the poem's audience and that they are to learn something from the blacksmith, Longfellow continues:

And children coming home from school
    Look in at the open door;
They love to see the flaming forge,
    And hear the bellows roar,
And catch the burning sparks that fly
    Like chaff from a threshing-door. (155; lines 19–24)

The poem goes on to describe the blacksmith going to church on Sunday, listening to his daughter sing in the choir, thinking about his dead wife, and then resuming work. It concludes thus:

Toiling—rejoicing—sorrowing,
    Onward through life he goes;
Each morning sees his task begin,
    Each evening sees it close;
Something attempted, something done,
    Has earned a night's repose.

Thanks, thanks to thee, my worthy friend,
    For the lesson thou hast taught!
Thus at the flaming forge of life
    Our fortunes must be wrought;
Thus on its sounding anvil shaped
    Each burning deed and thought! (lines 37–48)

I ask my students, How does this work as a schoolroom poem? How does it envision the social order? What is the role of the children? Whose voice is speaking in the last stanza? How, in short, does the poem teach its readers to read?

We then discuss the larger context of *McGuffey's Fifth Eclectic Reader* and whether it adds to the poem's meaning. Students might note the valorization of common labor in "The Generous Russian Peasant" (158), the emphasis on finding a (male) vocation in "Little Victories" (314), and the overt Christianity reflected in selections from the Bible (84), despite the text's use in public schools. All these other passages reflect on the values performed by the village blacksmith, who is hardworking, masculine, and Christian—and therefore exemplary. That he is also preindustrial, working at his own forge rather than in a factory setting, is important, because *McGuffey's* advances a doctrine of self-sufficient individualism regardless of circumstances. And herein lies one among many contradictions. Why is the blacksmith so exemplary?, I ask my students. Is it because he accepts his fate without complaint, or because he forges his own destiny? Is he ambitious to rise or content to labor? How does the poem—read alongside other *McGuffey's Fifth* lessons—teach children to act?

The notion of teaching children to act has further ramifications when we turn to the question of oral performance. *McGuffey's Fifth* begins with a long rhetorical lesson, designed to help children control their voices. I sometimes go over this rhetorical lesson orally, asking students to practice the exercises aloud—a task that they tend to find amusing. The "Emphasis" section, for instance, teaches "absolute emphasis," "relative emphasis," "emphatic phrases," and "emphatic pauses," so that students can learn to signal, with their voices, what is important in a poem (28–29). Attention to rhetoric can help students see how reading aloud can change the meaning of a poem. "Thanks, thanks, to thee, my worthy friend / For the lesson thou has taught!" seems like the most unambiguous of phrases, and yet it can play in a number of ways, as students will find if asked to read it rhetorically, with attention to emphasis, pitch, compass, and other oral variables. To what extent, I ask them, is *McGuffey's* standardizing our reading by teaching us rhetorical reading? How is learning to read aloud different from learning to read interpretively? Or is reading aloud a form of interpretation?

Just as the blacksmith stands, framed by the tree and highly visible, in order to teach his lesson, so too were public schoolchildren expected to stand in front of the class, in a highly visible position, to recite the poem. Did students' bodies then become exemplary "forms of labor," like the blacksmith's body? Were students performing not just a poem but also their acceptance of the poem's values, when they read it aloud? How can a poem's meaning—both as literary text and social artifact—be affected by the circumstances of its oral performance?

Once they are aware of the performance component, students will begin to notice the pervasive theatricality of schoolroom poetry—the way it lends itself not just to reading aloud but to reading aloud dramatically. Subtle indirection is avoided in favor of exclamatory apostrophes, as in Holmes's "Old Ironsides," which begins, "Ay, tear her tattered ensign down!" (Hollander 1: 556). Images are vivid and easy to picture, so that auditors can understand the poem even if it is not in front of them. Colors are splashy; in "Old Ironsides," the deck is recalled as "red with heroes' blood" as the waves appear "white below." While Shakespeare was not a schoolroom poet per se, he was widely recited in American classrooms, and his influence—and the influence of nineteenth-century theater—is in evidence. I stress this theatricality to my students as a way of asking them to appreciate moments in the poems that can seem merely melodramatic. Melodrama was not a misstep among the schoolroom poets; it was an expressive option for them, as it was for playwrights of the period.

Repetition was another important part of the schoolroom experience: children read, and heard, the same poems repeatedly. The poems themselves also tend to be repetitive, in the sense of relying on predictable image patterns and conventional rhymes and meters. Like melodrama, these formal features can seem weaknesses to twenty-first-century readers, but there were reasons for avoiding too much innovation. Practically speaking, predictability aided in memorization. The repetition of refrains also gave rhetorical readers a chance to practice their skill. All eight stanzas of "The Heritage," by Lowell, for instance, end with variations on the lines, "A heritage, it seems to me, / One scarce would wish to hold in fee" (McGuffey, *Fifth Eclectic Reader* 228; lines 6–7). Since readers must repeat these lines so often, they are forced to vary the readings in response to the changing circumstances of each stanza. The refrain thus serves as a kind of exercise in emphasis, pitch, and compass. Innovation was also suspect on an ideological plane: exemplary *McGuffey's* characters are industrious, but the good ones are never eccentric. Likewise, the poems display an industrious attention to the rules of prosody, not venturing into experimentalism. The point of these poems, and of *McGuffey's* as a whole, is to teach children about conventions so that they can fit into American society.

Teaching the schoolroom poets also raises the issue of heritage from a different angle. One notable thing about *McGuffey's Fifth* is that even though it is not diverse in a contemporary sense (white Protestant people and values are very much the norm), it is eclectic in the sense that it draws on a fairly wide assortment of writers—male and female, English and American. One of the most common recitation pieces in American nineteenth-century classrooms was by a British woman, Felicia Hemans: "Casabianca."

Yet neither Hemans nor her American counterpart, Lydia Sigourney, became schoolroom poets. There are few, if any, Hemans or Sigourney schools, the poets' portraits were not distributed, and their birthdays were not celebrated. By the same token, Poe, despite having written one of the most popular of all schoolroom recitation pieces, "The Raven," was not considered a schoolroom poet. The term was reserved exclusively for men from the antebellum East Coast literary establishment. When schools chose names, they wanted to emphasize a particular heritage: the New England past of pilgrims, Puritans, Yankee farmers, and snowy Christmas scenes. Even Western schools, located on land colonized by the Spanish, framed their history in this way. Longfellow, Lowell, and Holmes were all New Englanders from "good" Boston Brahmin families who knew one another and published one anothers' work. Whittier came from a long line of Quakers and built a strong social and literary network through the abolitionist cause. Bryant, while he was a New Yorker, was also a well-connected public intellectual with an established lineage. Jane Tompkins has described the dense web of connections that helped elevate Nathaniel Hawthorne to classic status (*Sensational Designs*). Certainly, something similar happened to these poets, who were led by the monumentally influential figure of Longfellow. For nineteenth-century educators, teaching the schoolroom poets, especially the four New England schoolroom poets, was a way to establish the authority of New England as a metonym for America, a project reflected everywhere in the school curriculum. In my classroom, students are always eager to discuss the idea of an invented tradition and the role schools play in propagating such traditions. We also discuss why poetry in particular might be recruited as a repository of tradition.

The schoolroom poets developed cults of personality, like the political figures of George Washington and (in certain states) Abraham Lincoln. As Washington's and Lincoln's birthdays eventually became holidays, poets' birthdays too began to be celebrated in the schools. This practice was extremely widespread by the later nineteenth century, just as marking Dr. Seuss's birthday is widespread today. I sometimes quote from primary sources, such as *Exercises for Authors' Days, for School and Evening Exercises* (1888), to give a sense of how the ceremonies proceeded. This excerpt is from a skit performed on John Greenleaf Whittier's birthday:

> Three little girls bring forward the initials J-G-W and place them (upon hooks for that purpose) beneath a picture of the poet—if one can be procured—reciting in concert:
>
> We bring the letters of his honored name,
> Yes, they did well
> Who named this man to make these letters spell
> Three priceless jewels that he ever wears
> More ornament even than the powers he bears
> Of writing matchless poems.
>
> First girl: The first in **J**ustice, crystal clear and fair
> Second girl: Then **G**enerosity, o gem most rare.
> Third girl: Then **W**isdom, rich far than all the rest,
> Whose gleaming shows God's Way is always best. (13)

I then ask the students, How is Whittier being presented? What is considered important about him in a play like this? Nineteenth-century schoolchildren were taught to read poems for their moral content, so that they could learn and perform this morality themselves, as the three girls are doing in the Whittier play. Behind the poet's name had to stand a moral authority, which such plays helped establish. As we read schoolroom poems in my classes, then, we continue to discuss how the poems work, not just to assert morals but also to establish their own authority (through invented traditions and mandatory performances) as moral texts.

As most instructors are aware, the social status and moral authority of poetry were a problem in the nineteenth century, especially after the Civil War, when so many technological innovations were transforming the nation. What was the good of poetry? I pose this question to my students and let them answer in the present tense, if they choose, since the same question could be asked today. Poetry does not sell, it cannot cure cancer, and most people do not even find it all that entertaining. So what is the point?

Nineteenth-century schools tried to answer this question from a variety of angles. First, there was the Arnoldian argument that poetry fed the spirit—that it was somehow noble (Levine 223). Second, some educators argued that poems like "The Village Blacksmith," which everybody seemed to know, bound the nation together. Third, there was the notion that poetry, precisely because it was an old-fashioned medium, could recover values that were being lost through industrialization. The schoolroom poets fed into all three of these discourses: they had led lives that could be held up as ideal; they were native-born American celebrities, able to show others how to be American; and they were products of an antebellum America, which many Gilded Age people were beginning to see, nostalgically, as a lost preindustrial utopia.

As role models, the schoolroom poets were important not just because of what they wrote but also because of who they were. Even though schools did not always observe the rigid separation of church and state, they by and large were not so bold as to mention Jesus, except at Christmas time. So the schoolroom poets filled a vacuum, acting as icons in an evolving civil religion. Their authority came from their literary reputations and perceived personal qualities. When we discuss how those qualities were deployed to authorize the poems and also to authorize the schools that taught the poems, I ask the students about the relation between biography and authority. Who is authorized to speak in a poem, and why? Does it, and should it, matter who wrote a particular text?

One way in which American schoolchildren internalized the authority of the schoolroom poets was memorization. Memorization is of course a specific kind of learning, and in the nineteenth century being a successful student was essentially synonymous with having a good memory. Memorization is sometimes dismissed by educational theorists such as Paulo Freire as merely banking knowledge, in which the students are the objects of education and thereby dehumanized by it (*Pedagogy of the Oppressed*). In my undergraduate classes, I put this theory to the test by asking students to memorize. For those instructors who have not asked students to memorize in the past, a few words of caution are in order. Some students will embrace the challenge, but others may balk or panic. Sometimes, I have avoided this problem by making recitation an optional, extra-credit assignment; when I do this, typically only a few people take the challenge. I have been more successful at making the public aspects of recitation optional: everyone must memorize, but less gregarious students can perform privately in my office. Generally, once they have memorized the poem and seen a few others perform it, students are willing (though never forced) to stand up in front of the group.

As a rule, I allow students to pick what they will memorize from the *McGuffey's* canon. One standard schoolroom recitation piece that works well is Bryant's "Lines to a Waterfowl" from *McGuffey's Sixth*. In eight elegant stanzas, the speaker addresses a bird as it slowly ascends; then, as in "The Village Blacksmith," he reveals the lesson in the final stanzas:

> Thou'rt gone; the abyss of heaven
> Hath swallowed up thy form; yet, on my heart,
> Deeply hath sunk the lesson thou hast given,
> And shalt not soon depart.
>
> He, who, from zone to zone,
> Guides through the boundless sky thy certain flight,
> In the long way that I must tread alone,
> Will lead my steps aright.
>
> (434–35; lines 25–32)

The poem is easy to gloss on one level because, like "The Village Blacksmith," it announces its lesson so boldly. In the context of *McGuffey's Sixth,* there is no question that "He" who guides the bird and the speaker "from zone to zone" is the Protestant God; and there is no question of what right is, either: "Observance of the Sabbath" (186–89) and "Labor" (398–400) are critical virtues, along with honesty and faith, and if models of right conduct are needed, students can consult the "Character of Columbus" (192–95). To read the poem as a *McGuffey's* lesson is to read it as a poem about the power of nature, but also as a poem that affirms and naturalizes authority.

Students are generally divided, though, over whether to memorize such a poem is simply to internalize the voice of authority. Surely, as presented in the *McGuffey's Reader*, "Lines to a Waterfowl" reiterates lessons, found elsewhere in the Readers, about Christian faith and obedience. But when the poem, or any poem, is memorized, the context changes—probably it changed in the nineteenth century as well as it changes today. I ask my students, How does your understanding of the poem change when you memorize it? When you recite a poem, are you mouthing an absent authority figure's words or are you becoming a kind of authority? How does the balance of power among the writer, the teacher, and the student shift when a poem is learned by heart? Answers to these questions will vary. I can say, however, that while I have heard many complaints about the memorization assignment beforehand, I have not yet had a student express regret at having accomplished it.

I never taught a class exclusively on the schoolroom poets, but I taught them as a unit in lower-division surveys, in upper-division courses in American poetry, and in courses on the Gilded Age. Most often, I present them about halfway through the semester as part of a larger discussion about nineteenth-century American poetry. I make sure that students understand the history of the schoolroom poets: when they wrote, and how they reflected the Romanticism and sentimentalism of the earlier nineteenth century. I want students to know the version of literary history that I am ignoring as I teach these texts in their primary social context. A brief lecture and time line conveys this background easily. Having established the basics, I am free to focus on the social significance of the work.

These poets can also be contrasted with more-innovative writers such as Whitman and Dickinson. I am careful to avoid the trap of setting up an author—Longfellow, for example—to be viewed as somehow inferior to Whitman or Dickinson. Not only is the comparison untrue but it is also comparing apples to oranges. Longfellow and Dickinson have very different aims, and their poems filled very different niches in American culture. Instead, I show how readers learned to read Longfellow in school and how that experience shaped their expectations. I can then introduce Whitman and Dickinson as poets who were in dialogue with social expectations and who made use of the notion of poems as lessons in many of their verses. Whitman in particular is a didactic poet (we may recall that he wrote *An American Primer*), although we might call his teaching methods experimental.

When I first began teaching the schoolroom poets, I expected to have to defend them against readers who, preferring Whitman and Dickinson, would resist Longfellow, Whittier, Lowell, Holmes, and Bryant as dated and preachy. I was surprised to find that many students like, even prefer, these verses, which are so straightforward and accessible. I have actually had to devote some energy to showing why schoolroom poetry has its limits, particularly in terms of its social use value: it drew its authority from a (very white, class-bound) New England past; it offered a fixed version of the truth instead of asking its readers to question the truth; and it elicited performances that showed how well students could learn, sometimes at the expense of allowing them to express their own feelings. In *McGuffey's*, at least, only one way of reading rhetorically exists; to fall into monotone, or to indulge in overemphasis, is to read not differently but incorrectly. Likewise, among schoolroom poets, that traditional forms display a correctness that is mirrored in the lessons taught again forecloses the possibility of writing (or thinking) differently. This regularity reveals how our contemporary approach is—at its best—more open: we read poems for their playful (instead of predictable) uses of language and for the ways that they complicate (instead of oversimplify) our responses to the world. Still, even as I make these points, I encourage my students to take pleasure in schoolroom poems—in their theatricality, their musicality, and even their ringing certainties.

While many scholars, myself included, do research grounded in cultural studies, it can be difficult to integrate this approach into the classroom, because working on nineteenth-century culture requires a fairly broad knowledge of that culture. Where to start? I have found the *McGuffey's* context satisfying in this regard: I can give a writing assignment that asks students to read intertextually, and every primary text they need is available in one volume—*McGuffey's Fifth*, for example—along with a clear sense of where and when this text was read and by whom. This material allows them to draw relatively accurate and specific conclusions, not just about the poems but also about aspects of the (school) culture that valued them.

Ultimately, teaching the schoolroom poets helps students become better readers. Many of my undergraduates expect to "read for the lesson" anyway when they encounter a poem: they want to boil it down and find out what it is teaching. Schoolroom poetry makes this process so explicit that students can begin to question it. Is poetry really just an ornate way of teaching lessons? Surely not, and while reading poems this way can help students appreciate their social history as classroom exercises, I hope that it also helps them rethink how texts acquire cultural value. At its best, the study of schoolroom poetry can encourage students to reevaluate their pedagogical experience and to reconsider how they, as students, interact with the authorities they find in the classroom and on the page.

Part II

Teaching Poets in Context

Paul Lauter

Teaching Lydia Sigourney

How should one teach Lydia Sigourney? Until recently—and still in many quarters—that question was always trumped by another: Why would you want to? But now the work of critics such as Nina Baym ("Reinventing"), Sandra Zagarell, and Patricia Crain, as well as of the editors of this book (P. Bennett, *Poets*; Kilcup, "Lydia Howard Huntley Sigourney"), has begun to move Sigourney out from under the evil shadow of her sole (and hostile) biographer Gordon Haight, allowing us to perceive her merits.

All the same, I doubt that Sigourney plays a major role in most American literature courses—even in Hartford, Connecticut, where she flourished and where I teach. That is unfortunate, for she not only wrote some quite good poetry but also offers a wonderful locus for many of the tasks central to the study of poetry: first, close reading; second, examination of contexts and the cultural work poems do; and third, editing, especially making decisions about the publishing and teaching value of different versions of a single text. Furthermore, precisely because she has been so marginalized, Sigourney comes without the baggage of settled canonical judgments that often paralyze students. In fact I offer a teaching strategy that approaches her work not through some preestablished aesthetic categories but through the historical processes that shape and reshape literary judgments. These canon questions are very helpful in opening poetry to students, most of whom have long since learned to regard "great authors" with a reverential breathlessness fatal both to appreciation and original analysis.

Various reasons contribute to a poet's neglect. First, a dialectic exists between teaching and research. As of this writing, the online *MLA International Bibliography* offers twenty entries on Sigourney, four of them dissertations, and *Literature Online* (which includes almost all her poetry) references twenty-four critical articles, seven of them contemporary reviews of Haight's 1930 book. By comparison, the champion among mid-century American women writers in the *MLA Bibliography* is, not surprisingly, Emily Dickinson, with 2,157 items. The drop-off is precipitous: Harriet Beecher Stowe has 503 items, Margaret Fuller 270, Louisa May Alcott 244, and Harriet Jacobs 137. No one else among women or minority writers comes close to these numbers. To get a sense of proportion, consider the statistics for some of the white men of the "American Renaissance": Emerson, 2,027; Thoreau, 2,057; Poe, 2,976; Hawthorne, 3,481; Melville, the early-nineteenth-century champ, 4,331. (Henry James, by the way, is the late-nineteenth-century champ, with 5,004). Let's go down the list of antebellum white men: Longfellow, 277; Bryant, 177; Whittier, 140; Bronson Alcott, 80; Lowell, 79; Higginson, 44; Orestes Brownson, 41. Contrast this list to additional figures for women and black men: Frederick Douglass, 274; Frances E. W. Harper, 74; Lydia Maria Child, 64; Catharine Maria Sedgwick, 62; William Wells Brown, 51; Susan Warner, 50; Harriet Wilson, 37; Caroline Kirkland, 33; Angelina Grimké, 30; Martin Delany, 25; Fanny Fern, 23; E. D. E. N. Southworth, 23 (many of them dissertations); Maria Susanna Cummins, 17; David Walker, 16; Frances Osgood, 12; and Sarah Piatt, so far but 3, one of these in Italian.

These huge discrepancies have consequences in the classroom, but not only for reasons having to do with materials available to support teaching unfamiliar texts. Teachers of literature are reluctant to move beyond the by now more traditional and safer choices: Stowe, Fuller, Jacobs—and similar later nineteenth-century figures (Jewett has 287 items, Freeman 139, Wharton 1,018). I do not mean to impugn the integrity or seriousness of any of my colleagues in making these choices. Rather, the dynamics of the constricted job market functions—as, I would argue, it was intended to function—to inhibit change and to make risk riskier. It is one thing to teach Margaret Fuller, much less Emerson or Thoreau, whose work is legitimated by the scholarship of many literary colleagues, some reasonably prominent. It is another to take on Sigourney or Alice Cary, whose poems and stories are scarcely vetted.

A more significant factor, perhaps, is the still-reigning paradigm for poetic value. Important poems, we are usually told, display such features as irony, complexity, internal tension, ambiguity. By contrast, a poem's functions or cultural work seldom determine decisions about teaching it. That constraint bears rather hard on Sigourney, since so much of her work was designed to serve particular purposes. These purposes could be quite private, as she indicates in her memoir, *Letters of Life* (1866). People asked her—she wrote with considerable irony—to produce: "an ode for the wedding of people in Maine, of whom I had never heard; the only fact mentioned by the expectant bridegroom, author of the letter, being that his chosen one was the youngest of ten brothers and sisters" (369); "a poem . . . on the dog-star, Sirius" (370); "elegiac verses" for the "owner of a canary-bird, which had accidentally been starved to death" (373); "elegiac lines on a young child" for a father who had supplied "as the only suggestion for the tuneful Muse, the fact that he was unfortunately 'drowned in a barrel of swine's food' " (373); "a monody for the loss of a second wife, fortified by the argument that I had composed one at the death of the first" (374). A vast majority of Sigourney's 945 poems, long and short, contained in *Literature Online* are in these and other senses occasional poems. Moreover, many of her best poems insistently engage the conflicted issues of her day: women's work, slavery, and particularly the genocidal Indian policy of the Jackson administration. But there is little room in still-prevalent modernist poetic theory for work so deeply implicated in particular historical moments, much less in movements for social change. In that respect, Sigourney's poetry has suffered a fate similar to that of most writers on the left of the 1930s–50s (A. Wald).

Modernist discourse has also taught us to despise, for reasons both good and bad, the culture of sentiment. Sentimentality is, of course, a very complex matter, involving issues of gender and class, artistic rivalries, and political conflict that I cannot address here—and need not, since Paula Bennett has addressed them in her rich and powerful *Poets in the Public Sphere*. But it seems to me that the establishment and enforcement of a modernist cultural hegemony may well account for the narrow-mindedness and hysterical tone of most of the screeds directed against Sigourney. The one full-length study of her was written by Haight, a Yale professor of Victorian fiction. It is a hateful book, filled like its title, *Mrs.*

Sigourney: The Sweet Singer of Hartford, with judgments like this one on the first page of the preface:

> I hoped to find among her poems some few pieces that would establish her right to the reputation she enjoyed for half a century as America's leading poetess. But before reading many of the forty-odd volumes through which the search ultimately led me, I was forced to agree that posterity had judged fairly in denying her claim. (ix)

One must wonder why he bothered to go on—perhaps they were distantly related or the city of New Haven had a stake in disparaging Hartford. Certainly, he does little to explain her popularity.

But Haight was hardly alone in his steady denigration of Sigourney. Consider the following quotation from Martha Bacon's *Puritan Promenade* (1964):

> Lydia Sigourney was arch-priestess of an order which had taken vows to prosperity, fatuity and sentiment. She blurred the outlines of the Evangelical scheme of thought and softened its severities while retaining its direct appeal to the emotional surfaces. She made it possible for her audience to love, to suffer, to act and to die vicariously and at no personal inconvenience while lounging in a hammock or warming the feet by the fire. She echoed the opinions of her readers and flattered their egos. What Lydia Sigourney said was exactly what they thought. To a generation emerging into the comfortable materialism of the nineteenth century she was balm to the nerves and a sedative to the conscience. She restated and justified every platitude that the era had coined for its comfort. (49–50)

By contrast, here is Sigourney's own discussion, in her autobiography, *Letters of Life*, of her 1822 volume *Traits of the Aborigines of America*:

> An early acquaintance with the Mohegan tribe of Indians, who resided a few miles from Norwich, and a taste for searching out the historic legends of our forest-people, deepened my interest in their native lineaments of character, and my sympathy for their degraded condition. In the notes of the volume, much information is concentrated respecting them, derived from various sources, in the revision of which I gratefully received the aid of the acute and discriminating mind of my husband. The work was singularly unpopular, there existing in the community no reciprocity with the subject.
>
> Indeed, our injustice and hard-hearted policy with regard to the original owners of the soil has ever seemed to me one of our greatest national sins. (327)

It sees to me almost impossible to reconcile what Sigourney says—and indeed what is in her book, and in her Indian poems generally—with Bacon's attack on her as a writer offering nothing but pap to sheltered consciences.

It is true, of course, that the ways in which certain subjects and certain expressive tactics resonate for readers change over time. T. S. Eliot's canon-establishing essay "The Metaphysical Poets" acknowledges the 250-year eclipse both of the style and the interests of John Donne, George Herbert, Andrew Marvell, and their peers. At the same time, Eliot effectively dismisses the ruminative style of Alfred Tennyson and his compatriots and many of their concerns as well. Not the least of these is a problematic theme for our students, namely, an obsession with death—death not so much a challenge to living ("Had we but World enough, and Time" [Marvell's "To His Coy Mistress"]) as the occasion for exhibiting and consoling loss ("Death found strange beauty on that polish'd brow, / And dash'd it out" [Lauter et al. (5th ed.) B: 1565]). As this last quotation from "Death of an Infant" may suggest, Sigourney was caught up in a Victorian culture of death. I turn more directly to this problem—and it is a problem for teaching her—later; here I wish to mark it as but one of the ways our culture is distant from hers. But before I try to construct a pedagogical bridge between cultures, I wish to consider certain aesthetic issues.

One might argue that however it functioned in its time, Sigourney's work is "weary, stale, flat and unprofitable" (Shakespeare, *Ham.* 1.2.135). Predictably, Bacon, like Haight, does make that argument. But such aesthetic judgments never exist outside culture and therefore outside politics. This truism offers a pivot for teaching, especially because it exposes for student analysis the historical processes by which value judgments are constructed and maintained. We can approach this issue of value by considering a text that Bacon excoriates, "Indian Names." She quotes a stanza from this poem and comments, "Lydia's language for the Indian was biblical, full of ye's and 'tis's and other archaisms, as well as metaphors with a tendency to lurch out of control" (62). Then, after quoting another stanza of the poem, she writes:

> Mrs. Sigourney's verse has one extraordinary quality. As poetry it fails in every respect. It does not challenge the imagination or stir the emotions or enflame the curiosity. But one is aware—just around the corner, as it were—of a haunting tendency to arouse mirth. . . . After plodding through volumes of intolerable stuff we find ourselves laughing, not at something so obvious as a mixed metaphor of waters from

> which we may not wash out names, but at accidents much more subtle. (62)

One might wonder what is behind the gratuitous nastiness, the over-the-top rage frying Bacon's prose. But more to our purpose, Bacon's judgments provide a useful challenge to the assumption most students make that writers who are anthologized and studied display literary values that are universally accepted. The poem itself effectively withstands Bacon's condemnation:

> How can the red men be forgotten, while so many of our states and territories, bays, lakes and rivers, are indelibly stamped by names of their giving?
>
> Ye say they all have passed away,
>   That noble race and brave,
> That their light canoes have vanished
>   From off the crested wave;
> That 'mid the forests where they roamed
>   There rings no hunter shout,
> But their name is on your waters,
>   Ye may not wash it out.
>
> 'Tis where Ontario's billow
>   Like Ocean's surge is curled,
> Where strong Niagara's thunders wake
>   The echo of the world.
> Where red Missouri bringeth
>   Rich tribute from the west,
> And Rappahannock sweetly sleeps
>   On green Virginia's breast.
>
> Ye say their cone-like cabins,
>   That clustered o'er the vale,
> Have fled away like withered leaves
>   Before the autumn gale,
> But their memory liveth on your hills,
>   Their baptism on your shore,
> Your everlasting rivers speak
>   Their dialect of yore.
>
> Old Massachusetts wears it,
>   Within her lordly crown,

And broad Ohio bears it,
    Amid his young renown;
Connecticut hath wreathed it
    Where her quiet foliage waves,
And bold Kentucky breathed it hoarse
    Through all her ancient caves.

Wachuset hides its lingering voice
    Within his rocky heart,
And Alleghany graves its tone
    Throughout his lofty chart;
Monadnock on his forehead hoar
    Doth seal the sacred trust,
Your mountains build their monument,
    Though ye destroy their dust.
  (Lauter et al. [5th ed.] B: 1572–73)

Forms of close reading usefully begin by opening the poem itself to students unfamiliar with the cultural and political conflicts of the particular 1830s moment. Paradox, a hallmark of familiar New Critical analysis, offers a starting point. Sigourney's poem turns on a fundamentally political paradox, precisely the one Bacon mocks: "Their name is on your waters, / Ye may not wash it out." It is useful, I have found, to ask students to unpack these strange yet resonant lines. They will sometimes point to the echoing guilt of Lady Macbeth or to the ways in which Sigourney elaborates on this central metaphor by having waters or other natural phenomena "speak" the presence of Native America. As Crain has nicely framed it, the Indians' continuing presence is "inscribed on and spoken by nature" itself in vivid verbs, as well as in striking proper nouns: the "everlasting rivers speak / Their dialect of yore"; Massachusetts "wears it," Ohio "bears it," Connecticut "hath wreathed it," Kentucky "breathed it hoarse," Alleghany "graves its tone," Monadnock and other mountains "build their monument." The Native presences are thus in a textual sense ubiquitous in the world from which whites have tried to exile them. Here it may be useful to bring in Chief Seattle's perhaps spurious but still resonant speech (though it is of suspect origin, the speech has ironically entered the discourse of Indian writers, and even more spurious versions are familiar to some students):

> And when the last Red Man shall have perished, and the memory of my tribe shall have become a myth among the White Men, these

shores will swarm with the invisible dead of my tribe, and when your children's children think themselves alone in the field, the store, the shop, upon the highway, or in the silence of the pathless woods, they will not be alone. In all the earth there is no place dedicated to solitude. At night when the streets of your cities and villages are silent and you think them deserted, they will throng with the returning hosts that once filled them and still love this beautiful land. The White Man will never be alone. (Lauter et al. [5th ed.] B: 1475)

The haunting presence of the Indian is likewise the subject of Sigourney's late (1854) "The Indian Summer," a poem of more nostalgic tone than "Indian Names":

Gorgeous was the time,
Yet brief as gorgeous. Beautiful to thee,
Our brother hunter, but to us replete
With musing thoughts in melancholy train.
Our joys, alas! too oft were woe to thee.
Yet ah, poor Indian! whom we fain would drive
Both from our hearts, and from thy father's lands,
The perfect year doth bear thee on its crown,
And when we would forget, repeat thy name. (1578)

Here, Nature itself speaks the Indian names that whites, from guilt and practice, "would forget." What provides the edge to "Indian Names" as a poem is the contrast between the language of presence spoken by nature and the distinctive verbs Sigourney puts into the mouth of "ye": "passed away," "have vanished," "fled away." In such verbs we engage the always difficult question of tone: who are the "ye" being addressed, and how does the speaker address them? Why are they made to speak thus evasively?

To answer such questions, one may want to bring Sigourney's poem into conversation with Philip Freneau's "The Indian Burying Ground" (1787 [Lauter et al. (5th ed.) A: 1223–24]); with the section on "The Destruction of the Pequods" from Timothy Dwight's *Greenfield Hill* (1794 [A: 1234–38]); and, more closely still, with parts of William Cullen Bryant's "The Prairies" (1832 [B: 2893–96]) as well as with Elias Boudinot's (Cherokee) "An Address to the Whites" (B: 1445–52). For example, after recounting how the "red man" had conquered the Mound Builders, Bryant writes:

Thus change the forms of being. Thus arise
Races of living things, glorious in strength,
And perish, as the quickening breath of God

> Fills them, or is withdrawn. The red man, too,
> Has left the blooming wilds he ranged so long,
> And, nearer to the Rocky Mountains, sought
> A wilder hunting ground. The beaver builds
> No longer by these streams, but far away,
> On waters whose blue surface ne'er gave back
> The white man's face—among Missouri's spring,
> And pools whose issues swell the Oregon—
> He rears his little Venice. (B: 2895)

In this verse, the dominant emotion is precisely that which goes with a sigh of regret and resignation, the outlook Dwight frames thus:

> Indulge my native land! indulge the tear,
> That steals, impassion'd, o'er a nation's doom:
> To me each twig, from Adam's stock, is dear,
> And sorrows fall upon an Indian's tomb. (A: 1238)

This sentiment also underwrites salvage anthropology, the assumptions that have long justified the looting of native cultures around the world. It seems to me that Sigourney designed her text actively to contest this kind of easy nostalgia, which came to support the politics of removal. The evasive verbs she puts into the mouths of the white speakers she implicitly confronts may be heard to mock verbs like those Bryant actually employs, "has left" or "sought," verbs that have the object of keeping the executioner's face well hidden (Dylan).

"Indian Names" directly challenges that form of casual, nostalgic consciousness, which saw the disappearance of Native peoples as a kind of natural phenomenon—like the turning of leaves in the fall or the displaced activities of the beaver, presented as functionally akin to those of Indians. Sigourney's "Indian Names," to bring historical context into play, is a poem of the mid-1830s, precisely the time when Cherokee removal would lead to the Trail of Tears, the forced removal of most Cherokees from Georgia to the Oklahoma Territory—a series of events with which today's students, unlike Bacon, are at least generally familiar. Sigourney's work, like most of her Indian poems, is part of the struggle for the consciences of Americans, a struggle then (and still) being carried out by Native Americans and their white supporters in a number of venues: Congress, the courts, and the pages of newspapers and magazines.

Sigourney was in fact an activist in the campaign against the removal of Creeks and Cherokees. In 1829 she worked closely with Catharine Beecher to draft, circulate, and file with the United States Congress an unprecedented women's petition against removal. Known as the Ladies' Circular, this petition was signed by thousands of women across the country and became a crucial tool for organizing antiremoval sentiment, especially in the religious community, into a potent political force (Hershberger). Despite the huge mobilization of antiremoval activism, the Congress at President Jackson's behest in May 1830 passed removal legislation that would ultimately—despite a Supreme Court decision favoring Cherokee rights and despite unremitting agitation for their rights—lead to the Trail of Tears.

Although the movement ultimately failed to achieve its political goal, it may have factored centrally in stimulating the transition in antislavery thinking from colonization to immediate and unconditional abolition. It surely was a significant factor in sharpening the rhetoric of Sigourney's agitational verse. In this context, Mary Hershberger also speculates that the experience of circulating and arguing for the Ladies' Circular liberated Sigourney at least to the extent of signing her writings, despite her husband's bitter objections. Stephen Brandon goes further, suggesting that the publication of Sigourney's poem "The Cherokee Mother" with its accompanying introductory materials in the *Cherokee Phoenix* newspaper "played a significant role in the entrance of women into the American public sphere" (191).

But of what real political importance, one might ask—and students do—is the preservation of Indian *names*? That question can itself generate an interesting discussion with respect both to the efficacy of language—naming—and to the function of language in contesting power. At one level the idea of naming engages a deeply atavistic anxiety. To name a thing is to have power over it: Adam names the creatures; Jacob, having wrestled the angel through the night, asks his name as a reward but is denied; religious Jews to this day are forbidden to speak the Hebrew name of their god, *Yahweh*, using a substitute, *Adonai* ("Lord") in prayers. More to our point, naming registers a deeper control over discourse itself. It matters whether a city is called Leningrad or Saint Petersburg, Canton or Guangzhou; whether an armed group is denominated "freedom fighters," "counterrevolutionaries," or "terrorists"; whether a nation can be characterized as part of an "axis of evil" or by some more neutral term.

To be sure, insisting on the presence of Indian names is not precisely the same as insisting on the presence of Indians themselves. A text like Boudinot's, in pointing to the increase in Cherokee population in Georgia and elsewhere, takes the latter approach and also helps students understand the "vanishing Indian" as an ideological construct. Boudinot flatly contradicts the notion that Indians were disappearing. He writes, "The population of the Cherokee Nation increased from the year 1810 to that of 1824, 2000 exclusive of those who emigrated in 1818 and 19 to the west of the Mississippi—of those who reside on the Arkansas the number is supposed to be about 5000." (James Parins, editor of this selection in the *Heath Anthology*, offers an even more precise count: "In 1808–1809 the Eastern Cherokee numbered 12,395. In 1819 the total was 15,000, one third of whom were west of the Mississippi. And in 1825 there were 13,542 in the East" [Lauter et al. B: 1447].)

But Sigourney is writing "Indian Names" in the mid-1830s, by which time removal is an all but inevitable consequence of Jacksonian policy. Moreover, her purpose is to question not the fact that the Indians are "disappearing" but the policies producing, indeed promoting, their disappearance as well as the culture underwriting that policy.

Something of the rage and desperation she feels emerges in the two additional stanzas contained in "Indian Names" when she published it in the 1834 volume of *Poems*:

Ye call these red-browed brethren
The insects of an hour,
Crushed like the noteless worm amid
The regions of their power;
Ye drive them from their father's lands,
Ye break of faith the seal,
But can ye from the court of Heaven
Exclude their last appeal?

Ye see their unresisting tribes,
With toilsome step and slow,
On through the trackless desert pass,
A caravan of woe;
Think ye the Eternal's ear is deaf?
His sleepless vision dim?
Think ye the soul's blood may not cry
From that far land to him? (B: 1573)

The verbs in these stanzas make explicit who is responsible for the vanishing of the red man, namely, Sigourney's Christian brethren. It is they who have produced the enforced migrations that will shortly culminate in the Trail of Tears. It is they whom she would therefore summon before the "court of Heaven." In her perceptive reading of the poem, Crain suggests that "Sigourney replicates her culture's nostalgic and pastoral view of the Indian, while at the same time excoriating that culture for its demonizing and demonic policies." Thus, Crain argues, Sigourney transforms the Indians from living people to dead names, to discourse. One might read the poem as a whole in this way. I do not accept that interpretation, however, any more than I would have accepted such an explanation of Denise Levertov's anti–Vietnam War poem "What Were They Like?"

> 1) Did the people of Viet Nam
> use lanterns of stone?
> . . . .
> 6) Did they distinguish between speech and singing?
>
> 1) Sir, their light hearts turned to stone.
> It is not remembered whether in gardens
> stone lanterns illumined pleasant ways.
> . . . .
> 6) There is an echo yet
> of their speech which was like a song.
> It was reported their singing resembled
> the flight of moths in moonlight.
> Who can say? It is silent now.

Like Sigourney, Levertov was engaged in an effort to redefine the cultural terms that attempt to justify warfare of the powerful against the seemingly weak. The poem poses a hypothetical result of United States war policy in order to generate opposition to that policy. Likewise, Sigourney is contesting the power that produces the Indians' disappearance. Her other Indian poems, such as "The Indian's Welcome to the Pilgrim Fathers" (1837) and "Burial of Mazeen" (1827), function similarly to challenge comfortable assumptions about white, Christian virtue, as does her book-length *Traits of the Aborigines* (1822). While it is certainly true that some of her Indian poems share the prevailing view of their passing—she wrote at least half a dozen poems about the death of warriors or Indian defeats in battle—even here one finds an unsettling edge, as in "Last Words of an Indian Chief" (1841):

> Hear my last bidding, friends! Lay not my bones
> Near any white man's bones. Let not his hand

> Touch my clay pillow, nor his hateful voice
> Sing burial hymns for me. Rather than dwell
> In Paradise with him, my soul would choose
> Eternal darkness and the undying worm.
> Ho! heed my words, or else my wandering shade
> Shall haunt ye with its curse! (lines 26–33)

Although students quickly grasp the politics Sigourney rejects, they have more difficulty understanding the values she is effectively promoting. Both Brandon and John Andrew argue that evangelical Christians like Sigourney and Jeremiah Evarts—who headed missionary activities directed toward Indians—saw removal as an evil in itself. But they also perceived it as a symbol of "forces such as the emerging marketplace economy, party politics, and individualism which, if left unchecked, would ultimately undermine" the specifically Christian community they believed to be central to maintaining civic morality in the American democracy (Brandon 200). The alternative to Indian removal (and, implicitly, to extermination) for which Sigourney argues is not really self-determination of Native Americans but their Christianization, which would bring them into the fold not just of the human community—where they are already located—but also the community of the saved. From this perspective, those promoting removal not only violated the treaties and human rights of Indians but threatened American democracy itself.

The additional stanzas of "Indian Names" open a new dimension for classroom discussion. The shorter version of the poem is the one that had been printed in most collections, including the one I edit, *The Heath Anthology of American Literature.* Two kinds of speculations, very useful in the classroom, arise from that fact. Why did Sigourney choose to print the shorter version in her later books? Was the reality of the Trail of Tears, which the last two stanzas cannot help but evoke, too painful, like one of Cassandra's predictions viewed in retrospect? Did her publisher object? Did it seem fruitless—Cherokee removal having been largely accomplished by the end of the 1830s—thus to confront white America with its guilty violence? Had the idea of a specifically religious justice come, at least with respect to Indian claims, to seem remote and even something of an evasion? After all, some abolitionists too were moving from the explicitly Christian arguments of Angelina Grimké to the skepticism, and ultimately rage, of Frederick Douglass and the Henry David Thoreau of "A Plea for Captain John Brown" (*Collected Essays* 396–417). Still, as one of my students pointed out:

> The waters that bear [the Indians' names] are baptismal and therefore consecrated ("But their memory liveth on your hills, / Their baptism on your shore"). The Indians themselves, it is implied, were "natural Christians," brothers to the white man who even were superior in living in pastoral harmony with nature. Their eradication is therefore fratricide, and it is just as much of a sin as the killing of fellow Christians. (Koller)

We will probably never have substantial answers to such questions, though it may well be that buried in Sigourney's voluminous correspondence is a letter explaining her choice.

Meanwhile, as editors and teachers, we must make our own choices. The basis for choosing provides a useful issue for classroom discussion. What is the difference between the two poems? What, if anything, does the longer version accomplish that the shorter does not? Do they affect the reader differently? Which is the better poem? And what constitutes "better"—aesthetic criteria, cultural power, political force? These and similar questions, I have found, lead to fruitful classroom interactions by destabilizing students' notions of the fixity of literary texts. Once editorial choices are no longer foregone, editorial processes—both of scholarly investigation and of critical valuation—come into view. We know that, of course, from studying the changing content and texts of *Leaves of Grass* as well as Emily Dickinson's poetry. But the Sigourney poem offers a peculiarly useful instance for classroom study.

I have concentrated on Sigourney's Indian poems, in part because they are among her best, in part because they engage issues of social justice with which today's students are at least familiar and even sometimes engaged. But limiting our view of her work to texts that appeal to twenty-first-century readers would give a distorted picture of her poetry. It would also limit our ability to understand the culture she expressed and helped construct. In nothing, perhaps, is Sigourney more a person of her time than in her many poems about death. Indeed, death—of Indians, of loved ones, of children especially—is the subject of a majority of her texts.

How are we to understand what may seem to our sensibilities—sated with cinematic and media representations of disaster, continuing war, and genocide—a strange, even obsessive concentration on death? Historians have a theory that helps explain why a kind of cult of death possesses Victorian culture in America. Here I am talking not just of supposedly sentimental writers but also of someone like Edgar Allan Poe, in whose work the *liebestod* of beautiful women like Annabel Lee and Ligeia plays at least as prominent a part as it does in Sigourney's. Death as subject and as source of sentiment is sufficiently prominent to be parodied by contemporary writers like Caroline Kirkland (and by much later authors like Twain). For others, the subject offers theoretical justifications for what might be seen as a morbid preoccupation. Alice Cary writes in "Conclusion" in her second collection of *Clovernook* stories:

> All things are beautiful in their time. Even Death, whom the poets have for ages made hideous, painting him as a skeleton reaper, cutting down tender flowers and ripe grain, and binding them into bundles for his darker garner, heedless of tears and prayers, is sometimes clothed with wings and the mercy of an angel. It was one of the most beautiful conceptions of Blake, displayed in those illustrations of the Night Thoughts which forever should cause his name to be associated with the poet's, that his countenance who is called the Last Enemy was all sweetness and pitying gentleness; and how many, who have trembled with terror at his approach, have found the dearest rest in his embraces, as a frightened child has forgotten fear in wildest joy on discovering that some frightful being was only its mother, masqued for playing. Through this still messenger "He giveth his beloved sleep." (361)

Virtually every element of the cult of death is here invoked: the metaphor of the child; the religious basis of the sentiments; the evocation of pity, tears, and prayer—these are the inescapable elements that present a challenge in today's classroom. Still, a strategy analogous to the one I have proposed may help bring to the surface the issues posed by these poems, even if it cannot resolve them to the extent that can be accomplished with the Indian poems. The issue here is not the continuing struggle for Native rights but why Victorian experiences and the Victorian preoccupation with death seem remote to us. We need not so much to recuperate such ideas but to understand how views of death and dying have changed in the last century and a half.

I am not proposing anything mystical: for the dead, death is what it has always been, the end. For the living, however, it has been taken out of the home, encountered personally ever less often, disinfected and sterilized, and at the same time familiarly projected on a scale unimaginable even to the Blakes and Goyas of the nineteenth century. That is, death is today less mediated by familiar hands and voices than by screens and charts, by professions and institutions designed to offer, among other things, distance. Death is packaged for us, a commodity of horror in the media, a medical fact of institutions, but as seldom as possible a personal encounter. Who among us has observed, much less participated in, the laying out of a corpse? Sigourney's verse arises from and speaks to a culture in which death was more commonplace and personal and in which the performance of grief was an integral part of everyday life. What from that culture has been lost, alongside what has been gained?

All this is not to propose that we should somehow make our own the sentiments about death that Sigourney expresses. The material conditions of her world cannot be reproduced in ours, even should we wish them to be. But it is useful to reach through her lines toward that world, so much like yet so different from our own, which leads us to that quintessentially American studies question: Why this thing in this way at this time? Why, in Sigourney's own moment, was "Death of an Infant" her most popular poem and perhaps the one most often associated with her name in subsequent years? And, to turn the case around, why is it that what was so unappealing to many of her compatriots (as she said of her Indian book) still works and lives? The goal of teaching Lydia Sigourney is to move students into answering for themselves precisely these kinds of questions.

Jeffrey Steele

"The Glorious Secrets of Sad Love": The Development of Margaret Fuller's Poetry

A leading cultural critic of her generation, Margaret Fuller has been remembered for her prose works. Challenging the restrictive gender norms that separated American "ladies" from the frontier, her 1844 literary excursion *Summer on the Lakes* explored the geographic and psychological limits of female identity (*Essential Margaret Fuller* 69–225). More notably, her 1845 treatise *Woman in the Nineteenth Century* reconfigured the ideological foundations of gender through the construction of new myths of manhood and womanhood (243–378). As a front-page columnist for Horace Greeley's *New-York Tribune*, Fuller commented extensively on the social conditions of New York and Europe. What is less known is that, throughout her literary career, she also produced an important body of poetry that echoed the concerns of her public writings and—in some cases—functioned as their textual unconscious. Like Emily Dickinson, Fuller published very few of her poems during her lifetime, circulating them among her closest friends instead. As a result, few nineteenth-century readers knew of her poetic aspirations until the posthumous publication of thirty-seven poems and seven poetic translations in the heavily edited collection *Life Within and Life Without*, which appeared in 1859, nine years after her death (see Steele, "Editing").

Although this edition provided a glimpse of her poetic output, it fell far short of revealing the literary and personal significance of the more than one hundred poems she wrote during her brief literary career. A number of Fuller's poems were anthologized in *The Essential Margaret Fuller* (1994; abbreviated *EMF* in the following discussion), but we still lack a comprehensive collection of her verse. Several of the poems referred to below are held in manuscript at either the Boston Public Library or the Houghton Library of Harvard University.

Starting around 1835, Fuller began focusing on the major topics of her poetry: female friendship and love, the pain of solitude, spiritual illumination, and personal transformation. In their concern with the vicissitudes of social ties (esp. relationships between women), as well as in their close examination of the stages of female spirituality, many of her poems can be profitably compared with those of Dickinson, who wrestled with similar issues twenty years later. Another useful strategy in studying and teaching Fuller's poetry is to link its concerns to similar passages found in her prose works such as "Leila" (*EMF* 53–58) and *Woman in the Nineteenth Century.* The most difficult of her poems deal with spiritual illumination and transformation. Here, Fuller's arcane interests necessitate some familiarity with classical mythology (esp. the myth of Isis) as well as with analogous accounts found in mystical texts and spiritual autobiographies. Ultimately, her poems, like many of her prose works, challenge readers to rethink gender identity and the sources of female self-empowerment.

Female Friendship and Love

Although Fuller argued persuasively that friendship and love form the most important foundation of human development, she often found herself separated from those she most cared for. Kindred spirits, she observed in her 1840 autobiographical sketch, "not only know themselves more, but *are* more for having met, and regions of their being, which would else have laid sealed in cold obstruction, burst into leaf and bloom and song" ("Autobiographical Romance" [*EMF* 40–41]). Later, in her *Dial* essay "Bettine Brentano and Her Friend Günderode," she celebrated the "true intimacy" of female friends as the "harmonious development of mind by mind, two souls prophesying to one another, two minds feeding one another, two human hearts sustaining and pardoning one another" (67).

But if Fuller's prose focuses on the mental and spiritual benefits of female friendship, her manuscript poetry reveals an emotional intensity and eroticism largely missing from her more public texts. For example, the important sequence of six poems written for Anna Barker between August 1835 and January 1836 highlights the intense emotional bond between Fuller and the person she once characterized as her "eldest and divinest love" (*Letters* 2: 93). But Fuller's poems to Barker, like most of her other poems addressed to women, idealized emotional bonds that were largely celebrated in their absence. In this respect, they resemble the texts in Dickinson's "sisterhood group," which—according to Vivian Pollak—"are concerned with some form of loss or renunciation," as they evoke a love that is "unrequited" (*Dickinson* 135).

Written in a Wordsworthian mode, "To____: Sunset, after Leaving New York, August 1835" commemorates a moment of shared vision reminiscent of the communion of William and Dorothy at the conclusion of "Tintern Abbey": "All this we both could see, together feel,— / Since then, no more alone at Nature's shrine I kneel." In a similar vein, the next poem, "To the Same, Glen-Anna, August 1835," meditates on natural landscapes emotionally charged by "the sweet company / Of the bright being I had held so dear." But the opening of the third poem, "To A.H.B.: On Our Meeting, on My Return from N.Y. to Boston, August 1835" (*EMF* 1), uncovers a depth of passion missing from the first two, as Fuller expresses a turbulent desire to escape with Anna to "some isle far from the haunts of men" (line 11). Longing to exist with Barker in "some Elysium set apart" (17), by the end she reluctantly acknowledges the spiritual benefits of accepting their separate existence in a realm of social tension that tempers passion in the heart's crucible ("it may be best / For thee as me, that fire the gold should test" [23]).

Like the woman addressed in Dickinson's poem "I showed her Hights she never saw" (T. Johnson, poem 446), the figure traversing Fuller's Barker poems becomes an imagined female companion whose afterglow compensates for the pain of physical separation. "And Lo," Dickinson later writes, "A Light, for her, did solemn glow, / The larger, as her face withdrew—." In the finest poem of Fuller's Barker sequence, the imperfect sonnet "To the Same: A Feverish Vision" (*EMF* 1–2), the figure of Anna takes on a similar imaginary resonance, as the speaker is rescued from "a day of wearying, wasting pain" (line 1) by a female figure who assumes the lineaments of a Homeric goddess:

> In a deep ghastly pit, bound down I lie,—
> About me flows a stream of crimson dye,
> Amid its burning waves I strive in vain;
> Upward I stretch my arms,—aloud I cry
> In frantic anguish,—"raise me, or I die!"
> When with soft eyes, beaming the tenderest love,
> I see thy dear face, Anna! far above,—
> By magnet drawn up to thee I seem,
> And for some moments was dispelled the fever's frightful dream!—
> (lines 6–14)

This poem recasts into a social drama Fuller's haunting childhood nightmare, motivated by reading Vergil, "of being among trees that dripped with blood, where she walked and walked and could not get out, while the blood became a pool and plashed over her feet, and rose higher and higher, till soon she dreamed it would reach her lips" (27). As Troy fell, Aeneas was rescued from the turbulence and destruction by his divine mother, Venus. In Fuller's poetic restaging of this dramatic moment, she replaces Aeneas's confusion with a debilitating migraine headache (and perhaps deeply rooted menstrual anxieties), while Anna Barker plays the gracious role of saving Goddess.

Eventually, Fuller's image of Anna (which she later associated with the goddess Diana) became one of the foundations of her feminist mythmaking. As Barker receded from Fuller's life after her marriage to Samuel Ward in 1840, idealized images of female power took her place in Fuller's imagination. By the mid-1840s, the syncretic goddess figure Leila (modeled in part on Isis) replaced Barker in the role of female savior. Anticipating that later mythic development, Fuller's early poems to Anna thus reveal one of the central biographical roots of her mythmaking.

More elusive but equally evocative are Fuller's undated manuscript poems "To E" and "To the Fair Unknown:— F.H.H." The ninety-two lines of "To E " (possibly addressed to the cynosure of her childhood, Ellen Kilshaw) celebrate Fuller's deep emotional attachment to an unnamed "Lady" who once stirred a "thousand deep heart-beatings, / So warmly felt, yet all unspoken" (lines 6–7). Idealizing her companion, Fuller responded to a "purity of soul" that filled her with "nobler love" and led her "nearer on to Heaven." Displacing the traditional poetic narrative of the inconstant lover onto the female friend, she pledges enduring loyalty to her "Lady" in the face of a "dark cloud of fear and pride / And cold distrust" (31–32). Particularly striking is Fuller's analysis, in the second half of this poem, of the psychological effects of failed love. "Love's waves," she observes, "turned backward on my breast / Must stagnate and grow bitter there" (53–54). At the moment, she can only participate vicariously in the reflected sunshine of her former friend's affection; but in her "secret heart" (69) she will continue to treasure scenes of former love, even as she longs for an end to "These trembling feelings, ill repressed" (86). In Fuller's imagery of selfhood, the pain of separation catalyzed many central symbols. Analyzing both the duration of affective ties and the psychological changes caused by their attenuation, she transmuted the heart's changes into a poetic vocabulary of personal transformation.

As in "To E," Fuller examined the emotional effects of separation in the enigmatic poem "To the Fair Unknown:—F.H.H.," which in its first stanza depicts her ties to an unnamed woman as an alternative marriage (anticipating the imagery of some of Dickinson's poems):

> There is one whom I love, there is one who loves me,
> Though neither yet knows who the loved one may be;
> We are wedded—long wedded, though bound by no vows,
> The world thinks us strangers,—the heart knows its spouse.

By the end of this poem, the distant lover, bound to Fuller's heart in a permanent affective "union," begins to transform into an "image" that opens the soul's doorway to an apprehension of "bliss," "rapture," and illumination:

> Tis long, fair Unknown, since the dawn of that bliss,
> Yet the thought of those moments lends rapture to this
> And oft, as I live o'er our meeting again[,]
> Thy image illumines my pathway of pain.
>
> (lines 25–28)

Like Petrarch catching a glimpse of his beloved, Fuller uses an imagined love as the platform for psychological and spiritual exploration. Eventually, her poetic image of such an imagined union would form the foundation of the spiritual archetype she termed the "sacred marriage"—the emblem of psychological and social harmony that formed the imaginative center of *Woman in the Nineteenth Century.*

Pain and Illumination

The geographic imagery of "To the Fair Unknown" links this poem to Fuller's most important mystical essay, "Leila." Just as the fair unknown served as a beacon guiding her along the "pathway of pain," Leila would become a glowing presence that Fuller imagined pursuing into "the secret veins of earth" and "through the caves where despair clings by the roof" (*EMF* 55). Much of this profound symbolism of pain, psychological questing, and illumination surfaced during her spiritual crisis of 1840–41. Each autumn after her father's premature death from cholera on 1 October 1835 became for Fuller a time of renewed grief and personal turmoil. The marriage of Anna Barker and Samuel Ward (she loved both) in October 1840 precipitated an even more intense period of turbulence and self-examination, which was exacerbated by her sense that all her closest friends (including her mentor, Ralph Waldo Emerson) were withdrawing from her. In the crucible of her imagination, the intense combination of pain, loss, and grief motivated many of her most profound literary experiments. Molding a personal mythology that rivaled the spiritual vocabulary of Emerson, she began exploring evocative psychological landscapes containing elusive goddesses who eventually coalesced into a figure she termed Leila. Reconfiguring the self in terms of mythological figures, Fuller's letters and journals during this period (like her poems) are filled with a densely textured symbolic language that formed the imaginary substratum of "The Great Lawsuit" and *Woman in the Nineteenth Century.*

One of the most striking poetic texts dating from Fuller's 1840–41 crisis is "River of beauty flowing through the life" (*EMF* 15–18). In this 136-line mini-epic, Fuller charts the progress of her alter ego Melodia, who finds the stream of love flowing into a womblike, underground "chasm" that she is forced to explore in order to heal her fractured self. Fuller's poetic commentary on Melodia's progress opens a critical distance between a figure of embodied pain and an interpretive awareness able to generalize principles of potential healing. Although Melodia passes through caverns filled with unseen crystals, it might be possible—Fuller observes—to transform pain into psychological insight, if "The inmost powers a strange convulsion cause" and reveal "the glorious secrets of sad love" (lines 43–44). In the dream logic of this psychological text, the wish for illumination coalesces into a change of setting: a "plain" where homeless "pilgrim angels" wander (50). Melodia asks for "a guide" in the hope to have her "sweetness harmonized" or to see "clear eyed, the Virgin Mother smile" (58–61)—a longing for a gracious maternal presence that would be fulfilled in Fuller's poetry in the deeply mythic texts of 1844. But in 1841, Fuller could not stabilize a harmonious bond between an imagined self and the divine other. As a result, Melodia sings a tune but "often lost the key" (74), for "the key-note was placed in other spheres / Whose echo her soul knew, but her ear missed" (75–76).

In a mystical response to Melodia's fervent voice, there stirs "from the rock" and "cradle tomb" (lines 83, 86) a godlike figure that Fuller identifies as "Paria" (named after the famous marble). Resonating with memories both of the lost Ward and Fuller's dead father, Paria functions as a muse whose presence allows a brief vision of "primal life" in an ecstatic region of incarnation where the "embracing Sun and Moon" briefly meet in "union" (103, 113, 106). But this vision of spiritual harmony and psychological equilibrium disappears when Paria flees back "into the secret caves" (127). Left behind, a distraught Melodia becomes a "wandering vestal of herself bereft" (133). In its failure to give her muse a permanent habitation, Fuller's poem thus lapses from the harmonious balancing of male and female principles that she saw as the key to personal fulfillment. Losing contact with her dream self or spirit guide, the poet is cut off from an essential part of her being and left alone in an ambiguous realm detached from spiritual fulfillment. (Among the many comparable poems by Dickinson are: "I've known a heaven like a tent—" [*Poems*, poem 257], "If I'm lost now" [poem 316], "I saw no Way—The heavens were stitched—" [poem 633], "We grow accustomed to the dark—" [poem 428], and "It would never be common more—I said" [poem 388].)

This pattern of spiritual illumination and loss structures a number of Fuller's most striking poems. For example, in her January 1840 text "God of the Splendid Stars," Fuller imagined herself on the "verge" of illumination, surrounded by strange, "starry eyes" and "Visions" of ethereal presences, "each enwrapt / In its own mental mystery" (lines 12, 15, 22–23). Although she senses among the "higher forms" a being "That seems myself and is not" (26, 29), she ultimately finds herself surrounded by inaccessible spiritual presences. The poet concludes:

> Yet is the spirit lone, its problem deep
> No other may work out, its mystic way
> No other wing may try, passionate hopes
> Mighty yet powerless . . . (57–60)

Similarly, in "Come!," Fuller unsuccessfully petitions the absent lover or spiritual guide to illuminate a world tinged with "heavy darkness," "weary loneliness," and "mournful silence" (lines 5, 7, 13). The poem concludes:

> Come to me, thou noble one,
> My sad soul longs for thee.
> Thou art my spirit's radiant sun,
> Thou art full of harmony. (13–16)

Here, nobility and spiritual radiance are defined through their negation. The challenge facing Fuller was to grapple with the forces separating her from her better self, identified with the absent beloved. A similar combination of insight and solitude marks the haunting "I wish I were where Helen lies," which she included in *Summer on the Lakes* (*EMF* 129–31) as the poem of another alter ego, Mariana. But a close reading of these texts reveals the pattern that Fuller underscored in her letters: in the psychic economy shaping her imagination, pain was paired with illumination, grief became the gateway to insight. As Fuller declared in a memorable October 1840 letter to Caroline Sturgis, "O, it has ever been thus, from the darkest comes my brightness, from Chaos depths my love" (*Letters* 2: 168).

For Fuller, the agony of separation—social, psychological, and spiritual—stirred a reciprocal imaginative response of mythmaking, as she articulated in moving images the passional forces that had started to shape her life. "My wings were just budded," she lamented in a January 1841 letter to Sturgis:

> they are pushed back upon my heart, but they are no longer tender with the plumage of the nest, they will not fold back over it and keep it warm again. So the breast must ache.
>
> Silent lies the pool, all nature crowded around in the prayer of conscious mutilation. Yet will it move no more till the true Angel descend.
>
> The ruined city lies beneath the moon, cold and barren falls her light on palaces, richly sculptured, but without a roof or a hearth stone, on temples of purest marble, but bereft of their gods. . . . (*Letters* 2: 199)

The drama of Fuller's intellectual and poetic development between 1841 and 1844 resides primarily in her growing capacity to nurture the "divine birds" of the heart, which—she asserted in *Woman in the Nineteenth Century*—"needed to be brooded into life and song by the Mothers" (*EMF*

344). In her most triumphant poems, written in 1844, the "true Angel" does descend to heal the mutilated soul and shed a warm, radiant light on the mind's "ruined city."

Personal Transformation

In order to appreciate the accomplishment of her 1844 poetry, it is useful to glance at a poem that Fuller included the year before in "The Great Lawsuit" (later reprinted in *Woman in the Nineteenth Century*):

> Each Orpheus must to the depths descend,
> For only thus the poet can be wise
> Must make the sad Persephone his friend,
> And buried love to second life arise;
> Again his love must lose through too much love,
> Must lose his life by living life too true,
> For what he sought below is passed above,
> Already done is all that he would do:
> Must tune all being with his single lyre,
> Must melt all rocks free from their primal pain,
> Must search all nature with his one soul's fire,
> Must bind anew all forms in heavenly chain.
> If he already sees what he must do,
> Well may he shade his eyes from the far-shining view.
>
> (*EMF* 252)

Conflating the familiar Romantic myth of the archetypal poet Orpheus with the classical image of Persephone languishing in the underworld, Fuller echoes the familiar cultural narrative of male heroism. In this poem, the recovery of "buried love," the retuning of the heart's "lyre," and the alchemical melting of "primal pain" through the "soul's fire" are all masculine accomplishments. Fuller never completely relinquished the model of male heroism; indeed, she bemoaned the absence of male heroes among her belated generation, born too late to fight a revolution and sliding toward ambiguous military intervention in Texas and Mexico. But her greatest writings supplemented such male agency with images of female power.

In some cases, Fuller had to recover what she termed "the idea of woman" from the dusty shelves of history and literature; but in others, she molded a vocabulary of female agency out of classical mythology,

European mysticism, and Christian iconography. What emerged in 1844 was an impassioned poetic meditation on the self's recovery. One of her central insights was that psychological and social harmony depends on the equitable balancing of male and female principles in all domains of existence. Her poetic texts were the workshop where she explored the transformative rhythms of such personal and cultural healing.

The reader is immediately struck by the sophisticated spiritual vocabulary structuring the 1844 poetry. In text after text, a richly textured language of meditation articulates Fuller's longing for personal fulfillment and transcendence. At times she uses the iconography of gem lore, as in the poetic prayer she sent Sturgis in May 1844, which opens with the image of a lost child protected by nurturing spirits who offer her talismanic gems:

> Slow wandering on a tangled way
> To their lost child pure spirits say
> The diamond marshal thee by day;
> By night the carbuncle defend
> Hearts-blood of a bosom-friend. . . .
> (*Letters* 3: 194)

In Fuller's personal mythology, the carbuncle (a glowing red gem) functions as the philosopher's stone in alchemy: the goal of a laborious personal quest, it embodies psychic wholeness and spiritual illumination. At times the glowing carbuncle morphs into the figure of Leila—a personification of the transfiguring power that Fuller (like Emerson) sought in the unconscious. In the essay "Leila," after the goddess has "retreated into the secret veins of earth," there "glows through her whole being the fire that so baffles men, . . . the blood-red, heart's-blood-red of the carbuncle. She is, like it, her own light . . ." (*EMF* 55). Evoking the saving power of the Goddess, Fuller concludes her poetic prayer to Sturgis with the hope that protective gems might "keep thee steadfast, chaste and wise."

In her writing, Fuller was molding a language of personal transformation that rivaled Emerson's model of self-reliance. Like Emerson, Fuller believed that the seeds of personal transfiguration, glowing with divine energy, lay in the depths of the psyche. But by necessity she took a different route from that of Emerson to the goal of personal independence. Sharing with him, for example, the ideal of priestly vocation, she was forced to recognize that ecclesiastical privileges were gendered in an age that prevented most women from filling ministerial roles. As a result, lines such as the following (printed in *Woman in the Nineteenth Century*) take on an ironic tension missing for a writer like Emerson, who had the luxury of resigning his pulpit:

> In the inmost shrine
> Stands the image divine,
> Only seen
> By those whose deeds have worthy been
> *Priestlike* clean. (323; emphasis added)

Imagining the soul's "flight" as a "lark-like spiral seeking light" (228), Fuller lamented the cultural forces that threatened to bind her. As a result, she carefully nourished the seeds of light that she found within the "Soul / . . . Cradled in the will" (235). The "birds of my thought," she asserted in the poem "Lead, lunar ray" (235–36), needed to be brooded in the "nest" by "mother thought" (lines 21–25). Only when the self's "wings grow strong" could one take the next step toward psychic harmony: the psychic quest toward "the distant zone / Where glows the throne / Of your phoenix king so lone" (26, 28–30).

Despite this sense of struggle, several 1844 poems achieved a powerful sense of personal and mythic attainment. Building on the powerful figure of Isis found in Apuleius's *The Golden Ass*, "Leila in the Arabian Zone" depicts the syncretic goddess Leila equipped with the sistrum (sacred rattle) of Isis, as she transforms both the self and man:

> The magic Sistrum arms her hand
> And at her deep eye's command
> Brutes are raised to thinking men
> Soul growing to her soul filled ken. (233)

In the classical narrative, Lucius was both transformed into an ass and restored to human form by Isis. Generalizing this dynamic into a principle of political transformation, Fuller imagines a female figure powerful enough to lift men and women to their full human potential, which—at present—has been perceived only in occasional "gleams" (268).

Even more triumphantly, "Double Triangle, Serpent and Rays" refers to the mystical symbol on the title page of *Woman in the Nineteenth Century*, as it profoundly evokes the cosmic and political harmony lying at the core of Fuller's utopian vision:

Patient serpent, circle round,
Till in death thy life is found;
Double form of godly prime
Holding the whole thought of time,
When the perfect two embrace,
Male & female, black & white,
Soul is justified in space,
Dark made fruitful by the light;
And, centred in the diamond Sun,
Time & Eternity are one. (233)

Solomon's seal (interlocking triangles similar to the Star of David) was an ancient symbol of psychic wholeness, as were the alchemical images of the snake swallowing its own tail (the ouroboros) and the glowing rays of the soul's sun. In Fuller's overdetermined figure, this archetype evokes a personal and cosmic harmony made visible and thus accessible in time (a manifestation of divine energy evoked by the theological term "justified," since justification is the alignment of the soul with a divine source). Most notably, Fuller both genders (and possibly racializes) the actualization of this harmony as a balancing of "Male & female, black & white." The poem as a whole thus functions as a highly condensed formulation of the central political argument of *Woman in the Nineteenth Century*—that social justice depends on equalization of the gendered forces configuring the values and social roles of men and women.

In order to achieve such balance, Fuller asserts, one must lift to the surface of individual awareness the seeds of illumination trapped in the personal and political unconscious. Dramatizing this process of surfacing, "Winged Sphynx" (*EMF* 234) is one of Fuller's finest poetic achievements:

Through brute nature upward rising,
Seed up-striving to the light,
Revelations still surprising,
My inwardness is grown insight.
Still I slight not those first stages,
Dark but God-directed Ages;
In my nature leonine
Labored & learned a Soul divine;
Put forth an aspect Chaste, Serene,
Of nature virgin mother queen;
Assumes at last the destined wings. . . .
(lines 1–11)

The latent seeds of self-development (glimpsed in "Lead, lunar ray") have now germinated, as "inwardness"—in Fuller's memorable formulation—crystallizes into "insight." In the psyche's darkness, she now recognizes a "Soul divine" laboring to break forth into the light of conscious awareness. Identified with both the Virgin Mother and the Sphynx (a classical goddess), the transfigured self is now able to soar on its "destined wings," which were always there but previously folded in the psyche's chrysalis. According to the ancient myth, the answer to the Sphynx's infamous riddle was "Man"; but in Fuller's poem the answer is the Sphynx's "own form" (13): transfigured "Woman," a new self-reliant being rarely seen in the nineteenth century.

As is evident from the poem's title, "Sub Rosa—Crux" (236–38) gives a mystical, Rosicrucian spin to Fuller's portrait of the self's transformation. Imagining a secret society of knights dedicated to the soul's rebirth, Fuller depicts them wearing the "glistening ruby bright" (line 9) or carbuncle, an external symbol of the glowing heart within. Seeking "the vein of gold," these spiritual explorers struggle to actualize a "faithful band" of "kindred angels" (34, 40) in her poetic narrative. Achieving the nobility of soul that she took as one of her highest ideals, this faithful company then dedicates itself to aiding those momentarily left behind, as they "marshal others on the way; / Or waited for them, fainting and way-worn, / By burdens over borne" (58–60).

Fuller's prose works as well as her poems testified to the difficulties of this spiritual struggle. Near the end of *Woman in the Nineteenth Century*, she envisioned a "society of novices" dedicated to "the capacity of man for virtue" in order to fulfill "the destiny promised him as a son of God" (*EMF* 333–34). Following discussions of prostitution and women's incarceration, this passage projected a model of newly transformed men and women who might escape from prejudice and become "the harbingers and leaders of a new era" (334). But as Fuller knew all too well, the route to this utopia of gender equality was dangerous and arduous.

In "For the power to whom we bow," the poem appearing immediately before the appendices of *Woman in the Nineteenth Century* (348–49), this difficult quest can be undertaken only by those "of pure and stedfast [sic] mind" (line 3). If they can endure the "rabble rout" that threatens to beat them "senseless" (lines 10–11), the seekers of social justice might achieve self-awareness. The end of this journey through the wasteland of barbarity is "what few have seen, / The palace home of King and Queen" (349; lines 15–16). To value the import of this final image, one must linger over the conjunction "and." The nineteenth century, Fuller had argued earlier in *Woman in the Nineteenth Century*, had no difficulty stabilizing images of the "King": "Man, in the order of time, was developed first. . . . [H]e misunderstood and abused his advantages, and became her temporal master instead of her spiritual sire" (343). But images of queenly, female power needed to be brought from the darkness of the cultural unconscious into the sunlight of awareness. (It is striking that Dickinson later wrestled with similar issues, as she too imagined the independent female self as a "Queen" with "Will to choose" her own "Crown" [poem 353]).

In addition to articulating woman's queenly power, Fuller argued that "equal union," both in society and the self, could be attained only by the harmonious balancing of male and female principles, the King and Queen. The product of such gender equity, in her mystical vocabulary, would be the achievement of "the sacred marriage" (the title of the poem she placed at the end of *Woman in the Nineteenth Century*). Recognizing the strength of "mutual action energizing love" (378; line 26), men and women—Fuller envisioned—might learn to work together in mutual cooperation and respect, neither party attempting to dominate the other. But as the conclusion of the poem reminds us, her vision encompasses both social and psychological domains. Achieving a utopia not yet realized on earth, those who actualize a "sacred marriage" will inhabit harmonious social relationships but also find "A Home in Heaven,—the Union in the Soul" (line 30).

Winning "the Secrets of the Tomb"

But it would be a mistake to suggest that Fuller's poetic development culminated in a tone of unalloyed spiritual triumph. For throughout her poems runs a vein of mournfulness. Although she was able to articulate powerful images of transfigured womanhood and perfected social relationships, Fuller also recognized that her existence was marked by the deep sorrow of living in the right place at the wrong time. Excoriated for unconventional ideals that challenged the comfortable contours of nineteenth-century gender roles, she often saw herself as an outsider trapped in a world of pain. For example, the extraordinary opening of "To the Face Seen in the Moon" (*EMF* 240–42) reveals the confession of a divided self who struggles to actualize the harmonious balance of masculinity and femininity, King and Queen. Gazing on the moon, the poet perceives a "human secret like my own" (line 8): "For through the woman's smile looks the male eye / So mildly, stedfastly but mournfully . . ." (9–10).

Existing in a society that provided only male images of inner strength, Fuller found in her own reflection the deep gender divisions that scarred her society. To bring the "male" strength of women (or the "Minerva" side) to the surface, her society needed to recognize in women's faces the "male eye" forbidden them. Given the love poems discussed above, it is likely that part of the mournfulness of this text resulted from Fuller's bisexuality. Deeply attached to a number of female companions, she also became emotionally entangled with several men: Ward, Emerson, James Nathan (in New York), and Giovanni Ossoli (the Italian father of her son). But for a variety of reasons, Fuller found it easier to express her heterosexual than her homosexual impulses. As a result, her most important relationships with women tended to remain on the plane of imagined and sublimated unions. This narrowing of identity—in the words of Judith Butler—produced a "gender melancholy" precipitated by the "foreclosure of possibility" (*Psychic Life* 135). Shaped by the restrictive gender roles of her society, Fuller's grief, transformed into a profound process of poetic grief work, was motivated by her perception that the women of her time had "much to mourn" (*EMF* 267).

In some of her strongest poems, Fuller confronted "the tomb" within through a process of mourning that began to heal the sources of pain and trauma. Brooding both on the image of crucifixion as well as the grief of Mary (the Mater Dolorosa immortalized in Renaissance art), "Raphael's Deposition from the Cross" (238–40) focuses on the transformative dynamics of such mourning. Exacerbated by the limitations of her social relationships, Fuller's sorrow (to the end of her life) was magnified by the painful recognition that the "divine child" of spiritual rebirth might be stillborn. Longing for "a love that cannot be crucified" (in the memorable phrasing of *Woman in the Nineteenth Century*), she argued that "could we give a description of the child that is lost, he would be found. . . . But we say not, see not as yet, clearly, what we would" (250). Having lost the "heavenly child, / Crucified within my heart" (238; lines 12–13), the poet finds herself in a posture of grief parallel to that of the mourning Mary. Repairing to the "tomb" of her bereaved soul, she envisions a process of fiery renewal (a powerful alchemical image) that might "Purify the veins of Earth, / Temper for a Phenix [sic] birth" (lines 29–30).

But as Fuller argues in the second half of this poem, only a circuit through the "deepest of distress" can open the closed pathways of feeling and imaginative renewal. Only those who have "force to bide the storm" of emotional upheaval can pass through to the realm of spiritual transformation (47, 50). If it is kept closed by fear, the door to Leila's domain is sealed with tears. The challenge is to move beyond "tears" into a realm of illumination, where "A muse-like form as thine appears / . . . new-born in primal light" (61, 63–64). Invoking her 1841 alter ego Leila and her most radiant symbol of transfigured womanhood, Fuller calls to her muse to take her "wand again" and "Listen to the throbbing breast," where "nightingales have made their nest" (65, 68–69). In the process, the scene of mourning transforms into a powerful symbol of the self's divine potential: a "Rosary" clasped with a "Ruby heart" and "cross of gold and diamond" (73–75). Fulfilling the promise of "Sub Rosa-Crux," this poem concludes with a utopian vision of the self's rebirth from grief into spiritual radiance:

> In the coffin hides thy blight;
>   All transfused the orb now glowing,
> Full-voiced and free the music growing
>   Planted in a senseless sod
>   The life is risen to flower a God. (80–84)

Reborn out of the tomb of grief, Leila reappears, bearing the Rosicrucian emblems ("Ruby heart," "cross of gold and diamond") celebrated in "Sub Rosa-Crux." Joining the spiritual band of illuminati, she assumes her rightful place in the realm of light.

But characteristically, Leila (a profound symbol of Fuller's hidden self) is a half step ahead of the poet and thus functions as an ego ideal beckoning the way toward future fulfillment. Marked by the painful knowledge that "Night is coming," the poet knows that she must remain awhile in the tomb, a region of "blight." Only by moving through the house of pain can she reach psychological and spiritual renewal. In the final four lines, the "orb" of the self starts to glow with a transfiguring power, as the self is reborn to self-reliance, "risen to flower a God." Perhaps the truest measure of Fuller's literary significance is the distance between these concluding lines and the almost frictionless spiritual renewal imagined by Emerson. "As fast as you conform your life to the pure idea in your mind," Emerson had exhorted at the end of *Nature*, "that will unfold to its great proportions" (*Works*).

Like most of her female contemporaries, Fuller discovered that the unfolding of identity carried a steeper price for women, who were barred both from personal independence and from the cultural forms that might help them actualize it. Ultimately, the power of her poetry—like that of the rest of her writing—is that it provides a repertoire of motives, images, and postures that helps unlock the gates of a more expansive female identity. Glimpses of her most powerful symbols are found in her published prose (most notably in the mystical essay "Leila"). But a complete understanding of Fuller's achievement, as a cartographer of the human soul, depends on a careful reading of her poetry.

Frances Smith Foster
and Valerie L. Ruffin

Teaching African American Poetry of the Reconstruction Era: Frances E. W. Harper's "Moses: A Story of the Nile"

Many of us have witnessed the enthusiasm and transformative knowledge that result from teaching fugitive-slave narratives. We know their value for teaching formal elements such as plot and theme, even as students are mesmerized by reading about Frederick Douglass's climatic victory over the slave breaker Covey or Harriet Jacobs's manipulation of Dr. Flint from her attic loophole of retreat. But as compelling as such antebellum slave narratives are, they are only one genre representing one theme and one relatively brief period of African American literature. Moreover, as significant as the slave narratives are, they were not that important to most nineteenth-century African American readers.

Poetry, on the other hand, was very important. In nineteenth-century African America, a poet was the New World griot. Poems were the wisdom of a people, messages of inspiration and models of behavior. Elocution was entertainment; and hardly a gathering, whether religious, political, or social, did not include the recitation of poems. The two most popular and prolific nineteenth-century African American writers, Frances E. W. Harper and Paul Laurence Dunbar, were famous primarily for their poetry.

The poetry of the Reconstruction era is especially useful for teaching the genre as well as for better understanding the aesthetics and significance of literature to nineteenth-century African Americans. During that period, most poets deliberately wrote to be as accessible as possible to less sophisticated readers. At the same time, their consciously crafted works reveal African American poets interpreting, incorporating, adapting, and transforming tropes, techniques, and motifs from writers such as Shakespeare, Milton, Pope, Whittier, and Longfellow. Reconstruction poetry can expand our students' literary universe with useful comparisons in form and content between the literatures of African America and other nineteenth-century literatures. Teachers seeking resources can consult earlier works, such as those by Benjamin Brawley (*Early Negro American Writers*) and William H. Robinson (*Early Black American Poets*) as well as substantial recent works, both primary and secondary—some of it specifically on poetry—by such scholars as Henry Louis Gates, Jr., and Nellie Y. McKay (*Norton Anthology of African American Literature*), Joan R. Sherman (*Invisible Poets*); William L. Andrews, Frances Smith Foster, and Trudier Harris (*Oxford Companion to African American Literature*). Fortunately, in addition to these print resources, the online *African American Poetry* full-text database makes the poems themselves more widely available than ever before, enabling our students to examine Reconstruction-era poetry with ease.

Especially in the postbellum period, African American poets wrote to inspire and inform; to celebrate and motivate; to warn, forearm, and challenge individuals and communities to work toward a nation that adhered to the blueprints of Protestant Christianity and the United States Constitution. Through their poems we can trace the development of African American aesthetic and intellectual culture. Though some, such as Harper and Charlotte Forten, published both in non–African American and African American media, the primary venue for most nineteenth-century African American poets was the African American press. This lesson is especially important for students who might otherwise be inclined to believe that since most African Americans were enslaved, there was no literature readership or there were no themes in antebellum African American literature beyond abolition.

One obvious advantage of teaching nineteenth-century African American poetry is its brevity. Because many poems are fairly short, we can use more writers and more texts in our classrooms and can make comparisons more quickly. For example, we juxtapose the measured meditations or prayerful pleas of James M. Whitfield that ask:

How long, O gracious God! how long,
Shall power lord it over right?
The feeble, trampled by the strong,
Remain in slavery's gloomy night?

with his "America" (1853):

America, it is to thee,
Thou boasted land of liberty,—
It is to thee I raise my song,
Thou land of blood, and crime, and wrong.
(*African American Poetry*; path: *Whitfield, America: And Other Poems* [1853], resp., 29 and 9)

And we still have time to include Joshua McCarter Simpson's grim but witty "Song of the Aliened America," which begins:

My country, 'tis of thee,
Dark land of slavery,
In thee we groan.
Long have our chains been worn—
Long has our grief been born—
Our flesh has long been torn,
E'en from our bones.
(path: *The Emancipation Car* [1874] 17)

Discussion can range from how rhythm, diction, and tone change to the implicit comparisons between social practice and the founding principles of our country to whether it is right or fair to satirize revered songs such as "America."

Before and after the Civil War, African Americans routinely compared their situations with that of the Hebrews enslaved in Egypt. Moses embodied the inextricable relation between the personal and the political, between the antebellum and postbellum. Writers emphasized resistance to slavery and oppression as a divinely sanctioned mandate. They characterized Moses as a person who sacrificed personal privilege and risked personal safety in order to lead people out of bondage and into freedom. African American poets frequently made references to someone standing "Moses-like," to slaves making an "exodus / From cursed bondage," to "When Israel sat by Babel's stream and wept" and "Israel's hosts" seeing their oppressors "utterly destroyed."[1] Many, like Harper in "The Burial of

Moses" (1854), called Moses a "bard" and a "sage" and depicted the honorable ends of those who are both poets and freedom fighters as lying "in state while angels wait" and being buried by "God's own hand" (*Brighter Coming Day* 78, 79). In an antebellum essay, "Our Greatest Want" (1859), Harper wrote, "I like the character of Moses. He is the first disunionist . . ." (103). In the postbellum era, like other African Americans, she wanted to create a new union. Moses, again, was their man.

In teaching this poetry, we suggest introducing it by reminding students of how post–Civil War America was changing. A pressing issue, of course, was what to do with or about the millions of freed African Americans. The Thirteenth and Fourteenth Amendments to the Constitution were intended to solve that problem. But slavery was more than a human rights issue. It had enabled the Southern states to prosper, as agricultural economies brought the Northeast to prominence in shipping and industry, and had given a large boost to Western expansion. The nation's economy was inextricably linked with African American labor, and the waves of immigrants coming into the country did not appear adequate to sustain vital redevelopment, let alone territorial expansion. At the same time, greater access to public education helped produce the laborers and managers, civic and religious leaders necessary for the newly re-United States to expand and prosper. But that education, combined with the new freedoms that the realities of the war presented to white women and people of color, also produced a cacophony of voices, ideals, and demands with which the mid-nineteenth-century populace and those who would lead them had to contend. A new social space had to be found for former slaves as well as for free African Americans, European and Asian immigrants, Native Americans, and for women and children of all cultures. In short, the Reconstruction era was a time of great transition and reconsideration, fraught with conflicting desires of some to return to the past and others to revise it. Strong leadership was essential. But Abraham Lincoln, the Moses who had saved the Union—even though his methods disenchanted many people—was assassinated. America as a whole was looking for a new leader to articulate a national vision and reunite the masses.

In African America, unity was also essential. Many poets revised the ideal of Moses to emphasize individual leadership less and to focus more on cooperative responsibility or nationalism. They tended to represent Moses less as a heroic or mythic symbol and more as a regular person, as an individual who would renounce personal privilege in favor of a fight for equity for all.

Albery Allson Whitman's epic poem *Not a Man and Yet a Man* (1877) exemplifies a postbellum Moses figure. One of the eight great-grandparents of Rodney, the poem's protagonist, was African. According to the science and law of that era, Rodney was black. But he was physically indistinguishable from white men. He could have enjoyed first-class citizenship by ignoring his social heritage, but, like Moses who left Pharaoh's palace, he chose to identify with the oppressed. Students might find the class and color distinctions here disconcerting, because this Moses figure is light-skinned and literate. But the poem allows discussion of class and caste as well as of the uses of mulatto protagonists in antebellum abolitionist literature and the modifications that postbellum writers made to these figures. For example, the use of mixed-race characters may reflect some writers' acceptance of Eurocentric standards of excellence. But there are other significant and pragmatic possibilities. Historical circumstances made it easier for light-skinned people to have the experiences and knowledge that leaders of the Reconstruction period needed. Most African Americans with the necessary wealth, education, and professional skills were of mixed ancestry. They had the option of passing—that is, they could move to another location, eschew their racial identities, and live more comfortable lives as whites.

But the problem of unity was not limited to physical appearance. In 1850, more than a half a million African Americans were not enslaved, and, regardless of physical appearance, these free African Americans could be persuaded to set themselves apart from the newly emancipated. Such class or caste difference was a serious challenge to any attempt to construct or reconstruct a unified African America or a United States of America. The biblical Moses was a culturally mixed, free, and favored figure, who, as Harper had pointed out, had rejected personal advancement in order to "subserve the cause of crushed humanity and carry out the greatest idea . . . of human brotherhood" (*Brighter Coming Day* 104 ["Our Greatest Want"]).

As in *Not a Man and Yet a Man*, the diction and the tone of the Moses Reconstruction poems were generally elevated and serious. One interesting exception to the grave and mythic portrayals of Moses is James Madison Bell's "Modern Moses; or, 'My Policy' Man," a humorous yet excoriating attack on President Andrew Johnson as an anti-Moses figure. Bell signifies continually on the man who he says fooled the country by feigning "hatred to the South" and promising the enslaved that "he their *Moses* would become, / And lead them to a freeman's home" (lines 115,

211–12 [*Poetical Works* (1901)]). In charges that presage those of Ida B. Wells some twenty years later, Bell also indicts Johnson for his sexist and unintentionally deprecating comments about Euro-Americans:

> He next reversed the bill of rights,
> Lest all the girls—that is the whites—
> Should Desdemonia's become,
> And fly each one her cherished home,
> And take to heart some soot moor,
> As Fathers did in days before.
> (lines 337–42)

Providing a comparison with those works mentioned above, Harper's Reconstruction-era poem "Moses: A Story of the Nile" (*African American Poetry*; path: *Complete Poems* [1988]) is an excellent case study of postbellum poetry. Poems of this type show how African American poets reconstructed certain tropes and ideas such as bondage and freedom to take into account physical oppression, economic exploitation, and racial and sexual discrimination as well as to emphasize the primacy of spiritual and moral freedom over materialistic gains. The poems highlight aspects of Reconstruction politics that—in response to Constitutional amendments and other laws of redress—created new racist codes that exacerbated African American oppression. As Harper's "Moses" recounts a biblical narrative on truth, justice, and activism, it also recasts American dualities of race (black and white), class (laborers and elite), and gender (male and female) into more complex concerns.

The subtitle "A Story of the Nile" emphasizes Moses as an African. Building on the Exodus narrative, Harper models a meditation on the characteristics and challenges of leaders and on the relations among individualism, sectionalism, and nationalism. Her poem is a dramatic work of about 1,100 lines divided into chapters. The first is called "The Parting." In the beginning scene, Moses is already a young man and comes to inform Charmian, Pharaoh's daughter, that he has decided "to join / The fortunes of [his] race, and put aside / All other bright advantages" (34; ch. 1, lines 4–6). Charmian is devastated, and in the ensuing conversation she recounts how she rescued him from the river; persuaded her father to make Moses an exception to her father's decree of death to all Hebrew infants and enslavement of all other Hebrews; and provided Moses, her adopted son, with every advantage. The first section of the poem emphasizes the mutual love and respect of Charmian and Moses, the difficult sacrifice that Moses is making, and the reasons for his decision. He feels solidarity with his fellow Hebrews and understands that as long as some must suffer for their lifestyle, no one can be truly free. Like most Euro-Americans and some free African Americans of Harper's own era, Moses could try to achieve material success or social security by separating himself emotionally and physically from the less fortunate. But, Harper shows him recognizing that individual success and ambition come at a cost: as long as one ignores the hardship of others, neither one's conscience nor soul is free. Charmian, seeing the "lofty / Faith and high resolves" "with silent lips but aching heart," acquiesces (41–42; ch. 1, lines 222–23, 249).

The next three chapters focus on Moses's return to the Hebrew community, the oppressive conditions under the Egyptians, and the challenges that Moses faced as he developed the character and courage necessary to do his duty to his God and his people. He worked as a lowly shepherd, "the calling / Most hateful to an Egyptian" (49; ch. 4, lines 5–6). He needed to share authority with his brother Aaron, who possessed skills that Moses did not have. He had to endure the fears and reproaches of those he was trying to rescue. In these and the following chapters, Harper details various injuries and issues that beset the leader and his followers as they try to form a new community. In the final chapters, she shows Moses's greatest disappointment: Moses would not enter the Promised Land with his people. But Harper asserts that his "life had been a lengthened sacrifice, / A thing of deep devotion to his race," and he died with "another, fairer, vision" as his "ransomed soul" entered heaven (64–65; ch. 9, lines 4–5, 68, 72).

"Moses: A Story of the Nile" shows, too, the complicated and changing ideas of gender in Reconstruction America. Students will benefit from learning that in the mid-nineteenth century, women's roles changed rapidly. Agitation for women's rights, for education, for leadership in abolition and other political arenas had reached unprecedented proportions in all segments of American society. Women of all colors were demanding access to education, public forums, and church pulpits. The exigencies of war required many who would have preferred to stay in the parlor to move to the stores and fields to provide food and shelter while the men were away. Like Moses's mother and sister, some surreptitiously defied edicts and protected the lives of both kin and strangers. Like Charmian, some came to love strangers as their kin and to rethink the politics of class and race, even if they themselves could act on these defiant thoughts only in individual and personal ways.

The women in Harper's "Moses," like many women of the Civil War era, transform or transgress against prevailing notions of domesticity and passivity. They both challenge and stabilize community and nation. Charmian, saving Moses's life, does not express obligatory or smothering love; she chooses not to limit his development, encouraging his independent thoughts and actions, which are, after all, reminiscent of her own. Moses's birth mother not only nurses him physically but also nurtures his spirit and sense of morality and social justice. Moses says that he learned "of the grand tradition of our race" from his mother (39; ch. 1, line 170) and observes that her stories about Abraham, Isaac, Jacob, and Joseph became "messengers of light to guide / My steps." Thus he was compelled to leave "the pomp and pride of Egypt / To cast my lot among the people of my race" (46; ch. 2, lines 135–36, 143–44).

In Harper's narrative, women—Moses's birth mother, foster mother, wife, and sister—help form his character and influence his actions. They are responsible for giving Moses life, for saving his life, and for helping him lead the oppressed toward a new land of liberty. In a twist on the biblical story, when the people successfully cross the river and their pursuers drown, Harper mentions the song that constitutes the first twenty verses of Exodus 15 and that the King James version of the Bible attributes to "Moses and the children of Israel." But she expands the one biblical verse about Miriam's song into four stanzas that recount the history of the people, and she precedes Miriam's song with twenty lines of description as to how Moses's sister led the "women / in music, dance and song" (60; ch. 6, lines 93–94). This kind of innovation suggests that including and expanding women's voices, experiences, and contributions was important in the reunification of a nation divided not only by racial but also by gender inequality.

Concerns about religion, morality, social justice, and human rights were characteristic of the nineteenth century. For many, the Civil War represented a struggle between good and evil. In the process, slavery was abolished and the nation was preserved. But unity remained a major concern. Harper's poem, like the works of many African American writers of the Reconstruction era, tried to move beyond a singular perspective. While Moses remains an icon, his value lies in his commitment to his community. In the process, his character, beliefs, and actions were shaped by many others. Moses learned Egyptian courtly behavior, and he knew therefore how to address Pharaoh. He listened to his mother, the historian of his race. And he knew from whence he came and to what he should aspire. Harper's poem shows interdependence between individual and community in history and in the present. As such, it is a true Reconstruction poem.

Note

1. The quotation "Moses-like" is from Albery Allson Whitman ("In the House of the Aylors"); "exodus / From cursed bondage" is from Alfred Gibbs Campbell ("Warning"); "When Israel sat by Babel's stream and wept" is from Whitman ("Lute of Afric's Tribe"); and "Israel's hosts . . . utterly destroyed" is from Campbell ("Warning"). Both Whitman and Campbell are in the *African American Poetry* database.

Gregory Eiselein

Emma Lazarus and Jewish Poetry

Almost every college student can recite lines from Emma Lazarus's Statue of Liberty sonnet, "The New Colossus," but few know anything more about nineteenth-century American Jewish poetry. These poems can seem to many students unfamiliar, even bewildering at first. The distance separating twenty-first-century readers from these texts is often vast; between them stands the Shoah, the modernist revolution in poetry, the development of electronic mass media, and more. I try to bridge this gap with various pedagogical approaches. Sometimes I ask students to look for connections between then and now. If students see parallels or identify with the content or affect of a poem, I encourage such associations, because they develop interest and investment in the poem. At other points in a semester, it works better to draw attention to a text's strangeness so as to invite students to become literary-historical detectives: How are we going to figure out how this text works? To whom would such a text be important or beloved and why? Whether one emphasizes similarities or differences, contextualization is an indispensable strategy for fostering interest and encouraging close reading and critical inquiry.

Context can be understood as background information—religious, historical, cultural, or biographical data that clarify a poem's meaning. I find it more useful, however, to think of context as the weaving together of relevant texts to be read with the poems, a definitional strategy consistent with the Latin verb *contexere* ("to weave together"). In practice, this weaving usually amounts to providing the class with two or three texts that we read alongside the poetry. Instructors may select texts, but students piece together contexts by figuring out how those texts mutually inform or intertwine with one another. In such contexts, perplexing poems can become dynamic, meaningful, perhaps even fascinating. This essay elaborates such an approach to teaching nineteenth-century American Jewish poetry and focuses on four overlapping contexts: social and political history, periodical publication, Jewish religious traditions, and poetic genres popular in nineteenth-century America.

Social and political contexts for understanding American Jewish poetry can be established by assigning selected historical documents to be read with the poems. For example, I often teach Lazarus's *Songs of a Semite*, which contains a poem on the Russian pogroms ("The Crowing of the Red Cock"), a verse tragedy on the mass execution of Jews in medieval Germany (*The Dance to Death*), dramatic monologues about anti-Semitic hatred, translations of modern and medieval Jewish poets, and numerous other Jewish-themed pieces. For students with little knowledge about the persecution of Jewish people in nineteenth-century Russia, documents from the period—such as a series of London *Times* articles (Lazarus, "Persecution") or a congressional report (S. Cox)—provide descriptions of the riot, arson, theft, rape, and murder that were part of these pogroms. In the light of such events, the representation of anger ("Maccabean rage" [*Selected Poems* 182]) in "The Banner of the Jews" seems warranted and Lazarus's decision to focus on the medieval persecution of Jews in *Dance to Death* becomes comprehensible. While offering students ways to discuss her passion and her apprehensions about anti-Semitism, the pogrom accounts also clarify specific phrases and images. Lazarus's "The Crowing of the Red Cock," for instance, seems more immediate and engaged when read alongside her *Times* article that describes "the systematic firing of the Jewish quarters" ("Persecution" 343) and explains that the crowing of the "red cock" is a Russian euphemism for the burning of Jewish towns (344). The horror of the pogroms is also an appropriate context for helping students fathom why a life of "heavy toil" in rural Texas might become an "unbroken paradise" (*Selected Poems* 178) for the Russian Jewish refugees in Lazarus's "In Exile."

Because of "The New Colossus," Lazarus is ever associated with the immigrants of the 1880s and an idealistic vision of the United States as a nation of exiles. Perhaps because of its classic status and familiarity, students find this poem appealing, even though its immigration politics do not always match student views. Such friction can spark energetic class discussions. I start by encouraging students' fondness for the ideal and asking about immigration in their family histories. Since some students are recent immigrants, some claim relatives in North America before the United States existed, some identify with one Old World nationality, and some maintain multicultural identities, their stories introduce a useful variety to the discussion of immigration; and they raise the themes that appear in Lazarus's poems: poverty, coercion, hardship, and freedom, among them.

We then return to the poem to explore the tension between the poem's idealism and American society's anti-immigrant hostility from the nineteenth century to the present. I might ask, If so many United States citizens have immigrant origins and if immigrants have contributed so much to American history and culture, why has the United States so rigorously restricted immigration? I provide students with documents from the 1880s about the rise of anti-Semitism (brief portions from a vicious but popular tract by Telemachus Thomas Timayenis, *The American Jew* [see Lazarus, *Selected Poems* 357–61 ("The American Jew: An Exposé of His Career")]) and anti-immigrant legislation (the Chinese Exclusion Act of 1882, which ended America's long-standing policy of open immigration). Few students are shocked to learn about anti-Semitic or anti-immigrant hostility, but when read alongside Lazarus's immigration poems—like "The New Colossus," "In Exile," or "1492"—these documents frame Lazarus's representations of America as the land of exiles in ways that highlight the oppositional aspects of her work. "The New Colossus" then becomes not so much a restatement of patriotic sentiment or high ideals as a deliberate, politically motivated attempt to counter anti-immigrant public opinion by defining American ideals and national pride around recent immigrants.

I begin the study of Lazarus in a way that permits students to appreciate her achievement as a poet and American Jewish writer. But because she can generate deep admiration, a class may begin to talk about her as a kind of Jewish saint. It is then time to invite students to think critically about her work, her global politics, and her relation to recent Jewish immigrants. I often jump-start such conversations by introducing thought-provoking scholarship. I ask students to think about Bette Roth Young's biographical examination of Lazarus's class privilege and her father's commercial ties to slavery; or we might read and discuss Paula Bernat Bennett's analysis of Lazarus's distance from the specific Jewish identity Lazarus idealized in her verse (*Poets* 97–103).

These conversations that complicate our understanding of Lazarus are followed by discussion of nineteenth-century documents that amplify this more complex perspective. For example, several of Lazarus's works speak about the creation of a Jewish homeland in Palestine. Alongside poems such as "The New Ezekiel," where the Lord speaks to Israel of renewal and return, or her poems about the restoration of Jerusalem and the Temple ("The Banner of the Jew," "The Feast of Lights"), we study her prose essay "The Jewish Problem," excerpts from George Eliot's *Daniel Deronda* (1877), and Abram S. Isaacs's "Will the Jews Return to Palestine?" Placing Lazarus's proto-Zionist writings alongside her Judeophilic but non-Jewish inspiration (Eliot) and the reasoned opposition to Jewish nationalism from her Jewish critics (Isaacs) situates her work in an intellectual and political dialogue that highlights the cultural work of her poetry. Such an approach also raises questions about her politics, while forestalling a straightforward equation of Jewish identity with Jewish nationalism or a simple approach to the Jewish identity politics in her work.

Lazarus is the nineteenth-century American Jewish writer I teach most: she is the most famous American Jewish writer before the twentieth century, the one with the largest body of verse, the most gifted as a poet, and the one whose work I have found consistently teachable. Nevertheless, historical contextualization enhances student learning about other American Jewish poets. Documents on industrialization, sweatshops, and working conditions, for instance, help make the protest verse of the Yiddish poets Morris Rosenfeld and David Edelshtadt seem less obscure and perhaps even inspirational. Most of my students love Rosenfeld's "My Little Son," a poem about a father who can see his much-loved son only "sound asleep" and "late at night" (135) following a long day of work. Some of my students (working parents, for example) identify with the speaker's depression over how the demands of work prevent him from developing a closer bond with the child he loves ("The time clock drags me off at dawn, / at night it lets me go" [136]).

Reading Rosenfeld alongside Jacob Riis's *How the Other Half Lives*, particularly the photographs and two "Jewish" chapters, supplies a broader and more fully described setting for a poem like "My Little Son."

Riis not only describes the crowded tenements but also recounts how the laborers work from sunrise to 9:00 p.m.; indeed, he says, "Life here means the hardest kind of work almost from the cradle" (105). Yet the most interesting discussions and student papers emerge when students contrast these two contemporaneous authors, both immigrants familiar with poverty and immigrant life in New York. Riis is the more diligent reformer; he has more details and statistics and a wider, more sociological perspective. So, I'll ask, doesn't that make Riis's work better and more socially useful? Don't most of Rosenfeld's poems from *Songs from the Ghetto* merely portray the hardships of individual, unnamed, stock characters? Students respond by arguing that Riis's stereotyped depictions of Jewish people are condescending and insulting; some in the class take particular issue with his description of Jewish women over thirty as "hags" (104). When I point out that Rosenfeld uses clichés, sentimental conventions, generalized figures, and stereotypes, some students concur, but others defend him on various grounds: the insider status he occupies in the Jewish immigrant community in contrast to Riis's outside-observer role; the warm respect and attachment Rosenfeld has for those about whom he writes, compared to Riis's distance (in the form of horror, outrage, or bemusement); or the poignancy generated by focusing on individuals and their specific pain rather than on the "huddled masses" (Lazarus, *Selected Poems* 233) or "endless panorama of the tenements" (Riis 119).

Another way to situate the Yiddish sweatshop poets in their social and political contexts is to devote attention to how the poems were used. Several were set to music and sung by workers and labor organizers. When I teach poetry as song, we listen to recorded performances of the songs. (Conveniently, some inspiring Jewish labor songs, including Edelshtadt's "My Testament," are available on Zalmen Mlotek's *In Love and in Struggle* [Mlotek et al.].) I suspect that students do not enjoy nineteenth-century popular songs as much as I do. Nevertheless, hearing the songs and imagining the workers who sang them help make Edelshtadt's swaggering, lurid lyrics stirring:

> when I am dead
> carry our banner to my grave;
> the freedom-banner—flaming red
> with all the blood that workers gave.

Moreover, consideration of the occasions for these songs allows me to shift attention from What does this poem mean? to What did this poem do?—an important cultural studies question for students of nineteenth-century Jewish verse.

The specific context of a poem's original periodical publication can also bring a text alive. Many Jewish poems first appeared in one of the over two hundred Jewish periodicals published in the nineteenth century. While most were short-lived, some of the major publications—the *Israelite / American Israelite*, the *American Hebrew*, the *Jewish Messenger*, the *Occident and American Jewish Advocate*—are available in libraries, microfilm, and electronic databases. Jewish poets also published in the non-Jewish press: many in local newspapers—Penina Moïse in *Godey's Lady's Book*; Adah Isaacs Menken in the New York *Sunday Mercury* and San Francisco *Golden Era*; Lazarus in a range of mainstream media; and so on. With access to such publications, teachers can develop assignments that ask students to search for anonymous and lesser-known Jewish poets or to examine the stories and issues that literally surround the poems studied in class.

For example, when the *Israelite* published Menken's "To the Sons of Israel," it also ran prose articles condemning the Catholic Church's kidnapping of Edgardo Mortara. Some of these articles retell the story of Pope Pius IX's decision to take the six-year-old Jewish boy from his family so that he might be raised as a Christian, while others cover the protests from Jewish communities around the world. When read alongside these news and opinion pieces, Menken's poem denouncing "Popish Rule and Power" becomes a more interesting, meaningful, and less randomly anti-Catholic document of cultural history.

An alternative for those with limited access to nineteenth-century serials is to invite students to compare the Jewish poems studied in class with the rich collection of periodical verse in the Blackwell anthology of *Nineteenth-Century American Women Poets* (Bennett). Points of connection are numerous, and the periodicals section of the Blackwell anthology presents students with a convenient survey of poetic themes and forms circulating in magazines and newspapers of the era. Students might seize on a poem in a popular genre—a jingoistic poem, for example, like Rose Hawthorne Lathrop's "The Cadet" (from *Harper's New Monthly Magazine*) whose macho young speaker celebrates his national identity: "Thank God! I'm an American!" (493). The nationalism of "The Cadet" invites comparison with a number of American Jewish poems: Moïse's "The Bird of Paradise," Menken's "Pro Patria" (Infelicia), Minna Kleeberg's "Das Land der Freiheit," or Lazarus's "The New Colossus," among others.

Although patriotism can be a difficult theme for classroom conversation, an emphasis on the poems as objects for analysis encourages critical thinking about the function of poetry in national culture. I explore with students the historical contexts that give rise to each expression of patriotic verse: the Civil War in Menken, Jewish refugees and immigration in Lazarus, American imperialism in Lathrop. Questions about the connotations of various symbols (the eagle in Moïse, the uniform and flag in Lathrop, the maternal Deborah figure in Lazarus, the cosmopolitan ship in Kleeberg) typically follow, and students should be encouraged to distinguish between explicit ideals and implicit policies represented in each poem. As contrast to these effusions of American nationalism, I conclude by introducing another periodical poem from the Blackwell anthology, Ella Wheeler Wilcox's "Goddess of Liberty, Answer" (504–05 [from the *Chap-Book*]), a poem that explicitly talks back to Lazarus's "The New Colossus" and critiques idealistic pronouncements of American liberty that ignore poverty, suffering, and worker exploitation.

Valuable online resources have also made the study of American Jewish poems in their original periodical context less troublesome. A paper or homework assignment might ask students to find an "unknown" poet or poem in the first enduring United States Jewish magazine, the *Occident*, which is available online for volumes from 1843 to 1850. Using the *Making of America* site, students can explore Lazarus's work in the *Century Magazine*, the *Galaxy*, and *Scribner's Monthly*. Examining her poems in this context makes it clear that she wrote on a wide range of issues; indeed, a survey of her magazine pieces begins to resemble the array of topics covered in the magazines themselves. Lazarus writes about the queen of Romania in one issue ("To Carmen Sylva"), Talmudic legend in another ("The Birth of Man"), the death of the French Prince Imperial in another ("Destiny"), and so on. If students browse these serials while studying her poems, instructors can raise questions about her erudition and reading. I also invite students to think critically about her range of topics: Does it indicate learning or suggest dilettantism? Is she remarkably multicultural and multidisciplinary in her interests, or do the poems represent the globalist perspective of a well-educated Westerner in an era of colonialist expansion?

A third important context for these poems is Jewish religious tradition. Focusing on holidays because of their importance in Jewish tradition and appeal to students, I like to emphasize a variety of perspectives on a similar holiday or tradition. For instance, an instructor can weave together a context for understanding Hanukkah by bringing together the story of the Maccabees' revolt and the rededication of the Temple (in 1 Maccabees 1–4), information about the history of Hanukkah celebrations in America, a nineteenth-century text about Hanukkah (Max Lilienthal's "The Festival of Chanuckah" in the *Occident* online), and a small group of poems—Lazarus's "The Feast of Lights," Moïse's hymn "Great Arbiter of human fate" for the "Feast of Dedication" (158), Rebekah Hyneman's "Song of Judas Maccabeus, before the Battle of Maspha," and Kleeberg's "Hannukah." I start by mentioning changes in Hanukkah through the course of American history: regional variations in celebrations, its gradual commercialization, its construction as a Christmas equivalent in the late nineteenth century, its growing importance for children, and so on. For instance, the lighting of the *hanukiyah* or menorah was a customary practice in the nineteenth century, but the holiday was not as widely or enthusiastically celebrated as it is now. I then ask the students to focus on the poems. Read together, the poems begin to mutually inform one another, which expands the comprehension of each; they do not, however, provide a uniform interpretation of the celebration or its meaning. In coming to see the differences between, say, Moïse's emphasis on mercy and the cleansing of "the blemished heart" (159) and Lazarus's call for a Jewish homeland, students are in a position not only to understand varying conceptions of Hanukkah but also to appreciate the distinct style of each poet. Following an introduction to historical changes in Hanukkah celebrations, such comparisons can lead to a discussion of the differences between Hanukkah's songs in the nineteenth century and the present. We might, for instance, contrast the deadly serious, bloody, God-glorifying "Song of Judas Maccabeus" to the song my students know best, Adam Sandler's "The Chanukah Song" (from *What the Hell Happened to Me?* [1996]). Associating nineteenth-century pieces with songs they already know has its advantages: it enlivens the conversation and pulls students into a discussion of material that may seem distant.

Rosh Hashanah provides another effective context for situating nineteenth-century Jewish poetry. In introducing the celebration of the new year, instructors might acquaint students with Rosh Hashanah as a time for introspection and self-examination and note that the event it celebrates is the creation of the world and humanity. It is also useful to mention the practice of *tashlik*, in which the participants gather at a body of water and toss bread crumbs or the contents of their pockets into the water as a symbolic gesture of casting off their sins and beginning the year anew. With this briefest of introductions to one of Jewish tradition's holiest days, a class might begin a conversation about a cluster of nineteenth-century poems. I start with a pair that address this holy day directly, Moïse's "Look down, O God! with gracious eye" and Menken's "Rosh Hashanah," both of which emphasize contrition and self-reflection. Deploying traditional symbols such as the sounding of the shofar (ram's horn) and the sea, Lazarus's "The New Year" identifies this holiday with autumn, abundance and suffering, departure and return. Rosenfeld's "September Melodies," not explicitly a Rosh Hashanah poem, draws on a similar set of images. I invite students to contrast the somber, expectant image of the new year in these poems with the revelry of the 1 January holiday. Moving from Rosh Hashanah itself to the event it celebrates, I conclude with poems that retell creation myths: Rosenfeld's "Creation of Man," Lazarus's "The Birth of Man," and her hilarious "The Creation of Man" (based not on a Jewish but a Miwok Indian creation story). Students might compare these different versions with other accounts of creation: American Indian and African stories, Genesis, and the big bang.

Finally, selected poetic traditions are another ideal context for teaching American Jewish poetry in a way that elicits interest and understanding. Just as ancient Hebrew poetry had a significant impact on free verse, Walt Whitman influenced Menken, Lazarus, and Rosenfeld. A second possibility is a discussion of ballad stanza and common meter that moves into an exploration of the relations between Protestant hymns, Moïse's adoption of the hymn form, and Emily Dickinson's transformative use of the form. The danger of such comparisons is that they easily lead to what seems like a predetermined outcome: an emphasis on Whitman's or Dickinson's genius and the perception of other nineteenth-century poets as conventional in comparison. I avoid the pedagogical approach that includes "other" nineteenth-century poets on the syllabus simply to illustrate how much better Whitman and Dickinson were than their contemporaries. Such an approach assumes literary value is a static quality rather than a hotly debated question; it encourages teachers and students to think about Whitman's and Dickinson's poems apart from historical and cultural contexts; and it discourages careful attention to other poets in the era.

A livelier and pedagogically more successful approach for me has been to use texts about women in the Bible as a tradition in which to contextualize Jewish poetry. Throughout the nineteenth century, Christian women of different races authored poems about biblical heroines: Maria Gowen

Brooks's "Esther" and "Judith," Eloise Bibb's "Judith" and "The Expulsion of Hagar," Francis Ellen Watkins Harper's "Vashti" (*Complete Poems*), and many others. Jewish women wrote similar kinds of poems celebrating these figures, from Moïse's maternal "Miriam" and Hyneman's catalog of "Female Scriptural Characters" in *"The Leper" and Other Poems* to Menken's shocking portrayal of "Judith" caught up in "the wild sweetness of Love and agony of Revenge" (Infelicia 52). Jewish periodicals could serve as yet another source for poems about women from ancient Hebrew scripture (the Norton anthology *Jewish American Literature* [Chametzky et al.] includes an anonymously authored "Miriam" from the *Israelite*, while the *Occident* published several pieces in this genre). A course might also include selected prose commentaries on female biblical figures from Jewish-authored texts like Grace Aguilar's *The Women of Israel* (1845) and Christian ones like Harriet Beecher Stowe's *Woman in Sacred History* (1874).

Studying these texts alongside one another has the paradoxical effect of both constructing a common genre and highlighting the differences among these writers: Jewish, Protestant, and Catholic; white and black; feminist and antifeminist; conservative, subversive, and rebellious; traditional and modern; and so on. It creates a specific context in which students can understand how Menken makes distinctive use of "Judith" and how it both situates her in a poetic tradition and differentiates her stylistically and thematically from other American poets. Such contexts will not necessarily make these poets seem less strange, but they will allow students to see how the same character can have divergent meanings for various communities of readers and how the meanings of these poems resonate differently in specific cultural traditions and historical moments.

Contextualization works well in the teaching of nineteenth-century American Jewish poetry, because it allows what may seem distant, strange, or obscure to become comprehensible and interesting. Associating the poems that elude them with texts, events, or ideas they do understand, students gradually learn to appreciate the poems by figuring out what they do and did and what they mean and meant. Moreover, contextualization is an approach that problematizes the poems. It turns them into puzzles or mysteries that can be examined, wondered over, and figured out. Such solutions (provisional and subject to further discoveries) require critical thought, close reading, additional research and inquiry, and complex analysis that asks students to see points of contact or conflict among different texts and contexts.

Alfred Bendixen

Charlotte Perkins Gilman's "Toolbox": The Value of Satiric Poetry and Social Reform

Charlotte Perkins Gilman's "The Yellow Wall-Paper" is now among the most anthologized and most taught works of American short fiction. Students of American literature may also be exposed to her utopian novel *Herland*, and they are likely to read or be told something about *Women and Economics* and her other nonfiction work. Unfortunately, the revival of interest in Gilman has not yet drawn sufficient attention to her poetic achievements, which were the foundation of her literary reputation in her own time and which ought to assume greater significance in our evaluation of her place in both the canon and the classroom. Gilman deserves to be ranked as one of the finest political poets of her generation and as one of the foremost satirists in the history of American verse. Incorporating the study of her poems into the traditional American literature survey will enable skilled teachers to challenge many of the preconceptions about literary and political culture that are embedded in the current curriculum. By introducing our students to Gilman's verse, we introduce them to the extensive role that American poetic humor has played in serious philosophical and ethical discussions about social justice, human rights, and feminist issues. We can also replace the currently overly simplistic picture of this writer, literary feminism, and traditional poetic form with a fuller portrait of our literary history. This essay aims to provide teachers with both the factual background and the specific strategies needed to bring these poems into the American literature classroom in ways that will enlarge our students' comprehension of the complex nature of our literary culture.

An understanding of the crucial role poetry played in Gilman's life and career challenges many of the notions current in traditional survey courses, which tend to privilege the brilliant literary experiments of Walt Whitman and Emily Dickinson in ways that denigrate traditional poetry. Like most educated Americans of her time, Gilman regarded poetry as the greatest of literary forms and valued the wide range of emotions and ideas that were expressed in the traditional verse of her time. The two scholars who have done the most valuable work on Gilman's poetry, Gary Scharnhorst and Denise D. Knight, have emphasized her admiration of Whitman and his influence on her verse (Scharnhorst, *Charlotte Perkins Gilman*; Knight, "With the First Grass-Blade"). Although ample evidence shows that she regarded Whitman as one of our greatest poets, her poems demonstrate little evidence of his influence. On some level, the attempt to exalt Gilman's verse by connecting it to Whitman's reveals some of the presumptions and problems entrenched in our current view of American poetry, particularly the implicit argument that any relation to a canonized poet like Whitman endows a writer with special importance and that neglected nineteenth-century American poets need to be connected to an established figure to merit inclusion. We need to challenge assumptions like this, because they distract us from deeper considerations of both the question of intrinsic literary merit and from a more accurate view of our literary history.

Although she spent much of her adult life in New York and California, Gilman was foremost a child of New England, and her primary literary debt as a poet is to that part of the New England tradition that dominated American literary study before World War II but has now been almost lost in oblivion: the poetry of James Russell Lowell, Oliver Wendell Holmes, and John Greenleaf Whittier, who are now unfortunately known as the "schoolroom poets." At the time that Gilman began her career, these three poets, along with Henry Wadsworth Longfellow, constituted the American poetic tradition. Unlike Longfellow, however, these three writers produced verse with several clearly distinctive qualities that shaped Gilman's own practices: the reliance on a bold and vibrant American voice (sometimes affirming the democratic vernacular at the expense of regular poetic meter), a commitment to assailing social and political injustice (especially in the cause of abolitionism), a belief in the didactic as one of several diverse uses of poetry (perhaps most evident in the tendency to view scenes of nature in moralizing frameworks), the use of a variety of traditional forms and metrical schemes (often using a refrain to highlight key points and move to a culminating moment that has both intellectual and emotional resonance), and a mastery of satire and comedy in the deflation of bigotry and hypocrisy (perhaps most evident in Lowell's *Bigelow Papers* and Holmes's "The Chambered Nautilus" and "The Deacon's Masterpiece"). For these poets, as for Gilman, the creation of a democratic poetry demanded the recognition of both private and public modes of expression in verse and an aesthetic in which morality, religion, and nature were directly connected to the exploration of domestic life in the United States.

In short, the figures we now call the schoolroom poets showed Gilman that conventional poetic forms could provide ideal ways of presenting unconventional ideas. Offering our students this awareness of Gilman's place in a poetic tradition that is now unfashionable but dominated the aesthetics of her time changes the dynamics of our literary culture. Instead of praising Gilman for having been influenced by Whitman, we end up rediscovering the importance of Lowell, Holmes, and Whittier (and the broader tradition they represent) for shaping the poetic achievements of Gilman and contributing to the development of a uniquely American feminist voice in poetry. Perhaps more important, we can acknowledge the existence of a powerful poetic tradition in the United States with clearly political aims and trace its development from mid-nineteenth-century abolitionism to turn-of-the-century feminism.

Although teachers of poetry presumably no longer speak of the didactic heresy, those who teach Gilman's poems will need to confront her belief in an aesthetics devoted to clear political and social aims. When Gilman spoke of aesthetic principles, she almost invariably emphasized some underlying didactic purpose and tended to disparage the purely literary qualities of her work. Thus when William Dean Howells asked to reprint "The Yellow Wall-Paper" in an anthology of American fiction, she assented "but assured him it was no more 'literature' than my other stuff, being definitely written 'with a purpose.' In my judgment it is a pretty poor thing to write, to talk, without a purpose" (*Living* 121). She also clearly emphasized the political and social purposes of the poems collected in *In This Our World* in an 1896 interview, proclaiming, "I don't call it a book of poems. I call it a toolbox. It was written to drive nails with" (qtd. in Scharnhorst, *Charlotte Perkins Gilman* 40). Although she publicly regarded her literary productions as tools, ones that could hammer down obstacles and help build a new society, comments like these seriously understate the extensive role that poetry played in almost every facet of this writer's life.

In fact, the creation of poetry was deeply interwoven with the fabric of Gilman's life. For her, it was a powerful way of addressing large public issues, of pleading for causes and assailing social injustice, but it was also a crucial mode for confronting her most private and intimate feelings. As Knight has demonstrated (*Diaries*), Gilman's papers include over one hundred unpublished poems dealing with various aspects of her private life: there are occasional poems commemorating a birthday, Valentine's Day, or some gift; spiritual meditations detailing and defining the poet's relationship to God; and a large body of intimate verse recording the joys and pains of the major love relationships in her life. At its best, this intensely private poetry offers us revealing glimpses into the passions and pains that marked her inner life.

For Gilman, poetry was both therapy and ritual. The discipline of verse enabled her to acknowledge, express, and cope with a range of emotions that she could not render in more public forms. Poetry also provided an ongoing ritual of self-assessment, which enabled her to commit and recommit herself to a gospel of work and duty. Her spiritual meditations in verse were crucial components of this process of self-definition, enabling her to fuse a conversation with God and an exploration of the self into a continuous affirmation of her chosen identity as social reformer. Poetry was her means of responding to private pains and joys—of recognizing the beauty of a landscape and coping with the loss of a lover. It was also her means of expressing her faith in a religious sensibility that recognized that social justice and Christianity shared a fundamental vision of the place of men and women in the world. It is important that our students understand the role that poetry played in the private and public lives of individuals in nineteenth-century America, and Gilman can stand as a crucial representative figure.

It is tempting to view her published poems as the public face of a carefully and sometimes painfully constructed private identity. Thus, private pains find expression in the public outrage at social injustice and the oppression of women, and in the sometimes fierce satire of the mindlessness that she finds underlying much of the conventional social philosophy of her time. Poetry remained a vital part of her public identity throughout her adult life. She justly dated the establishment of her literary career from the acclaim that greeted her witty masterpiece and most famous poem, "Similar Cases," on its publication in 1890. In her time, her literary reputation rested largely on her poetry, especially her satiric verses, which were widely quoted, often reprinted, and extensively praised on both sides of the Atlantic. Howells told Gilman that the poems collected in *In This Our World* contained "the wittiest and wisest things that have been written this many a long day and year . . . you speak with a tongue like a two-edged sword" (qtd. in Karpinski, "When the Marriage" 216). Upton Sinclair proclaimed her "America's most brilliant woman poet and critic," and Floyd Dell described her poems as "the best satirical verses of modern times" (qtd. in Scharnhorst, "Reconstructing" 249).

Although those sympathetic to Gilman's special brand of socialism and feminism greeted her verse with special enthusiasm, her poetry found a surprisingly large and appreciative audience. The diversity of her poetic achievements and her audience can be best represented in the simple fact that during her life her poems were reprinted in such fundamentally different collections as Edmund C. Stedman's *An American Anthology, 1787–1900* (1900), the anonymously edited *A Book of American Humorous Verse* (1904), Burton Stevenson's *Home Book of Verse* (1912), Sinclair's *The Cry for Justice* (1915), W. J. Ghent's *Socialism in Verse* (1916), Emanuel Haldeman-Julius's *Poems of Evolution* (1920), Louis Untermeyer's *Modern American Poetry* (1921), and Catherine Miles Mills's *The World's Great Religious Poetry* (1926).

Gilman relished the praise her poetry earned, and she attempted, with limited success, to ensure a permanent place for it. Her first published book was the collection of poetry *In This Our World*, which first appeared in California in 1893, was reprinted (with minor variations) in Great Britain in 1895, then expanded into a second American edition in 1895, and then extensively revised and again expanded for the 1898 Small and Maynard printing (which unfortunately omitted a few of her most powerful political poems). She continued to write and publish poems but did not produce another collection in book form. Toward the end of her life, her final preparations for death included extensive plans for the production of a second collection of poems, one that would gather the best work published after *In This Our World* into book form. In fact, she even hoped that this volume, to be entitled "Here Also" and edited by her friend Amy Wellington, could appear alongside a new edition of *In This Our World*

(*Later Poetry* 26). Although these plans did not come to fruition and Gilman's later poems would not be collected in book form until Knight's edition of *The Later Poetry* in 1996, the energy devoted to them during the poet's final days suggests a deep underlying recognition of the enduring importance of her work in verse.

For the classroom teacher, Gilman's poetry offers an opportunity to illustrate the ways in which American poetry was inextricably bound up with political, scientific, and ethical issues in the nineteenth century. Before moving on to a discussion of possible classroom strategies, however, I must remind readers that Gilman was a complicated thinker whose thoughts evolved over time and that the poems she wrote in the twentieth century reflected her reactions to a rapidly changing world. Some of the later poems, particularly "To Isadora Duncan" and the sequence of impressionistic poems about New York City collected as "River Windows," demonstrate the remarkable growth of her poetic imagination. Although many poems effectively continue her fight for social justice, some are surprising.

One of the leading intellectuals of the feminist movement in her time, Gilman despised Freud and favored a type of socialism closer to Fabian ideals than to Marxist ones. "A Psalm of Lives" converts Longfellow's famous poem into a fierce assault on the pessimistic view of human nature she found in Freudian ideas. Although she produced several poems explicitly affirming the value of tolerance, she also produced some verse that is remarkably intolerant. World War I radically changed her thinking about the virtue of internationalism and led to some poems attacking both Germany and pacifism. She was never comfortable with the idea of racial equality; "The Melting Pot" reflects her deplorably racist feelings about the masses of new immigrants into the United States. Although these poems represent a small fraction of the verse she produced, anyone concerned with doing justice to the complexity of political ideas in the United States needs to be aware of this contradictory element in the work of a poet whose major works satirize conservative and reactionary thinking.

A good selection of Gilman's verse can be found in Knight's Penguin anthology Herland, *"The Yellow Wall-Paper," and Selected Writings*, but an instructor may simply wish to use a handful of her poems from editions of *In this World* or *The Later Poetry*. For most survey courses, I recommend focusing on a handful of the satiric poems, especially "Similar Cases," and on Gilman's view of nature, and I encourage students to explore other poems for their paper assignments. The focus of class discussion may well depend on the authors and themes that have been emphasized in the course, but it is relatively easy to engage students by asking them to compare and contrast Gilman's view of the natural world and natural forces with that of Emerson, Thoreau, Twain, Dickinson, Whitman, Crane, or a number of other writers commonly covered in survey courses. Students will not only come to appreciate the special qualities of Gilman's verse, especially her clever use of humor and manipulation of point of view, but also understand the ways in which these poems take part in a larger conversation about the meaning of nature that runs throughout many American literary masterpieces.

"Similar Cases," the most famous and most reprinted of Gilman's poems, offers teachers an ideal place to begin. This satiric masterpiece enables instructors to provide a fuller picture of our literary culture by moving students from an appreciation of the literary comedy to a larger awareness of the impact of Darwin's evolutionary theories on American thought and ultimately to a consideration of how underlying views of nature and the natural shape political and social ideas. Gilman was among those swept up in the vision of a socialist future inspired by Edward Bellamy's utopian novel, *Looking Backward* (1888). Bellamy's followers were eager to form Nationalist publications and clubs, which provided important outlets when Gilman launched her career as a lecturer and author. In fact, "Similar Cases," which first appeared in the April 1890 issue of the *Nationalist*, assails those who failed to grasp the virtues of a future world based on cooperation instead of conflict.

Bellamy's opponents had argued that the egalitarianism at the heart of this socialist vision was fundamentally unnatural, a violation of human nature. In particular, they turned to the ideas of social Darwinism developed by the British philosopher Herbert Spencer, who argued that social evolution, like its biological counterpart, depended on a competitive struggle that would lead to the survival of the fittest. The social Darwinists adamantly opposed any state interference in economic schemes, vigorously affirmed individualism, and despised almost all forms of collectivism. Gilman's answer was to pull the evolutionary rug out from under their arguments.

In the 120 lines of "Similar Cases," Gilman humorously traces three stages in our evolutionary history to demonstrate that radical change is not only natural but also inevitable. In the opening, an eohippus provokes scorn from the Dinoceras and Coryphodon, "the heavy aristocracy / In days of long ago," when he declares his intention of becoming a horse (In This 96). They note the impossibility of this goal with a remark that passes for reasoned argument: "*Why! You'd have to change your nature!*" Then, an Anthropoidal Ape, who is "Far smarter than the rest," receives a similar response from the less intelligent apes when he aspires to become a man (97). Finally, a Neolithic Man prophesies the advent of civilized life to his neighbors, promising them, "We shall be civilized!," and moving to an ironic list of civilized qualities that culminates in "We are going to have Diseases! / And Accomplishments!! And Sins!!!" (99). They reply with the same arguments used against Bellamy's collective utopia:

> Said One, "This is chimerical!
> Utopian! Absurd!"
> Said another, "What a stupid life!
> Too dull, upon my word!"
> Cried all, "Before such things can come,
> You idiotic child,
> *You must alter Human Nature!*"
> And they all sat back and smiled.
> Thought they, "An answer to that last
> It will be hard to find!"
> It was a clinching argument
> To the Neolithic Mind! (99–100)

Students will enjoy the ways in which Gilman's clever rhymes portray the opponents of progress as dinosaurs, apes, and cavemen, but the central focus of the class discussion should be an exploration of the underlying philosophical issues. At the core of the poem's power is the view of human change as natural. She pinpoints the absurdity of using the dynamic process of evolution to argue that change is unnatural or progress impossible. In fact, in her revision of evolutionary thought, change is inevitable and natural and those opposing it are doomed to extinction.

Because Gilman always understood the intellectual stakes at the center of any political game, we can use her poetry to make our students more conscious of these issues. She knew that the belief in an unchanging human nature would be invoked to block political and social progress, and she knew that conservatives would invoke poorly conceived notions of nature and the natural to oppose any change in the condition of women. Her poetry often challenges these assumptions by enlarging our awareness of nature and redefining what is natural. For Gilman, nothing in the world is more natural than progress and the ability of human beings to develop. As I write this essay, the nation is engaged in a debate about the possibility of legally recognizing gay marriage, and the underlying issues directly concern views of what is natural or unnatural and the relation between radical political change and concepts of normal human nature. It is up to each instructor to decide whether to link Gilman's argument to the specific issues that dominate our current political discourse, but we have a responsibility to make our students think about our concepts of the natural and how they have been used to formulate political arguments.

In many of her poems, Gilman explicitly connects notions of the natural to feminist issues. For example, "Wedded Bliss" (1890) brilliantly demolishes the idea that it is natural for man to work and woman to remain at home. In the poem, Gilman suggests that any social order that confines women to passive roles is as unnatural as the mating of eagles and hens, lions and sheep, salmon and clams. In these comically unnatural marriages between different species, she identifies the injustice of gender divisions. Ultimately, the poem argues that a more natural world would eliminate the nonsense that prevents men and women from learning how to be better mates, better partners, and better human beings. In her poetry, feminism is natural, and the established order is merely an absurd violation of nature.

Gilman employed animal fables frequently and skillfully as part of her satiric arsenal. Instructors may wish to compare and contrast her depiction of animals in the natural world with that of Dickinson, many of whose poems also move her readers to a surprising new awareness of our relation to nature. Gilman's purposes are usually more overtly political, but there are crucial connections between these two female voices, including the use of a playful voice that ultimately transforms our awareness of our position in nature. Of course, there are also important differences. One of Gilman's most effective tactics as a political poet is to take an opponent's argument and express it in words that render this perspective ridiculous. Much of feminist criticism has emphasized the ways in which women are silenced and the need, as Alicia Ostriker has eloquently put it, for women poets to steal the language. Gilman's usurpation of sexist and reactionary voices for comic ends reminds us that skillful women writers have the ability to steal language in many different ways. For example, in "A Conservative" (1892), the speaker finds a young butterfly unhappy about its transformed state:

> "I do not want to fly," said he,
>   "I only want to squirm!"
> And he dropped his wings dejectedly,
>   But still his voice was firm:
> "I do not want to be a fly!
>   I want to be a worm!"
>
> (In This 101)

Gilman here employs the conventional image of the butterfly as an emblem of the human soul (transformed from the crawling worm to a creature of beauty and air) to argue that conservatives who resist change are actually resisting a natural order that liberates and elevates humanity to a new and higher spiritual element.

In "The Lion Path" (1893), Gilman also employs animal metaphors to play with and ultimately reject the social Darwinists' notion that the world is a dangerous jungle. She argues that personal courage is a sufficient response to all the forces that oppose meaningful progress. After depicting the terror of those who see lions in the path, her poem provides "one who dares" because he is on "such high errand as no fear could stay." At the end, the sources of terror are transformed into "Some spitting kittens, maybe, in the grass" (In This 13). Gilman focuses on a similar transformation in one of her most notable satiric poems, "An Obstacle" (1890), in which the speaker finds that the best way to confront a "Prejudice" that blocks his path and his view is to walk right through it (102). In her best satiric poetry, the laws of nature have chosen to be on the side of progress.

The satiric poems that established Gilman's literary reputation are part of the complex reenvisioning of nature and the natural that occurs throughout her poems, and they deserve to be put into the context of the great tradition of nineteenth-century American writing on this theme. It would be a mistake, however, to oversimplify her concept of nature by relying on a single poem. Her poems expose us to a wide variety of landscapes, some lovely and some deadly, as though asking us to recognize the variety of possibilities inherent in nature itself. While working in a settlement house in the grim Chicago neighborhood known as Little Hell, Gilman penned "The Beds of Fleur-de-lys" (1898), a lovingly described account of the view from the Presidio in San Francisco. She also fashioned a very effective poetic tour of San Francisco's urban landscape into the poem "Powell Street" (1894). Her ability to render the qualities of certain natural scenes with both precision and artistry is demonstrated in very different ways in the grim landscape of "A Nevada Desert," which was originally published as "Nevada" (1886), and the short evocative masterpiece, "A Moonrise" (1893). Some of the other nature poems, perhaps most notably "Wings" (1895) and "Tree Feelings" (1898), offer surprising moments of affirmation, in which the speaker achieves a significant communion with important symbols of nature.

But Gilman was usually most effective when she was most original.

Both "Nature's Answer" and "A Common Inference" achieve their power through shocking the reader into a confrontation with a nature that is both detached and dangerous. A similar theme may be found in "The Rock and the Sea" (1893), which opened the first three of the four editions of *In This Our World* and which should be ranked among her finest achievements in poetry. The poem consists of two dramatic monologues—each spoken by a representative of one of nature's most powerful forces, the masculine rock and the feminine sea, each declaring its superiority over the other. "The Rock and the Sea" is ultimately a powerful depiction of natural forces beyond human comprehension or control. It is one of the late nineteenth century's most poignant reminders that the forces of nature are beyond what the poem calls "the folly of man" (11). In this respect, all three of these poems should be ranked among the important achievements of American literary naturalism, which undercuts humankind's pretension by situating all forms of life in the midst of natural forces that are either hostile or indifferent and almost always unfathomable. For the most part, the treatment of American literary naturalism in the classroom tends to emphasize male voices working in fiction. The poems discussed here are a reminder that women poets played a role in this philosophical and literary conversation.

The points noted above should provide instructors with an introduction to some of the ways in which Gilman's poetry can enhance the traditional survey course in American literature. The teacher who brings these poems into the classroom will discover that the issues raised by them will lead to a fuller confrontation with the philosophical issues underlying American literary culture and ultimately to a richer view of the relation between poetry and ideas.

Nassim W. Balestrini

Paul Laurence Dunbar and Postbellum African American Poetry

African American poetry written between Reconstruction and the Harlem Renaissance reflects the poets' struggle to come to terms with the legacy of slavery, to define their relation to the United States and to Africa, and to find an acceptable position in contemporary American culture. In the thematic and stylistic contexts, each writer tried to find his or her own voice, while necessarily responding both to already existing African American poetic and lyrical works (including spirituals or slave songs as well as Phillis Wheatley's poetry) and to traditional and contemporary English-language traditions mostly represented by white poets. The demands of a predominantly white readership (as well as critics and publishers), the desire to attract readers of any color, and the realities of the book and magazine markets complicated the constant pressure to choose or mediate between African American and Anglo-American cultural models.

Paul Laurence Dunbar, born to former plantation slaves in 1872, wrote poems in dialect and in Standard English. He won acclaim from critics such as William Dean Howells and from his fellow poet James Weldon Johnson. Like other African American writers, he has been criticized for catering to a prejudiced taste that applauded dialect poetry to restrict black poets to their own, implicitly substandard, poetic form. But Dunbar has also been appreciated for his flawless technique in any style. Even a small selection of the several hundred poems he wrote during his short life (he died in 1906, at the age of thirty-three) helps students avoid monolithic associations between specific stylistic features and themes, between certain formal elements and meanings, between a poet's race and his art. I do not deny the significance and the signifying interactions among form and style, contents, and cultural factors, but students should be encouraged to approach a literary text from multiple perspectives in order to garner a variegated bouquet of implications.

Dunbar's poems illustrate his awareness, critical evaluation, and partial appreciation of Anglo-American culture inspired by Christian values and the ideals of the American Revolution. Aware of gaps between ideals and reality, he clearly condemns slavery and its aftermath when verbalizing the psychology of both. These attempted explanations are often a desperate cry or its muffled correlative.

In this essay, I suggest a variety of teaching approaches intended to foster an understanding of Dunbar's and other African American writers' poetry in the historical context of a recently reunited country caught in the paradox of racial discrimination and pride in the achievements of liberty. Unless otherwise noted, all page references are to Henry Louis Gates, Jr., and Nellie Y. McKay's *The Norton Anthology of African American Literature* (1997); this collection also contains Johnson's preface to the *Book of Negro Poetry*, which appreciates Dunbar's achievements and underscores the crippling effects of Howells's criticism (see esp. 872, 877–78). Students and teachers can also consult Joanne M. Braxton's edition of Dunbar's poetry (including its introduction) and its e-text counterpart at *Literature Online* (excluding the introduction and notes); Houston Baker's important 1974 essay; and the *Paul Laurence Dunbar Digital Text Collection*, which contains about half of Dunbar's poems, along with Howells's introduction to *Lyrics of Lowly Life*.

Color-Blind Reading

As a first step, I suggest a discussion of poems without explicit references to race. One may consider giving the students these poems at first without information on the poet's life and background. Students could begin their analysis by identifying formal features such as meter, rhyme, and stanzaic pattern. The discussion could then focus on theme and especially voice in the Victorian love poem "Her Thought and His" (897–98), on the one hand, and "Worn Out" (887–88) and "The Poet" (905), on the other hand. "Her Thought and His" evokes romantic associations with a moonlit evening on a shore. Water imagery reflects the speaker's submerged desire for his loved one ("And I thought of the flood-tide of infinite bliss / That would flow to my heart from a single kiss"), and it implies his potential to quench the equally subdued "flame" (lines 7–8, 11) that he perceives in her countenance. In contrast to this rather conventional love poem, written in a softly rocking, mostly anapestic meter, the other two works are richer in implications. The analysis of opposing images (light/darkness, coldness/warmth, life/death, high/low) related to an assessment of tone will help students ponder each speaker's situation. The persona in "Worn Out" addresses, in incessantly drumming iambic trimeter, an unknown "you." The anonymous "you" expects the speaker to ". . . hold [his] peace / And dry [his] fruitless tears," to ". . . smile / And drive the gloom away" (lines 1–2, 5–6). In contrast to "Her Thought and His," the persona's suffering goes beyond romantic suspense and culminates in analogies of waste and destruction—

> Like to an ash-stained hearth
> When all its fires are spent;
> Like to an autumn wood
> By storm winds rudely shent

—as well as in the speaker's heart crying out for "release" (lines 17–20, 24). The question of "release" should be compared with the closing lines of "The Poet": "But ah, the world, it turned to praise / A jingle in a broken tongue" (lines 7–8). What are the connotations of "jingle"? Whose "world" bestows praise? Which sense of artistic quality does this world promote? Why is the jingle expressed in "a broken tongue"? Once the instructor has collected answers, she or he could introduce the students to Dunbar's life and could discuss how familiarity with biographies and ethnic backgrounds influences and contributes to reading literary works.

As an alternative to this group, one could compare "Not They Who Soar" (894) and "Sympathy" (900), both of which depict suffering people. "Not They Who Soar" contains several juxtapositions connected to either flying majestically through the air or bending one's back in bone-breaking earthly labor. Students will want to discuss why the oppressed and depressed rather than the eagle-like creatures are heroes. One could ask them to consider the origins of this attitude (as indicated by references to God, which invite discussion of, for example, the Sermon on the Mount) and to try to imagine who could have written such a poem and in which historical context. "Sympathy" also revolves around an image of flight by creating an analogy between the speaker and a caged bird (one of Maya Angelou's autobiographies takes its title from the line "I know why the caged bird sings" [lines 15, 21]). Once the instructor has disclosed the context of slavery and of continued discrimination, students could consider this poem as an introduction to related poems on the same theme. As they will realize, the juxtaposition of a free and a caged bird, an actual face and a mask, a song of joy and a cry of pain also informs other texts on life's ambiguities. For a comparison of two poems on liberty, the class could study "Sympathy" alongside the elegiac "Ere Sleep Comes Down to Soothe the Weary Eyes" (893–94).

The Dimensions of Dialect Poetry: Self-Portrait or Stereotype?

After students have learned about Dunbar's racial identity and about the problematic expectations concerning a particular African American literary idiom, they may be curious to study both his dialect poems and his other poems. One of the goals of analyzing several dialect poems is to recognize the relation among surface features (the characteristics of the dialect, the form of each poem), the theme as indicated by the title as well as by related events or described phenomena, and whatever may be simmering underneath or run counter to the expectations of readers who want dialect literature to be nostalgic in the manner of humorous local-color stories or minstrel-show songs. A comparative study of a local-color story or of minstrel show lyrics (such as a Stephen Foster song) with Dunbar's poems may serve as an eye-opener.

To facilitate access to these poems, I would select "Little Brown Baby" (897) to conduct an exercise in annotation and in attention to detail. Once the instructor has read the poem aloud, students could work in groups on identifying linguistic patterns in one or more stanzas (pronunciation, grammatical features, diction). Printing the poem in double-spaced lines on a sheet of paper with wide margins on all sides allows students to circle or otherwise mark specific features, to use colors, arrows, or related methods of highlighting repetitions and further links among sounds, semantics, and grammar. As this topographic analysis will indicate the coherence of dialect features, the class should then discuss the validity and meanings of Standard English and dialects. Depending on the students' age, this discussion could be assisted by information on the controversy about speaking, writing, and publishing in African American forms of English. With regard to the poem itself, students could analyze the tension between the traditional theme of parental love and stereotypes about African American babies and families. They could ask themselves which features are traditional. Students may easily pinpoint playful behavior between parents and children. They could also discuss the rhyme pattern and the meter (a comparison with nursery rhymes or poems like Clement Clarke Moore's "The Night before Christmas" could be interesting). Students could also scrutinize familiar images as well as the function of the "buggah-man" tale (line 21).

One possibility of further developing the discussion of stereotypes would be a comparison between "A Negro Love Song" (888–89) and the nondialect poem "Dinah Kneading Dough" (901), which could be complemented by referring back to "Her Thought and His" (897–98). Again, reading the poems aloud and identifying the meter will contribute to understanding the atmosphere of each poem. If one recited "Dinah Kneading Dough" without showing the students the printed text, one could test whether they hear "kneading dough" or "needing dough." As a consequence, one could discuss the relation between the visual and acoustic elements in poetry and between the description of a woman's domestic work and the necessity of earning money in an occupation that society assigns to her. The fast-paced, dance-inspired "Negro Love Song" with its insistently repeated line ("Jump back, honey, jump back") may be related to images of the dance-club milieu, to the cakewalk and ragtime culture. One could also discuss it in comparison with song lyrics of the 1890s (see Paymer). Students could contrast the type of physicality portrayed in this poem with the physical aspects of Dinah's domestic duty of "kneading dough" and discuss how the speaker transforms an everyday activity into poetry. For instance, the first six lines list clichés that one expects to find in love poems; furthermore, the speaker compares the physically strong Dinah with ladylike maidens; finally, Dinah's aloofness and the swiftly drawn portrait of her beauty contrast with the soft malleability of the dough and of the speaker's heart. Students may want to discuss why Dunbar wrote one poem in dialect and the other in Standard English, why each of these poems achieves its particular effect on the reader, and how both poems relate to "Her Thought and His" (897–98). In this context, one should consider the question of the intended audience(s).

The relation between pride in African American looks and talents (especially in music and dance) and the danger of stereotyping through stressing abilities appreciated or accepted by whites also takes center stage in "When Malindy Sings" (894–96), one of Dunbar's most famous and debated poems. This poem can be studied in conjunction with "Dinah Kneading Dough" because of its depiction of black women in the stereotypical roles of domestic servant or religious singer and because one can again contrast the stylistic features and effects of nondialect and dialect poems.

The comparison of "Negro Love Song" and "When Malindy Sings" juxtaposes the popular music associated with late-nineteenth-century African American culture and the religious music of the antebellum slave songs. A close reading of "When Malindy Sings" (covering the approaches mentioned above) and a discussion of stereotypes could be complemented by the biographical portrayal of African American female singers of classical music, the blues, and jazz (such as Elizabeth Taylor Greenfield [1817?–76], Sissieretta Jones [1869?–1933], Marian Anderson [1897–1993], Ma Rainey [1886–1939], and Bessie Smith [1894–1937]). The career of the Fisk Jubilee Singers and the popularization of slave songs during the postbellum period (see *Jubilee Singers* [Fisk U] and *Jubilee Singers* [PBS]), especially after the turn of the century, when Harlem was becoming an increasingly popular cultural site, as well as the marketing of various types of singers (e.g., as expressed by promotional photographs) could all be part of the discussion of Dunbar's poetic rendering of Malindy. The Audio Companion CD to the *Norton Anthology of African American Literature* provides ample material, which could be complemented with texts and images from books (see Paymer; Toll; Lott) or Web pages provided by various universities and the Library of Congress (see the "Resources" part in this volume for more information on the Fisk Jubilee Singers, including the singers Elizabeth Taylor Greenfield and Sissieretta Jones; the blues; and musical renditions of Dunbar's works, some of which are included in the Audio Companion). The thin line between appreciating and defining a genuinely African American artistic genius on the one hand and limiting singers to a specific style on the other should become clear.

No matter if one discusses all these poems about parental and romantic love, women, and music—poems that mostly confirm specific norms and values instead of criticizing them—one should study dialect poems that may prompt stereotyping alongside those with a subversive streak. Significantly, two dialect poems set in the antebellum period encode their messages by using other textual conventions, the fable and the sermon, to cover up the substratum of meaning.

"A Cabin Tale" (898–900), a narrative poem in which a male slave tells his owner's son a fable, invites comparison with "Little Brown Baby" (897), the poem discussed earlier, about a father's love for his son. Dunbar's "A Cabin Tale" introduces a trickster figure into a David-conquers-Goliath tale of the witty weasel delivering the arrogant and greedy bear into certain death at the farmer's hands. As this poem embeds the fable into a narrative frame in which the stereotypically warm-hearted slave humors the white child while also reminding him of the correct manners of a future slave master, students can peel off the various layers of meaning by analyzing the frame and the tale separately and by then discussing the repercussions between the two. Who are the weasel and the bear in the human realm? Which circumstances allow the speaker to tell his listener an ambiguous tale? How does the poem hint at the child's expectations and play with the reader's expectations? The camouflage method of telling a fable that requires the reader to identify analogous situations and characters in the human world effectively illustrates the two levels of this poem.

The second example, "An Ante-bellum Sermon" (891–93), depicts the slaves' situation through the Israelites' predicament in Egypt. Students need, as a first step, to understand the biblical context and the tradition of this analogy, as indicated by the lyrics of the spiritual "Go Down, Moses." The lyrical "I" addresses his "brothahs," who have convened "In dis howlin' wildaness" (lines 1, 2) to hear about God communicating with Moses. The sermon juxtaposes statements and disclaimers: the preacher emphasizes God's power and His intention to free the oppressed; these statements alternate with disclaimers concerning the implications of the speaker's words for his listeners' current predicament. This rhetoric should be scrutinized in terms of strategies of confirmation and negation, of the double meanings of terms like "liberty" and "master." Most prominently, the slave master eventually yields his place to Jesus Christ, "de gracious Mastah / Dat has gin us liberty" (lines 83–84). As in the previous poem, the stereotype of an African American man perceived from a proslavery white perspective contrasts with the more subtle understanding of his fellow slave, based on the code that the community developed as a safety net.

The Smiling Mask and the Suffering Soul

The poems "Philosophy" (903–04) and "We Wear the Mask" (896) deal with the theme of a Janus-faced African American existence imposed by the pressures of race-based expectations. Again, coupling two works written in different idioms indicates that the dismissal of Dunbar's dialect poems as light, entertaining, and necessarily affirmative misrepresents the poet's art. The speaker of "Philosophy" straightforwardly expresses puzzlement at asking people to smile and pretend they are not miserable ("But it's easy 'nough to titter w'en de stew is smokin' hot, / But hit's mighty ha'd to giggle w'en dey's nuffin' in de pot" [lines 15–16]). The disarming directness of this poem, which plays with variations of words expressing the act of smiling, invites comparison with "We Wear the Mask." In order to approach "We Wear the Mask," one could ask students to locate all details pertaining to the mask motif, to identify all contrasts between surface appearance and inner emotional states, to explain the apostrophe to Christ as well as the clay image (lines 10, 12), and to then contemplate the following questions: Who created the mask, and who is responsible for keeping it on the speaker's face? Why does the mask look the way the speaker describes it? Why does the speaker exhort his listeners to keep wearing the mask? Which psychological effect has the mask exerted on the speaker over time? How do the functions that white and black people ascribe to the mask differ?

As an illustration of this "mask," it is helpful to discuss blackface minstrelsy, either through cover pages on nineteenth-century sheet music, photographs of minstrel show performers, or excerpts from movies such as *Show Boat* (1936; the Broadway musical premiered in 1927) or *The Jazz Singer* (1927). *Show Boat* includes a plantation song (sung by the female protagonist in blackface, plucking a banjo). The exaggerated lips, the rolling of the eyes, the costumes, and other features should easily spark discussion of derogatory depictions of African Americans, for which Al Jolson's blackface performance of "My Mammy" in *The Jazz Singer* serves as another example. The glamorous metropolitan setting in the North for Jolson's song as opposed to the claptrap show boat touring the rural South can serve as another point of departure for discussion. As Dunbar wrote his poems decades before these films were made, one should ponder the continuing existence of racial stereotypes. One could also illustrate the product history and appearance of Aunt Jemima or Uncle Ben or how African Americans have tried to combat certain masks and to replace them by other faces (or masks?) (for images of Aunt Jemima, see the Web sites of the Museum of Public Relations [www.prmuseum.com/kendrix/jemimas.html] and Advertising Age [www.adage.com/century/icon07.html]). Depending on the format of the class, one could also discuss current racial stereotyping and self-stereotyping found in popular culture, especially in music, television, and movies.

United States History and Contemporary Life: Heroes and Victims

Three poems may be selected to illustrate Dunbar's awareness of African American contributions to United States history and his patriotic attachment to this country. The poems serve to emphasize the pain Dunbar expresses in texts about the paradox of pride in the American ideals of liberty and equality coexisting with the continued oppression of African Americans.

The historical poems "Black Samson of Brandywine" (904–05), "The Colored Soldiers" (889–91), and "Douglass" (903) introduce heroes of the American Revolutionary War, the Civil War, and abolitionism. The first example, a ballad, partakes in the traditional rhetoric of heroic achievements in battle (stanzas 1 through 4) but then contrasts the hero's reduction to "chattel" (line 37) with his kinglike triumphs that inspire all artists. In addition to the vivid imagery depicting the hero, one should also consider that Dunbar selected a 1777 battle won by the British army. Does he want to imply that white American soldiers did not fight as valiantly as Black Samson? Or that the black hero fought with all his strength although the cause was lost at that point? Is the royal imagery for the hero meant to pique the descendants of antiroyalist American revolutionaries? Does the speaker pinpoint the irony of historiography, which remembers high-rank leaders more than simple soldiers? And what about the biblical allusion? Was Black Samson blinded by the desire for a liberty that was not meant for him? Was America his Delilah, who deceived him? This poem certainly requires discussion of allusions, images, and diction as well as of the speaker's attitude toward hero worship.

"The Colored Soldiers" connects neatly with "Black Samson of Brandywine" in first mentioning the poet's task to celebrate heroes as well as the disdain toward African American soldiers during the Civil War (lines 9–16), then launching into lavish praise of black soldiers as the bravest and fiercest of men. But again, Dunbar does not merely celebrate heroes who have been neglected and deserve to be remembered in historiography. More important, the speaker posits that black soldiers' participation in their own liberation and in the nation's reunification "has cleansed completely / Every blot of Slavery's shame" (lines 75–76). Although a detailed analysis of the form, style, and imagery of the poem is interesting in itself, I would rather focus the discussion on the speaker's argumentation concerning the soldiers' place in American history at a time of intense crisis and concerning their status as "noble sons of Ham" (lines 6, 78). Dunbar's poem reflects the debate of nature versus nurture, the question of whether one is marked for eternity by association with Ham and slavery or able to replace a badge of low status with a badge of honorable masculinity. Various possibilities for contextualization come to mind. One could discuss the poem after collecting facts about African American regiments of the Civil War and the fate of veterans. One could also analyze an excerpt from Mark Twain's novel *The Tragedy of Pudd'nhead Wilson* (1894), in which the narrator contemplates the nature-nurture debate.

The third example in this section takes us into Dunbar's own day, a time of lynchings and other horrific forms of persecution. Before discussing "The Haunted Oak" (901–02), one could read Dunbar's prose text "The Fourth of July and Race Outrages" (905–06), which stresses the paradox of celebrating (supposedly) all-American Independence Day while segments of the population fear harassment by those who rejoice only in their own freedom. Understanding "The Haunted Oak" requires sensitivity to poetic strategies of indirection but also familiarity with accusations of sexual transgressions leveled at black men who were subsequently lynched by vigilante racists.

First, students should be asked to identify the speaker (the personified oak) and the occasion for the speaker's narrative (the unnamed person's questions addressed to the oak in lines 1–4). Second, the depiction of the events and of the persona's emotions could be listed in parallel columns. Indirection plays a central role here. For instance, the speaker indicates the hanged victim's suffocation by referring to his "gurgling moan" (line 10). Furthermore, the persona evokes associations with Johann Wolfgang von Goethe's "Erl King" ballad when he asks "Who is it rides by night, by night?" (line 21), thus foreshadowing the victim's death. By describing the murderers' garb and by referring to their professions ("judge," "doctor," "minister" [lines 41, 42, 43]), the speaker identifies them not as mythical figures like the Erl King but as real persons and members of the Ku Klux Klan, whose crimes remain unpunished in court. Third, the various meanings of "riding" in the last two stanzas need to be clarified in order to understand who is riding whom or what and which associations (apocalyptic or other) such riding may trigger. The persona's use of ambiguity implies that the murderers cannot escape divine retribution, no matter how fast they ride. Finally, a close look at the symbol of the leafless bough and the reasons for making a tree the speaker of a poem on lynching will assist the students in merging all the details of their analysis into a coherent reading.

African Heritage: Addressing Ethiopia

Dunbar's "Ode to Ethiopia" (886–87) addresses many of the themes described above. In the attempt to identify the particular theme of this poem, students may be struck by the realization that the speaker does not depict the African continent or culture but rather the development from the enslavement of Africans to their arrival in the New World. A discussion of the stylistic features, the images, and Dunbar's decision to use the traditional poetic form of an ode can thus be connected with questions of African American self-image, African American history, and the African American perspective on the future. Students may also be interested in Dunbar's reasons for adopting a mythical Ethiopia as representative of the African continent for descendants of slaves who may not know their ancestors' origins. Furthermore, one could ask the class to identify American ideals in the poem (freedom, hard work, pride in one's achievements, Christian beliefs, the idea of progress) and to explain why the last stanza invokes the poets' role. When the speaker describes "bards who from thy [Ethiopia's] root shall spring, / And proudly tune their lyres to sing / Of Ethiopia's glory" (lines 46–48), he proclaims Ethiopia's capacity to bring forth genuine artists who will combine their poetic creativity—expressed in the conventional terms of a muse-inspired Orpheus singing to the accompaniment of his lyre—with loving appreciation of their African heritage.

Another approach to teaching this poem, especially if one does not plan to study a broad array of Dunbar's works, is to discuss it in conjunction with several poems on the theme of African heritage written before and after the Civil War and during the Harlem Renaissance. Frances E. W. Harper's 1853 poem "Ethiopia" (Gates and McKay 412), Gwendolyn B. Bennett's 1923 "Heritage" (1227), and Countee Cullen's 1925 "Heritage" (1311–14) would here complement Dunbar's 1893 "Ode to Ethiopia."

Harper's speaker assures personified Ethiopia that God will hear her cries and that her descendants will live in a harmonious world, which is depicted in terms of a tropical paradise, with "sheltering vines and stately palms" (line 17) and a peaceful Christian society. Bennett's lyrical "I" first romanticizes the clichés of an exotic northern African race, then closes by saying "I want to feel the surging / Of my sad people's soul / Hidden by a minstrel-smile" (lines 16–18), thus positing an aesthetically pleasing and attractive Africa against the distortion of her people on the popular stage. While both Harper and Dunbar integrate their vision of African American society into the mainstream through the adherence to ideas of liberty and Christianity, Bennett finds "a heathen fire / Of a strange black race" (lines 11–12) fascinating, without pledging allegiance to it.

Cullen's poem—which repeats the question "What is Africa to me" (lines 1, 10, 63), then transplants the conflict between white and black Americans into the speaker's soul—negotiates current clichés about life in the jungle, about the animal nature of nonwhite peoples, about the wild qualities of African flora and fauna. The poem offers a panorama that culminates in the speaker's central dilemma of alienation from African religion (which people want to foist on him to stress his otherness and his exoticism) and his ambivalent feelings about Christianity. On the one hand, he continuously wishes Christ were African; on the other hand, he has trouble accepting Africans as people on his own level of development: "Not yet has my heart or head / In the least way realized / They and I are civilized" (lines 126–28).

This discussion of a selection of works on the same topic by several African American authors may fulfill the same goal as the study of a variety of works by Dunbar alone: to prevent a limited and limiting perspective on a whole body of poetry—a perspective a student could develop from a preoccupation with only one text by a writer belonging to a specific ethnic group. Comparisons of this kind tend to be more memorable and instructive than the analysis of isolated examples, as they foster salutary amazement at the distinguishing individual facets of literary texts.

Dunbar's poems grant students the opportunity to learn about the most prominent African American poet of international repute between the end of Reconstruction and the early twentieth century. His poetry not only fascinates in aesthetic terms, it also lends itself to a discussion of historical and cultural contexts. Studying poetry of the postbellum period in the manner described above should provide insights into a time of major social upheavals, a time during which the American nation began to cope with the legacy of the Civil War. The painful clash between African Americans' high expectations and their cruel disappointment can be felt in Dunbar's poems. At the same time, his works foreshadow some of the stylistic and thematic concerns of twentieth-century African American poetry. For instance, his poem "Why Fades a Dream?" (*Collected Poetry* 77–78) prefigures one of the most famous poems of the Harlem Renaissance: Langston Hughes's "Harlem" (1951), which is better known by its first line, "What happens to a dream deferred?" (Gates and McKay 1267). A discussion of these two poems offers yet another approach to teaching Dunbar's works in the context of their aesthetic and social history. As has become clear, my main concern has been to develop methods that combine an in-depth analysis of individual texts with comparative analyses of various related or contrasting texts as well as with discussions of political and cultural developments. Even students who are suspicious of poetry may thus glimpse the relevance of poetry for an understanding of history and people.

Judith P. Saunders

Stephen Crane: American Poetry at a Crossroads

The manifest idiosyncrasies of Stephen Crane's poetry may be understood, at least in part, as the culmination of innovations pioneered by his two most important nineteenth-century American predecessors, Walt Whitman and Emily Dickinson. Written in the final decade of the century, Crane's poetry builds on formal experimentation in progress since 1855, when the first edition of *Leaves of Grass* was published. It reflects with striking clarity, moreover, his familiarity with Dickinson's work, which was only beginning to reach wider audiences by the time Crane began his career as a poet. He found ways to combine in his writing radical principles borrowed from the two earlier poets' defiance of poetic tradition. Like them, he embraced the identity of a rebel: "the impulse to shock, to make something new" was strong in him (Bergon 24). Formally and thematically, in consequence, he is an important precursor to the generation of the modernists; his gnarly, gnomic work provides significant links between nineteenth- and twentieth-century modes of literary expression. To help students situate Crane in the evolution of American poetics, instructors may present his work in conjunction with selected examples of poetry by Whitman and Dickinson, on the one hand, and that of William Carlos Williams, E. E. Cummings, and Wallace Stevens, on the other. Such comparative examination illumines the nature of nineteenth-century influences on Crane, at the same time confirming the forward-looking characteristics of his verse. Classroom discussions and written assignments can rely, for the most part, on well-known and readily available texts, including the volume cited in this essay, *The Complete Poems of Stephen Crane.*

Crane's oeuvre is modest, 136 short poems, most of which appeared in the two volumes published during his lifetime: *The Black Riders and Other Lines* (1895) and *War Is Kind* (1899). Clearly, his poetic achievement lies in the innovative quality of his work rather than in quantitative output. His indebtedness to Whitman emerges most prominently in his wholehearted embracement of free verse. In a decade when the lyrics of American schoolroom poets (Longfellow, Bryant, Holmes, Lowell, Whittier) continued to be canonized by popular taste, Crane's abandonment of rhyme and of accentual-syllabic meters is decisive. He signals his rejection of traditional devices in a parody of Henry Wadsworth Longfellow's immensely popular "Psalm of Life":

> Tell me not in joyous numbers
> We can make our lives sublime
> By—well, at least, not by
> Dabbling much in rhyme. (148)

He questions the validity of "rhyme" and "numbers" as vehicles for profound communication, jeering at the vapid content and self-conscious sentiment of Longfellow's "Psalm." Elements of his own poetics are implicit in his mocking criticisms. First, the role of poetry is to explore ultimate questions; that is, it strives for genuine rather than contrived sublimity. Second, a preoccupation with the melodious effects of meter and rhyme tends to undermine—indeed, impede—the expression of harsh truths or tragic insights.

Here it is relevant to invoke Ralph Waldo Emerson, who in his often anthologized poem "Merlin" (1845–46; *Collected Poems* 91–93) sought to free poets from reliance on the "trivial" effects of merely pretty sound. The "tinkle" and "jingling" of regular rhythms and predictable rhyme schemes are not suited, he argues, to the expression of powerful emotion or spiritual exploration. A poet is constrained tortuously by "the coil of rhythm and number," his creativity inhibited by bloodless calculations of "rule and pale forethought." Emerson's conception of "the kingly bard," as articulated in "Merlin," opens the way for the aggressively untraditional, seemingly antipoetic achievement of Crane at the century's end.

To probe the "mystic springs" of human striving, the bard must "smite the chords rudely and hard." Such metaphors appear apt indeed as descriptions of Crane's unadorned, hard-hitting, often abrupt pronouncements. Certainly, too, Crane's unsparing comments on human nature and the human condition correspond well to Emerson's demand for poetic utterance that is "peremptory" as well as "free."

Crane valued his poetry over his prose fiction precisely because the poems represent, as he explained, a "more serious effort" to articulate his "ideas of life as a whole" (qtd. in Joseph Katz xi). Because such a purpose was far more important to him than the aesthetics of form, he hesitated even to label his work poetry (Dooley 110). He generally referred to his poetic efforts as "lines," choosing for his first collection, for example, the title *The Black Riders and Other Lines* (thus avoiding the typical phrasing of "and other poems"). His relegation of traditional formal expectations to distinctly secondary consideration was also anticipated by Emerson, who in "The Poet" (1844) criticized would-be practitioners of the art for subordinating "argument" to "the finish of the verses" (*Ralph Waldo Emerson* 200). Given Crane's dissatisfaction with dominant nineteenth-century poetics, it is no surprise that he moved along paths laid out by Emerson and first traveled by that still more adventurous literary forebear, Whitman. Indeed, it is impossible to imagine Crane's poetry, or anything like it, springing into existence without the impetus provided by Whitman's forty-year career of confident rule breaking. The conspicuously ungenteel, "barbaric yawp" of Whitman's *Leaves of Grass* (line 1330) served Crane—and after him generations of twentieth-century poets—as a liberating model, a pattern of possibility for bold revisionings of an ancient art.

His most important legacy from Whitman was clearly permission to discard many long-standing conventions of lyricism. In Crane's hands, free verse becomes prosodically even more radical than in his predecessor's. Eschewing the long lines, swinging rhythms, and expansive effects of Whitman's verse, Crane favors verbal creations that look and sound like small, tight outbursts on the page. The brevity of his poems tends to prevent the construction of even loose rhythmic units, while short and inconsistent line length further impedes any regularity in the flow of words. Thus his poems not only fail to scan, they lack virtually all rhythmic qualities that might distinguish them from prose. Readers need to see the text on the page and reflect on the deliberate formation and placement of lines in order fully to appreciate Crane's compositions as poems.

With this emphasis on the visual dimension of poetry, Crane

anticipates the future, pointing the way most immediately to the work of Cummings and Williams. Direct students' attention to Cummings's "o sweet spontaneous," "in Just—," and "Poem, or Beauty Hurts Mr. Vinal," for instance, and to Williams's "Landscape with the Fall of Icarus" and "Iris." Crane's habit of achieving special emphasis by the insertion of conspicuously short lines (often a single word) among longer ones shows an attention to line breaks more acute than Whitman's and anticipates composition methods that would characterize coming generations of American poets. An excerpt from "In Heaven" illustrates his deliberate wielding of the short, singular line:

> Then all save one of the little blades
> Began eagerly to relate
> The merits of their lives.
> This one stayed a small way behind,
> Ashamed.
> Presently God said:
> "And what did you do?" (20)

By allowing the thematically significant word *ashamed* to occupy a line all by itself, he underlines its importance without resorting to auctorial comment, figurative decoration, or linguistic playfulness of any sort. Stylistic starkness is in any case a hallmark of his work; beside Crane's poems, Whitman's look lush.

Like the structure of his verse, Crane's vocabulary and syntax are simpler and leaner than Whitman's. There is a surface flatness to his statement that facilitates its underlying irony. Individual pieces often read like "tightly compressed epigrams or highly condensed parables" (Dooley 111). If his laconic posture differentiates him decidedly from the earlier poet, an uncompromising rebelliousness, which is simultaneously ideological and formal, places him squarely in Whitman's lineage. Crane does not accept Whitman's affirmative worldview but nonetheless joins Whitman in debunking a host of culturally imposed opinions and institutionalized prejudices: "creeds and schools" (*Walt Whitman Archive*; path: *Leaves of Grass* [1881–82], "Song of Myself" [p. 29]; all Whitman references are to this source).

Both poets are suspicious, if not downright contemptuous, of orthodoxy, fervently discontented with the narrowness of received authority in any realm, whether metaphysical, intellectual, or sociopolitical. Crane's depiction in "I stood upon a highway" of "many strange pedlers," each offering for sale the "pattern of God" he prefers (36), must remind his readers of section 41 in "Song of Myself." There Whitman's speaker collects drafts, lithographs, and sketches of a massive cross-cultural selection of deities, "taking them all for what they are worth and not a cent more" (67). Both poets point out the great number and variety of human conceptions of the godhead, and both shake their heads at the exclusiveness with which each individual clings to one particular theological "pattern" or "sketch." Crane's speaker condescendingly rejects the "little images" offered him by various believers ("I said: 'Hence!' "), highlighting his confidence in the superiority of his own vision by attributing smallness to all others: "I can't buy your patterns of God, / The little gods you may rightly prefer."

In their antagonism to culturally imposed beliefs and practices, both poets tend to ally themselves with the humblest forms of existence, questioning whether humanity, with all its pieties, prejudices, and hypocrisies, really merits a privileged place in the great chain of being. Whitman announces that he may "turn and live with animals" rather than with "dissatisfied" and "demented" humans, who are all too typically driven by a desire for wealth and status. Animals are free, moreover, from religious self-abnegation and cant: they do not make him "sick discussing their duty to God" (54). Gleefully he extols "dung and dirt," declaring that "the bull and the bug [are] never worshipp'd half enough" (67). In the poem " 'Think as I think,' said a man" (50), Crane, in his turn, identifies with a supposedly lesser creature in his scathing reply to a dogmatist. "Think as I think," an unnamed sectarian abruptly demands, "Or you are abominably wicked: / You are a toad." Instead of refuting the contention that nonconformity makes him less, or other, than human, Crane's speaker deftly removes the barb from his opponent's taunt by accepting demotion to amphibian status. "And after I had thought . . . / I said: 'I will, then, be a toad.' "

Like Whitman, Crane implies that the price of being human is often too high to pay. Throughout his work, "nonhuman perspectives . . . fascinate Crane," and frequently "animals offer direct and poignant critiques of human actions" (Dooley 35, 138). Crane's empathetic identification with brute beasts manifests itself with special force in one of his most frequently reprinted poems, "Fast rode the knight—." Repudiating violence undertaken for the sake of romantic ideals, the poem conveys the awful waste of warfare by portraying not the death of the knight but the death of his horse:

A horse
Blowing, staggering, bloody thing
Forgotten at foot of castle wall.
A horse
Dead at foot of castle wall. (89)

The two repeated elements, "horse" and "castle," emphasize the juxtaposition of two disparate realms: animal and human. In their striving for glory, wealth, and power, human beings exploit animals ruthlessly as means to strictly human ends. In death, the horse is seen as the "thing" to which, from the knight's point of view, it was already reduced.

In another Whitmanesque assault on culturally prescribed behavior, Crane's "Two or three angels" subjects a "fat church" to satiric comment. The supernatural visitors are bewildered by the "little black streams of people" who visit the church "continually": "and the angels were puzzled / To know why the people went thus, / And why they stayed so long within" (34). Here Crane attacks religious practices on two fronts. He criticizes first the institution that grows rich ("fat") off its congregation without providing genuine spiritual enlightenment or solace. He aims equally stinging barbs at the "streams of people" who continue to conform unquestioningly to empty religious usages, meekly complicitous in their own exploitation. Here, as elsewhere, his contempt for "the mob" makes itself evident (Wolford 3). The compliant behavior of the "black streams of people" saps the soul and thins the wallet. The presence of the observing angels indicates the possibility, moreover, of positive supernatural forces or meanings elsewhere in the cosmos. Crane's speaker, like the angels, is "puzzled" at the tendency of the masses to retreat from real encounters with the metaphysical and to take refuge instead in institutional authority, dogma, and ritual. Locating spirituality outside the walls of any humanly constructed church, he is only slightly more pessimistic than Whitman, who makes similar points in sections 41 and 43 of "Song of Myself," asserting that "my faith is the greatest of faiths and the least of faiths" (69).

Crane's "Two or three angels" also may be read for the sake of contrast alongside Whitman's well-known "When I Heard the Learn'd Astronomer." That eight-line poem records an A-to-B progression: initially part of the audience at a scholarly lecture on astronomy, the speaker proceeds outdoors to enter into personal communion with the stars. Literally speaking, he moves from indoors to outdoors, from noise to silence, from crowd to solitude. Less literally, he moves from rational knowledge to intuitive understanding, from passive comprehension to active engagement, from mathematical abstractions ("figures," "charts," "diagrams") to sensory impressions ("moist night air"). This is exactly the kind of progression the "streams of people" in Crane's poem are unable to conceive or undertake. Stuck forever "within," as the final position of that word in the poem emphasizes, they cannot enact the self-liberating action the angels envision. Only the superhuman observers are able to stand outside institutionally sponsored experience and make assessments or imagine alternatives. Whitman's poem is more optimistic than Crane's in that Whitman creates a confident persona who readily decamps when institutional auspices grow oppressive; and he does so in a framework that contains an individually crafted as well as a culturally molded response to nature and to its "mystical" sources.

Crane's debt to Dickinson is at least as large as that to Whitman. His introduction by William Dean Howells to Dickinson's poetry in 1883 appears to have exerted an inspiring influence on his art as Crane assembled his first collection of poetry (Joseph Katz xiii–xiv; Dooley 111). If Whitman's example released him from a host of prosodical strictures, Dickinson's unveiled the subtle possibilities of irony and concision. Since he ignored her innovations in oblique rhyme and compressed syntax (at least for his own purposes), his poetry does not sound like hers but resembles it strongly in its breathtaking economy. His spare, nugget-like poems are also suggestively Dickinsonian in the slenderness of contextual detail they offer. Like her, he leaves his poems deliberately untitled, thus forfeiting a significant opportunity to convey the who, what, when, and where of a poem. His work frequently proves disorienting in exactly the same fashion as hers: both writers leave readers searching fruitlessly for clues (biographical, sociopolitical, or other) to the situations framing poetic utterance. One need only remember how Dickinson evokes emotions such as pain, or grief, or renunciation, for instance, with exquisite precision but without revealing surrounding circumstances or causes. To illustrate the starkness of situation characteristic of Dickinson's work, instructors may choose often anthologized poems such as "After great pain a formal feeling comes" (*Poems*, poem 372), "Renunciation is a piercing virtue—" (poem 782), "I measure every grief I meet" (poem 550).

Crane's portrait of "a creature" eating its own heart in "In the desert" is similarly bare of explanatory context; readers are uncertain, even, whether or not to view the "naked" and "bestial" protagonist as an auctorial persona or as a version of Everyman:

In the desert
I saw a creature, naked, bestial,
Who, squatting upon the ground,
Held his heart in his hands,
And ate of it.
I said: "Is it good, friend?"
"It is bitter—bitter," he answered;
"But I like it
Because it is bitter,
And because it is my heart." (5)

The symbolic or psychological meaning of eating one's own heart resists immediate understanding, nor is the relation between environment ("desert") and human action obvious. Does the creature resort to emotionally cannibalistic behavior because the land is barren and provides no nourishment? Keith Gandal understands the poem in terms of Crane's personal emotional experience. In his reading, the "creature" feeds on itself because it is rejected by others: no other emotional sustenance is available. Thus the consuming of one's own heart is an act of both self-affirmation and self-hatred ("Stephen Crane's 'Mystic Places' " 117). Taking the heart as the locus of feeling, particularly of love or passion, readers may infer that emotional deprivation has led to a perverse and self-consuming wallowing in personal misery. The speaker refrains from comment, except to note the animalistic appearance of the central character. Although the grotesque details of the story summed up in these nine lines are clearly intended to shock, the speaker expresses no revulsion and offers neither judgment nor interpretation. Readers are left with a picture of self-conscious reveling in bitter, destructive self-love.

Both topic and method in this disturbing, enigmatic poem are reminiscent of Dickinson. The almost perversely exalted detailing of emotional agony or deprivation is an important recurring theme for her—for example, in "the hallowing of Pain" (poem 871) or the relishing of "An insufficient Loaf—" (poem 872). In a similar vein, she observes that the "Rehearsal to Ourselves / Of a Withdrawn Delight— / Affords a Bliss like Murder—," adding that "We will not drop the Dirk— / Because we love the wound" (poem 664). Such uncomfortable insights into human psychology deliver a distinct jolt. Reminding readers of often unacknowledged impulses, they forecast Crane's portrait of the excruciating satisfactions of self-cannibalizing emotion.

From Dickinson, Crane seems to have learned, above all else, to cultivate a carefully bland or casual speaking voice for the exploration of taboo topics and the expression of unconventional points of view. Carefully crafted ironic disparity between tone and content serves both poets well, especially in articulating metaphysical protests. In both "I shall know why when time is over" (poem 215) and "I reason, Earth is short—" (poem 403B), Dickinson ponders the inefficacy of Christian promises of justice in the hereafter. "Christ will explain each separate anguish / In the fair schoolroom of the sky—," she assures herself mockingly, hinting that Christian theodicy reduces human beings to a humiliatingly childlike state of docility (poem 215). The image of Christ as schoolmaster carries much of the satiric thrust of this poem, which questions how posthumous understanding of earthly suffering ("when . . . I have ceased to wonder why—") can offer any meaningful solace. The speaker's "anguish" is immediate, as the repeated final exclamation ("that scalds me now—that scalds me now!") vividly emphasizes, and so extreme that deferred explanations of its purpose appear pointless, even ridiculous.

"I reason, Earth is short—" pursues the same argument, reframing the schoolroom metaphor as a mathematics problem. A "new Equation," in which earthly pain is perfectly counterbalanced by supernatural compensation, will be provided later, "in 'Heaven,' " but Dickinson once again questions the adequacy of a posthumous New Deal supposedly awaiting the faithful:

> I reason, Earth is short—
> And Anguish—absolute—
> And many hurt,
> But, what of that?
>
> I reason, we could die—
> The best Vitality
> Cannot excel Decay,
> But, what of that?
>
> I reason, that in Heaven—
> Somehow, it will be even—
> Some new Equation, given—
> But—what of that?

She weighs the "absolute" experience of present misery, including the ineluctable frustration of mortality itself, against the hope of eternal compensation, judging this orthodox "Equation" to be utterly unsatisfying. Deftly she manipulates the rhetorical question that is the poem's refrain so that in its final recurrence its meaning is inverted. The first two iterations of the query appear to offer theological comfort in answer to human wretchedness: the implied answer to the speaker's question is that mortal "anguish" does not matter because of the promise of consolations after death. Unexpectedly, in stanza 3, the same words indicate that now it is the deferred, immaterial solace that does not matter: "what of that?" Thus the poem dismisses with laconic offhandedness the conventionally pious logic so frequently employed to keep the miserable many from protesting their lot.

One of Crane's better known poems ("If I should cast off this tattered coat") echoes Dickinson's contemptuous rhetorical question in compressed form:

> If I should cast off this tattered coat,
> And go free into the mighty sky;
> If I should find nothing there
> But a vast blue,
> Echoless, ignorant,—
> What then? (70)

He poses the same problem Dickinson raises in "I shall know why when time is over" and "I reason, Earth is short—" but moves further from explicit reference to Christian theology. Christianity becomes, by inference, one among many human attempts to impose morally meaningful designs on the cosmos. Crane imagines the profound bafflement of a dying human being when anticipated revelations and comforts fail to materialize in the beyond. If "the mighty sky" in fact contains no supernatural order or significance, if the theologically primed, dying spirit is to be confronted instead with "nothing," then doctrinal reassurances about an afterlife are no more than a setup for disappointment. Such disappointment is aggravated by the suspicion of deliberate deception.

Crane's poem is a six-line question directed at those who have encouraged the speaker to anticipate a posthumous *something*, thus infusing a "mighty" and "vast" universe with meanings "echo[ing]" (or corresponding to) human conceptions of justice, solace, and sublimity. The implications of the question "What then?" are perhaps still more bitter than those of Dickinson's "But, what of that?"—encompassing not only perplexed rage at having been misled but also a shocked reevaluation of assumptions that have shaped the speaker's life: What shall I do if my whole approach to living, including crucial ethical and intellectual choices, has been predicated on expectations now exposed as false? Like Dickinson,

Crane treats otherworldly-based interpretations of human experience with a sarcasm fueled by outrage.

Crane's scorn for conventional metaphysics is more sweeping than Dickinson's though hardly less disillusioned. Her criticisms tend to target institutionalized doctrine, exposing its logical, emotional, and moral flaws. Crane more often launches his attacks on human nature itself, whose frailties he sees as the wellspring of doctrine and institution alike. In "A god in wrath," for instance, he portrays the worship of a deity as unvarnished affiliation with the powerful against the helpless. An angry god is observed to be "beating a man" without apparent provocation, yet "the people" side unquestioningly with the aggressor, exclaiming, " 'Ah, what a wicked man!' / And— / 'Ah, what a redoubtable god!' " (21). Only cowardice or sycophancy can explain this reaction to a divinity who is nothing but a bully.

In "A man said to the universe," Crane singles out human complacency for sarcastic treatment, portraying with tongue-in-cheek wonderment the tendency to see the self as the center of all:

> A man said to the universe,
> "Sir, I exist!"
> "However," replied the universe,
> "The fact has not created in me
> A sense of obligation." (102)

As in "A god in wrath," the poet offers no direct comment; human beings damn themselves by their own words. Readers surely notice, too, that the enormous vanity displayed by the speaker provides the foundation for much of Christian theology. Only the idea that human beings stand at the center of the universe can account for the Book of Genesis, with its species-centric assertion that the earth and all its creatures were created expressly for the use of humankind.

In the parable-like poem "The wayfarer," Crane strips human beings of several layers of pretension in the context of a search for an abstractly defined "truth" that encompasses religious enlightenment while extending beyond it:

> The wayfarer
> Perceiving the pathway to truth
> Was struck with astonishment.
> It was thickly grown with weeds.
> "Ha," he said,

"I see that none has passed here
In a long time."
Later he saw that each weed
Was a singular knife.
"Well," he mumbled at last,
"Doubtless there are other roads." (94)

The complexity of this poem's judgment on human nature lies not in the allegorical association between piercing truth and sharp knives, which clearly is not new, but in Crane's recognition that falseness inevitably is embedded in a constellation of other flaws.

The wayfarer's initial observation that few before him have traveled down the "pathway to truth" is full of smugness. His exclamatory "Ha" simultaneously jeers at predecessors who have turned aside and sets a seal of self-approbation on his own intent. Only I am committed to truth, is the essence of his thought. Once he discovers the reason others have turned back (the truth hurts) he too comes to a halt, but without acknowledging that he is in fact abandoning his quest. His final, evasive comment, "Doubtless there are other roads," shows him dissembling even before himself. In readers' eyes, he stands condemned four times over: first, for his failure to pursue truth, no matter how painful; second, for his egotism in assuming that he alone is interested in truth; third, for his failure to acknowledge that he is in fact abandoning his quest; fourth, and most tellingly, for his failure to correct his earlier judgment of his predecessors and to admit that he is no better than they are. Simple on the surface, this poem lays bare human weakness unrelentingly, exhibiting a deluded self-love at the core of our common nature.

Less high-spirited than Whitman's, more bitter than Dickinson's, Crane's apostasy moves in the direction of existential and nihilist philosophies influencing much early-twentieth-century literature. The formal spareness of his poems fits undeniably well with their uncompromising philosophical bleakness. His largely negative assessment of human nature hints at the emergence of the antihero, while his heavy reliance on dialogue foretells the receding of auctorial presence in both prose and poetry of the coming century. His commitment to linguistic plainness, coupled with the almost fragment-like brevity of his poems, makes it possible to read his work as a preview of imagism in its formal economy, its simplicity and directness of expression, its repudiation of abstract generalization and philosophical comment, its commitment to organic and innovative form in place of established prosodical conventions, and its openness to new and unorthodox topics.

Crane shows interest, as well, in problems of phenomenology that were to prove central to the work of Wallace Stevens and many of Stevens's contemporaries. One of Crane's central preoccupations is, as Chester Wolford observes, "to penetrate memory, imagination, and related faculties which order the chaotic events occurring in the universe" (34). A number of Crane's poems explore the perplexities of changing perspectives or the difficulties of distinguishing between competing realities. In "A man saw a ball of gold in the sky," for example, he presents without resolution the dilemma of a man who perceives a distant sphere as "a ball of gold," only to discover that once he has "climbed for" and "achieved" the object, it reveals itself as clay. The poem depicts an unending cycle of disappointment, in which the rejected clay object transforms itself again to gold once the perceiving human being is again distanced from it; "this is the strange part," Crane's speaker confides (37). Like the protagonist in Stevens's "This Solitude of Cataracts," Crane yearns for a seemingly unattainable "permanent realization" (Stevens 366). In his investigation of Crane's "pluralistic philosophy," Patrick Dooley justly points out that, for Crane, "there is no Reality, only realities; no Truth, only truths" (xxi).

Crane combines his investigation of perception with theological rambunctiousness in "A god came to a man," where he retells the story of the Fall. After "a god" explains to "a man" that a "glorious apple" has been positioned within his grasp but forbidden to him, the man complains that the interdiction has wrought a profound change in his psyche: "Behold, thou hast moulded my desires / Even as thou hast moulded the apple" (132). Quite apart from the theological debate it initiates, the poem raises intriguing questions about human psychology: the workings of the complex intellectual and emotional structure experienced as the self. Consistently, Crane is interested more in "hidden levels of consciousness" than in "literal representations of social reality" (Bergon 143). Much like post-Freudian writers yet to come, he suggests the frustrating elusiveness of an identity that is "moulded" from without as well as from within. His insight that even the most powerful of desires can be generated outside the self, that these cannot be said to exist until externally defined, is very close to some of Stevens's observations. Preoccupied with the question of whether human beings know anything "without external reference," often persuaded that "final belief / Must be in a fiction," Stevens turns repeatedly to investigation of the relation between inner and outer realities (226; "Asides on the Oboe," lines 2–3). Like Crane's protesting Adam, whose desires are given shape through outside intervention, Stevens posits that nothing exists until it has been named: "Life consists / Of propositions about life" (310; "Men Made out of Words," lines 3–4). Thus Crane joins "with Whitman and Melville and a few others as precursors of Wallace Stevens's search for a supreme fiction" (Wolford 34).

Crane's most elaborately developed consideration of the "propositions" composing human reality may be found in "A youth in apparel that glittered," his cryptic story of a young man whose dreams of a fictive glory prove stronger than the instinct for self-preservation:

> A youth in apparel that glittered
> Went to walk in a grim forest.
> There he met an assassin
> Attired all in garb of old days;
> He, scowling through the thickets,
> And dagger poised quivering,
> Rushed upon the youth.
> "Sir," said this latter,
> "I am enchanted, believe me,
> To die, thus,
> In this medieval fashion,
> According to the best legends;
> Ah, what joy!"
> Then took he the wound, smiling,
> And died, content. (29)

From the opening lines, details inspired by fairy tales inject a note of humor, even mockery, into the poem. The youthful protagonist appears to be obsessed with romantic tales of quests, dangers, and martyrdom. Walking purposely into dangerous territory ("a grim forest"), wearing what appears to be armor-like garments ("apparel that glittered"), he is concerned only that the atmosphere correspond to that which he cherishes from "the best legends." Because the scenery, props, and costumes all speak to his fiction-fed imagination, he is "content," even "enchanted," with the prospect of his own murder. The hope of entering into a reality glorified by human fantasy overwhelms all other considerations; if the "fashion" of his death meets his expectations, nothing else matters.

Confronted with this pointless, well-costumed, all but rehearsed death, readers may hesitate between horror and derision. The irony directed against the mesmerized boy emerges indirectly, as his own extravagant language and exaggerated delight are juxtaposed against the harsh finality of his meaningless and violent death. Unlike the heroes of the tales his imagination has feasted on, this boy has completed no quest and defended no cause: all the elements that might invest his death with moral or social significance are missing. "Content" with props alone, he has confused surface with substance. The effect of the poem is to underline the almost unfathomable strength of the human imagination, here fostered by both literary and folk tradition. Insofar as imagination is shown in the poem to be the cause of a death without purpose, Crane may seem to be questioning its value. Just as a misplaced dedication to romantic notions of glory leads to the "bloody" death of the innocent horse in "Fast rode the knight—," the legend-based fantasy life of the youth overrides reason and common sense; it is antithetical, even, to survival.

Yet it is difficult to argue that the poem constitutes a wholly negative judgment of the human imagination, if only because the force attributed to it is so strong. Even though the shaping of this particular youth's inner reality has proved grotesquely fatal, the poem nonetheless offers a backhanded salute to the realm in which Crane himself, as a literary artist, is active. The ambivalence the poem deliberately elicits is, again, reminiscent of that inspired by Stevens's ever shifting, multifaceted representations of a miraculously seductive "interior paramour" (444), the fecund mind itself. Thus we see Crane persistently intrigued by issues that were to occupy literary artists for decades to come. Only eight years older than Stevens (a fact his early death tends to obscure), Crane stands poised on the cusp between centuries, an idiosyncratic presence bridging the distance between two distinctive generations of voices in American poetry.

Part III

Strategies for Teaching

Eliza Richards

Poe, Women Poets, and Print Circulation

Locating Edgar Allan Poe's poetry in a cultural field can pose difficulties, not least because so many of his poems dislocate themselves from knowable surroundings: their focus is not this world but other worlds. His speakers report on their wanderings in "Dream-Land," that "wild weird clime that lieth, sublime, / Out of SPACE—out of TIME" (*Poetry* 79). They struggle to describe the horrors of the deathly "City in the Sea" (67) or the "ghoul-haunted woodland of Weir" (89 ["Ulalume"]). Even when they do not travel in other worlds, his speakers insist on their aberrant, isolated status; they "have not been / As others were" (60 ["Alone"]) and have "dwelt alone / In a world of moan" (80 ["Eulalie"]). Their mental horizons are often defined by the melancholic longing for a lost, loved woman. Unearthly even while alive and perfected in her death, her memory haunts the male lover and cuts him off from his surroundings.

Just as their names borrow syllables from one another—Lenore, Irene, Helen, Annabel Lee, Eulalie, Ulalume—Poe's female figures blend into a single emblem of supernal beauty. The poems reiterate a romantic model of desire predicated on absence, famously codified in "The Philosophy of Composition": "the death, then, of a beautiful woman is, unquestionably, the most poetical topic in the world—and equally is it beyond doubt that the lips best suited for such a topic are those of a bereaved lover" (*Essays* 19). Poe's work renders analogies between a man's loss of his beloved and the poet's doomed attempts to reproduce in language the melodic realm of celestial beauty:

> The struggle to apprehend the supernal Loveliness—this struggle, on the part of souls fittingly constituted—has given to the world all *that* which it (the world) has ever been enabled at once to understand and *to feel* as poetic. (77 ["Poetic Principle"])

The paired portrayals of mental distress—melancholic responses to a lost love and to an inaccessible form of utterance—link Poe to his lyric speaker and underwrite biographical and psychological interpretations of his work.

Poe encourages readers to understand his poems as singular expressions of a damaged man, and readers have consistently attributed to the author the *"Mournful and Never-ending Remembrance"* of his poetic figures (25 ["Philosophy of Composition"]). Stressing Poe's early and repeated loss of loved women—mother, foster mother, and wife, among others—anthology introductions frequently encourage this identification. Teachers, then, must work against cues in the poems, resilient psychological trends in Poe criticism, and the initial responses of students familiar with popular Poe mythology (his supposed drug addictions, sexual perversions, and mental derangement) if they wish to set his poems in a historical frame.

Their energies will be rewarded by the pedagogical opportunities that historicist modes of interpretation provide. Psychological approaches minimize, for example, how Poe's figures of isolated suffering circulated in ephemeral publications as a form of cultural currency; such approaches therefore limit an understanding of how his work informed and responded to nineteenth-century American print culture. A historical lens can place Poe's speakers in the spectrum of the period's conventional lyric figures: the tortured genius, the domestic mourner, the spiritual seeker, the chivalric lover, and so on. The seemingly signature formal properties of Poe's poetry, moreover, bear an intimate relation to prosodic conventions of the period, which he exaggerates in order to tag them as his own. Poe's renditions of sonnets, odes, and ballads firmly, if somewhat oddly, relate him to his peers. His imitation of the practices of his British contemporaries or near contemporaries—Lord Byron, Samuel Taylor Coleridge, Elizabeth Barrett Browning, and Alfred, Lord Tennyson, to name a few—also place his work in the mainstream of the period's transatlantic poetic exchanges. Attributing conventional forms of expression to a single practitioner limits students' opportunities to explore cultural and transcultural workings of genre. Finally, reading Poe's poems as extensions of a troubled male consciousness screens out the creative contributions of many writers, women poets in particular, who influenced and were influenced by Poe and whose work circulated through the same print networks. Many of these writers engaged in public lyric dialogues, critiquing, appropriating, mimicking, extending, and complimenting one another's work. Reading Poe in relation to his female contemporaries can help us understand the interactive, transsubjective modes of expression favored in the periodical publications that were a primary venue for poetry in his time.

Devoting a substantial number of reviews to celebrated women poets of his time, Poe broadcast his interest in their work—and in their popularity, which eluded him. In a review of Rufus Griswold's *Female Poets of America*, he categorizes and recategorizes these women.

> In point of actual merit—that is to say of actual accomplishment, without reference to mere indications of the ability to accomplish—we would rank the first dozen or so in this order—(leaving out Mrs. Brooks for the present.) Mrs. Osgood—very decidedly first—then Mrs. Welby, Miss Carey (or the Misses Carey,) Miss Talley, Mrs. Whitman, Miss Lynch, Miss Frances Fuller, Miss Lucy Hooper, Mrs. Oakes Smith, Mrs. Ellet, Mrs. Hewitt, Miss Clarke, Mrs. Lewis, Mrs. Nichols, Mrs. Warfield, (with her sister, Mrs. Lee,) Mrs. Eames and Mrs. Sigourney. If Miss Lynch had as much imagination as energy of expression and artistic power, we could place her next to Mrs. Osgood. The next *skilful merely*, of those just mentioned, are Mrs. Osgood, Miss Lynch, and Mrs. Sigourney. The most imaginative are Miss Carey, Mrs. Osgood, Miss Talley and Miss Fuller. The most accomplished are Mrs. Ellet, Mrs. Eames, Mrs. Lewis, Mrs. Whitman, and Mrs. Oakes Smith. The most popular are Mrs. Osgood, Mrs. Oakes Smith and Miss Hooper. ("Mr. Griswold")

This rather absurd shuffling exercise shows not only that the names of women poets carried evocative powers that are lost on today's readers but also that Poe wished to position himself as a judge and connoisseur of women's poetry. At the same time, his lists level difference and turn the women into a generic crowd, one that nevertheless encroaches on the reviewer's sovereignty, so that he must contain them in his discerning categories. In both his reviews and in his poetry, Poe entered into active competition and collaboration with women writers.

I'd like to suggest ways to read Poe's poetry and reviews alongside the poetry of his female contemporaries as a means of understanding nineteenth-century print economies of lyric poetry and the intellectual transactions that they enabled. This goal might initially appear to be poorly suited for the classroom, requiring an unwieldy amount of preparation and contextual materials. I've found, however, that the simple act of juxtaposing interrelated works by Poe and women poets provokes discussion of modes of lyric exchange. Such an approach both expands our understanding of Poe's work and offers fruitful ways to read nineteenth-century women's poetry, which has proved resistant to psychological modes of interpretation. Although the primary materials that support such an approach have long been difficult to access, they are increasingly available on the Web.

The following sections of this essay set Poe's work in relation to that of Elizabeth Barrett (she was not yet married to Robert Browning), Frances Sargent Osgood, and Phoebe Cary. Even when cited in book form, all Poe materials cited below, including reviews, are available on the Edgar Allan Poe Society of Baltimore Web site (Poe, *Works*).

Elizabeth Barrett and Secondariness

In undergraduate classes, before situating Poe in relation to his peers, I first present his poems as they appear in anthologies—in isolation on the page, with a biographical preface—and elicit interpretations derived from close textual analysis. In this scenario, interpretations inevitably lean toward the psychological. Students read the poems as reflections of the poet's life as depicted in the preface, or they evaluate the lyric speaker's troubled state of mind. In "The Raven," we conclude that Poe or his speaker has been shattered by the loss of his Lenore, that he fetishizes her name as a substitute for the living woman, that he is unable to detach himself from his love object, that he sustains his melancholy by interrogating the raven, and that he stages his grief in a hysterical bid for the reader's sympathy. The insistent trochaic octameter and saturation of perfect rhymes, alliteration, and assonance, we decide, numb the speaker's and readers' sensitivity to language's meaning. This distancing strategy keeps the speaker from feeling the pain of loss, but it also transmits that state of shock to the reader.

On the next day we return to "The Raven," this time considering the poem in the context of contemporary print circulation. I introduce materials that set the poem in conversation with the work of Poe's peers. The class then generates an entirely different reading of the poem, learning in the process about the ways that classroom frames influence interpretation.

Resurrecting a beloved woman may be impossible, but attempting the impossible attracts readers who sympathize with the male lover's plight. Poe himself acknowledges and promotes this idea in "The Philosophy of Composition," when he insists that he embraced his theme in "The Raven" in order to generate a "*universally* appreciable" "effect" (*Essays* 16). He succeeded, to judge by the wave of reprintings following the poem's publication, the outpouring of enthusiasm for the "wild and *shivery*" poem, and the number of poetic replies—parodies, valentines, commercial jingles, mimic renditions of all sorts—generated by readers, not least among them the women poets who published in the same venues as Poe (qtd. in Silverman 237). Their enthusiasm owes less, perhaps, to Poe's savvy calculations than to the affinities his poems shared with theirs, affinities that he highlighted.

Poe drew attention to one instance of his indebtedness in his review of Barrett's *"The Drama of Exile" and Other Poems*, which appeared in the *Broadway Journal* on 11 January 1845, shortly before the first publication of "The Raven." "Lady Geraldine's Courtship" received special notice:

> With the exception of Tennyson's "Locksley Hall," we have never perused a poem combining so much of the fiercest passion with so much of the most ethereal fancy, as the "Lady Geraldine's Courtship" of Miss Barrett. We are forced to admit, however, that the latter work is a very palpable imitation of the former.

Even as Poe accuses Barrett of imitation, he prepares readers to understand his poem as an imitation of hers, quoting lines that draw attention to his future debt. Those lines are spoken by Bertram, the lowly poet who fears that Lady Geraldine is a vision rather than the living woman he loves:

> Eyes, he said, now throbbing through me! Are ye eyes that did
> undo me?
> *Shining eyes like antique jewels set in Parian statue-stone*!
> Underneath that calm white forehead are ye ever burning torrid
> O'er the desolate sand desert of my heart and life undone?
>
> (*American Poetry, 1600–1900*;
> path: *Poems* [1844] 214, lines 9–12)

Of the line he italicized, Poe says:

> From the entire range of poetical literature there shall not, in a century, be produced a more sonorous, a more vigorous verse—a juster—a nobler—a more ideal—a more magnificent image—than this very image, in this very verse, which the most noted magazine of Europe has so especially and so contemptuously condemned.

Just over two weeks later, "The Raven" first appeared in the *Evening Mirror*, carrying substantial echoes of Barrett's poem, particularly that sonorous line Poe admired:

> This I sat engaged in guessing, but no syllable expressing
> To the fowl whose fiery eyes now burned into my bosom's core;
> This and more I sat divining, with my head at ease reclining
> On the cushion's velvet lining that the lamp-light gloated o'er,
> But whose velvet-violet lining with the lamp-light gloating o'er,
> *She* shall press, ah, nevermore! (*Poetry* 84; lines 73–78)

"The Raven" dramatizes Poe's displacement of the charismatic presence of female contemporaries like Barrett in order to make room for the male poet. The trochaic octameter alone identifies Poe's debt, but his sly rearrangement of symbols suggests a commentary on gendered traditions of poetic production. Whereas in Barrett's poem Lady Geraldine commands Bertram's attention, in Poe's poem the lady is dead, the male poet holds center stage, and the raven now possesses Lady Geraldine's riveting eyes. Poe's speaker feels the raven's probing gaze as an accusation, as if the bird were asking where the lady went. In the raven's mouth, Lady Geraldine's speech is reduced to a single borrowed word. The speaker's expressions of grief fill the place where Barrett's living lady once commanded Bertram's attention.

While Poe may stress the importance of "novelty" in "The Philosophy of Composition," "The Raven" foregrounds and thematizes practices of borrowing, repetition, inspiration (or the lack of it), and poetic transmission. Both Poe's and Barrett's poems are indebted not only to Tennyson's "Locksley Hall," which shares the unusual metrical form, but also to Coleridge's "Christabel" (*Bartleby.com*), whose Lady Geraldine is spectral, demonic, corrupt, and corrupting; the poem suggests that she has been violated and violates the innocent Christabel in turn. Barrett recuperates Lady Geraldine from Coleridge's treatment by purifying her dark powers. Poe, in turn, reallocates her ability to arrest attention by evacuating her from the poem and shifting the spotlight to the male lover's professions of sorrow. These engagements suggest that secondariness in both gendered and nationalist traditions interest Poe: just as women writers like Barrett had to justify their entry into masculine literary traditions, so Anglo-American writers like Poe struggled to define their relation to established British literary traditions. Recognizing their common dilemma, Poe both allies himself with and distinguishes himself from his female peers.

Presenting "The Raven" in this poetic hall of mirrors provides opportunities to explore the transatlantic traffic in gender and genre that puts Poe's poem in a complex network of interliterary imaginings. Setting "The Raven" in relation to "Lady Geraldine's Courtship" generates questions—unavailable when Poe's work is considered in isolation—about the difference gender and nationality make for poetic production and reception.

Frances Sargent Osgood and Fancy

Poe may raise to the level of a "poetic principle" the claim that the death of a beautiful woman is the most poetical topic in the world, but a glance beyond his oeuvre shows that poetical women of the period, and the female muses they patterned themselves after, were as closely associated with animation as they were with marmoreal stillness. The mobile figure of Fancy showers linguistic gifts on the poet in Thomas Gray's "Progress of Poesy": "Bright-eyed Fancy, hov'ring o'er, / Scatters from her picture'd urn / Thoughts that breathe and words that burn" (lines 108–10). In "Fancy," John Keats insists that the poet must "let winged fancy wander / Through the thought still spread beyond her" (lines 5–6). Other female muses of the male imagination share Fancy's ethereal, spritelike mobility. William Wordsworth's "phantom of delight" is "a dancing shape, an image gay, / To haunt, to startle, and waylay" ("Perfect Woman," lines 9–10). Percy Shelley's female aspect in "Epipsychidion" is "made / By Love, of light and motion" (376; lines 93–94).

Drawing from this male-centered tradition of poetic inspiration, many of the American women poets who rose to prominence in the first half of the nineteenth century on the wave of the popular press appropriated Fancy for their own professional and expressive purposes. Cutting out the middle man, Fancy spoke directly to the people, with a disembodied female "voice" unmediated by the male pen. Hannah Gould, whose book of poems Poe reviewed favorably in the *Southern Literary Messenger* in 1836, embraces this identification in "To Mrs. L—." Speaking of her poems as flowers and contrasting them with the intimidating works of the "darling sons of song," Gould writes:

> . . . all I bring are wild and pale,
> And humble natives of the vale,
> Which I have plucked, where oft I stray,
> On fancy's wild and devious way,
> In playful, or in pensive mood,
> As chanced to pass my solitude.
> (*American Poetry, 1600–1900*;
> path: *Poems* [1839] 172, lines 37–42)

Straying on fancy's "wild and devious way," Gould's speaker becomes the sprite-like muse. This identification gives her license to gather and distribute her flower-poems, even as it marks them as lighthearted and ephemeral, in contradistinction to the darling sons' more enduring songs. Personifications of Fancy, "poetesses" in Gould's tradition were boisterous and whimsical, with strong passions and a short attention span; they professed unconsciousness of their expressive capacities; they cast poetry as a form of saying and doing, of singing and dancing, rather than as an arrangement of written words on a page. In this way, women poets dramatized their newly minted claim to poetic expression while appealing to the men they were competing against. Instead of casting themselves as full-fledged poets, they posed as muses on the loose, tempting male poets and readers of genteel magazines and newspapers to harness their inventive powers.

Because motionless, speechless women so frequently figure in Poe's poems as stimulants to the grieving male lover's reverie (e.g., in "Lenore," "Ulalume," "The Sleeper," "The Raven," and "Annabel Lee"), it is perhaps surprising that in his reviews Poe associates women poets with the embodied, expressive mobility of the dancer, the singer, the actress, and Fancy. Poe and Osgood, who published in the same periodicals and were personally acquainted, negotiate the poetics of female mobility. I consider Osgood's female flights of fancy alongside Poe's attempts to define and contain active female forms. Juxtaposing his poetics of female immobility with her poetics of female mobility suggests that figurations of femininity in the period were not static or monolithic but multiple and multifaceted, deployed strategically in a competitive literary market.

For Poe, as for a large, admiring readership, Osgood incarnated Fancy. In a *Marginalia* entry for April 1849, he proclaims that "Mrs. O. has lately evinced a *true* imagination, with a '*movement*' (as Schlegel has it) or energy, of which I have been considering her *incapable*" (*Essays* 1441). Her "careless abandonment of manner" is "an indication of the vigour, the wealth—in a word—of the genius of the poet." His word for her moving poetic form is "grace": Mrs. Osgood is "unrivalled" in this aspect "as evinced, for instance, in a wave, in a curl, in the petal of a flower, in the motion of a child or of a dancer" (Rev. of *A Wreath*). Abandonment and grace signify a soulful, gestural movement that brings language to life. He makes no distinction between Mrs. O.'s verbal representation and the physical thing, as if she directly transmitted the moving object to the reader's eye.

Underscoring his embodied reading of Osgood's poems, Poe admiringly quotes a poem about a dancer in a review of her work. Osgood's "Letter to an Absent Friend," Poe tells us as he cites it in his review, is a tribute to Fanny Ellsler, an internationally renowned Viennese dancer who appeared in ballets at the New York Park Theater during her United States tour. The woman poet whom Poe admires for her movement—her grace and abandonment—represents those traits in a dancing female form:

She comes! The spirit of the dance!
And but for those large eloquent eyes,
Where passion speaks in every glance,
She'd seem a wanderer from the skies.

So light, that, gazing breathless there,
Lest the celestial dream should go,
You'd think the music in the air
Waved the fair vision to and fro.

Or that the melody's sweet flow
Within the radiant creature played
And those soft wreathing arms of snow
And white sylph feet the music made.

Now gliding slow with dreamy grace,
Her eyes beneath their lashes lost,
Now motionless with lifted face,
And small hands on her bosom crossed.

> And now, with flashing eyes, she springs,
> Her whole bright figure raised in air,
> As if her soul had spread its wings
> And poised her one wild instant there.
>
> She spoke not; but so richly fraught
> With language are her glance and smile,
> That when the curtain fell, I thought
> She had been talking all the while.
> (Rev. of *A Wreath*)

For Poe,

> this is, indeed, poetry, and of the most unquestionable kind—poetry *truthful* in the proper sense—that is to say, breathing of nature. There is nothing forced or artificial, no hardly-sustained enthusiasm. The poetess speaks *because* she feels and *what* she feels—but what she feels is felt only by the truly poetical.

Just as the speaker cannot discern where the music leaves off and the dancer begins, Poe elides distinctions between speaking and writing, dancing and poetry, and Osgood and Ellsler. Because they share a single "poetical" "spirit," the dancer becomes a lyric figure of Osgood's vivacious imagination. More than an analogue, then, the poem is portrayed as a metonymic extension of Osgood's feelings; because her feelings are true, they are unified with the dancer's motion. In Poe's review, Osgood becomes the dancer in her poem, expressed by it as well as expressing it. Women for Poe are capable of the natural production of art. Poetic themselves, they cannot help but produce poetic offspring that "breathe" and "speak," that render words transparent and spring from the page as living, dancing forms.

Osgood anticipates her readers' expectations that women write as if they were poems and that they produce poems that behave like women. The title "Letter to an Absent Friend" codes the poem as a tribute from poet to dancer, two women renowned for their "grace" and "mobility"; it suggests that the readers are viewing an exchange between friends who share both spirit and name—a name closely resembling "Fancy," their sister muse. By associating sister arts and artists, Osgood encourages readers to contemplate the difference between women's bodies and their verbal representations. Fanny Ellsler dances, Frances Osgood represents the dance in words that seem to disappear in a visual representation: one speaks with her body, one evokes a female body through verbal sleight of hand. Osgood may portray a woman with flashing eyes who springs and glides, but in fact there are only words on the page. Osgood has indeed "been talking all the while" while denying it; or rather she has been writing in a way that readers understand as talking. She is an "absent friend" that readers cannot grasp; she harnesses the desire for the muse sustained in masculine poetic traditions in order to cultivate a fascinating, elusive author figure. Her poem offers a sophisticated commentary on artistic representation and reception that also proleptically critiques Poe's review. She challenges expectations for female authorship in a poem that Poe seeks to contain in his review's frame. Reading poem and review together reveals a struggle over definitions of female authorship in a shared system of poetic norms.

In a pair of poems that share the same title, Poe and Osgood extend their discussion of female mobility and containment, addressing the structural inequalities enforced by nineteenth-century coverture laws, which make women men's property in marriage. Poe's "Eulalie: A Song" takes the emotional implications of this inequality to its logical extreme. The male speaker begins innocently enough, professing his love in the terms of romantic convention, but his effusive praise turns sinister by the third stanza:

> Now Doubt—now Pain
> Come never again,
> For her soul gives me sigh for sigh
> And all day long
> Shines, bright and strong
> Astarté within the sky,
> While ever to her dear Eulalie upturns her matron eye—
> While ever to her young Eulalie upturns her violet eye.
> (*Poetry* 81; lines 14–21)

Praising his love in terms of its deadening effect, the speaker characterizes his bliss as an escape from doubt and pain. His ecstasy derives from Eulalie's reduction to a spectral echo of himself: she gives him "sigh for sigh." His requirement of total fidelity exacts the toll of physical passion. A "blushing bride" in the first stanza, "radiant" in the second, by the end of the poem Eulalie's ever-upturned "matron eye" suggests that achieving complete devotion requires purging herself of desire.

Instead of praying to God, as her posture conventionally suggests, Eulalie is gazing into the star eye of Astarté, an ancient Middle Eastern goddess of war and sexual passion. Eulalie's steady gaze both night and day—when the star may or may not be visible—suggests that sexual repression has frozen her body and driven her mad. Her deadening is underscored by the way she averts her face from the speaker's: strangely, the lovers do not gaze into each other's eyes. Though her fixed gaze may signify many things, none bode well for the relationship: perhaps she spurns the speaker, but his narcissism prevents him from noticing; perhaps she has died of deprivation and lies on her back, staring blindly at the sky, eyes unclosed in death. Poe foregrounds the absurdity of the male speaker's insatiable desire for adoration. His monomaniacal love is satiated only by his female companion's obliteration.

Osgood's "Eulalie" converses with Poe's. In addition to the title, the poems share seven-beat lines in accentual meter, the alternation of long and short lines, and the deployment of repetition and refrain; both poems are associated with traditions of song. They also both stage a dialogue between an eloquent male speaker and a silent female lover, but in markedly different ways. Instead of expressing joy in having fully arrested Eulalie, Osgood's male speaker celebrates her signature, chronic mobility:

> If my soul, on calling, 'not at home,' is told, Eulalie,
>   I would make free
> To wait till yours came back, tired and cold, Eulalie!
> And then it will be glad its wings to fold, Eulalie,
>   And I should see
> How long I might the glorious truant hold, Eulalie!
>
> They say that more domestic and more tame, Eulalie,
>   It ought to be!
> But if heaven gave it wings, were you to blame, Eulalie?
> Ah, no! to tie a Peri were a shame, Eulalie!
>   And they might see
> It always carried joy where'er it came, Eulalie.
>
> (*American Poetry, 1600–1900*;
> path: *Poems* [1850] 452–53, lines 19–30)

Not anti- but counterdomestic, the male speaker reverses gender roles with Eulalie, insisting that he will wait until she tires of wandering and returns "home" to him. Eulalie's wings of fancy sanction her mobility; it would be perverse not to let a fairy fly. If she decides to "fold" her wings, the speaker does not presume to think that she will stay with him forever; he must try to "hold" the "glorious truant" with her consent and release her at her will. Though this speaker, like Poe's, celebrates a union of souls, here "soul" comes to stand for "body," politely signifying sexual attraction.

While Poe underscores the deadening effect of the marriage bond, Osgood proposes a more positive alternative. Instead of marrying and becoming her husband's property, Eulalie remains a free agent whose mobility inspires the male speaker's admiration and attraction. Poe, in other words, stages the caged-wife poem, while Osgood portrays a male lover who repudiates the social expectation that Eulalie should be "more domestic and more tame." Considered together, the poems caution against assuming that the author's gender determines the gender politics of the author's poetry.

Other Osgood poems that work well in conjunction with Poe's "Eulalie" in a teaching cluster on fancy and female mobility are "Flight of Fancy," "The Fan," "Caprice," "To My Pen" (all available at *American Poetry, 1600–1900*), and Poe's essay, "Fancy and Imagination." A cluster on the wife could include sources as diverse as the entry "Coverture" (on the *Encyclopedia of Women's History* Web site), Dickinson's poems "I'm 'wife'—I've finished that" (poem 225) and "She rose to his requirement—dropt" (poem 857), Osgood's "Oh Hasten to My Side" and "Happy at Home," and Lydia Huntley Sigourney's "The Bride" (all at *American Poetry, 1600–1900*).

Phoebe Cary and Parody

I have been suggesting that restaging the poetic conversations enabled by antebellum print circulation illuminates relations between psychological and cultural interpretations. In the context of his engagements with Barrett, Poe's "The Raven" not only portrays a man deranged by extreme sorrow but also revises and appropriates a powerful female contemporary's work. When set against Osgood's rendition, his "Eulalie" showcases the crippling emotional effects of marriage inequality but also stills Osgood's mobile forms of Fancy.

In yet another scenario, Phoebe Cary's parody of Poe's "Annabel Lee" turns a man's deranged mourning into a sociological study of New York City lust, challenging the gendered terms of romantic desire that underpin the exchanges among Poe, Osgood, and Barrett. "Samuel Brown" offers a hilariously instructive treatment of the gendered conventions informing

Poe's poem by inverting its tenets. Cary transplants his love affair from a remote fairy kingdom to the gritty, class-based geography of New York City and lets the female speaker tell the story of her separation from her male partner. Whereas Poe's lovers were children, possessed of a pure and ethereal passion for one another ("*I* was a child and *she* was a child, / In this kingdom by the sea; / But we loved with a love that was more than love— / I and my Annabel Lee"), Cary's lovers are adults driven by a lust undeterred by Samuel Brown's marriage to an uptown girl:

It was many and many a year ago,
In a dwelling down in town,
That a fellow there lived whom you may know,
By the name of Samuel Brown;
And this fellow lived with no other thought
Than to our house to come down.

I was a child, and he was a child,
In that dwelling down in town,
But we loved with a love that was more than love,
I and my Samuel Brown,
With a love that the ladies coveted
Me and Samuel Brown.

And this was the reason that, long ago,
To that dwelling down in town,
A girl came out of her carriage, courting
My beautiful Samuel Brown;—
So that her high-bred kinsman came
And bore away Samuel Brown,
And shut him up in a dwelling-house,
In a street quite up in town.

The ladies not half so happy up there,
Went envying me and Brown;
Yes! that was the reason, (as all men know,
In this dwelling down in town),
That the girl came out of the carriage by night,
Coquetting and getting my Samuel Brown.

But our love is more artful by far than the love
Of those who are older than we,—

Of many far wiser than we,
And neither the girls that are living above,
Nor the girls that are down in town,
Can ever dissever my soul from the soul
Of the beautiful Samuel Brown.

For the morn never shines without bringing me lines
From my beautiful Samuel Brown;
And the night's never dark, but I sit in the park
With my beautiful Samuel Brown.
And often by day, I walk down in Broadway,
With my darling, my darling, my life and my stay
To our dwelling down in town,
To our house in the street down town.

(*Literature Online;* path: *The Poems of Alice and Phoebe Cary* [1903] 458–59)

Cary's verbal play both demonstrates an appreciation of Poe's sonic effects and offers a savvy commentary on the ways that his mastery dematerializes love by aestheticizing the female form and moving the woman into the realm of male fantasy. Poe's recurrent rhyming of "me," "Lee," and "sea" enacts the speaker's obsessive fixation on his lost love; the persistent assonance of long *o*'s and *e*'s mimics mournful cries. By closing off the vowel sounds at the line endings, Cary's "Brown," "down," and "town" substitute urban pragmatism for romantic elegy. In doing so, she juxtaposes Poe's disembodied male melancholia, predicated on the death of a beautiful woman, with mutual lust between a living man and woman.

Poe's "Annabel Lee" is itself almost a parody of the ways that romantic ideals of love operate in the service of killing women into art. His speaker's story begins like a fairy tale ("It was many and many a year ago / In this kingdom by the sea") and unravels until the reader must notice that the speaker has become unhinged:

The angels, not half so happy in Heaven,
Went envying her and me—
Yes!—that was the reason (as all men know,
In this kingdom by the sea)
That the wind came out of the cloud by night,
Chilling and killing my Annabel Lee.

The speaker's assertion that envious angels murdered Annabel Lee signals that he is paranoid. Because readers cannot trust his account, they cannot know how Annabel Lee died. The speaker wallows in sorrow instead of explaining. When he finally reveals that he still "lie[s] down by the side" of his "beautiful Annabel Lee," we see that he is not only haunted by her spirit but also delighted to possess her corpse. Perhaps only through death has Annabel Lee become "my darling, my darling, my life and my bride," a fetish object evacuated of female subjectivity.

By portraying a love affair between two consenting adults, Cary casts Poe's speaker as incapable of imagining or tolerating female agency; she foregrounds his implication that he prefers Annabel Lee dead. Poe's women die inexplicably; the male lovers mourn but distance themselves from responsibility for deaths they seem to desire. Turning Poe's "chilling and killing my Annabel Lee" into "coquetting and getting my Samuel Brown," Cary substitutes direct, aggressive female desire for the violence that Poe's male speaker displaces onto the envious "angels in heaven." Contrasting the unilateral structure of elegy with the reciprocal structure of a love affair, Cary foregrounds the narcissism of Poe's speaker, who loves Annabel Lee because "she lived with no other thought / Than to love and be loved by me." Cary's speaker, in contrast, actively "loves" Samuel Brown, regularly meeting him "down in town"; she freely expresses her sexual desire and easily entertains herself with writing poems while Samuel is with the woman who pays his bills. The lovers part midway through the poem not because one dies but because one marries; the strength of their love or lust is proved by their ingenuity in sustaining contact despite Samuel's marriage. The reversal of gender roles—Samuel is like a kept woman while the female speaker resembles an adulterous male lover—draws attention to the socially constructed nature of gender and the space for gender experimentation provided by lyric poetry: it is easier, Cary suggests, for a woman to act like a man in a poem.

I have offered three juxtapositions that demonstrate how ideas about gender and poetic production took shape in public lyric transactions in the antebellum period. I have briefly performed the types of readings the selected materials generate in classroom discussion, with the help of directed questions and framing lectures that set the works in the context of print circulation. Such juxtapositions allow students to challenge received ideas about gender, poetic production and reception, authorship, and attribution. They generate such questions as, Why is Poe understood as an important author while the women poets have been forgotten? What is the difference between the author's and the lyric speaker's gender? How did antebellum print circulation both enable and disable gendered forms of expression? How do cultural conditions inform psychological states? Exploring these questions depends on understanding poetry as an active mode of communication that has aesthetic, personal, and political stakes and consequences for writers and readers alike, then and now.

Katharine Rodier

Poetry and the American Renaissance: Another Reconsideration

As a reader and writer of poetry myself, as well as a contextual critic of nineteenth-century American literature, particularly of women's writing, I include a range of poetry when I teach American Literature, 1830–1865, my version of an upper-level course titled The American Renaissance at many universities. At this point in twenty-first-century literary studies, F. O. Matthiessen's original conception of the American Renaissance has been reconsidered, revisited, looked beneath and beyond, reenvisioned, othered, and otherwise reinterpreted to encompass more than five writers and their work over a span of five antebellum years. In fact, even those students who can appreciate Matthiessen's ideological focus may be surprised that his canon nonetheless excludes a writer whose work most of them already know, like Edgar Allan Poe, or another writer whom they believe they know something of, at least in a murky tabloid-style sense, like Emily Dickinson: that weird lady who wore a white dress and stayed in her room writing about death? Primarily, as this essay elaborates, I organize this course to develop my students' critical reading, thinking, and writing skills through the challenge of responding to a diverse cultural and literary legacy that many may not already recognize or affirm and that some may in fact hesitate to engage.

Quite a few students are surprised to find that a historically based course on the so-called American Renaissance includes so much poetry, and not only "great" poetry by two superluminaries like Dickinson and Walt Whitman. In particular, those students already acquainted with Dickinson's and Whitman's protopostmodern proclivities may question how those poets could have had any contemporaries worth reading now: wouldn't such writers already be familiar to us if, as Susan K. Harris asks, they were "any *good*"? (263). Others may claim that high school "ruined" all poetry for them, perhaps because of a teacher's solipsistic insistence on singular yet unconvincing readings of inexplicably significant texts. I am of course overlooking students' curious yet abiding admissions of affection for Poe's "The Raven," fostered in part perhaps by *The Simpsons*' television revival of the same, originally broadcast in 1990. Notably in that episode, as Lisa prepares to read the poem aloud to Bart from what he suspects might be a schoolbook, she reassures him, "Don't worry. You won't learn anything" (Kogen and Wolodarsky).

As Lisa's barb suggests, for any number of respondents these days poetry, if it belongs anywhere, belongs in school, if not in schoolbooks best left closed. Moreover, contemporary students who do not themselves read poetry unless they must—mainly to fulfill class assignments—may not readily apprehend the significance that the genre held in the nineteenth-century United States as a vehicle of philosophical, political, moral, or spiritual thought. It was also a form of entertainment: a pleasure to read, if the interpreter was literate, but equally a pleasure to hear or to recite. "Really?" I've been asked. "You're kidding," I've been told. But I've been surprised by other students who after reading a broad selection of nineteenth-century American verse take to heart the most sentimental or didactic of poems. Furthermore, those readers who will not call a poem a poem unless it rhymes, usually predictably, are often captivated by a nineteenth-century poem's rhythmic patterning, its formulaic descriptions, and the easy morals that I in my sometime capacity as a creative writing teacher have spent semesters trying to exorcise from college students' beginning work. While such students may not and may never see a poem as I do, I count myself fortunate to find out from and with them the sometimes unanticipated ways that earlier American poetry may still speak to its readers.

American Literature, 1830–1865, a course at Marshall University in Huntington, West Virginia, enrolls mostly undergraduates—both English majors and nonmajors—as well as up to five master's students, sometimes more with overenrollment. Total enrollment usually runs between twenty-five and thirty students, readily enabling a discussion-based approach. My section of the course qualifies as writing-intensive because informal and formal writing assignments, the formal in a proposal-draft-revision format, compose more than half a student's assigned workload. As gender-based inquiry grounds a significant part of the course activities, the class also counts toward the women's studies minor, and by virtue of its reading content, it fulfills the university's multicultural requirement.

A state university, Marshall serves many first-generation and many part-time students, not all of whom would identify themselves as readers let alone as scholars or academics in any traditional sense. As I plan the course to anticipate such varied levels of student preparation, I select poems to represent major thematic or critical issues that may or may not surface in prose texts, seeking examples to clarify, to confirm, or even to confound the students' readings of the other works of the period. What did nineteenth-century Americans care about? What did they believe? What did they purport to believe? How does literature reflect or distort or perpetuate these trends? Accordingly, poetry becomes as central to the course as it was to the culture that the class investigates through the readings, although I tend to understate that point from the outset in the interests of posing a challenge to those persistent poetry-phobes who may otherwise have fled the class the first day.

Following the work of Walter Benn Michaels and Donald E. Pease, Jane Tompkins (*Sensational Designs*), Susan K. Harris, Joanne Dobson ("American Renaissance"), and others, I also extend in scope and in time coverage the content base of a traditional American Renaissance course. This is my description in the course syllabus:

> In his 1941 study, *The American Renaissance*, F. O. Matthiessen examined the contributions of Emerson, Thoreau, Hawthorne, Melville, and Whitman to "America's way of producing a renaissance, by coming to its first maturity and affirming its rightful heritage in the whole expanse of art and culture" (vii). More recent inquiry into mid-nineteenth century expression in the United States has situated Matthiessen's canon of visionaries within a dynamic range of alternative, authentic American voices, male and female, some commercially successful, some historically silenced. Focusing on the 1830s through the Civil War, this course reconstructs in part the cultural milieu that inspired and provoked Matthiessen's major writers. More specifically, it contrasts these figures and other frequently studied American roman-

> tics like Poe and Dickinson with some of their once popular but now lesser-known contemporaries. It also interposes some overtly political or social texts, as well as transcriptions from oral multiethnic traditions.
>
> In this course, you will read, question, discuss, and write about a range of writing, dating from this specified time span. Based on our readings as outlined below, we will consider, What is—or was—American literature of the time? What themes, conflicts, or trends define or complicate our historical sense of a "national" literary flowering? Which of these issues persist in our culture today? (1)

Clearly, my approach reinterprets Gerald Graff's recommendation from his 1992 *Beyond the Culture Wars* to "teach the conflicts": I help students articulate and consider ideological conflicts between and within the texts that I assign, certainly, but also recognize their possible connections as well as the aesthetic and generic tensions inherent in recovering a sense of the nineteenth century's developing literary marketplace. More explicitly, my course design revisits Paul Lauter's strategy of "teaching passages and themes that bring differences into relief" ("Teaching" 290), often moving beyond his important pedagogical recommendation of "pairing" texts (295) to considering a group of texts in juxtaposition, more as a constellation of comparative or interpretive options. Poetry provides a useful reference point for such an endeavor.

While my direction in the classroom follows my own creative and critical leanings, it nonetheless draws in part on models that my professors in college and in graduate school supplied over a period spanning two decades, a time of rich critical developments in academia. At the University of Virginia in the 1970s, I studied the American Renaissance with Stephen Railton. Almost twenty years later, I began doctoral studies at the University of Connecticut and took a graduate seminar there with the same title from Milton R. Stern. Strikingly, as new-historicist trends began to flourish in the field, Railton's class juxtaposed texts from Matthiessen's canon with the work of popular writers like Henry Wadsworth Longfellow and Harriet Beecher Stowe; with texts by Margaret Fuller and Dickinson as well as Poe; and with writing by a lesser-known regionalist like Joseph G. Baldwin, author of *Flush Times of Alabama and Mississippi.* If poetry was not emphasized as a genre in that course, its presence proved key in enabling the class's study of high and low literary canons of the time period as signified, to be sure, by largely aesthetic standards, even as our inquiry could not overlook political and historical issues. In this context, I first heard Nathaniel Hawthorne's complaint to his editor William

D. Ticknor about a "d——d mob of scribbling women" (*Letters* 304). In the light of what would become my own future work as a scholar, I recall that rather than nod or smirk at the line, as some did around me, I wondered, "Who *were* they?"—a question that I have happily continued to explore as a professional.

If returning to graduate school in 1989 exposed me to a world of critical inquiry more insistent than the one I had experienced as an undergraduate some years before, it also reminded me of the worth of a comparative approach to texts. My director for a dissertation on Dickinson and other American women writers of her time was not an Americanist but a comparatist, Margaret R. Higonnet. And I owe my choice of the topic to a reawakening to the significance of Dickinson's cultural milieu that I developed in the American Renaissance class with Stern. In that seminar, student reports on criticism and context as well as class discussions served to amplify the course content beyond a reading list that at first seemed to duplicate Matthiessen's, even if it did add Dickinson and Poe. While Stern's syllabus may not have blasted the most traditional of American Renaissance canons, the pedagogy and perspectives that the professor advanced did impel his students to look on their own for the wider resonances of the works they read, a technique that I extend in my own teaching today.

In this seminar, we considered Ralph Waldo Emerson and Poe as poets, not only as prose writers, and compared their poetics even as we investigated how those perspectives might infuse their prose texts. Because of this background, in my teaching I approach Poe and Emerson through multiple genres, pointing out that these writers embedded selections of poetry in their prose and asking about the implications. What's that passage about the "subtle chain of countless rings," added in 1849, doing at the beginning of Emerson's transcendentalist manifesto in "Nature"? Why does "The Conqueror Worm" appear in the middle of Poe's "Ligeia" and "The Haunted Palace" in "The Fall of the House of Usher"? Even students who confess to skipping "the parts that were poems" can see on reviewing these authorial strategies—through informal writing, through guided discussion, through group consultations, or other means—how they may intensify or encapsulate themes. In Poe, the poetry foreshadows or accompanies action or directs the reader's attention to what else is occurring in the story's plot at the same time. Similarly, in Stern's course, Dickinson and Whitman emerged as prose writers as well as poets, and we read the novels of Herman Melville, himself a poet, and of Hawthorne with as close attention to critical considerations of language as we gave to the more formal aspects of their fiction.

So when as an assistant professor I conceived my own approach to teaching what was sometimes still called the American Renaissance, my thinking on the subject owed much not only to Matthiessen and the other teachers who recast his work but also to my recasting those perspectives to include scribbling women, fireside men, and writers or transcribed speakers of color—as well as drama. More important, I had come to understand how studying a range of the poetry of the period might help students synthesize a picture of a culturally vital if remote era. At any rate it could help even the least politically or aesthetically minded member of my class learn to read more reflectively. I organize the course along a rough chronology, but only after introducing the literary period in the first class meeting through short readings, in particular through shared close readings of longer poems by William Cullen Bryant and Lydia Sigourney, which I conclude by assigning Longfellow's *Evangeline* and Lydia Maria Child's "The Quadroons" for the next week.

In a discussion-based course that meets once a week for two and a half hours, even the initial meeting to me warrants more than a cursory introduction to the syllabus followed by dismissal to the bookstore with a promise that the real semester will begin next week. I start the class by having students brainstorm aloud about their knowledge of the period from 1830 to 1865 in the United States and of its culture. I am prepared to prompt; to ask leading questions, more questions, vexing questions; to fill in; to move further back and forward in time; and to point to the stack of handouts that I have lugged in. These include excerpts from Child's 1828 *The American Frugal Housewife* ("Odd Scraps for the Economical"); from Tecumseh's address from the winter of 1811–12, which begins, "Brothers— We all belong to one family" (qtd. in Oskison 115), and in which he threatens whites that "we will stain the earth red with their blood" (116); and from unnamed slaves' 1777 petition to the House of Representatives at the Massachusetts Bay Colony (Elliott et al. 419). To share these texts, *PowerPoint* or an overhead projector might do as well. After this introduction, I shift to other texts, assuming more overtly the role of oral interpreter. I also play the parts of interrogator and coach, performative strategies that lead to discovery and that I encourage my students to try themselves.

First, I present aloud, stanza by stanza or sometimes phrase by phrase, the full text of William Cullen Bryant's 1815 "To a Waterfowl," for which the students do not have print copies, pausing often in my delivery to ask, "What's going on here?" Former students of Stern's may recognize here a version of an in-class interpretive exercise that my 1990 seminar, surely not uniquely, came to identify as, "Where are you going, duck?" As our shorthand title suggests, such a stop-and-start reading affects not only our running paraphrase of the poem's content, what some students might call a translation; it also points out gaps between Bryant's elevated poetic treatment of his subject and our contemporary habits of speech and interpretation.

Beginning with Bryant's title, which I briefly classify and explain as an example of apostrophe, a good-natured critique of Bryant's heightened Latinate diction unfolds as students come to recognize that the poem conveys a comforting and by now conventional spiritual lesson. In a recent rendition, the poem's conclusion became, "That capital P Power from stanza 4 aka spirit probably God who guides and cares for you, duck in flight, will care for me over the lonely long haul, too." When we finish the poem, once the students have stopped laughing, I ask them why that was so funny. Answers range from "He's talking to a duck, which is pretty funny in itself" to "It's hard to hear someone say things like 'Seek'st thou the plashy brink' " to "A duck 'scream[s] among' his 'fellows'?" (Hollander 1: 125), to, very occasionally, "Those are pretty corny rhymes." We can now reconstruct a notion of the possible descriptive and formal standards of the era, as well as the role of erudition in literature at the time, discussing further why the appeal of such language might have been so widely popular, even among the less educated. And we establish a few precedents to revisit throughout the semester: that lyric poetry is an oral tradition, despite its sometimes befuddling manifestations through the ages; that reading passages aloud helps us understand them better, even or especially if the language is difficult; and that subsequent writers like Dickinson and Whitman, while radical in their departures from the styles of currently less familiar American poets of the age, sometimes share surprising affinities with those poets, including a personalized reverence for nature and an understanding of popular forms.

This exercise leads to a more detailed discussion of Bryant's "The Prairies," in which we interpret his 1833 construction of an American landscape to evoke a developing country, noting its depiction of losses as well as its promise. The class conducts its initial study of this literary artifact also in fireside fashion, in this case through a read-around of print copies that I distribute: the class members read aloud, in turn, a line or two or several, until every voice in the classroom has spoken, however briefly. I may interject comments as the students read, but mostly this presentation becomes theirs, creating a community of voices if not necessarily any consensus of response. When we discuss the poem afterward, we focus first on content: What's the poem about? Who speaks? What's going on? How do we know? I also ask what about its attitudes may seem dated or obscure and why as well as what might seem impenetrable, ponderous, or archaic about the language. I cite examples and explicate them further.

For instance, Bryant describes how Native American Mound Builders,

> . . . a disciplined and populous race
> Heaped, with long toil, the earth, while yet the Greek
> Was hewing the Pentelicus to forms
> Of symmetry, and rearing on its rock
> The glittering Parthenon. (*Poetical Works* 67)

Despite weighty phrases like "hewing the Penticulus," students on a first reading grasp the poem's dramatic situation: the speaker observes a prairie landscape and details his associations, both geographic and historical, which lead him to reflect on the negative consequences of westward expansion on land, people, and wildlife. But he envisages more positive possibilities of settlement as well. Ambiguously, Bryant's conclusion extends the progression of this reflection so that "[a]ll at once / A fresher wind sweeps by and breaks my dream, / And I am in the wilderness alone" (69). Usually, the class can conjecture many causes for this conflicted outcome, and through this new critical methodology the students reach a point where they may interrogate the further cultural or political repercussions of Bryant's perspectives as well as the concept of wilderness.

Thereafter, we turn to a much more compressed lyric on what seems to be a similar subject, Dickinson's poem 1779:

> To make a prairie it takes a clover and one bee,
> One clover, and a bee,
> And revery.
> The revery alone will do,
> If bees are few.

While Dickinson's undated poem surely postdates Bryant's, it shares some details, including key words and images, an appreciation of nature, and the like. But on closer reading, when I ask students to compare these treatments, they may assert more difference than similarity between Dickinson's cosmic recipe and Bryant's extended contemplation, largely thanks to Dickinson's brevity yet strong conflation of wit and awe, which in its ostensible simplicity puzzles many a reader. Recently, though, one member of my class said, "They are really about the same thing," and went on to elaborate the connection among Bryant's "dream," Dickinson's "revery," and the possibilities of creation, both artistic and divine. Bemused, exasperated, admiring, stunned, the students at my prompting at such a point may argue whether either poem is religious and, if so, how. Assessing the implications of their very different responses, they begin to identify some thematic issues that will recur throughout the semester but also begin to see their classroom in terms of a conversation that is transpiring among more than two sides.

Another longer poem that I introduce through the fireside method in the first class meeting is Sigourney's 1849 "Oriska," a narrative that perpetuates a noble savage stereotype through a tale of cross-cultural Romantic exploitation and betrayal leading to the twinned outcomes of infanticide and suicide for its Native American heroine. A close reading of Sigourney's account of this "awful pathway to eternity" opens a discussion on the power and the pitfalls of sentimental writing, drawing first on the students' typically immediate responses: "That's wrong," "She had to do it," "She was so loyal," "She was so stupid," "He was terrible"—few if any readers will deny the villainy of Oriska's betrayer. After these first impressions, we revisit the sentimental manipulations of the poem, asking what larger persuasive or otherwise significant purposes such freighted appeals might enable. Later in the semester, when I incorporate critical passages from Nina Baym ("Reinventing"), Harris, and Dobson ("Reclaiming") about the deeper strategic possibilities of sentimental discourse to protest as well as to affirm, the students can think back to this example, moving to a more overtly critical understanding beyond simply avowing the poem's morals about suicide or murder.

Already, the possibility of female agency in the nineteenth century in the Unites States has become grounds for debate in the course, whether or not in examples bound further by race, as in Oriska's case. Authors I also assign who reconfigure versions of these issues include Longfellow in *Evangeline*, Harriet Beecher Stowe in *Uncle Tom's Cabin*, Child in "The Quadroons," Hawthorne in *The Blithedale Romance*, Harriet Jacobs in *Incidents in the Life of a Slave Girl*, Fanny Fern in *Ruth Hall*, Civil War nurses like Louisa May Alcott and Phoebe Yates Pember in both fictionalized and biographical accounts, and Rebecca Harding Davis in *Life in the Iron Mills*. The informal writing prompts that I assign week by week help prepare students to discuss dissonances and connections that occur across this generic range.

Poetry figures strongly in other groupings or pairings that I may intentionally arrange over the semester through the reading, writing, or discussion assignments or that students themselves may notice, point out, and reconsider. When I bring in antebellum poems by African Americans, George Moses Horton's defiant "The Slave's Complaint" serves as a marked counterpoint to Ann Plato's more docile "Advice to Young Ladies," wherein religious consolation seems not racialized in any specific terms. Frances Ellen Watkins Harper's "Eliza Harris" (1853) provides an obvious intertextual reference to *Uncle Tom's Cabin*, which students familiar with both texts may readily scrutinize and debate, while Harper's 1858 "Bury Me in a Free Land" suggests another perspective on Stowe's sometime solution of relocating former slaves to Liberia, which twenty-first-century readers tend to denounce as no solution at all. Harper's 1857 "The Slave Mother," with its dramatic conclusion, may cause some students to reconsider "Oriska" and set both those texts for comparison against Stowe's abolitionist appeals to mothers, which Stowe herself complicates through the character Cassy in the last section of her novel. Moreover, the issue of child mortality, untimely or intended, also links Sigourney's 1827 lyric "Death of an Infant"—which even now moves some students to tears—and the abolitionist Maria White Lowell's 1845 poem invoking slave infanticide, also entitled "The Slave-Mother." Many students here draw ready connections to Toni Morrison's *Beloved*.

In a similar example, before our first discussion on transcendentalism, students read Emerson's "Nature" and "Self-Reliance" (for searchable online full-text versions of all Emerson's work, see *Works*) and excerpts from Margaret Fuller's "Woman in the Nineteenth Century" (*Essential Margaret Fuller*) and write informally about the connections and differences in subject, style, or perspectives that they perceive among these texts. To open the class meeting, I read to them Emerson's poem "Brahma," asking about the title allusion and explaining it if necessary. Then I read the poem aloud again and ask what its conflations and convergences may or may not have to do with the essays they read before class. Focusing mostly on Emerson, students generally posit a few parallel or tangential concepts, alerting me to how much I need to explain about the basics of transcendentalism, which I illustrate through references to both "Brahma" and the prose selections. Students then organize into smaller groups of no more than five and seek three passages from Emerson that also suggest the connections between these poetic and philosophical treatments. Each group presents at least one example to the entire class, explaining the relevance of what it found and noting any further parallels or complications. I conclude by asking the class to refer to their preclass writing and compare Fuller's gendered interpretations of a transcendental mode of thought, usually now clearer through the lens of the poem that opened the discussion as well as through the discussion itself.

The following week, when the class has read Henry David Thoreau's *Walden* alongside Alcott's satiric "Transcendental Wild Oats," I distribute copies of Alcott's poetic tribute "Thoreau's Flute." As we note the natural imagery that dominates the poem, we consider how this admiring portrait amplifies our sense not only of Thoreau but also of Alcott's attitudes toward the communal living enterprise and the personages that she lampoons in her acerbic memoir. Including the poem allows us to review our previous commentary on sentimental appeals, to speculate on the fictional element of poetry even with a "true" subject, and to discuss yet again to what purpose an author might sketch a remembered person, situation, or event through multiple genres.

These insights offer a strong link to our eventual consideration of Whitman, first through "Song of Myself," then as a Civil War witness and survivor who published prose war memoirs and continued to revise them and who also wrote very different types of poetry to render his impressions. To illustrate, we consider first "The Wound-Dresser" against what the class might retain of Whitman's "barbaric yawp," and I question how the visionary compassion of the earlier poem becomes modified through the particular experience that the second invokes. We develop the idea further by comparing the beloved and form-driven "O Captain, My Captain" with the expansive Lincoln elegy "When Lilacs Last in the Dooryard Bloom'd": Is this the same Whitman? Is either the Whitman who wrote the brief pictorials "Cavalry Crossing a Ford" and "Bivouac on a Mountain Side"? What considerations of audience, purpose, experience, or other influences might account for his various efforts? What does such a range of writing indicate about Whitman's artistry?

Studying other Civil War literature provides additional opportunities to interpose various styles of poetry in order to highlight examples of prose testimony. Having discussed war memoirs by Whitman as well as by others who worked as nurses, like Alcott and the Confederate hospital administrator Pember, my class close-reads the apocalyptic imagery of Julia

Ward Howe's "Battle Hymn of the Republic" and discusses how its religiously inflected language functioned to rally and unite popular support for what would prove a devastating conflict. To contextualize further, we look at excerpts from war letters by the reputedly disengaged Dickinson, one mourning the death of the Amherst soldier Frazer Stearns (letter 255; letter 256; 397–99) and one to Thomas Wentworth Higginson during his service in the Union Army, in which she calls war "an oblique place" (letter 280, 423): so was this writer really remote from the conflicts of her day? To set up the following week's class on Dickinson, which is also the last class of the semester, I distribute copies of her poems "They dropped like flakes" (poem 545) and "When I was small, a woman died" (poem 518), which we question as war poems. Why might people who do not directly experience war feel compelled to write about it? What do Dickinson's treatments suggest about the repercussions of a United States Civil War even on a well-to-do, reclusive Massachusetts woman safe at home, far from the battlefront? Then, looking back to Whitman, we ask, How might the challenge of actual witness determine the artist's will to embrace or reject the heretofore confirmed conventions of expression in his preferred craft? And why might such involvement engender multiple responses?

Finally, my approach to teaching a revised American Renaissance curriculum entails a juxtaposition of texts in which poetry figures crucially and handily. Nineteenth-century American poems, if not short, can be aphoristic, quotable, or quickly interpreted, at least in a paraphrase—as impromptu oral interpretations as well as assigned readings may underline. But including these works in such a class will also crystallize other issues, artistic and cultural, that concurrently written prose or dramatic texts espouse. Requiring students to read poetry in the class does not guarantee that their resistance to the genre will drop away, but it does reinforce the notion that the class chronicles a transitional era in this country, particularly in terms of artistic and individual expression. Also, such a tactic may enhance and extend a reader's ability to question and wonder, whether privately, aloud, or in writing. Most simply, the poems that I incorporate into the syllabus for this course may illuminate a student's comprehension of other literary, historical, or personal impulses that existed at the time. They further clarify my own, as our classroom conversations on the subject affirm.

Jane Donahue Eberwein

"Told in Story or Sung in Rhyme": Narrative Pairings in Prose and Verse

We often forget that the nineteenth century, which saw the rise of the novel as the most popular format for imaginative fiction, was also a lively period for narrative poetry. Historically, storytelling in print has been associated with verse—epic, ballad, romance, satire, verse histories, and retellings of biblical episodes. When Romanticism sent poets back to these roots, it encouraged writing of many kinds. Widespread literacy in the United States and a growing publishing industry created a mass market for literary entertainment. Novels provided much of this demand, but so did narrative poems. If we hope to familiarize students with nineteenth-century reading experiences, we should recognize the balance that then existed in a literary culture that took equal pleasure in tales, to borrow John Greenleaf Whittier's distinction from "Skipper Ireson's Ride," whether they were "[t]old in story or sung in rhyme" (*Complete Poetical Works* 55). I have found that pairing narrative poems with prose narratives of the period (nonfictional ones as well as short stories and novels) helps restore this balance.

Among pedagogical advantages gained by introducing a few narrative poems as companions for the prose works now dominating college English curricula is the breathing space they open for students feeling overwhelmed by more extended readings. In my survey of American literature, I often encounter students who report they have never read a whole novel and feel oppressed by my expectations. For them, a day or two devoted to a poem comes as a relief. This attitude holds especially true when poems can be approached by methods students are learning to apply to short stories, novels, and autobiographical works—when they can talk about plot structure, narrative method, temporal perspective, characterization, setting, style, and tone. Many arrive with defenses up against lyric poems, apprehensive that each comes encrypted with some secret meaning intelligible only to teachers. If they bring any experience with narrative verse, it is more likely to be with Dr. Seuss's books than anything studied formally, but there is something reassuring about that. In decades just before and after the Civil War, Henry Wadsworth Longfellow and other Fireside or schoolroom poets created a general reading audience for poetry greater than Americans have known in any other period. They did so largely by telling memorable stories. I find that these poets and their contemporaries still empower readers by easing anxieties and that, in the process, they help us achieve instructional goals.

Angela Sorby makes a good case elsewhere in this volume for the benefits of experimenting with those teaching methods used when the most popular of these writers became established as the country's schoolroom poets. Basically, however, we can treat nineteenth-century narrative poems in the ways most of us now analyze and appreciate other texts. Simply pairing them with prose stories inevitably highlights issues of reader response, and these texts can be explored variously as reflections on American culture in terms of race, class, and gender tensions; as responses to social conflicts—especially over slavery and the treatment of Native Americans; as representations of natural and psychological geographies; as sentimental or gothic imaginative fictions; and as indicators of conditions of authorship, publishing, and readership in nineteenth-century America. When my students read Longfellow's "The Day Is Done" (*Poetical Works of Longfellow* 64–65) with its modest claims for the comfort provided by verses with "power to quiet / The restless pulse of care," they often draw a connection between families gathering to read poems aloud as evening entertainment and their own families' television-viewing practices. Narrative poems from an earlier time offer insights at least comparable to currently fashionable cultural studies of recent sitcoms. Nor need we take all our examples from the once-canonical Fireside Poets: there are narrative poems by women and minority authors as well.

The juxtaposition anthologies make easiest is one many of us already routinely explore by reading "The Raven" alongside Poe's tales; it works especially well with "Ligeia" in terms of gothic resemblances that prompt questions. Why does each story employ a first-person narrator who is sole witness of eerie events and who withholds basic information from us—even the name of his beloved? Did these ladies ever exist except in the imaginations of madmen? Or, as my students are prone to wonder, did the student who speaks to us in "The Raven" murder Lenore? Has the narrator of "Ligeia" dispatched Rowena? What are we to make of such vague time schemes? Why did Poe set both stories in sumptuous locales sealed off from the world? Many more resemblances come to mind, but the most interesting difference to confront is the generic one between gothic narrative in prose and poetry. What difference does it make that Poe chose to relate "The Raven" in verse?

The effect of poetic condensation is evident, as is the impact of sound. Students in my introductory course generally know nothing of prosody, so I am content if they complete the semester hearing the difference between iambic meter and whatever is noniambic. "The Raven," fortunately, is so insistently noniambic as to register with them as unusually lilting and even fun to read; though we find that the poem's musicality conflicts with its gothic narrative devices. While searching for examples of Poe's artistry, students typically point to his rhymes and repetitions, especially his famous refrain and the way it calls attention to stanzaic divisions. Even without resort to his "Philosophy of Composition," we find all sorts of signals that Poe meant us to respond to this story as an especially ingenious poem. How do the versifying effects influence reader responses? That students tend to be more kindly disposed toward the poem's grieving speaker than to Ligeia's widower might be, in part, because they try to read "The Raven" autobiographically and anachronistically as a lament for Virginia Clemm Poe. The rollicking meter further contributes to their goodwill by providing a pleasurable experience that dulls awareness of the way this man heightens his own agony by directing a sequence of increasingly pressing questions to a creature whose limited response is guaranteed to reinforce his despair. There is a comic element to the poem's diction and versification ("Much I marvelled this ungainly fowl to hear discourse so plainly" [*Works*]) that Poe almost manages to keep out of the tale by virtue of its grimly suspenseful tone, even though his explication suggests that he had no intention of making us laugh. He would probably be happy to know that students tend to condole with his narrator as a sentimental figure or tremble with him as a victim of gothic horror rather than smile at the extravagance of the language.

This poem, perhaps because of its concentrated form, presents us with a more memorable and evocative symbol than "Ligeia" does. If one wants to relate that symbol to nineteenth-century America, one can call attention to the sentimental cult of mourning, to Romantic personifications of birds as sources of inspiration, and to the racial apprehensions suggested when a troubling black stranger takes possession of the marble bust epitomizing white, Eurocentric culture in a poem by an author troubled by his own hybrid mix of Northern and Southern identities—an issue less clearly raised by the German and English settings of "Ligeia." A revealing question remains: Why did Poe always want to establish himself as a poet even though his preferred genre revealed itself from the start as less marketable for him than prose?

A particularly rewarding juxtaposition of poetry and prose I have lately introduced into my survey course picks up on Frederick Douglass's salute to Whittier as "the slave's poet" (*Narrative* 92). Students respond powerfully to the *Narrative of the Life of Frederick Douglass* because they know Douglass recounts his personal experience. While they begin by regarding the book as a straightforward and even "simplistic" text, we gradually move on to discussing its rhetorical and political strategies as I guide them toward a recognition of the conscious artistry that shapes Douglass's storytelling. We consider, of course, his vulnerability as a fugitive slave in contrast to William Lloyd Garrison and Wendell Phillips, whose writings provide the book's framework.

Adding some Whittier poems to the discussion creates another opportunity to discuss rhetoric. An obvious choice is "The Farewell of a Virginia Slave Mother to Her Daughters Sold into Southern Bondage," part of which Douglass quotes directly:

> Gone, gone,—sold and gone,
> To the rice-swamp dank and lone,
> From Virginia's hills and waters;
> Woe is me, my stolen daughters!
>
> (Whittier, *Complete Poetical Works* 278; Douglass 92)

In six twelve-line stanzas, Whittier writes in the slave mother's voice though in sophisticated poetic diction resembling the elevated style Douglass uses in passages particularly admired by his original readers—for example, his lament for his grandmother and his apostrophe to ships plying the Chesapeake. "The Farewell" is more elegy than narrative, though it implicitly conveys a story of daughters who are sold off the Virginia plantation on which they were living as slaves. From an environment of family and church support, they are cast into one of brutal toil, irreligion, loneliness, and sexual abuse. The relative abstractness of Whittier's poem is fleshed out when one recalls Douglass's stories about beatings of women or remembers the story of little Frederick being separated from his mother. Students reading Whittier's poem find themselves guessing the age of the daughters, unsure whether they should be envisaging children, adolescents, or young adults; such uncertainty reflects the generality of the societal horror Whittier deplores.

Why did Douglass think his narrative improved by references to Whittier? Although a black slave's voice had authenticity, that of a white journalist-poet offered greater authority and in 1845 helped Douglass connect with the abolitionist readership Whittier had been helping to form since the early 1830s. As is obvious from the appendix Douglass added to deflect concerns about his sarcastic attacks on America's hypocritical Christianity, he had reason to worry about alienating an important part of his audience. Whittier, known for Quaker piety and prophetically scriptural denunciations of societal sin, could speak more freely than Douglass and, as a poet, was liberated from demands that he present nothing but literal fact. In "A Sabbath Scene," for example, he narrated a dream vision of an escaped slave seized when fleeing to a church for asylum (312). When worshippers offer the runaway protection, the parson intervenes to protect the owner's property rights both by citing Scripture and by using the Bible to gag the fugitive while her owner reasserts physical control.

More easily than Douglass, Whittier inveighed against Northerners whose greed and moral indifference perpetuated the slave system. He was in a better position to challenge readers with dormant antislavery sympathies. Students realize that the first-person narrator of "A Sabbath Scene" is not himself a slave and not even a member of the congregation but someone safely removed in a comfortable home. Where Douglass conveyed the trauma of the slave witnessing horrors to which he himself could be subjected, Whittier expressed the guilt of those in the story who should have rushed to the fugitive's rescue but stepped back when confronted by the preacher's claims to legal and scriptural authority. His speaker imagines himself intervening in their stead only to awaken and find his heroic response a dream.

Beyond this Douglass/Whittier pairing, which Douglass himself explicitly called to his readers' attention, many possible links can be established between either his narrative or Harriet Jacobs's *Incidents in the Life of a Slave Girl* (both of which are written from the author's personal experience) and poems by Frances Harper (which are written by a free black woman on the basis of imagination and empathy). Harper also conveyed the anguish of disrupted families and the desperate courage of slaves intent on freedom. Her most ambitious narrative and dramatic poem, "Moses: A Story of the Nile" (*Complete Poems* 34–66), retells a biblical story of particular interest to slaves though without direct reference to conditions in the United States. Divided into nine chapters, "Moses" relates the hero's experience from infancy to death, but Harper (like Jacobs) chose to foreground women's roles in this story: Princess Charmian's adoption of the seemingly abandoned Hebrew baby, his birth mother's watchfulness over her child, his sister Miriam's protective care and later prophetic celebration of triumph when God liberated his people from Egypt. Although Harper showed Moses defying Pharaoh, she devoted greatest attention to his boldly generous choice in committing himself to his mother's enslaved people. Readers interested in a sustained discussion of Harper's "Moses" should consult Frances Smith Foster and Valerie Ruffin's essay in this volume.

Other parallels emerge when reading Harper's antislavery poems in relation to *Uncle Tom's Cabin*. Both "Eliza Harris" (6–7) and "Eva's Farewell" (22–23) take their titles and intensely concentrated story lines from Harriet Beecher Stowe's tremendously influential popular novel. "Eva's Farewell" dispenses with most narrative elements to give readers the child's hymnlike proclamation of faith addressed to her father. One would have to know the novel to grasp Eva's relationship with Augustine St. Clare or the context of slavery that gives special poignance to this child's death. "Eliza Harris," by contrast, selects from Stowe's sprawling book one episode to treat with intense narrative concentration: the scene in which Eliza leaps ice floes on the Ohio River to rescue little Harry from being sold. Although Harper's debt to Stowe is frankly acknowledged, readers comparing her twelve anapestic tetrameter quatrains with Stowe's chapter 8 will discover differences in treatment as well as resemblances. Most important, Harper's repeated emphasis on the frantic mother's fleeing "the tramp of the horse and the bay of the hound" conflates this crossing of the Ohio with later episodes: George Harris's defiance of an armed posse led by slave hunters and the family's escape into Canada. Students familiar with Stowe's novel and the historical context of the Fugitive Slave

Law will recognize the sadly ironic falsity of Harper's concluding line, "For the child of her love is no longer a slave!"

In "The Slave Mother: a Tale of the Ohio" (28–30), Harper told a different story, closer to Toni Morison's *Beloved*, about a mother who stabbed her infant daughter to death after fleeing with all four of her children into a free state only to find that "Ohio cannot save." Beyond subject matter, Harper paralleled Stowe in her tendency to address her readers, drawing us dramatically into the action: "Heard you that shriek," she demands in "The Slave Mother," "Saw you those hands?" (4–5). Like Stowe, she focused chiefly on the mother-child bond to challenge legal definitions of property. "The Slave Auction," for example, calls to mind the episode in *Uncle Tom's Cabin* where Simon Legree buys Emmeline away from her mother, and the poet seeks empathetic response from, "Ye who have laid your love to rest" (10). Both writers used the literary forum to denounce laws violating American ideals. When Harper asked in "Eliza Harris," "Oh! How shall I speak of my proud country's shame," her voice resonated with Stowe's "Concluding Remarks."

Other relatively brief and therefore readily reproduced narrative poems present instructive contrasts to frequently taught short stories. Reading Nathaniel Hawthorne's "My Kinsman, Major Molineux" and struggling to visualize everything that happens in the murky climactic scene of the major's tarring and feathering, students might appreciate "Skipper Ireson's Ride" with its imagery of a "[b]ody of turkey, head of owl, / Wings a-droop like a rained-on fowl" (*Complete Poetical Works* 55–56). Hawthorne's tale is gothic, Whittier's ballad has a comic quality, yet both texts address the links among pain, guilt, and laughter. Reading the poem may shift students' attention back to Hawthorne's ambivalent treatment of mob behavior. It also raises questions about the author's moral responsibility when retelling history. Whittier—who came to believe that Ireson had actually made an effort to save the doomed Marblehead sailors whose drownings motivated the community's collective revenge—worried that his popular and often memorized ballad revived misleading charges of cruelty he drew from folk sources. This same ballad, treated as an example of local-color fiction, with its Marblehead setting and dialect (except, revealingly, when Ireson himself talks), can readily be coupled with stories by Sarah Orne Jewett—especially because the imbalance of power between the ballad's formidable women and its "Sea-worn grandsires, cripple-bound" who stumble after them anticipates the gender disruptions of Jewett's coastal villages.

Although not fully developed narratives, Sarah Piatt's "A Pique at Parting" and "Her Word of Reproach," like Phoebe Cary's "Dorothy's Dower," relate well to stories by Charlotte Perkins Gilman and Edith Wharton that confront tensions in marriage that became increasingly pressing topics late in the century. In advanced undergraduate classes, longer and more famous narrative poems provide contrast or reinforcement to widely taught American novels. James Fenimore Cooper's *The Last of the Mohicans* can be paired with a section or two of Longfellow's *Hiawatha* or Lydia Sigourney's "Pocahontas," Catharine Maria Sedgwick's *Hope Leslie* with Longfellow's *The Courtship of Miles Standish* (*Poetical Works*).

The most rewarding combination matches the century's most admired novel, Hawthorne's *The Scarlet Letter*, with Longfellow's *Evangeline*, its most popular long narrative poem. This pairing creates a particularly fascinating contrast, because both authors, friends since their Bowdoin College days, considered trying their hands at the basic story line, which the Reverend H. L. Conolly first called to Hawthorne's attention and which both Conolly and Hawthorne then discussed with Longfellow. Only when it became apparent that Hawthorne had no interest in developing this folklore about separated Acadian lovers did Longfellow ask for his consent to render it in verse. When the poet later thanked Hawthorne for a friendly review of *Evangeline*, he added:

> Still more do I thank you for resigning to me that legend of Acady. This success I owe entirely to you, for being willing to forego the pleasure of writing a prose tale which many people would have taken for poetry, that I might write a poem which many people take for prose. (*Poetical Works of Longfellow* 70)

Reading *Evangeline* more or less as we approach a novel or prose romance and doing so in connection with *The Scarlet Letter*—published only three years later—reveal striking similarities. Both works present long-suffering, isolated heroines who seek reunion with their lovers and almost achieve it, only to lose them in death. Both texts make powerful appeals to readers' visual imaginations and rely heavily on their authors' evocation of settings. Both begin and end with memorably gloomy images that establish the dominance of tonal effects: Longfellow's "forest primeval" and wailing ocean; Hawthorne's prison, scaffold, and graveyard. Both encompass a long time span and have a narrator who taps into the story at intervals of several years. Neither plot involves much action.

There are major differences, of course, reflecting Hawthorne's and Longfellow's imaginative and artistic dispositions. One reason Hawthorne may have rejected this story was that it involved none of the guilt that adds moral and psychological depth to his fiction. From first to last, Evangeline remains a flawless exemplar of "the beauty and strength of woman's devotion" (72); when Longfellow likens her to saints, he does so without the irony attending Hawthorne's reference to the mother of Christ as he introduces Hester on the scaffold. Hawthorne balances sections of the novel focusing on Hester and Pearl with others focusing on Dimmesdale and Chillingworth, to the extent that some critics identify Dimmesdale as his protagonist. Longfellow, on the other hand, switches only once (for five lines) to Gabriel; it is his father's account and the reports of others that assure us of his continuing grief over Evangeline's absence, even as that sorrow expresses itself in a perverse pattern of wandering that virtually ensures the lovers' continued separation. By the end of her story, Evangeline's social situation has become much like Hester's—marginal yet appreciated because useful—though she never encounters the communal scorn that torments Hester and is not hardened by isolation. *The Scarlet Letter* confronts us with tragedy; *Evangeline* settles for pathos.

Hawthorne was probably wise in resisting Conolly's pressure to develop this story, but Longfellow aptly recognized ways in which a skeletal plot could be exalted by translation into poetry. His chosen genre allowed him to cast a saintly aura over his heroine and sometimes exalt her to epic nobility. Evangeline embodies the virtues of her people, her faith, and the land itself that French colonists won from the forest by virtue of their pastoral care. If Hawthorne took some risks in sharply critiquing the Puritan origins of his native region, students should recognize the generosity of spirit that inspired Longfellow to pay homage to a French Catholic colony at a time when most Anglo-Americans of his class and area felt threatened by Catholic immigration.

More controversial among literary critics of his time was Longfellow's choice of dactylic hexameter rather than iambic meter. As with Poe's choice of trochaic octameter in "The Raven," this decision meant that readers would respond more consciously than usual to sound effects and that the more sophisticated among them (Poe included) would judge Longfellow by the loftiest classical standards. His prosody harks back to Homer and Vergil, and many readers of his time would have heard in the cadence of "This is the forest primeval" an echo of "Arma uirumque cano" (1). But whereas Vergil sang of weapons and the hero who wielded them, Longfellow attempted the paradox of a sentimental epic with a heroine exemplifying the pacific Christian ideal of "affection that hopes, and endures, and is patient" (72).

Longfellow's challenge was to exalt Evangeline's simple story while expanding its range of reference beyond the lost Acadie. She reflects the rootedness in tradition that sent *pius* Aeneas into exile from the ruins of Troy, fleeing with his old father, young son, and their household gods toward the new Troy that would become the Roman Empire. Longfellow directly alluded to this transfer of empire in the opening of "Part the Second," where he wrote of ships "[b]earing a nation, with all its household gods, into exile," and he showed through Basil's prosperity in Louisiana how the promise of America rewarded at least some of those Acadian fugitives. Praying, "Let me essay, O Muse! to follow the wanderer's footsteps," however, he focused his readers' thoughts on his heroine, whose story remains one of loss despite her optimism, purposefulness, mobility, and other traits associated with masculine success in the United States (84, 85). If this is an epic, it is one without the traditional military hero, without battles, without a descent into anything the reader recognizes as hell, with only modest feasts, and without a victorious ending.

A change Longfellow made to the original story reflects his intention of celebrating America more generally rather than simply Acadie. Where Conolly spoke of the bride's wandering about New England (a geographic setting more than ample for Hawthorne), Longfellow sent Evangeline along the Ohio River, down the Mississippi into the bayous of Louisiana, far into the western wilderness to the foothills of the mountains, north to Michigan, and finally to Pennsylvania. The only major region Longfellow omitted in his depiction of the United States was, in fact, New England, though alert readers may discern that the "English" envoys who enforced King George's edict probably came from Massachusetts—a point of historical irony on which Hawthorne would have seized.

Longfellow's choice of William Penn's City of Brotherly Love for the final scene seems odd in its distance from the French settlements, but Evangeline in her long search has come to know other cultures; she has even found brief solace in the companionship of a Shawnee widow of a Canadian killed by Comanches. There are references to Spanish outposts as well as French ones on the frontier, and the continent's diversity is finally best represented by the Quaker city offering general refuge. On the day of her reunion with Gabriel, Evangeline hears bells from an Episcopal church and psalms from a Swedish service; she and Gabriel lie together in the city's Catholic cemetery. If this is an epic, it is one that celebrates tolerance and diversity as well as quiet dutifulness as virtues befitting the natural amplitude of this continent. Its lesson for generations of European immigrant children reading *Evangeline* in schools would have been one of cultural inclusion.

Although decidedly not an epic, *The Scarlet Letter* differs less from Longfellow's poem than students might expect. By comparing the novel with *Evangeline*, students may discover that Hawthorne took almost as many liberties with conventions of the romance as Longfellow did with those of epic. Yes, there is conflict, but most of it is internal—morally and psychologically profound but not especially suspenseful. Of the book's two quests, Pearl's and Chillingworth's, neither results in a showdown comparable to Ahab's confrontation with the white whale. Hester and Dimmesdale struggle for inner peace in such divergent ways that, despite the seeming hopefulness of the forest scene, readers must realize that Hester's dreams could only spell Dimmesdale's defeat. A ghostly air of supernatural possibility suffuses Hawthorne's writing, much more than it does Longfellow's, but that air has little effect on action.

We cannot generally expect to find in American narrative poems (aside from Melville's *Clarel* [1876]) the psychological depth we encounter when reading Hawthorne. Evangeline matures but remains unchanged at heart; Gabriel's restless torments reach us only by hearsay. But poets like Longfellow successfully stressed tone—in this case the somber melancholy introduced by the sea and the forest in contrast with the idyllic pastoralism of Grand Pré. In similar ways, *The Scarlet Letter* also draws power from its grave sadness of tone.

Another characteristic of narrative poems is pictorial emphasis, which we find in *Evangeline* or even in short poems like Whittier's "Maud Muller" and "Barbara Frietchie"; it is also one of Hawthorne's strengths in the three scaffold scenes and other symbolic groupings of characters. Poets use musical qualities of rhythm, rhyme, refrain, and alliteration to heighten the drama of a situation (as in Longfellow's "Paul Revere's Ride"); to contribute to atmosphere and setting (as in *Hiawatha*); to distract the reader from what is happening (as in Poe's "Annabel Lee"); and (esp. in *Evangeline)* to soften the impact of sadness and frustration, in much the same way that René Leblanc comforts Evangeline by telling his favorite tale about heaven's sending a storm to vindicate the honor of an orphan girl just after her execution. Although prose severely limits the use of rhythm and rhyme, students comparing these two texts may grow more alert to the poetic aspects of Hawthorne's verbal and imagistic repetitions.

Reading narrative poems alongside short stories, novels, and nonfictional narratives, then, expands students' reading experience and encourages students to become increasingly aware that artistry informs all good writing. It also challenges them to consider their reading behavior and how their expectations relate to those of nineteenth-century readers. That narrative poems tend to devote a surprisingly high percentage of lines to pictorial effects may surprise members of a generation that looks to visual media for the kind of imaginative stimulus people once sought in language. Cross-genre contrasts also encourage readers to recognize narrative choices made by prose writers as well as poets, and they certainly intensify awareness of stylistic and tonal decisions. They are likely to confirm Longfellow's belief that there is an element of poetry in artfully deployed prose just as there is an element of prosaic familiarity in versified tale telling. Overall, the goal is to foster an appreciation of literature, both "[t]old in story" and "sung in rhyme," by sharing some of the pleasure readers of another century found in their favorite books.

Elizabeth Petrino

Discordant American Vistas: Teaching Nineteenth-Century Paintings and Poetry

When I teach nineteenth-century American poetry, I find visual materials useful in developing students' perceptions about the cultural memory of the United States. Paintings, sculpture, photography, textile design, book design, and the material arts provide visual analogues to the texts and attune students to their ideological meanings. My essay describes how classroom discussion of paintings by Edward Hicks (1780–1849), Thomas Cole (1801–48), and George Catlin (1796–1872) can facilitate students' understanding of the arguments supporting or critiquing nineteenth-century theories of human progress—theories that justified western expansion and the disappearance of the Indians as necessary correlates of Euro-American civilization's establishment on the continent.

Roughly two centuries ago, American artists and writers struggled with the consequences of westward expansion and the declining frontier. Although many could not accept genocide of the Indians and wholesale environmental destruction, most believed in nineteenth-century views that linked clearing the land with civilization. Their works introduced the most popular arguments in defense of westward expansion even while they challenged government policies and settlement's effects. The internal contradictions in these paintings and poems, considered together, offer students a way of seeing that exposes the conflicts embedded in cultural perceptions, raising fundamental questions such as, Did writers and artists deliberately or unconsciously express these conflicted views in their works? How do images help students understand the range of perspectives on Indian removal policies and the decline of the frontier? Do they offer students a model for confronting how artists and poets create alternate histories, or do they simply report events?

Rewriting History

I begin with Hicks for several reasons. As an early folk artist, he draws attention to the struggle of American artists and writers such as Lydia Maria Child and Washington Irving to establish a national tradition distinct from Europe's. Like these writers, he was committed to exploring themes relevant to the founding of the new nation. A sign painter by trade, Hicks was practiced at copying ready-made motifs onto signs, furniture, and other household objects, and he drew his artistic vocabulary from the Bible, maps, and other sources at hand. Colored by his Quaker background and religious evangelism, his retelling of the Puritan and colonial arrival in America is, even in its contradictions, consonant with the views of his era. Most scholars agree that from the Puritans on, there were two competing views of America—as a howling wilderness and as an Arcadian pastoral. Both are embedded iconographically in Hicks's works.

Peaceable Kingdom of the Branch (1826–36; *American Originals* 35), one of at least sixty such scenes Hicks painted between 1820 and 1849, incorporates these views to hold out hope for the future while suggesting present dangers. Bisected along the diagonal, the painting depicts on the right a view of the Christ child swathed in a red cloth strip, embracing a lion, and holding an olive branch. On the left appears the Natural Bridge of Virginia, below which, on the child's side of the stream running beneath the bridge, Hicks situates William Penn signing a treaty with the Indians. In the foreground, a blasted tree mars this Edenic landscape, while in the background threatening clouds appear in the distance and isolated fir trees cling to a hillside.

The odd choice of the Natural Bridge as part of the peaceable kingdom's symbology can be explained by its association either with the sublime or with Thomas Jefferson—or, most likely, with both. According to Jefferson, who owned the land on which the bridge was discovered, the steep formation, which was 215 feet high and 90 feet wide, inspired nineteenth-century viewers with awe. Looking down, they found the view "painful" while from below it was "delightful." The mysterious origin of the bridge as well as its height led Jefferson to conclude that "some great convulsion" formed it, a myth further supporting its divine origin. For Jefferson, the bridge—"so elevated, so light, and springing, as it were, up to heaven"—offered a transcendent spiritual experience (Cain 1: 351). Given the bridge's close association with one of the nation's most prominent founders, its dangers to crossing travelers may well have inspired Hicks to see in it an apt symbol of the nation's future, grand and perilous at once.

In filling his painting with such conflicting signs—danger on the one hand, symbols of a new millennium of peaceful brotherhood and harmonious coexistence on the other—Hicks may have hoped to allay fears among settlers who imagined cruel Indians and wild animals lurking behind every tree. But the wild elements in his landscape hold other meanings also. Most important, he uses them allegorically to suggest those unruly elements in human behavior that, he believed, could be brought under control only through Christ. The word "branch" in the title refers to Isaiah 11.1, which describes the Messiah as a branch of the royal house of David. Around the frame of the picture, Hicks inscribed a commentary:

> When man is led and moved by sovereign grace,
> His grim carnivorous nature then shall cease,
> And not one savage beast be seen to frown,
> A little child shall lead them on in love.

The words echo the sentiments in Isaiah: "The wolf also shall dwell with the lamb, and the leopard shall lie down with the kid; and the calf and the young lion and the fatling together; and a little child shall lead them" (6 [King James Vers.]). Hicks identified these wild animals with the four temperaments—melancholic (the wolf), sanguine (the leopard), phlegmatic (the bear), and choleric (the lion)—and his painting suggests that in the New World's peaceable kingdom such qualities will be transformed into their domestic opposites: the lamb, the cow, the kid, and the ox. His historically (and geographically) inaccurate placing of Penn's meeting with the Indians in proximity to the Natural Bridge could then suggest that Penn is meant typologically to represent Christ, whose "sovereign grace" will transform human nature in the New World. Hicks's belief that civilization required the taming of the wild elements in human character as well as in the environment thus could, from the Indians' perspective, be said to run directly counter to his hopes for a peaceful accommodation such as Penn's with the aboriginal population.

By the mid-eighteenth century, natural-law models of human development argued that civilizations progressed through several distinct, consecutive stages: "hunting (savage), herding (barbarian), agriculture, and commerce" (Lewis 9). David Rich Lewis claims that agrarian idealism fueled the government's desire to reform Indians into independent yeoman farmers, as Euro-Americans viewed "settled western-style agriculture as the most appropriate means of making the Indian over in their own image" (7). Ironically, however, this theory of progressive human development from savage to civilized could also be used by United States policy makers as a powerful tool to justify the appropriation of Native people's lands, since the Native people had not improved it or themselves through farming. As Henry Rowe Schoolcraft, one of the first American Indian agents, wrote, "Civilization . . . cannot permanently exist without the cultivation of the soil" (qtd. in Lewis 9). But those Indian societies traditionally reliant on hunting for much of their sustenance resisted becoming farmers, putting their land-use needs in direct opposition to those of Euro-Americans.

Turning to poets, one finds that their works also encode competing accounts of America's founding and the colonists' encounters with Indians. Like his contemporaries, the famous Connecticut Wits—Joel Barlow, author of *The Columbiad*; James Kirk Paulding, who wrote *The Backwoodsman*; and Richard Henry Wilde, who penned *Hesperia*—Philip Freneau (1752–1832) sings the praises of America and argues for conquering the West even as he is deeply troubled by the motivations driving westward settlement and its environmental destruction. In his ode "On the Civilization of the Western Aboriginal Country," for instance, he contends that human history is cyclic, a movement he symbolizes through the wheels of fate turning in opposite directions, with civilizations rising and falling, including that of the Indians, whom he disparages and idealizes at once as "Nature's ruder child[ren]" (Hollander 1: 1; line 16).

Addressing the settlers who would travel west in search of land, Freneau cautions that unbridled greed will leave "Forests destroyed by *Helots*, and by slaves, / And forests cleared, to breed a race of knaves" (Hollander 1: 2; lines 49–50). He enjoins settlers to weigh their motives carefully, and he sees religion as the only reason for colonization:

> But, if devoid of subterfuge, or art,
> You act from mere sincerity of heart,
> If honor's ardor in the bosom glows
> Nor *selfish* motives on yourselves impose,
> Go, and convince the natives of the West,
> That *Christian* morals are the first, the best.
> (1: 2; lines 53–58)

Students are intrigued that the poem ends on a self-contradiction, endorsing the idea that "the child of Nature is the *better* man" (3; line 70) but rationalizing the acquisition of Indian lands under the guise of Christianizing them. After exploring the roots of Freneau's commitment to the expansion of Euro-American culture, they are better able to see how his fatalism reflects his generation's belief that, by the very nature of human progress toward civilization, Indians must assimilate or perish.

Lydia Sigourney's "The Indian's Welcome to the Puritan Fathers" (1836) is far more straightforward in its criticism of utopian expectations such as those Hicks's painting establishes. Her poem reconstructs the first meeting of the Wampanaoags and Pilgrims as described in William Bradford's *Of Plymouth Plantation*, turning this iconic moment in Indian-white relations into one of bitter irony. Far from "England's velvet green," the Pilgrims settled on a "sterile plain" bounded by a "rock-bound coast" and "wrathful main" (P. Bennett, *Nineteenth-Century American Women Poets* 14–15; lines 13, 3, 4). Strangers in a strange land, they hid their feelings of regret under a "stoic mien" (16; line 15) and went about planning their community—where corn would be raised and church and schools built—when a "red-brow'd chieftain" walked out "from the forest wide" to greet them. The Indian does not know that this overture marks the beginning of the end of his race, "a blast and ban" on future generations (lines 18, 25). "No wrath he breath'd, no conflict sought," Sigourney writes, "To no dark ambush drew, / But simply *to the Old World brought, / The welcome of the New*" (lines 21–24). The settlers will not reciprocate once they are in the stronger position:

> But who to yon proud mansions pil'd
> With wealth of earth and sea,
> Poor outcast from thy forest wild,
> *Say, who shall welcome thee?*
> (lines 37–40)

If, like Freneau, Sigourney saw the disappearance of the Indians as inevitable, unlike him, she explicitly blames European colonizers, not some nebulous concept of the cyclic rise and fall of nations.

The fissures and shifts in tone in Margaret Fuller's "Governor Everett Receiving the Indians" (1845) suggest that she also found problematic the narration of America's rise as a civilization. (P. Bennett, *Nineteenth-Century American Women Poets* 56–60). Critics have argued that the breaks in thought, generic shifts, and tonal variety of Fuller's early memoir, *Summer on the Lakes* (1844), reflect her inability to reconcile the representation of the Indians with their tragic fate. As Jeffrey Steele explains, point-of-view shifts throughout the work reveal "her ongoing effort to escape destructive cultural values infecting both her consciousness and the lives of those she was examining" (*Transfiguring* 136). Other scholars have concluded, like Christina Zwarg, that Fuller "wrestled with the failure of interpretation underlying the widespread perception that the Native American was doomed to a tragic fate" (97).

Fuller may have felt called on to examine the oppressive ideologies because the notion of progress itself was so central to her feminist beliefs. In "Governor Everett" she shifts back and forth between seeming admiration for Everett's rhetorical finesse in his famous 1837 address to the Sauk and Fox tribes and disapproval of how he and other Euro-Americans used their oratorical skill to mislead the Indians with false promises and assurances. To help students appreciate these shifts, it is useful to analyze Everett's actual text in relation to Fuller's apparent—or ironic—endorsement of its author, which makes Everett's calculated effects so obvious. Repeatedly calling the Indians "brothers," Everett creates a specious family history for whites and Indians based in part on shared location, turning waters and lands contested between Indians and settlers into signs of their kinship. Thus he compares the "red man" and the "white man" to the eastern (Mississippi) and western (Missouri) rivers that "flow . . . into one great stream." They are, Everett claims, "all one band—one family" with "many branches and one Head" and a single "great father," the president, to whom they all owe filial loyalty (258–59).

But Everett's manipulation of some of the basic gambits of Indian oratory—the emphasis on family and brotherhood, in particular—provides a thin veneer at best for what is in fact his determined effort to rationalize (and naturalize) his people's land grabbing. What Fuller sees in white-Indian relations is, rather, one people's unjust oppression of another and plains steeped in the blood of the defeated: "Must they not think, so strange and sad their lot, / That they by the Great Spirit are forgot?" (P.

Bennett, *Nineteenth-Century American Women Poets* 58; lines 88–89). Shifting from an earthly to an empyrean view, she registers her rage:

> We take our turn, and the Philosopher
> Sees through the clouds a hand which cannot err,
> An unimproving race, with all their graces
> And all their vices, must resign their places;
> And Human Culture rolls its onward flood
> Over the broad plains steeped in Indian blood.
> (lines 94–99)

"We take our turn" aptly sums up Fuller's, Everett's—and our own—complicity in using the entitlements of civilization to support genocide against people conveniently deemed an "unimproving race." The "flood" of culture destroys tribal ways and human lives, a fate that, however inevitable it appeared, Fuller nevertheless condemns.

Manifest Destiny

In 1893, reading before the American Historical Association, Frederick Jackson Turner promulgated his now-famous thesis on the foundational role of the American frontier in shaping American character and social life. Extolling the expansiveness of American democracy under the doctrine of manifest destiny as a native phenomenon, Turner argued that the appropriation of free land had relieved poverty and encouraged economic equality. "American democracy," he claimed, "was born of no theorist's dream. . . . It came stark and strong and full of life out of the American forest, and it gained new strength each time it touched a new frontier" (qtd. in H. Smith 259). But while belief in the United States' democratic mission legitimated the taking of land for most nineteenth-century Americans, there were many writers and artists who were deeply troubled by the effects expansion had on native forests as on indigenous peoples.

Cole's *Home in the Woods* (1847; *American Originals* 49) captures a liminal moment in American history, when settlement was just beginning to change the landscape, and subtly registers the artist's unease with such incursions. The painting depicts a pioneer family's dwelling in the White Mountains of New Hampshire. In the misty distance rears Mount Chocorua, where, according to legend, an Indian chief, fatally wounded by settlers, was said to have cursed their lands and waters before he died. To the right, a house and garden have been carved out of the woods. Ax-hewn stumps and broken limbs litter the clearing where the cabin stands, mutely testifying to settlement's destructive effects. A sprouting garden and a ightning rod perched atop the roof point to the settlers' domestication of nature.

Symbols of death and temporality include a scythe and hellebore, a poisonous plant of the buttercup family, which grows in the split stump of a tree that Cole places prominently in the picture's foreground. Centrally located, a butter churn is turned away from the drying effects of the sun, implying that a transitional moment between afternoon and evening has arrived and inviting the viewer to speculate on themes of change and loss. Some critics contend that the painting's Christian iconography, including several supports that resemble crosses, intertwined vines, crossed tree trunks, and the fish carried home at twilight, as well as the cheerful family welcoming the father home at dusk, evoke Cole's turn, late in his career, toward conventional religious themes (see, e.g., *American Originals* 50). But if so, the painting offers little else to console viewers responsive to its underlying melancholy. Although the lake might serve as a transcendental medium of contemplation and the towering mountain peak as a symbol of nature's permanence, both are visually subordinated to the settler's cabin and to the tiny figures who inhabit it, irrevocably changing the wilderness with their presence.

Many critical and literary texts can help students situate Cole's discomfort with the expanding frontier and the environmental devastation it wreaked. In his highly influential study *The Machine in the Garden* (1964), Leo Marx argues that nature and technology were viewed as coexisting harmoniously in the nineteenth century. His famous example of a middle ground between civilization and wilderness—Walden Pond—may offer a parallel to Cole's painting. Critiques of Marx's study, however, allow students an alternate way to assess Cole's presentation of expansion's effects. David E. Nye's *American Technological Sublime* (1994) contends that sublime landscapes, which included the Natural Bridge, Niagara Falls, Yosemite, and the Grand Canyon, fulfilled the desire of viewers to identify themselves as Americans. However, Nye goes on, the Americanness of this "sublime was inseparable from a peculiar double action of the imagination by which the land was appropriated as a natural symbol of the nation while, at the same time, it was being transformed into a man-made landscape" (37). His discussion of the way technological and natural symbols combine in this period seems appropriate for Cole's painting, where household objects, furniture, and tools reflect the intrusion of people into the wilderness rather than their harmonious coexistence with it.

That environmental destruction occurred as a result of settlement was, in fact, well known in the century. As the ecological historian William Cronon has charted, deforestation in New England resulted in a series of widely acknowledged detrimental effects: weeds multiplied, temperatures fluctuated, flooding as both the consequence and the cause of soil erosion became commonplace, and wild animals were pushed out of their territories. This destruction made frontier settlements like the one depicted in Cole's painting increasingly controversial, as those who favored such economic progress squared off against those who wished to preserve the wilderness intact or see it developed more slowly.

Informed by these critical perspectives, students are prepared to read nineteenth-century poets who were similarly divided among those who took deforestation as the price of progress, those who saw it as unambivalently good, and those who objected to it. One striking example is a comparison of Sigourney's poems on settlement with Longfellow's placidly nostalgic *Evangeline*. Used as stage-setting devices, the introductory lines of Sigourney's blank-verse poems imaginatively evoke the place where the poems occur, while they generate sympathy for the denuded landscape. Longfellow opens *Evangeline* with a melancholy evocation of what was:

> This is the forest primeval. The murmuring pines and the hemlocks,
> Bearded with moss, and in garments green, indistinct in the
> twilight,
> Stand like Druids of eld. (*Selected Poems* 3)

But one cannot lose oneself in the past reading "Fallen Forests" (1845), as Sigourney writes in outrage of the present—"Man's warfare on the trees is terrible" (P. Bennett, *Nineteenth-Century American Women Poets* 20; line 1)—and warns her generation to stop acting as their despoiler, "a thief to prey / On Nature's bosom" (21; lines 46–47). Similarly, in "The Western Emigrant" (1843)—a poem about a Connecticut native who resettles his family in Illinois—she again treats deforestation as a kind of sacrilege: "Amid these forest shades that proudly reared / Their unshorn beauty towards the favoring skies, / An axe rung sharply" (13–14; lines 1–3).

Students can also compare Sigourney's approach with that of Walt Whitman in "Song of the Broad-Axe" (first published as "Broad-Axe Poem"). Whitman's ax symbolizes the progress and development of American society. Both destructive and creative, it serves a dual purpose: building a "sylvan hut" and clearing "space . . . for a garden" (Leaves 156; line 26) and demolishing cities in "the hell of war, the cruelties of creeds" (158; line 91). But whereas Whitman acknowledges the ax's baneful uses, unlike Sigourney he does not present the land-clearing ax as itself making war on trees. On the contrary, he celebrates the "shapes" that "arise" as a consequence of the ax's work: "Citadel, ceiling, saloon, academy, organ, exhibition house, library" (162; line 192). Part of the popular genre of ax poetry, Whitman's and Sigourney's poems, when read together, point to the deep and widespread division among writers about how to register the price that settlement entailed.

Instructors can broaden the discussion of settlement to include those artists who openly protested the destruction of the forests in prose and verse, one of whom was Cole. In his 1827 *Sketchbook*, Cole lists ideas for future projects, including "Lost Indian—Dead Hemlock," linking the demise of the Indian and the forests, as well as an idea for a never-realized painting, "The Past and Present": "This might be American scenery—a scene in its primeval wilderness—with Indians—the land changed under the hand of Civilization." In 1835, he reviled the destruction of old-growth forests in his poem "The Complaint of the Forest," written while he was touring the Catskill Mountains. Like Ralph Waldo Emerson, who in "Hamatreya" represents the voice of the earth exalting over human arrogance, Cole dramatizes the forest's voice: amid the sounds of nature, a human being, "the destroyer," has "utter'd responses sharp / And dissonant—the axe" (4; lines 107, 112–13). His blank-verse poem of over two hundred lines characterizes the forests as primeval places where once only the voices of "Cataracts" and "sylvan habitants" sounded, but now "crashing branches frequent lash'd the ground" (4; lines 111, 115), and

> the little streams
> That oft had rais'd their voices in the breeze
> In joyful unison with ours, did waste
> And fled [pin'd—added] away as though in deep despair.

Although Cole does not mention Indians explicitly in "Complaint," his frequent allusions to past civilizations, as in "Lebanon's / Dark ranks of Cedar" (5; lines 122–25, 132–33) and "scatter'd Israel's [people] 'mid the tribes of man," link the rapidly disappearing forests to the simultaneous disappearance of indigenous peoples (8; line 239).

Also in contrast to the troubled depiction of settlement in Cole's painting, William Cullen Bryant's "The Prairies" (1832) defends expansionism by calling on a cyclic view of history. Examining the speaker's vision of a prehistoric race of Mound Builders who became extinct, students might explore the themes of regeneration, violence, and renewal that underlie Bryant's portrayal of their passing. Describing the Midwestern flatlands as "the Gardens of the Desert . . . For which the speech of England has no name" and a "temple" (Hollander 1: 162; lines 1, 3, 162), Bryant takes the view that the prairie is cultivatable land beneath which lies the remains of a lost civilization. Richard Slotkin writes:

> In his dreams he [Bryant's speaker] sees the history of the first conquest of the continent, in which the conquering role now played by his own people is transferred to the present Indians, who come to destroy the native Mound Builders and lay their cities waste. (455)

Students might discuss how Bryant rationalizes the demise of the Indians as part of a civilization's natural decline. Does the poem simply reveal his era's preference for a classical, agrarian civilization over a nomadic existence? Or does he mean to predict the Indians' future in the assimilation of the prehistoric Mound Builders, who were defeated and who intermarried with the victors?

Inventing the "Indian"

Portraiture paintings of Native Americans, virtually a subgenre in nineteenth-century art and photography, provide another opportunity to study arguments supporting or critiquing Indian removal. In their portfolio of American Indian sketches, *History of the Indian Tribes of North America with Biographical Sketches and Anecdotes of the Principal Chiefs* (1838–43), Thomas McKenney and James Hall express the paternalistic ideology on which were based the national policies of land appropriation and Indian removal. Perceiving the Indians as idle and unable to adapt to white civilization, they argued that taking Indian lands was justified, since the Indians' tendency to "vice" and "bad propensity," because they were "savages," only exaggerated the effects of the corruption they contracted from white people (12). But whites had to assume responsibility for Indians, since "the burden of guilt must be conceded to lie upon the party having all the advantages of power, civilization and Christianity, whose position placed them in the paternal relation towards these scattered children of the forest" (12–13).

Catlin, the greatest of the nineteenth-century Indian portraitists, also believed that Indians were disappearing before the advance of Euro-American civilization, but he desired to preserve Indian traditions through his art, and his Romanticism helped counteract the dehumanizing effects of popular invective. Karl Bodmer and Frederic Remington, both painters who developed images of the American West, also created extensive archives of Native American life, but Catlin was the most successful at bringing sympathy to his studies.

In *Osceola, the Black Drink, a Warrior of Great Distinction* (1838; Gurney and Heyman 222), Catlin portrays a young Seminole leader who became famous when he defied the United States government, reputedly plunging his knife into a treaty that would have forced his people to emigrate west of the Missouri River, a gesture that precipitated the Second Seminole War. A Romantic hero and freedom fighter for many intellectuals, Osceola attracted the attention of Lydia Maria Child, who in her protest fiction and journalism integrated the plight of the Indians into the pro- and antislavery debates that gripped the nation before the Civil War. The fate of the Seminoles, who had intermarried with runaway slaves, epitomized for Child, according to Carolyn Karcher, "the historical intersection of the abolitionist and Indian causes" (*First Woman* 549). Like Sigourney's epic *Traits of the Aborigines* (1822), Child's "An Appeal for the Indians" (1868) rehearses some important causes of the Indians' devastation and raises questions for students about the prejudices and sympathies of nineteenth-century accounts.

If Sigourney's and Child's works document the mistreatment to which Indians were subject, Catlin's portrait of Osceola conveys the Romanticism that Indians embodied. Unlike Catlin's hastily executed portraits, often blocked out in the field, Osceola's was painted in careful, even brush strokes, and the sculpted head and fine features suggest that Catlin intended to idealize his subject in a way more befitting an American revolutionary hero than a savage. The details of dress, such as his hat with three ostrich plumes and the colored sash, evoke an Eastern prince. The art historian William Truettner comments that "Catlin's solution was to convert the Seminole into a character who might have stepped from the pages of a Chateaubriand novel—a true *Chactas*, the prince of an exotic nation" (Truettner and Anderson 228). Traveling to meet Osceola shortly before he died in prison in 1838, Catlin recorded his impressions and admiration: "This gallant fellow . . . is grieving with a broken spirit, ready to die, cursing the white man, no doubt, to the end of his breath" (Letters 1: 219–20). Catlin's portrait and comments both suggest that he saw Osceola as a tragic figure and that he deliberately sought to garner sympathy for him as a hero. Yet his concern did not prevent him from profiting from Osceola's popularity: rather than convey the painting to the commissioner of Indian affairs in Washington, he added it to his "Indian Gallery," as he called his collection of portraits, and sold lithograph copies to the public.

Catlin's painting might serve as a backdrop for a discussion of the ways he and many other nineteenth-century artists and writers both sympathized with and profited by the Indians. Students might find it interesting that nineteenth-century artists staged their exhibitions dramatically, erasing the boundary between fake and real Indians. When Catlin traveled to England in 1839, for example, he transported craft work, traditional clothes, and a Crow lodge. He even hired resident Londoners to perform tableaux vivants. These staged reenactments of eleven war and eight domestic scenes were meant to place the Indians in their native environments for the audience, but they also pandered to the belief that Indians were violent savages (Gurney and Heyman 66). Eventually, actual Indians joined Catlin's entourage and danced before audiences, reduced to self-parodies for a public that treated them as curiosities.

Aware of the predicament Indians were in as well as party to it, Catlin sardonically portrays the change they suffered as a result of their contact with civilization in *Wi-Jun-Jon, Pigeon's Egg Head (The Light) Going to and Returning from Washington* (1837–39; Gurney and Heyman 202; see *Search*), a famous diptych that concludes his book. The Assineboin chief had traveled to Washington to meet President Jackson, and Catlin portrays him in full ceremonial dress. In the second portrait, when the chief returns to his people, he is tricked out in a military uniform, carrying bottles of whiskey in his pocket, an umbrella, and a fan. According to Catlin, he wore "a pair of water-proof boots, with high heels, which make him 'step like a yoked hog' " (Gurney and Heyman 202). Students might explore the reasons for Catlin's ironic coda and his derogatory comments as well as his pandering to his audience's taste for the exotic in presenting his Indian Gallery. His paintings memorialize a traditional way of life, but his message—that civilization destroys it—is nowhere more evident. How he viewed his own role in enabling this destruction is far less clear but gives students something to ponder.

Glancing through Rufus Wilmot Griswold's *The Female Poets of America* (1849), we find many writers who were prepared to sentimentalize the removal of Indians, even while they defended the government's actions as an inevitable consequence of the gulf between Indian savagery and white civilization that mandated the Indians' disappearance. Lucy

Larcom's "The Burning Prairie," for example, mentions the Indians in a conventional sentimental aside—

> for Mississippi's water
> Speeds no sachem's light canoe,
> And beside the dark Missouri
> Are the Indians' wigwams few.
> (361; lines 29–32)

—but only to contrast their savagery to the improving labor of white farmers, who use fire as a "mighty besom" to "swee[p] the fertile plain" (lines 33, 34). Other poems, like Frances H. Green's "A Naragansett Sachem," idealize the Indian male—tall, impressive, and anatomically perfect—associating him with classical precedents (as in the "day-dreams of Praxiteles" [124; line 8]), but then take back what they give by stressing the incongruities of his dress, which includes scalp locks, wampum, and human teeth. Like the vanished Romans and Greeks, the Naragansett chief and his people, no matter how noble and beautiful, have no place in a modern, civilized world. Eliza L. Follen's "Sachem's Hill" seems to lament the Indians' disappearance also but then consoles the reader with the thought that, were the Indians to return from the "land of spirits" (121; line 25), they would rejoice to see what whites had done with their land.

Interestingly, African American poets writing on Indians also tended to romanticize them, even while accepting their disappearance. In "The Cherokee," Mary Weston Fordham, a late-nineteenth-century African American poet, provides an intriguing comparison with white, Northern poets. Like Sigourney but unlike the three white poets cited above, Fordham lays the blame for Native Americans' disappearance squarely on the "Pale-Face[s]" who appropriated their land. However, she also ennobles the Cherokee's decision to join his deceased wife in death, as if it were the only solution (Kilcup, *Nineteenth-Century American Women Writers: An Anthology* 515; line 29). Like the self-willed death of Chingachgook in James Fenimore Cooper's *The Pioneers* (1823) and the self-imposed exile of the Indian hero in Child's *Hobomok* (1824), this (fictional and voluntary) choice on the Indian's part—effectively, to disappear—not only frees the white audience from guilt, it rewrites history, which actually tells the story of Native American survival. The tragedy behind such Romanticism is that it encouraged even writers who were deeply and genuinely sympathetic to the Indian, Sigourney, for example, to distort and treat reductively what actual Indians were like and how diverse and complex their lives, customs, and fates were.

Far from providing a comprehensive survey of American painting, these examples hint at many visual analogues available to the instructor: the magnificent scenes of the Sierra Nevada by Alfred Bierstadt; the allegorical depictions of the Hudson River Valley by Jasper Francis Cropsey and John Kensett; the impressionist portrayals of climatic change and rural life by George Inness; and the smaller, more meditative luminist paintings by Martin Johnson Heade and Fitz Hugh Lane are all worthy of discussion. Their themes, such as agrarian values versus nomadic life, manifest destiny, environmental change and deforestation, and the stereotyping of Indians as noble savages, resonate in rich and complex ways with the nation's history and literary tradition and, through discussion, become immediately accessible and even exciting to students.

Elizabeth Savage

Understanding Sentimentalism

Over the past three decades, scholars in pursuit of a diversified American literature and an explanation for the canon's homogeneity have succeeded in expanding the canon and revealing how discourses shaping American literary history have fortified the predominantly white, male canon against any serious challenge to its aesthetics (Avallone; Lauter, *Canons*). Research into American literary criticism in the nineteenth and twentieth centuries explains that terms of literary merit, like "transcendent," and of period demarcation, like "American Renaissance," valorize writing by white men associated with (if not exactly members of) the upper classes of New England. This research makes clear how writing by women and authors of other racial, social, and economic backgrounds have been excluded from the canon, but it does not explain why even authors of social privilege, because they are perceived as sentimental, have failed to regain the literary clout in the classroom that would make their recovery meaningful. This approach to teaching nineteenth-century American poetry helps reveal the ways assumptions about gender held in the twenty-first century operate to authorize and to undermine the expression of emotion.

Several new anthologies provide the opportunity to inspect contemporary standards determining sentimentalism. The latest edition of *The*

Heath Anthology of American Literature (Lauter et al.) contains poems by Frances Osgood and poems by Lydia Sigourney, two writers whose poetry has for a long time been taken to exemplify the sentimental, unsophisticated, popular scribbling against which real literature is distinguished (my citations to their work are from Walker's anthology *American Women Poets of the Nineteenth Century*). The pedagogical approach proposed here moves discussions of nineteenth-century poetry outside the frameworks that tend to trivialize writers new and returning to the canon, in order, first, to relocate their poetry in conversations about nineteenth-century efforts to claim emotion and poetry as legitimate sources of knowledge and, second, to discover the gendered associations readers today bring to the poems. Osgood and Sigourney wrote a large range of poetry that defies their literary status as emotionally excessive, moralistic simpletons (Baym, "Reinventing"; De Jong, "Legacy Profile"; Dobson, "Sex"), so I have been tempted to select for classwork poems that prove their literary worthiness according to canonical standards. Yet because this approach discovers the criteria readers employ when they praise or condemn a poem for its emotional expression, I encourage teachers not to avoid poems most easily dismissed as sentimental but, instead, to commit themselves to learning, with their students, the processes by which they determine literary value and pleasure.

The contrast between students' reactions to Walt Whitman's "Out of the Cradle Endlessly Rocking" (first published as "A Word out of the Sea") and their reception of Osgood's and Sigourney's "dead baby" poems motivates this approach to teaching writers long absent from the canon (primarily women, but men as well) alongside their long-famous hosts, namely Whitman and Emily Dickinson. The same students who condemn Osgood's and Sigourney's poems as self-indulgent and emotionally manipulative often delight in the emotional candor exhibited in Whitman's poem and in Edgar Allan Poe's "dead girlfriend" poems. Students have gone so far as to confess in open class that Whitman's poem made them break down, but they have been unequipped to explain why the weeping, barefoot boy, motherless eggs, and mournful birdsong escape the judgments visited on women writers.

At first, I was ready to credit the double standard entirely to the authors' sex: students assumed these women wrote autobiographically and inappropriately sought sympathy from strangers, while Whitman and Poe wrote imaginatively, earning empathy by breaking masculine stereotypes and expressing emotion in public. But class discussions prove that, while the sex of the author does influence readings, the seemingly intuitive division of these poems into "sentimental" and "emotionally authentic" categories registers deeply embedded reading responses to particular poetic moves, responses often bound up with gender but not always tied to a poet's sex.

Three of the many conventions of the sentimental covered in Joanne Dobson's essay "Reclaiming Sentimental Literature" are accessibility of form and content, a generous use of typographic intensifiers, and a positioning in and a desire for empathetic relationships. This lesson invites us to compare Whitman's "Out of the Cradle . . ." with Osgood's "A Mother's Prayer in Illness," and Sigourney's "Death of an Infant" against the background of these conventions in order to consider how their presentations of emotional states inscribe their texts as masculine/literary or feminine/sentimental in the minds of today's readers. This method of rerouting discussions of sentimental poetry into conversations about reading practices is useful for integrating relatively unknown poets (like these two women poets or William Cullen Bryant) into courses traditionally featuring only major poets (like Poe). Closely comparing poems that undergraduates consistently identify as "timeless," "moving," and "universal" with poems that, despite similar emotional scenes, the same students consider sappy and merely personal, makes legible poetic gestures that convey emotional authenticity and those that do not; it helps students understand their judgments of poetic voice and disturbs the presuppositions underlying their judgments.

Teachers of American literature survey courses who want to introduce poets unfamiliar to undergraduates can begin the unit with this lesson as a way of preempting student assumptions that these writers are inferior to the poets they already know, like Poe, Whitman, and Dickinson. Classes that have addressed developing concepts of manhood and womanhood throughout, especially with regard to the role of the writer, will be more successful at avoiding the misunderstanding that gender concerns are relevant only when women writers or characters are involved. Upper-division courses in American Romanticism might use the same approach in conjunction with reading Poe's "Philosophy of Composition" (*Essays*) to illuminate the era's effort to rescue the office of the poet-writer from women—a struggle "Out of the Cradle" complicates in useful ways, perhaps deliberately and despite Whitman's infelicitous assessment of American poetry as having allowed foreign "dandies" to overrun it with "whimpering and crying about something" (*Walt Whitman Archive*; path: *Complete Prose Works* [1892], "Democratic Vistas" 975). Courses in literary criticism, American poetry, or modernism might follow this approach as a way of introducing students to inherited critical practices. Finally, this strategy could be adapted easily for use in writing classes in which understanding ethos plays a central role.

Introducing Backgrounds and Contexts

When, in 2001, Jonathan Franzen resisted having his book *The Corrections* chosen as an Oprah's Book Club selection because he thought it belonged to a "high-art literary tradition" unsuited to Oprah's audience (qtd. in Elliot 70), he unwittingly invoked a set of cultural associations that have accumulated since the seventeenth century to shape our modern understanding of what counts as literature. The idea of literature Franzen called on to protect his book from certain fame and fortune is itself sexist, racist, and classist: literature is inherently exclusive of women (Oprah and her predominantly female audience) and nonwhites (Oprah herself and, by association, her book club) and too sophisticated for a general readership (television's mass audience of stereotyped viewers). This example of shared but unexamined assumptions about the literary gives students a fresh perspective on their own attitudes toward the sentimental. They generally know about Oprah's Book Club, the cultural importance of which and the significance of Franzen's reaction to are studied in Cecilia Farr, and most of them do not expect to find popular works they adore (by Stephen King or J. K. Rowling, for example) in the literature section of a bookstore. Teachers of American literature are familiar with the division the Franzen flap publicized and have themselves encountered nineteenth-century literature through Ezra Pound's notorious figural assessment of the era as an "old bitch gone in the teeth" and his hope for poetry that is "harder and saner . . . as much like granite as can be . . . austere, direct, free from [that century's] emotional slither" (*Selected Poems* 64; "Retrospect" 12). Teachers of American literature also know this conflation of womanish writing with cultural erosion, but the association in the American literary imagination begins not with Pound but with the antinomian controversy.

On her arrival in New England, sometime between 1634 and 1636, Anne Hutchinson began holding weekly meetings in her home to discuss the Sunday sermons. Eventually, large groups of men and women participated regularly, and the meetings became more corrective, criticizing rather than reviewing the sermons. Hutchinson claimed that the church elders had allowed their doctrine to lapse into a covenant of works; she advocated a return to the doctrine of free grace and the removal of the erring ministers. As Amy Schrager Lang notes, Hutchinson's supporters and opponents divided the Massachusetts Bay Colony until she was brought to trial in 1637–38, excommunicated, and banished for heresy (2–5). According to historians like Cotton Mather, neither Hutchinson's persecutors nor her defenders ever "to their dying hour underst[ood] what their difference was" (qtd. in Lang 67), and accounts of the crisis focus not on her religious beliefs but on her violations of social decorum. By subjecting men to her convictions, Hutchinson exhibited "unnatural" sexual behavior that implied other kinds of sexual misconduct. These implications transformed her from a force of social dissent into a discredited example of unseemly emotional expression. By the end of the seventeenth century, Hutchinson, the publicly expressive woman, stood for social impotence and emotional excess (Lang 43, 52–71).

In the eighteenth century, the cultural categories signified by Hutchinson spread to other socially disenfranchised groups. During the First Great Awakening (1740–45), revivals featured a redistribution of religious authority by allowing all converts to preach. Reverend Charles Chauncy of Boston's First Church deployed the nexus of woman, powerlessness, social disorder, and "wrong religion" to link the awakening's support of invisible witness and congregational democracy with society's downfall. Chauncy and others denouncing the awakening applied a circular argument to nullify the empowerment afforded by revivalist practices: the preponderance of women, children, blacks, and illiterates—those persons highly susceptible to emotional excitement—was taken as proof of the objectionable nature of the revivals, which naturally attracted inferiors known for faulty beliefs and practices (Lang 72–106). The elements of the revivals Chauncy named and condemned as silly (yet dangerous) are the same ones activated when literature is dismissed as sentimental or not part of high-art literary tradition. In the nineteenth century, writing that was eagerly and easily consumed by the masses replaced the threat posed by the revivals, and writing that made money became equated with womanishness or unworthy literature.

Long before Pound and the New Critics began worrying about cultural effeminacy, some nineteenth-century male writers were concerned with reclaiming writing and emotion as manly provinces, which meant wresting not only the profession from women but also the creative resources necessary for writing—namely, individuality, intuition, emotion—from the trivializing applications charted in Lang's book. Hawthorne's infamous remarks on women writers who were his competitors provide the most egregious evidence of this anxiety. In his sketch "Mrs. Hutchinson," he links the antinomian upstart to the "girlish feebleness" of popular women's writing stunting the growth of American literature (18).

Hawthorne is hardly alone in his desire to define strong, mature writing against women's work. Despite the financial success and popularity of his own writings, Ralph Waldo Emerson conceives the transcendentalist as a guardian of a cultural-psychological space that is safe from the marketplace, and he asks his public reproachfully if they will "not tolerate one or two solitary voices in the land, speaking for thoughts and principles not marketable or perishable?" ("Transcendentalist" 110). For Emerson, what sells is interchangeable with what is doomed to disappear, a prophecy fulfilled by the twentieth-century disappearance of women writers like Osgood and Sigourney, but also Henry Wadsworth Longfellow and William Cullen Bryant, whose lucrative writing careers have provided the strongest proof of their literary inadequacies.

In a letter to Horace Greeley, Henry David Thoreau distinguishes himself from other writers and the consumers they serve by emphasizing the source of his income: "For the last five years, I have supported myself solely by the labor of my hands. I have not received one cent from any other source. . . . There is no reason why the scholar . . . should not do his work in the ditch" (W. Harding 2–3). According to Thoreau, good writing issues (sparingly) from a good life characterized primarily by manly labor and minimal need for money. This sentiment is applied by Greeley, who in response calls Thoreau "a thorough classical scholar," a "true poet (though he rarely or never wrote verses)," who "never sought to make a livelihood by his writings, though there are not six men in America who can surpass them" (2). Needless to say, Thoreau's literary model disqualifies women and emasculates scholars whose successful writing careers testify to their unmanly profession.

The nineteenth-century discourses binding masculinity to literature and femininity to perishable commodities easily developed into the critical lens of modernism and New Criticism. Literary instruction at all levels has absorbed these attitudes, which shape students'—and teachers'—responses to Osgood, Sigourney, and Whitman. I have had little success convincing students that certain poems aren't really sentimental and even less success valorizing sentimental works by separate but equal standards (e.g., social activism). Instead, I use students' biases as a way into the following critical problems: In what ways do nineteenth-century writers package emotional topics and states of mind as literary? And what, for twenty-first-century readers, marks emotion as legitimate or insincere? Nineteenth-century poetry can tell us much about the present: about our ways of authenticating emotion, our expectations of the poet, and our interpretations of emotional cues. Whether student responses are uniform or diverse, the exercise works because it moves evaluation away from the question of whether these poems are good or not.

Reading How We Read the Sentimental

The approach I outline below begins from a comparison of the poems' negotiations with sentimental features surveyed (but not necessarily endorsed) in Dobson's "Reclaiming Sentimental Literature." Under each summary of a general sentimental convention, I include questions for discussion, possible responses to the issues they raise, and speculative analysis of those responses.

Accessibility

One sentimental convention is accessibility of form and content, including conversational diction, meter (blank or free verse) and tropes familiar to students, and experience shared by many. Although the poems articulate various experiences remote to modern students, the topics are recognizable as poetic materials. How does each poem use poetic devices? Are these devices connected to certain images of the poet?

The periodic construction that makes up Whitman's opening stanza in "Out of the Cradle Endlessly Rocking" and employs anaphora (the repetitions of "out" and "from") anticipates that an important childhood memory is soon to be related, announces that the speaker is a weeping man, and ends with the lofty assertion that the speaker is a poet: "I, chanter of pains and joys, uniter of here and hereafter, / A reminiscence sing" (*Walt Whitman Archive*; path: *Leaves of Grass* [1860] lines 269–70). Apart from the stanza's concluding anastrophe, the poem straightforwardly presents a recognizable poetic situation, the recollection of an emotional event that moves the speaker to tears and to speech. The deliberate delay of the narrative element, however, syntactically enacts the distance between the emotional experience and its communication. Does the postponement imply effort to traverse the temporal distance and retrieve the powerful emotional experience? or a reluctance to speak of it? Does the poet's announcement that he is "A man, yet by these tears a little boy again" (line 18) suggest that he is or is not in control of accessing his childhood self? Which reading makes the emotional expression legitimate?

The distance between speaker and experience in "Cradle" contrasts with the direct presentation of death (also Whitman's topic) in Osgood's and Sigourney's poems. Sigourney's "Death of an Infant" relates the baby's death in the past tense (but not a specified past), assigns tears only to the child's mother, and describes in rather brutal terms (death binds the baby's eyelashes together, then silences it) and in the third-person ("its") beatific expiration. In Osgood's "A Mother's Prayer in Illness," the mother asks God to kill her children before she dies because, without their mother, "this rough world" (line 18) will embitter them as it has embittered her:

> Ah, let me stay!—albeit my heart is weary
> Weary and worn, tired of its own sad beat
> . . . —tired alike
> Of joy and sorrow, of the day and night.
> (lines 45–46, 48–49)

The poem's diction is relatively unornamented, the rhyme scheme relaxed and unintrusive, and its central action surprising: the poet-mother predicts bad things happening to her beloved but imperfect children were she to die before them.

While Sigourney's poem remains on one temporal plane, both Osgood's and Whitman's poems occupy at least two. Considering that the causes for emotion occupying Whitman's poem seem open to the accusation of sentimentality (a child feels sad about a dead bird, but an adult should not), teachers and students alike are led to think about how the temporal relation of the poet to the poem influences our sense of emotional importance. Does greater temporal unity imply limits on the poetic voice? Does the appearance of emotional immediacy or spontaneity add to or detract from poetic authority? Is emotional expression more welcome from one we expect to be reluctant to speak of emotion? Are expectations of silence and speech linked to our ideas about gender?

Typographic Excitement

Another sentimental convention is the "typographically excited mode" (Todd 85): liberal use of exclamation points, visually stressed words, and interjections ("Oh!"). How does each poem indicate emphasis, and how does each negotiate its reliance on punctuation to underscore emotional intensity, a method widely considered weak or immature in both prose and poetry?

Because Sigourney's poem contains no such typographic excitements, students might talk about the poem's avoidance of visual emotional cues as an alternative method of constructing voice. How, for example, do Osgood's and Whitman's intensifiers suggest their speakers' proximity to the emotional content? or to the emotion itself, which, in all cases, could be anger as well as sorrow? In what ways is tone registered by the typographic choices of each poem? Is sincerity affected by the understanding that the emotions are stated loudly or quietly?

Notably, while Osgood's speaker completes each thought with an exclamation mark, Whitman's poem places most of the visually stressed words in the bird's song and in the boy's (remembered) internal monologue. Although visually immediate, the excitement—the child-poet's reaction to the bird's song—is doubly removed from the man-poet, who recollects and, as poet, stresses the intensity of the boy's confrontation with death, perhaps to throw into relief the boy's ability to endure quietly his painful transformation into empathetic translator-brother. By comparison, the speaker of "A Mother's Prayer in Illness" may seem to speak impulsively, passionately, even blasphemously. What, then, can be included in the criteria for emotional sincerity: the urgency of utterance (Osgood), the containment of explicit forms of grief (Sigourney), or the persistence and consistency of emotion over time (Whitman and possibly Sigourney)? Do the poems link, oppose, or equate physical and emotional vulnerability?

The Desire for Bonding

Most important, Dobson offers the "ethos" of the sentimental as an "imaginative orientation" in "human connection, both personal and communal, [that] acknowledges the shared devastation of affectional loss" (266); the sentimental's theme is "the desire for bonding" on an emotional plane (267). This third category holds the richest possibilities for cracking the codes of expression in poetry. The very publication of a text presumes or seeks "human connection" (a readership, whether hostile or welcoming), and poetry often expresses loss, absence, or discrepancy between desire and reality. Looking at how readers interpret the poem's "desire for bonding"—what the poem wants from the readers and the demands it places on them—is, in my opinion, key to understanding attendant readings of its emotional import as sentimental (faked, trivial, an imposition) or powerful (real and important). The processes through which these poems move the private emotional experience into the public realm suggest several possible conclusions about the relation between the poem's perceived desire and the poem's claim to literary (and emotional) status. Thus, the contemplation of these poems (and any other poem) ought to address at least two questions: What explanation, implicit or explicit, does the poem provide for its expression of emotional experience? What does its expression require of the reader?

Interestingly, only Sigourney's poem does not provide a specific motive for describing the infant's death, nor does it prescribe an explicit emotional response. By the poem's end, death's callous erasure of the child's beauty and personality becomes a comment on death's ineffectuality against the powers of heaven rather than an invitation to communal grief: "there beamed a smile, / So fixed, so holy . . . / . . . [Death] dared not steal" (lines 12–14). Osgood's poem is a private prayer occasioned by serious illness from a mother to her "Father," insisting that He reconsider His plan to take her from her fragile children. The submission of the private prayer to a public readership can be interpreted as a appeal for sympathy and for judgment of her maternal worth in making such an outrageous request. Whereas Sigourney's poem reconciles the losses witnessed in its first eleven and half lines and therefore requires only agreement (it is consoling that the baby went to heaven) or disagreement (the afterlife is no consolation) from the reader, Osgood's poem, featuring a far more personalized speaker, invites the reader to sift through its complicated attitudes toward God, maternity, the mother's children, and human nature. Sigourney's poem contributes both an account of "shared devastation of affectional loss" and a palliative, potentially "bonding" image of death; Osgood's poem, conversely, risks breaking the social bonds that make maternal crisis a legitimate cause for distress: the mother of this poem prefers the death of her children to her own death but ultimately wishes that they all be spared life in a vicious world.

The meaning and purpose of death are also central to Whitman's poem, but "Out of the Cradle . . ." presents the poet as one who models sensitivity to the world's cruel realities. Unlike the anonymous voice of Sigourney's poem and the mother of Osgood's, Whitman's speaker identifies himself from the beginning as a man and a poet, which serves as an explanation for the public expression of private emotional experiences of the far past. The speaker maintains specialness with the title of poet and establishes distance from the readers he enlists in relating his tearful discovery of compassion, which initiates his manhood and his ascension to poet. The way Whitman's speaker partakes of the "shared devastation of affected loss" seems important: throughout the poem, he speaks to the bird as the boy and to the self as a child. The circuit of compassion, while it extends to the world or nature in an abstract way, is closed, and the poet as translator assigns his own meaning to the experience and, like Sigourney's speaker, his own consolation for the loss and grieving that the poem details. Also like Sigourney's speaker, Whitman's poet gives rather than solicits sympathy. Although the poem implies that great emotional vulnerability is the poet's primary trait, it conducts its own reading of the memory: the poem's self-interpretation authorizes the poem's emotional content. Do the speakers' assignments of meaning to the emotional experience mitigate the sentimental images and topics? Do the literal locations (sickbed, Long Island beach) of the emotional expression affect its authenticity?

Expanding the Context

The concerns and questions clarified by reading nineteenth-century American poetry with attention to how we interpret emotional experiences as important or not extend to contemporary American culture in both academic and popular realms. Without prompting, students involved in conversations central to this lesson begin to recognize over the course of the unit the ways that prefatory material in anthologies present biographical details that direct the reading of a writer's work. The most interesting and fruitful thinking about these literary problems, however, happens when students apply them to their everyday lives as consumers, critics, and social beings.

To conclude the unit on poetry and the sentimental, I ask students to identify devices these poems use to shape or to preempt the reader's judgment of emotional circumstances in other texts and genres. How are representations of personal experience categorized in terms of gender—for example, what makes a movie a chick flick, and what cues or contexts protect films like *Eight Mile* and *Forrest Gump* from the label, despite the abundance in them of emotional conventions typical of sentimentalism? What circumstances have converted near-constant phone contact—a habit that less than ten years ago was shorthand for the frivolity of adolescent girlhood—to become a hip, genderless, and virtually unremarkable extension of self? By insisting that students think through the ways in which assumptions about gender—as well as about race, class, and nationality—shape tastes, values, and experiences, I hope to impress on them the importance of nineteenth-century sentimental poetry. The history and substance of this poetry help us understand whose trouble we care about and why and identify and change attitudes that maintain social and literary hierarchies.

Cheryl Lawson Walker

Sex, Drugs, and Mingling Spirits: Teaching Nineteenth-Century Women Poets

It hasn't always been easy to teach nineteenth-century women's poetry to my students—smart young women in twenty-first-century southern California who know more about life than I did when I was their age. Some have complained that these poems are too distant from them, too alien, but other students have been all too ready to transform themselves into Victorians, without a clue that the world of these women was in important ways different from ours. These responses are problematic in different ways, but they share a failure to connect to history that prevents students from encountering the poetry on anything like its own territory.

I often try to alleviate this difficulty by assigning groups of poems—for example, poems that concern sex, drugs, and the otherworldly, topics that have some resonance with today's youth. It comes as a surprise to many students that women in the nineteenth century wrote passionately about sexuality, that drug use was fairly widespread among women of the middle class, and that religious feeling was beginning to express itself in less doctrinal and more ardently mystical terms. To give students some background about these matters, I have put several historical sources on reserve, assigning individual students to read parts of them and then give brief five-to-ten-minute reports about what they have found. This method has two advantages. The reports put the class on notice that the world of Victorian America was not quite as straight-laced as they might think. Furthermore, the students who have done the outside reading now have an investment in making sure that the poems are interpreted in accordance with the historical record. They are therefore more likely to want to get involved in the discussion.

Before I move to the texts we read, let me make some preliminary observations. The assignments suggested here might best be addressed in one long (two-hour) class or two short (one-hour) classes. My model is the American literature survey, but other kinds of courses can also accommodate these insertions. I have included Emily Dickinson in my groupings, but of course Dickinson's work deserves at least one class of its own. The suggestions I offer are not meant to be in any sense exhaustive. Other poems, other topics, and other historical works would do just as well, but these following clusters have been used successfully. Finally, I usually order the anthology I edited, *American Women Poets of the Nineteenth Century*, so most references in this essay are to this text. But the extracts can sometimes be found elsewhere, and in all cases I provide a few other sources. Dickinson, for example, is not included in my anthology, so her work is always supplementary.

Sex

It is not a bad idea to begin with sex. Despite what used to be said about the prudish Victorians, sex, as we know from many historical sources, was widely discussed in nineteenth-century periodicals, advice books, and literature—and not always negatively. Among social problems, prostitutes and unwed mothers were frequent topics of concern. Unwed mothers were often represented as likely to become prostitutes. Stories of seduction (one might think of the late example of Stephen Crane's *Maggie: A Girl of the Streets*, but one could also cite William Hill Brown's 1789 novel *The Power of Sympathy*) typically focused on a rake who takes advantage of an innocent young girl, causing her downfall while he escapes unscathed. Though much of this literature was moralistic, designed to warn young girls not to risk their reputations, some of it took a quite different tone, providing salacious entertainment for those who were not so interested in upholding bourgeois Victorian standards.

In *Beneath the American Renaissance: The Subversive Imagination in the Age of Emerson and Melville*, David S. Reynolds, exploring the "subversive" genre of sensationalist literature about sex, writes:

> Although reliable primary evidence of antebellum sexual habits is frustratingly scarce, enough evidence survives to explode the long-standing myth that there was an all-powerful cult of domesticity that governed daily behavior and kept America a prudish, highly moralistic culture. True, such a conservative outlook was promoted in popular ladies' magazines and etiquette books. But the cult of domesticity was itself, like conventional fiction, an ideological response to reading habits that were far more inclined to the scabrous and illicit than is commonly supposed. (211)

Students who read the chapter "The Erotic Imagination" in Reynolds's book will discover that the 1840s, a formative period for many women poets in my anthology, saw the full expression of many anti-Victorian attitudes and practices. "In this decade," Reynolds claims, "the awakening recognition of sexual desire was waging a titanic struggle against the residual repressiveness of the Puritan conscience" (222).

Popular literature, such as that written by George Thompson, focused on women's powerful sex drive. In his nearly one hundred novels, women are portrayed as nymphomaniacs; adulteresses; and partakers of many varieties of illicit sex, including incest. George Lippard's "voyeur style" made his novel *The Quaker City* infamous as "the immoral work of the age" (216). Yet he had a large readership. His heroines, the "animalistic" Dora Livingstone (217) and the virginal Mary Arlington, are treated to highly suggestive descriptions filled with sexually charged metaphors. Both writers contested the Romantic view of women as purer and more morally elevated than their male counterparts. In fact, if anything, the women in this popular and subversive literature were made to seem fiercer in their sexual demands than the men.

Though cult-of-domesticity literature—in which women are presented as pious, pure, domestic, and submissive—was also widely available in the nineteenth century, the very fact that so many advice manuals focused on the negative consequences of women giving vent to their passions suggests that female purity was in large part a patriarchal construct designed to keep women in their place rather than a generally accurate description. In 1846 Mary Gove Nichols, a sexual reformer, gave a widely publicized speech in which she declared that many women engaged in masturbation because they found it more satisfying (and safer) than relations with men.

Helen Lefkowitz Horowitz's *Re-reading Sex: Battles over Sexual Knowledge and Suppression in Nineteenth-Century America* is a more carefully researched history of nineteenth-century attitudes, and it picks up where Reynolds leaves off. Less interested in literary works, Horowitz deals more with social movements, such as the free-love crusade of Victoria Woodhull. Her study of obscenity trials over the course of the century allows her to chart changes in attitudes toward sexuality. She too finds the century multivalent in its attitudes about sex, she too notes the popularity of erotic materials and racy books, and she too mulls over the concern with masturbation in medical handbooks and obscenity trials. As more than one social historian has noted, public discourse became more repressive after the Civil War and "legal suppression, especially after 1873, had a powerful effect on what could be published about sex at that time" (14). Students would do well to read the introduction and then read around in the rest of Horowitz's book in order to find material specifically relevant to the poems.

I found two chapters particularly useful: "Placing Sex at the Core of Being" and "Sex Talk in the Open."

Karen Lystra's chapter "Secrecy, Sin, and Sexual Enticement" in *Searching the Heart: Women, Men, and Romantic Love in Nineteenth-Century America* also confirms the appetitive nature of female sexuality. She writes:

> Contrary to stereotype, American advisers from enthusiasts to restrictionists recognized the sexual appetites of women as well as men. Though post–Civil War sexual and moral advisers were much more explicit than their antebellum colleagues, there was considerable unanimity in guidebooks through the Victorian period that both men and women had a natural sexual urge. (102)

Lystra does caution, however, that in some of the most prominent medical manuals, women were represented as "less passionate than men, slower to be aroused, less knowledgeable, or shyer" (117).

Material from these historical sources can provide interesting and helpful background for the study of a cluster of nineteenth-century women's poems about sexual desire. The poems I often assign here are Dickinson's "Wild nights—Wild nights!" (poem 269) and "In winter in my room" (poem 1742), Frances Osgood's "The Cocoa-Nut Tree," Ella Wheeler Wilcox's "The Tiger," Julia Ward Howe's "The Soul-Hunter," and especially the poems of Rose Terry Cooke—for example, "A Story," "Captive," "Monotropa," "Semele," and "In the Hammock." Except for Dickinson's poems, all these are contained in *American Women Poets of the Nineteenth Century.*

Howe's "The Soul-Hunter" is a powerful poem whose imagery may well have influenced Crane's portrayal of Maggie's fate at the hands of a monstrous figure who "hunts so late, so dark." In any case, it, like Cooke's "A Story," corresponds in many ways to the monitory works that were addressed to young women who might be inclined to listen to the blandishments of a seducer. "The Soul-Hunter" is specifically addressed to a "maiden," and the poet tells her that she should drown herself, throw herself into the fire, or lock herself living in the tomb before listening to this evil man "who lures thee like a bird." It is impossible to miss the sexual overtones of the threat posed by this figure:

> He hath such promise, silver sweet,
> Such silken hands, such fiery feet,
> That, where his look has charmed the prey,
> His swift-winged passion forces way,
>   Who hunts so late, so dark.
>   (C. Walker, *American Women Poets* 152)

Whatever it is that he hides under his cloak, it suggests the potent virility that the poem presents in such terrifying terms. The poem therefore accords well with Dickinson's fantasy "In winter in my room" and Wilcox's "The Tiger."

Dickinson's poem is particularly responsive to Freudian interpretation. The worm, "pink lank and warm," becomes a snake "In feature as the worm before / But ringed with power." When the snake "to a Rhythm *Slim* / Secreted in his Form / As Patterns swim / Projected him," the speaker runs as fast as she can in the opposite direction (*Poems*, poem 1742). Given the fear of sexuality that some nineteenth-century texts seemed meant to evoke in young women, it is not hard to understand why Dickinson herself might find the fantasy of male sexuality so disturbing (it has been suggested that her proclivities were mainly lesbian [see M. Smith, "Belle" and *Rowing*; Bennett, "Pea"), though it must be said that in both the famous "man of noon" letter (*Letters*, letter 93) and in "In winter in my room" the specter of male lust is also strangely attractive.

Some poems reflect this ambivalence, whereas others seem blithely unconcerned about the power dynamic that made and still makes heterosexual relationships different and more dangerous for females than for males. Osgood, for example, gives us the overtly phallic "Cocoa-Nut Tree" as an enticement, "With its stately shaft, and its verdant crown, / And its fruit in clusters drooping down" (C. Walker, *American Women*

Poets 111). As I discuss in more detail in my book *The Nightingale's Burden* (40–41), like the Indian maiden who is imagined as lying beneath it, the speaker is clearly attracted to this symbol of male eroticism: "O, the lovely, the free, / The cocoa-nut tree, / Is the tree of all trees for me!" (C. Walker, *American Women Poets* 111).

Cooke (whom I overlooked in *The Nightingale's Burden*) offers some of the most salacious fare, and it is anybody's guess how she got away with the quite un-Victorian sentiments expressed by her speakers while remaining such a pillar of respectability. For example, "Semele" is striking both because it is unusually passionate and because its torrid address is so openly antimoral. One could assign a student to research the Greek myth, in which Semele, who has been badly advised by a disguised Hera, asks Zeus to appear to her in all his radiant divinity; when he does so, she is consumed by the fire of his lightning.

Cooke's "Semele" differs from the Greek version because she already seems to know the consequences of her choice:

> Burn, as the leaping fire
>   A martyr's shroud;
> Burn, like an Indian pyre,
>   With music fierce and loud.
> Come Power! Love calls thee,—come, with all the god endowed.
> (266–67)

Though one might well discuss the influence of literary Romanticism on this poet, the poem is better understood in the context of nineteenth-century reformist medical literature in which women are granted sexual appetites or in Reynolds's context of the popular sensationalism that gave prominence to the lustful woman. In this demon-lover poem much of the imagery is sexually charged: "persuade the bud to flower," "come, with all the god endowed," "in dread and glory rise," "the altar waits thy torch" (266–67). One could even call this work, in contrast to the much more benign "Cocoa-Nut Tree," a poem of satanic phallus worship.

Cooke married the much younger Rollin Cooke: she was forty-six, he thirty. The marriage seems to have brought an end to her experiments with sexually subversive literature, yet only a few years earlier she had published in the *Galaxy*, a respectable journal, a poem entitled "In the Hammock" that was a startling departure from conventional middle-class mores. The speaker of the poem is swinging in a hammock and thinking about her love life. "I'm a hang-bird in her nest, / All with scarlet blossoms drest, / Swinging where the winds blow free" (275). This young Latina contrasts herself with her more religious acquaintances, who spend their time in church. Though she has plenty of lovers—seven are tall; two are crooked, rich, and old—there is one with cold blue eyes who attracts her the most, possibly because (though small) he is the most indifferent. Obviously influenced both by the popular genre of dramatic monologue and by the new works coming from the West by such writers as Bret Harte and Ina Coolbrith, "In the Hammock" tells a racy story in a delicate but innovative form. Its heroine, who receives no moral indictment, explicit or implicit, from the poet, toys with ten lovers, mocks the Bridegroom provided by the convent, and fantasizes an illicit encounter with an earthy lover. She is indolent, self-indulgent, and unrepentant. In her scarlet regalia, she swings away in very immodest fashion. The ghost of masturbation hovers near: her cheek is pale, her eyes shine.

There will be plenty to talk about if students are asked to provide historical background about attitudes toward women and sexuality in the nineteenth century. This background provides a good basis for discussing both conventional and unconventional poems. Cooke's "A Story" is conventional: it offers a moral fable in which a lovely flower (a gentian) has an encounter with a bee (a conventional figure for the lustful male). She is foolishly responsive to his entreaties and then deserted by him. Dickinson's bee poems, such as "Did the harebell loose her girdle" (poem 134), "Could I but ride indefinite" (poem 1056), and especially "A bee his burnished carriage" (poem 1351), provide excellent opportunities for comparison.

The range of attitudes in these poems about sexuality should help students resist the temptation to generalize about the past. It should be possible to get them to talk about their own attitudes, which are also likely to represent a range. Professors who have read some social history can provide contextual material to keep the discussion on track.

Drugs

While sexuality (both sublimated and overt) is an important issue in many nineteenth-century women's poems, drug use is much less central. Nevertheless, there are some interesting works that do focus on this matter. It will come as a surprise to many students that most of those addicted to opiates in the nineteenth century were women, many of them from the middle class. In *Substance and Shadow: Women and Addiction in the*

United States, Stephen Kendall writes, "For much of the twentieth century addiction has been known as a 'man's disease,' yet the majority of morphine and opium addicts in the nineteenth century were women" (14).

David Courtwright claims that before 1900 "opium and morphine addiction was primarily an upper-class and middle-class phenomenon" (40), though Kendall argues to the contrary, that the physicians who treated such women tended to serve a more advantaged clientele. In any case, the quantitative data that we have available from the nineteenth century give us a picture of broad use among the privileged classes. In 1871 Alonzo Calkins described the typical addict as a high-toned lady "idly lolling upon her velvety fauteuil and vainly trying to cheat the lagging hours that intervene ere the 'clockwork tintinnabulum' shall sound the hour for opera or whist" (qtd. in Kendall 16). Though some women became addicted to opiates because of medical conditions for which such drugs were prescribed, boredom seems to have been a crucial catalyst for women seeking an escape from their humdrum lives. One anonymous lady admitted:

> I am the last woman in the world to make excuses for my acts, but you don't know what morphine means to some of us, modern women without professions, without beliefs. Morphine makes life possible. It adds to truth a dream. What more does religion do? (qtd. in Courtwright 59)

Several comments might be made about this set of statements. In the first place, students should be aware that in the nineteenth century such drugs were legal for a long time, so this woman is not confessing to a crime. Even after drugs became regulated in some states (in the 1870s), it was easy enough for women to obtain a prescription, as Lily Bart does in Edith Wharton's *House of Mirth*. Nervous women were given morphine with nearly the same frequency that women today are prescribed Prozac. Secondly, this anonymous woman comes close to admitting that her desire for drugs comes from boredom. She has nothing to claim her attention, neither a job nor a passion for religion. Finally, she vacillates between suggesting that she has her morphine addiction under control (unlike other women she could name) and calling herself "morphine mad." She claims to have enough will power to keep herself from going beyond her daily allowance. But Lily Bart, who dies from an overdose in the end, also makes this claim.

This woman likely belonged to the upper middle class, but women in rural areas, not so well off, isolated and lonely, also sometimes found relief by taking drugs such as laudanum. In 1872 F. E. Oliver published a report concerning the drug use of Massachusetts women, claiming that they had recourse to opium because they were

> doomed, often, to a life of disappointment . . . and in the smaller and more remote towns, not infrequently, to utter seclusion, deprived of all wholesome social diversion . . . opium being discreetly selected as the safest and most agreeable remedy. (qtd. in Kendall 16)

Though prostitutes were another group who used drugs, the women who frequented opium dens, along with "the Chinaman, the laborer, and 'longshoreman,' the young man in society" (18), were usually women of high standing.

In his more statistical account of drug use by women in the nineteenth century, Courtwright tells us that housewives constituted the largest group of female addicts. Most became addicted between the ages of 25 and 45 and chose opiates because they could be used at home; that way others, even husbands, would not know about their secret vice. Opium and morphine addicts were disproportionately white, native born, and Southern, though drug use was also well-known in New England, Philadelphia, Chicago, and among the Chinese in the West. Courtwright estimates that between 150,000 and 300,000 women were using opiates at any given time during most of the nineteenth century. Furthermore, he asserts:

> The majority of nineteenth-century female addicts were married and therefore stayed at home. Unmarried female addicts were observed among domestics, teachers, actresses, and especially prostitutes. Another type, mentioned as early as 1832, was the harried society lady, who downed opium or morphine to steady her nerve and enhance her wit. (40–41)

The material on women and drug addiction in the nineteenth century should help students find a context for such works as Maria White Lowell's "An Opium Fantasy" and Mary Tucker Lambert's "The Opium-Eater," both in *American Women Poets of the Nineteenth Century.* (Although Lambert is included in the Schomburg Library collection of black women's poetry, recent criticism has discovered that she was not the author of the poems included there; the actual author is Mary Eliza Perine Tucker Lambert, who was born in Alabama in 1838 and educated in New

York.) After her father and first husband lost their property in the Civil War, Lambert returned to New York, successfully selling her poetry and journalism (see J. Gray, "Passing"). "The Opium-Eater" clearly exemplifies the relief from the misery of their lives that some women found in opium. Its first-person narration contains no moralistic commentary about this practice, although in the second stanza the speaker raises a question about "inward sin":

Life's pathway to me is dreary,
I am ill, and cold, and weary;
Would my lonely walk were done,
And my heavenly race begun.

Once all things to me were bright,
Things that now seem dark as night:
Is the darkness all within?
Dark without from inward sin?
(C. Walker, *American Women Poets* 310)

The answer implied is no, since the speaker points to age; to problems with her feet (corns), head, and teeth; as well as to her dismal prospect for the future.

This section, however, is preceded by the phrase "before taking a dose." The second part of the poem—"after taking a dose"—describes the transformation effected by the drug:

Ah! now I sit in bowers of bliss,
Soothed by an angel's balmy kiss!
Delicious languor o'er me stealing
Is now my only sense of feeling. (311)

Each of her past miseries now reappears in a different guise. Her gray hair "is not so very grey," her teeth cause her no distress, and even her corns are nothing to make a fuss about. Students will no doubt see a degree of false optimism in the last line of the poem ("I know I'll never weep again" [311]) and may well want to talk about the insidious sense of confidence that attracts people even today to the roseate high of cocaine or ecstasy.

Like "The Opium-Eater," Lowell's "An Opium Fantasy" puts more emphasis on the pleasures of opium than on its harmful effects:

Soft hangs the opiate in the brain,
And lulling soothes the edge of pain,

Till harshest sound, far off or near,
Sings floating in its mellow sphere.
(C. Walker, *American Women Poets* 196)

Because Maria White was married to James Russell Lowell, we know more about her than we do about Lambert. She was well educated and grew up in an intellectual, middle-class family. Her life was far from easy, however, and she died at the age of 32 after having seen each of her four children die before her. Though Maria was active in several nineteenth-century reform movements, including abolition and temperance, she does not seem to equate the use of opium with intemperate behavior. If anything, Lambert raises more questions about it than she does. One suspects that Maria's ill health may have drawn her to the use of opium.

In any case, Lowell's poem demonstrates a more sophisticated use of language than Lambert's. There are memorable lines and images that may have influenced Dickinson, as I have argued elsewhere ("Dickinson" 189–93). Like Dickinson, Lowell renders her experience impressionistically:

What wakes me from my heavy dream?
Or am I still asleep?
Those long and soft vibrations seem
A slumberous charm to keep. (196)

In the context of opium use, "those long and soft vibrations" could easily refer to the drug experience itself, but since Lowell mentions the owl as the prince of poppies in later stanzas, they might also refer to the call of the owl. The most memorable lines are those in the third stanza, where time seems to be stopped and distance (space) unrolls "Like silver balls, that, softly dropped, / Ring into golden bowls" (197). Here Lowell captures the disorientation that drugs often induce; at the same time she creates a mysteriously compelling analogy that carries us beyond the physical effects of the opium into the realm of the aesthetic.

Mingling Spirits

Nineteenth-century women poets wrote many passionate poems about the convergence of human and divine energies, some quite mystical and others more traditional. Since many students in my classes have an interest in religion, I often include explicitly religious poems. Indeed, all the poems considered in this essay are in some sense about ecstasy—emotional, sexual, narcotic, spiritual—so one might also offer a section on nontraditional religious expression and its foundation in Catholic, evangelical, liberal, Jewish, and Native American cultural contexts. A selection of poems that feature such expression might include the following: Elizabeth Oakes Smith's "Strength from the Hills," Rose Terry Cooke's "Schemhammphorasch" and "An End," Emma Lazarus's "The New Ezekiel," E. Pauline Johnson's "Shadow River, Muskoka," Louise Imogen Guiney's "Borderlands," and Ella Wheeler Wilcox's "As by Fire." In her anthology *Nineteenth-Century American Women Writers*, Karen Kilcup lists works by topic, including "Literature of the Spirit," and these readings also might help students develop a sense of context.

The two books that I sometimes place on reserve are Catherine L. Albanese's *America: Religions and Religion* and T. J. Jackson Lears's *No Place of Grace: Antimodernism and the Transformation of American Culture.* Albanese's chapter "Original Manyness: Native American Traditions" will help students understand some of the background to Johnson's poem. I find that many students are interested in Native American culture, but Albanese is also a good resource for American Judaism (see Cooke's "Schemhammphorasch" and Lazarus's "The New Ezekiel") and liberal religious traditions such as those that influenced Oakes Smith and Wilcox. Lears is helpful as a background to the work of Guiney. His chapters "Medieval Vitality: The Erotic Union of Sacred and Profane" and "The Medieval Unconscious: Therapy and Protest" are useful for a consideration of the poems by Guiney and Wilcox. The remarks he makes, earlier in his book, about Guiney's militaristic vitality are not particularly relevant here.

Several of these poems are written in the voice of a woman who feels what Lears calls a "feverish yearning" for an encounter with the divine (161). Oakes Smith perfectly embodies the nineteenth-century woman Lears describes who longs to be freed from the tasteless actual. She had a strong mystical streak and believed that she could sense events before they happened. In 1887 she spent a year as a practicing minister to an independent congregation in Canastoga, New York. Her "Strength from the Hills," though it does not emphasize its religious underpinnings, can be read as part of the liberal Protestant movement that sought to breathe new life into the Puritan spirit of American culture. It recalls the Psalms, especially 95 and 121 ("I will lift up mine eyes unto the hills, from whence cometh my help" [King James Vers.]). Oakes Smith claims that in the hills

God comes near, cleansing and reinvigorating the spirit that feels stagnant in bourgeois society:

Yet come unto the hills, the old strong hills,
And leave the stagnant plain;
Come to the gushing of the newborn rills
As sing they to the main;

And thou with denizens of power shall dwell,
Beyond demeaning care;
Composed upon his rock, mid storm and fell,
The eagle shall be there.
(C. Walker, *American Women Poets* 76–77)

According to Albanese, "One early sign of what liberalism would come to embody" was the universalist transcendentalism that clearly influenced Oakes Smith and Lazarus. Albanese writes:

> For the Transcendentalists, intuition—the inner voice—became the key to the discovery of revelation; and nature, as the sacred space that evoked the inner perception of truth, was likewise privileged. Hence, both the inner space of the mind and the outer space of nature suggested for them the presence of a God who was immanent. (129)

Guiney's "Borderlands" also imagines the convergence of human and divine energies as occurring in nature, but her short poem, written in the 1890s, exemplifies a far different strain in nineteenth-century poetry, that of Catholic mysticism. It imagines a walk in the evening that seduces with "a too divine alluring":

Yet in the valley,
At the turn of the orchard alley,
When a wild aroma touched me in the moist and moveless air,
Like breath indeed from out Thee, or as airy vesture round Thee,
Then was it I went faintly, for fear I had nearly found Thee,
O Hidden, O Perfect, O Desired! O first and final Fair!
(C. Walker, *American Women Poets* 405)

A Catholic and an amateur medievalist, Guiney found an audience among those who looked to Catholicism (and medieval Catholic mysticism) for the intensity of feeling that Protestantism seemed to lack. Lears describes this late-nineteenth-century pursuit of psychic regeneration as highly eroticized. It especially drew female adherents: "Impatient with the stodginess of bourgeois virtue, many Americans imagined an ecstatic medieval piety—soaring to summits of spiritual exaltation, dropping to abysses of self-abasement, burning always with a white-hot flame" (161).

Wilcox's "As by Fire" is by contrast far more Puritan, especially in its emphasis on spiritual perfection as achieved by will or, as she puts it, "what we have resisted." Yet Wilcox, too, like the medieval vitalists whom Lears describes, uses the imagery of fire. At first, this fire is associated with her body: "This vigorous frame with healthful fervor burning" wages war with the spirit. However, in the end the image is elevated to the ranks of spirituality:

> The very fire which seems sometimes so cruel
> Is the white light, that shows me my own strength.
> A furnace, fed by the divinest fuel
> It may become at length.
> (C. Walker, *American Women Poets* 346)

Lears's "white-hot flame" seems especially relevant here.

One could play Guiney's vitalist "Borderlands" off against the more Protestant poem of spiritual renewal by Wilcox. But another late-nineteenth-century poem that provides similarity (in its themes of spirituality and nature) but also difference (in its cultural context) is Johnson's "Shadow River, Muskoka," recently republished in Kilcup's *Native American Women's Writing* anthology. It begins:

> A stream of tender gladness,
> Of filmy sun, and opal tinted skies;
> Of warm midsummer air that lightly lies
> In mystic rings,
> Where softly swings
> The music of a thousand wings
> That almost tones to sadness. (217)

As Kilcup points out, Johnson, of Mohawk descent, drew from both white and Indian literary traditions: "With a superb family library, well-educated and relatively affluent parents, and famous orator grandfather, Johnson was able to acquire a broad understanding of traditional English and Iroquois literature" (55). Students should find the discussion of Native American religious traditions in Albanese helpful. But in addition to representing Indian beliefs about the natural world (the "mystic rings" of summer air, for example), this poem is reminiscent of the work of Algernon Charles Swinburne, a British poet very popular in the late nineteenth century. The languorous sensuality, the multiple sequential rhymes, and the use of expanding and contracting line lengths are all Swinburnian.

Judaism in America also needs to be explored in a transnational context. Both Lazarus's "The New Ezekiel" and Cooke's "Schemhammphorasch" (in Axelrod, Roman, and Travisano) address the rites and traditions of the Jews as they were conserved in the Diaspora. Albanese's chapter "Israel in a Promised Land: Jewish Religion and Peoplehood" emphasizes the conservative nature of Jewish practices as a defensive strategy against threats to the community. But she also suggests powerful connections between Jews and Americans, who saw themselves as people of a covenant, and between Jews and Native Americans, who were sometimes seen as descendants of the lost tribes of Israel.

"Schemhammphorasch," as the anthology note tells us (Axelrod, Roman, and Travisano 511–14), stands for the mystical name of God that cannot be spoken except by the angels. Though a Congregationalist, Cooke here longs for the key to the universe that the Talmud says was given by the angel Michael to Pali and by Pali to Moses:

> If I could read Schemhammphorasch,
> My brain would burn with such a fire
> As lights the awful cherubim;
> My heart would burst with woe and ire,
> My flesh would shrivel and expire;
> Yea, God himself grow far and dim. (513)

But the speaker admits that she lacks the capacity to incorporate such knowledge, "For could I live, or love, or pray, / If I could read Schemhammphorasch?" (514). Thus she finds the mystical traditions of Judaism both tempting and intimidating. But she is not above appropriating some of its ideas for her own work in a manner familiar enough to us now but much more ecumenical than typical Congregationalism of her day.

"The New Ezekiel," by Emma Lazarus, also situates itself in Jewish culture, but Lazarus was born into a Sephardic Jewish family, and her poem expresses, unlike Cooke's, a personal sense of wrongs committed against Jews. Though she wrote, "Until we are all free, we are none of us free. Wherever we are free, we are at home" (C. Walker, *American Women Poets* 333), "The New Ezekiel" can be read as an early document of Zionism, dreaming as it does of Israel as the true Jewish home:

> The Spirit is not dead, proclaim the word,
> Where lay dead bones, a host of armed men stand!

I ope your graves, my people, saith the Lord,
And I shall place you living in your land. (340)

This poem (and others by Lazarus) should appeal to students who long for poetry as a passionate expression of political views. People may also wish to discuss the poem from a contemporary perspective that includes both Jewish and Palestinian claims. It could be juxtaposed with Lazarus's "In the Jewish Synagogue at Newport" and Longfellow's "The Jewish Cemetery at Newport."

Compare and Contrast: Is This Enough?

I do not believe that comparing and contrasting are enough. Clearly there is not time in one semester (let alone a quarter) to provide adequate context for reading these poems and to discuss their language, imagery, and meanings. But this difficulty is no excuse for ignoring history entirely. Through women's history, national history, cultural history, and literary history students can be encouraged to see poetry as one form of representation that carried significant weight in the nineteenth century, more weight than it carries now. Giving students some sense of these issues invites them to think in more complex ways about both poetry and the past. If you are planning to assign a research paper due at the end of the term, you can suggest that students investigate one of these poets and her cultural context in greater detail. All three of the anthologies I have suggested here include contextual material as well as bibliographies of works that are appropriate for such research.

We are always pressed for time, making the best of a bad bargain, hinting at some things, passing over others too quickly, and never fully covering all those issues we meant to make clear to our students. Adding some history, however inadequate, to the literary conversation encourages students to reflect on the ways in which we are all historically constituted, and this contextualization should make them more aware of the similarities and differences between us and our forebears. In the end, the poem of history, endlessly revisable and revised, is no less interesting than the poem of art.

Gregory Byrd
and Nan Morelli-White

Teaching Nineteenth-Century American Poetry in the Community College

Community college students, overwhelmingly, work full-time jobs and take a full-time class load. Time is of primary importance to them, and anything that does not command their attention will be pragmatically relegated to the "do later" pile in a decision that must consider work, other classes, family, housework, and social life. These students are often older than most college and university students. Saint Petersburg College, where we teach, has recently begun to offer bachelor's degrees in education, nursing, and technology; but the institution's primary mission is still to provide general education courses to undergraduate students and lifelong learners in the community. Our average student is a twenty-eight-year-old woman, though many are in their late teens and early twenties. Many of our returning students come to class hungry to learn. Some are beginning a new phase of life after a divorce or after their children have moved out. Some are beginning a career and find that a college degree will help them get ahead. Some are the best and brightest who, most often because of financial difficulty or family obligations, choose to remain in this area rather than head off to a state college or university.

One of the greatest challenges for teaching anything in a community college, and nineteenth-century American poetry in particular, is the open-door policy. While students must either pass minimum competency exams or enroll in remedial courses in order to take college-level courses, a community college instructor cannot take for granted that students know anything about poetry or about nineteenth-century American history. Community college students know quite a bit, but their knowledge may not be in the content area of American literature or history. A typical second-semester freshman composition course or American literature survey class will contain a great diversity of students whose varied needs must all be considered.

A lack of historical knowledge means that students have little or no context for the poems they read. Even worse, as James Loewen states in *Lies My Teacher Told Me*, their historical knowledge may be biased by class, race, or gender issues, inaccurate by omission or simply wrong. Combine this problem with the canonicity that is enforced by textbooks and occasionally by departments, and it becomes difficult for an instructor to teach American poetry of the nineteenth century in a meaningful way. A logical response to these problems might be to take a New Critical approach and to interpret poems as entities in and of themselves. This method avoids the problem of students' ignorance of history but does nothing to correct it. We prefer to see poetry as existing in a web of culture—connected to history, art, photography, music, and politics. One helpful approach to teaching American poetry of this period is therefore to ground it in the American culture(s) of the nineteenth century, not in order to place it in a museum with other artifacts but to show that this body (or bodies) of poetry is not outdated (as students may initially think) but current and relevant.

Sex, love, war, depression, greed, and disenfranchisement are not unique to the twenty-first century. They are all themes quite relevant to nineteenth-century America and may be used as the basis for approaching that era's poetry. We have selected four options for teaching nineteenth-century American poetry that were successful with our students in courses including composition, American literature, and women's literature. Gregory Byrd has used student presentations and the techniques described in the sections below on the Civil War and Native Americans; Nan Morelli-White has used the approach described in the section on sentimental poetry by women.

Student Presentations

Each of my students must sign up early in the semester to give a five-minute presentation on a writer, a movement, or a topic on our syllabus. This short presentation may lay the groundwork for the student's later research paper. On the days when we discuss a topic or writer, the student responsible for the presentation must hand out a page of notes marking the highlights of his or her talk. This talk must connect the literature to the author, time, and culture. The student then turns in a short essay of about two pages, a written version of the talk. This presentation assignment gives the student an important role in the class, allows each student to contribute something, enables students to practice speaking skills, and helps move the class discussion forward. I purposefully make the assignment count little—maybe 5% of the total grade—to remove anxiety and allow students to focus on the research. They become very interested in their chosen topic and enjoy the position of expert on it. At the end of the class, students have one handout from each of their peers to use as notes for writing papers or studying for exams, and the presenters have already done some research. Students may use the board, the World Wide Web, *PowerPoint* presentations, or any other sort of multimedia approach they choose, but they are only required to create handouts.

Student presentations decenter the classroom by moving the locus of knowledge, if only for a few minutes, from the instructor to the students. Such decentering requires students to become purveyors of knowledge as well as consumers of it. They must overcome any learned passivity in order to perform well in front of their peers, and their peers as well as the instructor are their audience for their presentation. I keep track of the requirements of the presentation as they are speaking to make sure they have answered the major questions (how is the writer typical or atypical of the period, what are the basic elements of the movement, etc.). If student presenters fail to address any of those required points, I ask about them in the question-and-answer period following the presentation.

After a few presentations, the class (and usually the presenters) anticipate these questions, and the class will raise them. As the semester progresses, students will also begin to make connections between the topic presented and earlier poems, poets, and movements. They might ask such questions as, "So how do you make sense of Dickinson's writing in a style so different from that of Sigourney?" Student presenters may or may not have happened on information that allows them to respond intelligently to such a question. If they respond successfully, they become more confident. If the question is too difficult for them, I either take it up myself or throw it open to the class. Of course, the class might ask more pedestrian questions, such as, "How did she die?" or "Was she married?," but any discussion that allows presenters to display their understanding is beneficial, and any interested discussion of the poets and poems provides a helpful starting place for approaching the poet, poems, or topic for the day.

Instructors are well advised to organize a class visit to the library based on this assignment. A good librarian can tailor a library visit to the specific sorts of sources students will need. This strategy is particularly important for a body of students who are not strong researchers (perhaps in an American literature survey or second-semester freshman composition class). Once students know where to find the information (appropriate library databases, the PS area of the reference section, and specific works) they will feel more at ease doing the research, asking questions of the librarian, and completing a good assignment. To prevent them from obtaining all their sources via the Web, I require them to use at least one specialized reference work, one book, and one Web site.

A presentation topic might be women's poetry, protest poetry, poetry about slavery, Romanticism, or working-class poetry; but any topic will work that fits into the particular class. I tell my students that their presentations help us understand the context for the poems we are reading, and I write students' names into the course calendar beside the topic on which they will present. As an example, one student recently gave a presentation on political poetry and focused on poetry about slavery. Her presentation opened the door to discussions of Henry Wadsworth Longfellow's "The Slave's Dream," Sarah Louisa Forten's "The Slave" and "My Country," and Phillis Wheatley's "On Being Brought from Africa to America." Although Wheatley is not a nineteenth-century poet, students were able to see poetry about slavery as a dialogue across temporal, class, and ethnic divisions. Another student's presentation, on Julia Moore, allowed students to laugh a little (the student misread her notes, saying "one of Julia Moore's most pathetic books" instead of "one of Julia Moore's most popular books"). This student's reading of the criticism of Moore, a popular and successful poet, as a hack led the class to a discussion of taste and value in nineteenth-century poetry and prepared us well for an in-depth discussion of sentimental poetry.

Instructors should be comfortable with occasionally turning over a small part of a class to students and not feel threatened if students offer something new about a poet or poem. Student presentations add energy to a class and give confidence. The only caveat is to be sure to structure the assignment carefully so that presentations do not stray from the overall class design.

Making the Civil War Real

I begin by asking my students to tell me the dates of the Civil War. Buffs in the group might know them. Often, though, I get guesses ranging from 1776 to 1961–65. When I ask students to list the reasons for the war, everyone knows this one: slavery. It may not be the wrong answer, but it is far too simplistic, not accounting for the amount of damage and death in the war or for the complex politics of westward expansion. Students' experience of this period are vague memories of Stephen Crane's *The Red Badge of Courage* or of a dozen TV miniseries on the Civil War. With luck, a few might have seen Ken Burns's *The Civil War* series on PBS, but I do not count on it. Their views are often ossified in terms of how people felt about the war: the North wanted slavery to end and the Union to endure; the South wanted slavery to endure and the Union to end. By using Web-based materials and a selection of poems about the Civil War, an instructor may give this frequently misunderstood period a face and may focus on the use of poetry both to chronicle and to protest the war.

Herman Melville is a good place to begin. Students often know him only as the author of *Moby-Dick*, and they tend to find the candor and clarity of his *Battle-Pieces* (in *Collected Poems*) refreshing and helpful. "The Portent" and "Misgivings" give students ample opportunity to practice with metaphor while helping them understand America's prewar mood. I discuss "The March into Virginia" in the context of Melville as both observer and protester. "A Utilitarian View of the Monitor's Fight" anticipates the detachment of the modernist era and the First World War and echoes the impersonality of the industrial revolution.

Walt Whitman was both an observer and a critic of the war, and his position as a pacifist may connect with student nostalgia about the 1960s and raise the question of nonviolent participation in war as an American tradition. (In the American Revolution, Quakers tended the wounded on both sides but did not fight.) Where Melville describes the impersonal, Whitman connects deeply with the personal, as students see in "Vigil Strange." "The Wound-Dresser" presents a view of the Civil War lacking even the little amount of excitement of "Vigil Strange." Both of these poems work very well together with the *Selected Civil War Photographs* online collection of the Library of Congress's *American Memory* site. The availability of a projector attached to a computer enables me to select the most appropriate photographs to leave on the screen as the class discusses the poems; after the discussion I often ask students to point out any differences or similarities between the poems and what they see on the screen.

In order to establish a contrast to the stark realism of Whitman and Melville, I assign John Greenleaf Whittier's "Barbara Frietchie" and Julia Ward Howe's "Battle Hymn of the Republic" (P. Bennett, *Nineteenth-Century American Women Poets* 85). I have students read these poems aloud, either in groups or to the class and then ask which view (Whittier's or Howe's, Melville's or Whitman's) is more accurate. The discussion can easily lead into questions of patriotism versus realism. Whenever I talk about war poems, I always ask first if there are any veterans in the room and then make use of them as experts on battle and soldiering. This is a good way to draw them into the discussion and to show respect for their service. It also makes a strong connection between 150-year-old poems and a person sitting in the classroom.

The Indian Question

One of the biggest misunderstandings students have about the nineteenth century in America is the role of Native Americans: how they were treated and how they treated others. Students may have heard of the Trail of Tears but probably not of the Cherokee removal; many do not know that Congress debated the removal of the Cherokee from Georgia and the Carolinas as it would any other legal bill. Students may be unaware that thousands of people—such as the poet Lydia Sigourney—appealed to Congress not to divest the Cherokee of their land. Sigourney's poems, such as "The Cherokee Mother" and "Indian Names" (P. Bennett, *Nineteenth-Century American Women Poets* 7–8, 12–13) allow students to see the treatment of Native Americans in a new way. An instructor might also consider having students read from Longfellow's *Song of Hiawatha* and compare his and Sigourney's approaches. Because I teach nineteenth-century poetry as part of the American Literature I survey, I also compare Sigourney and Longfellow with Benjamin Franklin's essay "Remarks concerning the Savages of North America," with Mary

Rowlandson's narrative, and sometimes with James Fenimore Cooper's *The Last of the Mohicans.* For our visually literate students, viewing Edward Curtis's later photographs provides an additional impetus for discussion with a focus on representation.

One difficulty with teaching Native American–related poetry of this period is that while Sigourney and Longfellow write with passion about Native Americans, much Native American oral poetry had not been translated or printed in mainstream publications when the Cherokee removal debates occurred in the early nineteenth century. I foreground the discussion of representation by asking students why there was so little Native American poetry then. Students should remember that Native American cultures transmitted poetry and narrative orally. As a result—with a few exceptions, for instance, the published poems of John Rollin Ridge, which sometimes reflected a white style and perspective—Native American poems were not commonly written in or translated into English until the end of the century. I remind students that the lack of a written language was evidence used by some whites to show that Native Americans were uncivilized. Ironically, the Cherokee who were forced from their homelands had created a written language well beforehand. Reading some of the prose Cherokee memorials may allow students to see how well the Cherokee represented their side of the removal debate. Students respond well to the discussion of poetry about Native Americans, often showing surprise that there was such a lively debate about the fate of the Cherokee. I help them see the breadth of the debate as a very American element, similar to debates about slavery and, later, civil rights.

Teaching Nineteenth-Century Sentimental Poetry by Women

The way instructors introduce sentimental poetry to their students will vary according to the kind of class being taught. In the chronological approach of an American literature course, students will already have some context for understanding the obstacles to self-expression faced by women; in a women's literature course, they will have a fuller understanding of women's history. But even so the instructor may find it necessary to provide some social and historical background.

Many students are unaware of the specific ways in which women have been disenfranchised. With an explanation of the industrial revolution, increasing urbanization, the perils of disease, the high infant mortality rate, along with other general socioeconomic conditions of the nineteenth century, students can contextualize women's lives. To assess students' specific knowledge, instructors might pose questions—for example, asking if someone can explain the suffrage movement or tell when women were able to vote in America. Perhaps a student can define the expressions "the angel in the house," "old maid" or "spinster," and "hysterical." Those terms can lead to a discussion of the paucity of social roles open to women and the limited means women had of self-definition and expression. I find that it is helpful to mention Silas Weir Mitchell's "rest cure" and how it was used to silence women such as Alice James and Charlotte Perkins Gilman, who were serious about perfecting their craft and voicing their ideas.

One method of engaging students' attention and making ideas vivid is to present them with images of women participating in stereotypical nineteenth-century social roles: the adoring and servile wife, the blissful young mother, the blushing young maiden. If time permits, a discussion of women's attire is quite revelatory. Images of women in bustles, petticoats, and corsets are amusing to contemporary eyes, but bringing these images into the classroom enables the instructor first to capture students' attention and then to instruct them in the unpleasant consequences of wearing these heavy and restrictive garments. The reasons for a woman's "charming breathlessness" and the need for "fainting couches" in this era quickly become apparent. There are many useful Web resources that help provide this historical context (e.g., *American Women's History; Fashion-Era*; "Infant Mortality").

To illustrate the spectrum of women's writing at the time, I like to focus on two poems, Moore's "Little Libbie" and Sigourney's "Death of an Infant" (in P. Bennett, *Nineteenth-Century American Women Poets* [6] and Kilcup, *Nineteenth-Century American Women Writers: An Anthology* [42]), both about the loss of children, which was faced so often by nineteenth-century mothers. Although both poems are sentimental, a comparison reveals Sigourney's skill with the subject matter in contrast to Moore's meretricious, unintentionally comic product. Students need the definitions for *sentimentalism* and *obituary poetry*, as well as a little background information about both writers. I also inform them about Mark Twain's parody of Moore in *Huckleberry Finn*. It is particularly ironic that the more talented Sigourney was self-critical while Moore apparently remained happily ignorant of the poor quality of her poetry. It is important that students have the texts of both poems available in the classroom for specific analysis, so that the differences emerge quickly and strikingly:

Little Libbie
Julia A. Moore

One more spirit to Heaven has flown,
To dwell in that mansion above,
Where dear little angels, together roam,
In God's everlasting love.

One little flower has withered and died,
A bud near ready to bloom,
Its life on earth is marked with pride;
Oh, sad it should die so soon.

Sweet little Libbie, that precious flower
Was a pride in her parents' home,
They miss their little girl *every* hour,
Those friends that are left to mourn.

Her sweet silvery voice no more is heard
In the home where she once roamed;
Her place is vacant around the hearth,
Where her friends are mourning lone.

They are mourning the loss of a little girl,
With black eyes and auburn hair,
She was a treasure to them in this world,
This beautiful child so fair.

One morning in April, a short time ago,
Libbie was active and gay;
Her Saviour called her, she had to go,
E're the close of that pleasant day.

While eating dinner, this dear little child
Was choked on a piece of beef.
Doctors came, tried their skill awhile,
But none could give relief.

She was ten years of age, I am told,
And in school stood very high.
Her little form now the earth enfolds,
In her embrace it must ever lie.

Her friends and schoolmates will not forget
Little Libbie that is no more.
She is waiting on the shining step,
To welcome home friends once more.

Death of an Infant
Lydia Sigourney

Death found strange beauty on that cherub brow,
And dash'd it out. There was a tint of rose
On cheek and lip;—he touch'd the veins with ice,
And the rose faded.—Forth from those blue eyes
There spoke a wishful tenderness,—a doubt
Whether to grieve or to sleep, which Innocence
Alone can wear. With ruthless haste he bound
The silken fringes of the curtaining lids
For ever. There had been a murmuring sound
With which the babe would claim its mother's ear,
Charming her even to tears. The spoiler set
His seal of silence. But there beam'd a smile
So fix'd and holy from that marble brow,—
Death gazed and left it there;—he dared not steal
The signet-ring of Heaven.

Once the two poems have been read aloud, the students are ready for some specific questions that elucidate the characteristics of sentimentalism in both poems as well as distinctions in the poems' quality.

1. Both Moore and Sigourney were given the designation "the sweet singer" ("of Michigan" and "of Hartford," resp.), and their poems were highly popular. What are the connotations of the word "sweet" here? Why "singer" and not "poet"?
2. Can you point out some of the clichéd phrases and ideas in both poems?
3. Examine the ways the poets express some similar ideas. How is Sigourney's flower imagery superior to Moore's? How is the child's silence in death expressed in each poem? Both poets refer to the sadness of those left behind, but Sigourney does it with just an allusion. How? For example, compare Moore's "dear little angels" to Sigourney's "cherub brow" and Moore's "sad it [Libbie as a flower] should die so soon" to Sigourney's "he touch'd the veins with ice, / And the rose faded."

4. Moore gives details about the child's appearance along with her manner of death. Why, and what is the effect? What is the effect of Sigourney's being less specific?
5. Both poets use personification and alliteration. Give examples and explain which you feel are superior ones.
6. Compare the rhythm and meter of the poems. What effect does sound have on theme? How does Sigourney's use of enjambment and caesura enhance her poem's meaning?
7. What lines in Moore's poem seem to be unnecessary or repetitive? How is Sigourney's use of repetition more effective?
8. Although both poets tried to evoke sadness and sympathy in their audiences, Sigourney's poem obviously better inspires these emotions. Why, then, was Moore's poetry also popular? What does the popularity of Moore's poetry in her time and our response to it today reveal about audiences then and now?

These questions are representative of some ideas instructors will wish to cover. I generally use questions for consideration as a point of departure to stimulate class discussion, which invariably takes its own form. I have found that the most useful role I can play is that of facilitator, adding pertinent commentary and redirecting students to the point at hand if necessary. There is also always a light side to the discussion, which makes students feel at ease and increases their confidence—for example, even those with minimal experience in literary analysis see that poor Libbie's choking "on a piece of beef" is unintentionally quite funny. When I use the above format of introduction, poetry reading, and discussion, students come away from the class with a clearer idea not only of sentimentality in poetry but also of women's roles in nineteenth-century society.

The approaches we have taken allow us to make ideas available to our students in specific ways. The inclusion of Internet images creates vivid and memorable associations with course material. Asking students to see connections between what they are studying and the world as they experience it makes their course work relevant. And when students are responsible for making oral presentations and answering discussion questions, they are drawn into the learning process. This involvement dispels the lethargy that is always a risk for those who are overburdened personally and academically. By varying classroom activities and appealing to different learning styles, we are best able to reach the diverse community college population.

Note

In this essay, Nan Morelli-White wrote the section "Teaching Nineteenth-Century Sentimental Poetry by Women"; Gregory Byrd wrote the other sections.

Coda

Edward Brunner

In Newspapers, over Radio Waves, on Envelopes: Nineteenth-Century Poetic Discourse in the Early Twentieth Century

Well into the twentieth century, Americans came into daily contact with lines of poetry and welcomed such contacts as useful adjuncts to living. Poetry today, of course, is largely confined to campuses and acknowledged mainly in classrooms. Those campus sites are more various, accessible, and evenly distributed through the nation than at any other time, but in previous years Americans instructed themselves not by relying on upper-level educational institutions but by extracting knowledge from the media around them—from newspapers, magazines, radio, film, and such early examples of the visual culture as the postcard. Around 1950, it begins to be easy to find poetry on campus, in literary magazines edited for a local audience, in ambitious publishing ventures aimed at a national audience (on the model of the *Kenyon Review* and the *Sewanee Review*), in contacts with poets cycling through a reading circuit or hired for a residency, and in classroom sessions that discuss recent poetry and encourage its practice. But before 1950, it was even easier to find poetry outside the campus, in locations at the very center of the culture.

Throughout the first half of the twentieth century, poetry remained one of the major discourses that the nineteenth century employed to think with—a way of compressing information into powerful summarizing moments, a chance for confronting large issues on a manageable scale, and an occasion for feeling part of a common experience. Nevertheless, producing classroom examples of this sometimes popular, sometimes political poetry requires some ingenuity. No comprehensive anthology of it currently exists, and the delivery systems for such poetry—from shows like the Mutual Broadcasting Network's 1930s *New Poetry* hour to the editorial pages of newspapers between the world wars to the envelope poems of World War II—are not easy to retrieve. Still, research projects to uncover this material can be compelling in themselves. Students can be involved in the process of recovering "lost" popular and political poetry. The college library is not a staid repository of neatly cataloged phenomena but something closer to a lost city or a fabulous ruin from which extraordinary treasure can be extracted.

Though students will eventually proceed to working with microfilm, with transcriptions on tape, and with even more arcane items, they should probably begin by examining easily accessible records, such as those in poetry anthologies. As these anthologies attest, the modernist revolution in poetry by no means vanquished its opposition. In the first half of the century, modernist and experimental poets appeared in anthologies alongside poets who employed traditional forms and cultivated popular and commercial success. A dramatic example is the Armed Forces edition of Louis Untermeyer's *Modern American Poetry* published during World War II. There, the pseudo Italian American dialect poet T. A. Daly ("Giuseppe, de barber, ees greata for 'mash,' / He gotta da bigga, da blacka mustache" [169]) rubs shoulders with T. S. Eliot ("The heavy burden of the growing soul / Perplexes and offends more, day by day" [437]), along with the proto-ecological poet James Whaler ("I flamed a water-beetle's fat vermilion, / I joined the water-striders' cool cotillion" [477]). Including African Americans like Countee Cullen, Paul Laurence Dunbar, Langston Hughes, and James Weldon Johnson, Untermeyer also makes room for poetry by women (22 of the total 93). Since he presents poets chronologically by birth date, a reader turning pages confronts first Elizabeth Madox Roberts, then Elinor Wylie, then Ezra Pound, all born in 1885. Such a "melting pot" anthology seems the ideal Armed Forces edition—able to remind soldiers of a diverse and liberal society that is under threat from single-minded totalitarian forces. This edition, moreover, is substantially the same as the editions by Untermeyer published in the 1920s and 1930s. Indeed, virtually all poetry anthologies up to 1950, from Leonora Speyer's pioneering *American Poets: An Anthology of Con-*

temporary Verse (1923) to Bliss Carman's *Oxford Book of American Verse* (1927) to Selden Rodman's Modern Library *New Anthology of Modern Poetry* (1938), emphasize diversity as the reigning characteristic of modern American poetry.

The situation changes abruptly in 1950, when the scholar and critic F. O. Matthiessen, producing a new edition of *The Oxford Book of American Verse*, departed from Carman's 1927 conception. Alan Golding has described this anthology as "one of the most radical revisions of the American poetry canon," calculating that "Matthiessen added 28 poets to Carman's selection and cut a remarkable 147" (25–26). Carman, well-known in his time as a founding member of the turn-of-the-century school of vagabond poets, which emphasized Whitmanesque camaraderie and produced ballads of the open road, had constructed an anthology that envisioned a nation of many different poets, some of whom wrote only a work or two that were memorable. By contrast, Matthiessen saw a nation guided by a small set of highly valuable poets so touched by genius that their minor works were more interesting than any of the single works that numerous poets might compose in their lifetime.

Matthiessen's radical recasting of American poetry reflected forces at work in mid-century. The multiversity was rapidly being invented as first-generation college students arrived on campus through the GI Bill. As institutions strained to educate these new arrivals, young instructors welcomed the pedagogy implicit in the New Criticism, which posited the self-sufficient poem. The text that was linguistically complete in itself never required that its audience possess cultural capital. All that was needed was a willingness to attend to rhetorical complexity. Superficially antielitist, this ahistorical reading technique severed any connection that poems might have to a particular social setting and its relevant social issues—settings and issues necessary to appreciate many poems that Carman had selected to underscore America's diversity. At the same time, Matthiessen's concentration on a handful of genius poets helped underwrite the New Critical focus on linguistic complexity. Since these genius poets were inventing new linguistic strategies, readers needed to accustom themselves to their voice as it evolved; it was essential, then, to comprehend their development by studying many of their works, even early ones.

This emphasis on a poet's linguistic evolution in turn lent powerful support to departments of English, for only in such departments could the discipline of close reading be mastered. History courses were not pertinent, because material from history was irrelevant before the iconoclastic genius of Emily Dickinson and Walt Whitman and other self-invented modernists like Ezra Pound and Eliot. When Randall Jarrell railed at the idea of an "age of criticism" in essays and lectures from the 1950s, he was identifying a professional class of scholars and intellectuals who made a case that the value of a poem rested on its linguistic and rhetorical complexity and redefined the literary so as to strengthen English as a discipline at a time when prestige in the university depended on casting a profile that was vividly professionalized.

Before 1950, however, a great deal of poetry was not written for professionals—as can be illustrated with special piquancy by the cover from any early issue of *Esquire*. That magazine's subtitle, "Entertainment for Men," and a glimpse into pages that feature glamour-girl cartoons by E. Simms Campbell and the airbrushed pinup girls by George Petty and Alberto Vargas (if library copies have any pages left) will allow students to identify the magazine's target audience. But in its inaugural years, men were presumably entertained by poetry written by other men. *Esquire* regularly solicited contributions from such poets as Edgar Lee Masters, Langston Hughes, William Rose Benet, and Witter Bynner. And on its cover, it blurbed the poet's name under the category "Poetry," which appeared in the same-size bold type as other specialties: "Articles," "Fiction," "Satire," "Sports," "Photography," and "Cartoons."

Esquire's commitment to poetry would not be enduring. After 1940, "Poetry" as a cover category would be replaced by "Verse," and the only lineated texts inside would be the racy doggerel that accompanied the Varga girl. (It is impressive that the editors made this semantic adjustment: they knew they were no longer publishing poetry.) But during the halcyon years, poems inside *Esquire* were not relegated to back pages or obscure corners; they were displayed within a customized graphic design on an entire page that was a striking blend of the verbal and the visual. Particularly fine for classroom usage is Hughes's "Air Raid Barcelona" from the October 1938 issue, which appears below a William Sharp lithograph of an anguished figure rising from the ruins of a city, holding in each hand the bodies of children as airplanes fly far overhead. This page, as Michael Thurston has noted, was "calculated to draw on the not necessarily political sympathies of its readers," for the graphic design was "pitched to almost any one who might object to the indiscriminate murder of children under cover of darkness" (128).

When *Esquire* links Hughes's words with Sharp's images, it is not simply framing the obscure poem with a clear picture to decode it. Rather, it is drawing on a long-time editorial practice in which poetry was envisioned as capable of reporting incidents as vividly as front-page headlines. America's involvement in World War I was debated in verse submitted to newspaper editorial pages, as Mark Van Wienen has argued in *Partisans and Poets* and demonstrated in his anthology *Rendezvous with Death*. These poems sometimes offered the consolation that an elegiac tradition made available, but just as often they promoted controversial discussion. The sinking of the *Lusitania* in 1915 generated numerous poems, in part because it was an event in which civilians became victims of hostile fire (Van Wienen, *Partisans* 5). Van Wienen's examples should assure students that even a few minutes with a microfilm of wartime newspapers will produce examples of poems driven by topical concerns, often appearing as extensions of editorial-page positions in partisan publications:

> Poems sought to interpret what the events reported in the papers meant, what the lived experience of the war mobilization meant, and what role the United States played, and should play, in those events and in the lives of its citizens. (*Rendezvous* 24)

Yet newspaper verse was not simply politicized. The names of those who contributed to those newspaper pages have been largely forgotten, though even a glance at the work of Rosa Zagnoni Marinoni (1888–1970), a writer and poet born in Italy in 1888 who moved to America when she was ten and lived in the Arkansas Ozarks, reveals work in an impressive variety of forms, from sonnets to free verse, much of it sharply engaged with issues of social justice. Beginning in the mid-1920s, Marinoni published in such large-circulation newspapers as the Chicago *Tribune*, the New York *Herald Tribune*, and the *Washington Post* as well as in small papers like the *Northwest Arkansas Times*, from her new home town in Fayetteville, where she had traveled in 1908 after marriage to the professor who had founded the Romance languages department at the University of Arkansas. *Side Show*, a 1938 collection of her verse that barely samples the "over 4,000 poems" that dust jacket copy credits to her, represents material that newspapers welcomed. Marinoni specializes in the vignette, understanding that newspapers value brevity and respecting that readers have limited time. Usually addressing an audience that is presumed to be female, she often works in less than a dozen lines, as in "Northern Exposure":

> The wind was blowing from the north today.
> I did not wish to open wide the door.

I only noticed when she walked away
That she was very old and very gray.
I did not need the needles that she sold.
And so I shook my head and closed the door.
I wish she had not been so thin—so old—
I wish the north wind had not blown so cold. (43)

The poem is not just about the invisibility of the elderly and the poor but also about how such invisibility is maintained, by whom, and under what circumstances. What are the responsibilities of the privileged? Only to "wish" others will be helped? Marinoni helps us see ourselves as peering into the world from behind the newspaper, which brings us news of the world yet keeps that world at bay—like a door that we may or may not choose to open more widely.

Marinoni has a special place in her poetry for the poor and elderly. Several poems center on women who die from want; others specify the hourly wages that the untrained can expect (between thirteen and fifteen cents); others depict the poverty of rural Arkansas, in which gray shacks lack glass for windows. Her upbringing in Italy perhaps prepared her for a sequence of poems set in Mexico, in a climate more benign than Arkansas's, in which poverty is present but not destructive. Through a window frame in Mexico, the faces of children gaze as a sort of compensation—though Marinoni's description of them as "lilies of the poor" (34) also acknowledges their mortality. Elsewhere, Mexican interiors are enlivened by singing birds and hummingbirds, as indoor and outdoor interpenetrate. But the rural Arkansas setting in other poems—a setting that must have begun almost at the edge of the university town of Fayetteville—takes grayness as its reigning color. Marinoni has her eye open for affirmative signs: on the single window of a shack, a homemade Christmas decoration offers a bright red-and-green mix of colors. But the brightness has an almost explosive effect in a landscape that is otherwise so deteriorated as to seem incoherent.

Marinoni claims her offerings are modest. In a prologue that glosses the title of *Side Show*, she compares her work with a circus that she imagines her readers just leaving. Yet apart from poems on domestic subjects, she also writes on the terrors of warfare. One poem gradually discloses it is about a lynching. Religion, when she invokes it, is never a successful bulwark against terror and destruction. And she is always careful to extend a sense of dignity to those who lack resources, as in "Apple Woman: Snapshot in November":

Proud as a mother cat with her new litter
Of healthy kittens frisking in the sun,
The Apple Woman sits beside her cart
And polishes the apples one by one.
She blows her breath upon each rosy swell.
And rubs it with her apron to a glow.
Around her black umbrella flutters down
A silver halo of November snow. (58)

The snapshot, as 1930s documentary photographers knew, could be a simple moment of picturesque time or a deeply disturbing human portrait. As aesthetically pleasing as this imagistic scene may be, it is powerfully complicated by its last two lines, which exist simultaneously as an intrusion of reality and a beatification of the woman in that reality. Is the nameless Apple Woman a derivation of Eve, a maternal figure as singular as a saint to whom snow is a halo? Or is she equated with a creature helpless beneath a death-black umbrella that offers no protection against the cold?

That poetry is a discourse in which complex questions can be posed, in which complicated representations occur, is evident no less when it appears in a medium that was construed along newspaper lines. The earliest radio stations were owned by publishing syndicates. WGN, whose call letters stood for "world's greatest newspaper," belonged to the *Chicago Tribune* and like that newspaper prided itself on resembling a bazaar in which every family member could find an area of interest; the newspaper and the radio station were both programmed for maximum appeal. Though poetry's allure was in one sense enhanced by the medium of radio, which obviously privileged the spoken word, in another sense radio's alliance with speed and electronics limited the kind of poetry that played best over the air. The live broadcast was embraced by radio as a feature that distinguished it from its competitor, the cinema. Live broadcasts transported listeners to faraway places at the moment events were unfolding. For poetry to succeed in such a medium, its words had to be strikingly modern.

Poetry's success on radio, then, often hinged on topicality. Radio dramas by Edna St. Vincent Millay and Archibald MacLeish dealt with front-page events such as the bombing of Lidice and the siege of Madrid. During World War II, the poet Norman Corwin, in conjunction with Orson Welles, offered panorama-like vistas that dramatized American values. But few examples of poetry were so well suited to the medium as the five performance-based texts collected as *A Day in Manhattan* (1941) by A. M. Sullivan, who combined his tasks as president of the prestigious

Poetry Society of America with a job on Wall Street as associate editor of *Dun's Review* and host of the hour-long *New Poetry* program broadcast (beginning in 1933) by the Mutual Network. (Since the Mutual Network was "formed cooperatively out of a string of local independent stations," most of its programming originated from affiliate stations, allowing it to offer "the unusual occurrence," in Barbara Dianne Savage's words—including such remarkable breakthroughs as tributes to African Americans produced by African Americans [121].) Like other members of the Poetry Society of America who contributed to its monthly journal, *Voices*, Sullivan favored traditional and formal styles such as the sonnet sequence. But he understood that poems performed on radio would be most successful if they emerged from that side of the Whitman tradition that emphasized the urban picaresque. *A Day in Manhattan* demonstrated Sullivan's skill in using a verbal and temporal medium to construct an experience that was primarily visual and spatial. The five sequences were conceived as broadcasting events, with parts assigned to different voices. "Psalm against the Darkness" is subtitled "A Symphonic Poem in Eight Voices—Four Male and Four Female." These lend themselves wonderfully to classroom performance, especially when students listen to other radio programs of the period to reproduce the stylized and dramatic deliveries of announcers.

A certain dated quality is part of the charm of Sullivan's "Transcontinental," subtitled "A Radio Poem in Six Voices." It opens by announcing the departure of "the Transcontinental on Track Twenty-One" as if we were to travel through space ("Chicago, Omaha, Denver and the Coast") but then a second announcement promises we will also travel back in time and "See what the French sold to Thomas Jefferson" (A. Sullivan 19). To signal the voyage is under way, a new voice speaks in lines that portray motion through repetition:

> Above the smear of oil in the sunset,
> Above the rhythm of steel on the river,
> Above the cattail plumes of the meadows
> We gather speed in the twilight. (19–20)

Sullivan understands that rhyme can increase pace, and to convey images in a series of swift glances, he uses three voices:

> 1st: I see a school
> 2nd: I see a church
> 3rd: I see a young lad
> Bending a birch. (21)

To some in Sullivan's audience, that birch bender will appear to be on loan from Robert Frost. Other place-names resonate with literary allusions: the train passes "the headstones of Spoon River" in homage to Edgar Lee Masters. Variations in line length, rhythm, and diction convey distinct settings. The names of the states are both savored and pronounced at different speeds as the voyage races to a close:

> Chorus: Slowly:
> Min-ne-so-ta, Min-ne-so-ta, Min-ne-so-ta,
> Col-o-ra-do, Col-o-ra-do, Col-o-ra-do.
> (Faster)
> A-ri-zo-na, A-ri-zo-na, A-ri-zo-na,
> (Faster) California, California, California. (23)

Having delivered us to the West Coast, the voices of the announcers resume. "Who wants to meet the sun?" one asks, and the other responds, "East Coast Limited on Track Twenty-One" (24).

Not only does "Transcontinental" take advantage of the opportunities radio offers for imaginative projection by encouraging audience involvement through associating the sound of words with visual descriptions, it also negotiates issues important to early radio. Michele Hilmes has described nighttime radio as a "commercialized medium with one foot in the vulgar popular and one foot on the ladder of social hierarchy" (187). Through poetic conventions like rhyme and meter, Sullivan delivered an experience nearly universal in the 1930s, when travel by rail was familiar to all. His audience traveled culturally upward, as it were, while it took delight in recognizing the poetic reproduction of such familiar sounds as the

> sad wavering of the whistle
> That cries "Be-w a r e," "Take c a r e"

and such familiar sights as the glimpse of heavy equipment in shadows that is a "A fluid string of darkness, lifting and falling / Over tool shed and cinder bed" (20).

In addition, Sullivan's "radio poem in six voices" strategically resolved a dilemma that radio encountered when it sought to bring high culture to the masses. How could a production like a radio show, clearly a work of collaboration, not clash with the idea that the work of art, as Hilmes phrases it, should "possess a sole creative author from whose individual genius the work stems"? Radio could finesse the problem, in some cases, by offering a "series drama dominated by a presiding genius" (Hilmes 212), as Orson Welles did in the *Mercury Theater of the Air*. But Sullivan's solution was to use multiple voices to orchestrate a cross-country trip that transformed the continent itself into the "genius" whose appealing and diverse geography attends to us all.

Another audio poem that lends itself to classroom performance, Sullivan's "Midnight Caravan (A Radio Poem in Five Voices)" is the working-class version of "Transcontinental," narrating from a trucker's point of view the night drive down US 1 from New York to Philadelphia. Instead of the "Transcontinental" landscape of vastness in which moments of diversity are celebrated, "Midnight Caravan" unfolds in a setting brutalized by the encroachments of the machine. The territory is scarred with a history of danger, its locations marked by death ("Here's the curve where Jerry hit the bus" [15]). Using workers' voices, the poem reveals the transporting of goods as a danger-filled trek. As Sullivan registers the numbing routine of the journey, he also conveys a sense of onward momentum:

> Glimmer, shimmer, brighter, dimmer,
> One light, no light, stop light, go light,
> No light, one light, two lights, no light,
> Glimmer, shimmer, brighter, dimmer. . . . (12)

The lines emphasize the deceptions of the visual—the hallucinatory images in the glare of the lights and the folds of the shadows—the better to rely on passages that convey authority through audible rhythms. Men bind themselves to their machines: "Now men whose being is fused by the hours to the rumbling torsos of metal / Measure the swinging bulk of their bodies by the breadth of the chassis" (14). When *Esquire* excerpted a passage for its May 1937 issue (in a full-page design by Arnold W. Ryan), the upland trek alone was presented in these alliterated seven- and eight-beat lines. The observations and commentaries by drivers that, in the radio version, were used to punctuate the journey, to restore it to a human dimension in which fear and pain were part of daily work, were effaced entirely. In *Esquire*, the drivers were powerful creatures, magicians who maneuvered "Elephants on roller skates, incredible behemoths who shoulder the breeze to a whirlpool" (A. Sullivan 11).

America as a work of art, poetically reconstructed through verbal representations of images and sounds, was especially significant in the Depression era. "In various ways, and to various political ends," Kate Lacey has observed, "radio was seized upon as a tool that could bind the various constituents of the nation together, wherever they were and whatever their circumstances" (28–29). Perhaps no poet was more aware of radio's potential than Archibald MacLeish, who early in the 1930s wrote dramas that used the medium's ability to encourage imaginative projection to convey the horror of aerial bombardment.

MacLeish was widely regarded in his time as a writer with strong roots in a modernist aesthetic. "A poem should not mean / But be" (*New and Collected Poems* 109) was the tagline from "Ars Poetica" in his 1926 *Streets of the Moon*, a breakthrough collection that borrowed images Eliot had used to convey despair and had refashioned them into a basis for expatriate urbanity. But his enduring achievement may well prove to be a single poem that he produced in a few minutes, a work that has never appeared in any of the major anthologies of American poetry (unlike the nearly ubiquitous "Ars Poetica") and that is not always identified with his name. The poem, which only received the title "The Young Dead Soldiers Do Not Speak" when it was modified for reprinting in his 1948 collection *"Act Five" and Other Poems*, may be the single elegy most often associated with modern warfare by individuals and organizations actually familiar with combat.

"The Young Dead Soldiers" began as a set of notes jotted in 1943 in response to a call for material for a Liberty Bond Drive that passed across MacLeish's desk—MacLeish was head of the Office for War Information. Shortly before, he had learned that the son of old friends, a boy his son's age, had died while piloting a combat aircraft (Donaldson 374). The writing of the poem, then, veers uneasily between personal anguish and personal responsibility—an intersection steeped in grief:

> The young dead soldiers do not speak.
> Nevertheless they are heard in the still houses; who has not heard
> them?
> They have a silence that speaks for them at night and when the clock
> counts.
> They say: We were young. We have died. Remember us.
> They say: We have done what we could but until it is finished it is
> not done.
> They say: We have given our lives but until it is finished no one can
> know what our lives gave.
> They say: Our deaths are not ours; they are yours; they will mean
> what you make them.

> They say: Whether our lives and our deaths were for peace and a
> new hope or for nothing we cannot say; it is you who must say
> this.
> They say: We leave you our deaths. Give them their meaning.
> We were young, they say. We have died. Remember us.
> ("Young Dead Soldiers")

This is MacLeish's 1948 version. In the 1943 original, the next-to-last line was longer: "They say, We leave you our deaths: give them their meaning: give them an end to the war and a true peace: give them a victory that ends the war and a peace afterwards: give them their meaning" (*Young Dead Soldiers*). In wartime, MacLeish felt compelled to spell out exactly what he meant by "meaning": a victorious end to the war that ushered in a glorious peace. Such a line was no doubt uncontroversial when battles raged. To remove it widens the poem's potential for usage. And the poem is constructed so it can be used; that is its power.

Cary Nelson has described this poem as a "form of public commemoration; it makes grief a national and historical category" ("Martial Lyrics" 270). Indeed, MacLeish appears not to produce words himself but to act as transcriber. By his own direction, the poem, when first printed, appeared unsigned. (In a note he appended to the typescript when he circulated it among friends, he wrote, "This text will be used by the Treasury Department. It will be published anonymously. I should appreciate it if it were treated as a private document until that time" ["Young Dead Soldiers"]). Still, his act of transcribing is unusual, for he does not pretend to record what the dead might actually say. Instead he is registering a moment of silence, a moment in which the young dead soldiers do not speak. It is a silence that we all know. By offering not words of grief but describing a situation in which a terrible silence is understood to be at once impossible to escape as well as necessary to move beyond, MacLeish opens a momentary space in which we, the living, can act to fill that silence with meaning. All our future, MacLeish understands, will now be a conversation with those no longer with us. At the same time, how we complete our lives will give their incomplete lives their only fulfillment. We listen, we speak, we live not for ourselves alone but within a powerful, loving memory.

Marinoni and Sullivan must be sought out in archives or in libraries; not so MacLeish's poem. Originally, it appeared in a context as remote from us today as hour-long radio broadcasts of epic poems or as short poems alongside editorial opinion pages. Nelson includes it among illustrations of poetry that first appeared on postcards and on advertising trade cards at the end of the nineteenth century and that reached an apogee during World War II ("Martial Lyrics"). Unsigned and without a title, its text located against a stark black-and-white drawing of three small crosses on a distant hill, the poem appeared on envelopes designed for sending victory letters. But Nelson has also located a half dozen different places where the text reappeared, in the pages of the *Reader's Digest* (Sept. 1945), on the daily bulletin for the Oakland (California) Public Schools, on the front page of the *San Francisco News* (25 Apr. 1945), and above all as a heading to that section of the newspaper where the names appeared of the local men and women who had recently died in combat.

After the close of hostilities, however, the poem did not fall into obscurity. It continued to circulate, a staple of occasions when the honored dead are held in memory. It continues to circulate. On the Internet, it can be found on the memorial pages of the Fourth Battalion of the 47th Infantry, recalling the Mekong Delta. It was included in an address to the Congress on 12 September 2001, by Rhode Island Senator Jack Reed. Portions of it were cited in a 1994 speech by Israeli Prime Minister Yitzhak Rabin, and portions reappeared in a speech five years later by Israeli Prime Minister Ehud Barak, commemorating the death of Rabin. And it was excerpted for the Web site of the Rochester, New York, police department. If there is another poem by a mid-century poet that has achieved the circulation of "The Young Dead Soldiers Do Not Speak," I am unaware of it. Indeed, as a final research project for a class on "lost" poetry that addresses public issues, asking students to find five references to the poem on the Internet and discuss how the poem is used in each of its appearances is an experience that strongly suggests that popular poetry may not be so absent from the last half of the century. We may simply have not yet discovered how to look for it.

Note

Permission to quote "Northern Exposure" and "Apple Woman: Snapshot in November," by Rosa Zagnoni Marinoni, was granted by Paula Marinoni.

Part IV

Resources

Philipp Schweighauser

Resources for the Study of Nineteenth-Century American Poetry: A Selective Guide

Anyone compiling bibliographic information on nineteenth-century poets will be struck by the discrepancy between these poets' popularity in their own time and the relative dearth of interest in them since. The once-revered Fireside Poets (William Cullen Bryant, Oliver Wendell Holmes, James Russell Lowell, John Greenleaf Whittier, and Henry Wadsworth Longfellow) and the sentimental-domestic tradition of immensely popular writers such as Lydia Huntley Sigourney, Elizabeth Oakes Smith, Celia Laighton Thaxter, and Lucy Larcom have suffered neglect, but so has the poetic output of major nineteenth-century prose writers (e.g., Margaret Fuller, Ralph Waldo Emerson, Herman Melville). The titles discussed in the "Critical Debates" section suggest some answers to why so much nineteenth-century poetry went unrecognized in the twentieth century. But my main purpose here is to encourage readers to investigate what is still a developing critical field.

I. Editions

On the heels of the invaluable Schomburg reprint collection of nineteenth-century black women writers (including Joan R. Sherman's four-volume *Collected Black Women's Poetry*), new editions of other women and minority poets have begun to appear. Independent editions of Alice Dunbar-Nelson, Margaret Fuller, Charlotte Perkins Gilman, Frances Ellen Watkins Harper, Emma Lazarus, Louisa McCord, and Sarah Piatt now stand on college library shelves together with standard editions of the major figures of the premodernist canon: Edgar Allan Poe, Walt Whitman, Emily Dickinson, and others.

Since 1998, R. W. Franklin's new variorum edition of Dickinson's poetry has become the standard, superseding the 1955 Johnson edition and correcting the latter's errors. A one-volume classroom edition was published in 1999. Franklin's edition of *The Manuscript Books of Emily Dickinson* enhances our understanding of her creative process and the original shape of her poems—as well as their dashes. Whitman's complete poetry is available in many good editions, including the Library of America's *Poetry and Prose*, which contains both the first edition and the 1891–92 "deathbed edition" of *Leaves of Grass*. Other dependable single-author editions of nineteenth-century poets' works published by the same press are Stephen Crane's *Prose and Poetry*, Longfellow's *Poems and Other Writings*—the most comprehensive selection of Longfellow's poetry readily available in print—John Greenleaf Whittier's *Selected Poems*, Ralph Waldo Emerson's *Collected Poems and Translations*, and Henry David

Thoreau's *Collected Essays and Poems.* The standard and most complete collection of Poe's poetry is Thomas Ollive Mabbott's University of Illinois Press edition *The Complete Poems.* A capacious selected edition of the Southern poet William Gilmore Simms appeared in 1990 from the University of Georgia Press.

The work of several African American poets is now accessible in good editions. For Harper, we have Frances Smith Foster's reader *A Brighter Coming Day* and the comprehensive *Complete Poems of Frances E. W. Harper*, edited by Maryemma Graham. For Paul Laurence Dunbar, Joanne Braxton's *The Collected Poetry of Paul Laurence Dunbar* is the best available source; for George Moses Horton, Sherman's *The Black Bard of North Carolina.* Dunbar-Nelson's work has been reissued in a three-volume edition edited by Gloria T. Hull.

Among anglophone Jewish American writers, two have received editorial attention. Lazarus's poetry is now accessible via Gregory Eiselein's scholarly edition, *Selected Poems and Other Writings.* Eiselein has also edited Adah Isaacs Menken's Infelicia *and Other Writings.* Among Yiddish poets, Morris Rosenfeld's *Songs from the Ghetto*, translated by Leo Wiener from the Yiddish in 1898, was reprinted in 1976.

Recently, Sarah Orne Jewett's 1896 selection of Celia Thaxter's poetry was reissued in an expanded edition and with an introduction by Jane E. Vallier. A substantial selection of Piatt's poetry is now available in Paula Bernat Bennett's *Palace-Burner*, and a large selection of Fuller's verse is included in Jeffrey Steele's *The Essential Margaret Fuller.* To date only one scholarly edition of the verse of a nineteenth-century anglophone Native American poet has appeared, Carole Gerson and Veronica Strong-Boag's very welcome *E. Pauline Johnson, Tekahionwake: Collected Poems and Selected Prose.*

Editions of poetry by two writers largely known for their prose work are now also available. For a first encounter with Melville's poetry, the revised *The Poems of Herman Melville*, edited by Douglas Robillard, is recommended. Edwin H. Cady's edition *"Pebbles," "Monochromes," and Other Modern Poems, 1891–1916* collects a large selection of William Dean Howells's late poetry.

2. Anthologies

Since the publication of Cheryl Walker's breakthrough *American Women Poets of the Nineteenth Century*, ten more anthologies have appeared: five mixed; one devoted to African American poets; and three, like Walker's, devoted entirely to women poets. Equally important, selections from nineteenth-century American poets other than Poe, Emerson, Whitman, and Dickinson are now regularly included in introductory anthologies of American literature such as the *Norton* (Baym) and the *Heath* (Lauter et al.), giving these writers wider exposure than they have had since their own day.

Among nonspecialized anthologies of nineteenth-century poetry, John Hollander's Library of America anthology *American Poetry: The Nineteenth Century*, which comes in two beautifully designed volumes, is a good starting point. The entries are arranged chronologically by authors' birth dates, the first volume covering poetry from Philip Freneau to Whitman, the second from Melville to Trumbull Stickney. Hollander's anthology is noteworthy both because it brings to the reader's attention many little-known authors and because its second volume makes available a good selection of nontraditional poetic texts, including spirituals, folk songs, and Native American poetry. An expanded CD-ROM version of this text is also available from Library of America. It contains all the poems in Hollander's print edition and has a search function, good biographical profiles of all the authors represented, nearly six hours of audio recordings, and a useful chronology of historical events. All these resources are explicitly designed for classroom use.

The first volume of the *New Anthology of American Poetry*, edited by Steven Gould Axelrod, Camille Roman, and Thomas Travisano, reaches up to 1900 and includes a very generous selection of nineteenth-century poetry that more clearly than Hollander reveals its debt to recent recovery work on nineteenth-century women writers. Especially notable are its Piatt selections.

The Axelrod, Roman, and Travisano selections would look very different if it were not for the work of Walker, Janet Gray, and Paula Bennett. Walker's *American Women Poets of the Nineteenth Century* was a groundbreaking anthology, highlighting the work of many long-neglected women poets. It contains a useful introduction, notes on all the authors, and poems by twenty-seven writers including Maria Gowen Brooks, Alice Cary and Phoebe Cary, Rose Terry Cooke, Ina Donna Coolbrith, Harper, Larcom, and Frances Sargent Osgood. Based on years of archival research, Bennett's *Nineteenth-Century American Women Poets* makes available poetry by 143 women poets. The volume is divided between multiple selections from thirty-eight "principal poets" (Sigourney to Dunbar-Nelson) and an innovative second section in which poems taken from nineteenth-century periodicals and newspapers are arranged chronologically. Gray's *She Wields a Pen* anthologizes fifty-three women writers, from the well-known (Dickinson) to the unknown (Frances Jane Crosby). Gray's introduction provides an excellent discussion of nineteenth-century poetry's popular culture context. Her volume also contains a chronology of the poets' lives, annotations, and selections from contemporary criticism.

Sherman's *African-American Poetry of the Nineteenth Century* is devoted to another group of poets that has suffered critical neglect. It comprises 171 poems by thirty-five African American writers, has a useful introduction to the historical and cultural concerns of the poems, and includes an extensive though now dated bibliography. Anthologies of nineteenth-century Native American poetry in both period and modern translations are relatively easy to find. George W. Cronyn's 1918 *American Indian Poetry: An Anthology of Songs and Chants*, reprinted in 1991, is a good choice.

Other recent anthologies of nineteenth-century poetry, all less ambitious in scope than the above named, are Robert Bain's *Whitman's and Dickinson's Contemporaries*, Paul Kane's *Poetry of the American Renaissance*, William Spengemann and Jessica Roberts's *Nineteenth-Century American Poetry*, and Shira Wolosky's *Major Voices: Nineteenth-Century American Women's Poetry*. Of these, Bain's is the most committed to representing the field's diversity and offers selections from the most poets. Spengemann and Roberts's is available in an inexpensive Penguin edition but contains no poetry by writers of color and only once ventures outside the traditional canon to reprint fourteen of Piatt's poems.

The poems collected in the more specialized *The Columbia Book of Civil War Poetry*, edited by Richard Marius et al., reach well into the twentieth century but also include standard works by Melville, Dunbar, Longfellow, and Whitman, plus patriotic war songs from both sides. Lee Steinmetz's much earlier *Poetry of the American Civil War* is even more limited but preserves some poetic voices largely forgotten today. (How many of us have read Claudian Bird Northrop's "The South Carolina Hymn Of Independence" or J. P. Randolph's "The Slave-Mongers' Convention"?) The Library of America has recently published J. D. McClatchy's anthology, the first among Civil War anthologies to include Dickinson's poems. Otherwise this volume is surprisingly conservative in its inclusions and approach. The same cannot be said of Faith Barrett and Cristanne Miller's selections: the editors split their anthology between sizable samplings of a small group of important figures (Horton, Whittier, Whitman, Melville, Harper, Henry Timrod, Piatt, Dickinson, and the newly discovered soldier-poet Obadiah Ethelbert Baker) and a rich selection of discrete poems arranged not by author but chronologically to follow the trajectory of the war itself, from rumblings to aftermath.

Several additional general anthologies are also useful to teachers of nineteenth-century poetry. Karen Kilcup's *Nineteenth-Century American Women's Writing* contains a broad range of women's poetry. Another literary anthology of hers, *Native American Women's Writing, c. 1800–1924*, has a good selection of traditional songs as well as poems by E. Pauline Johnson, Zitkala-Ša, and Jane Johnston Schoolcraft. *The Norton Anthology of African American Literature* (Gates and McKay) has extensive selections of African American poetry, including much oral poetry as well as more conventional poems by writers such as Dunbar, Harper, Horton, James Monroe Whitfield, and Charlotte Forten Grimké. The *Jewish American Literature* anthology (Chametzky et al.) makes available nineteenth-century poetry by, among others, Lazarus, Menken, Rosenfeld, David Edelshtadt, and Penina Moïse. For those interested in questions of social class, Philip S. Foner's *American Labor Songs of the Nineteenth Century* is an excellent resource. In addition, Benita Eisler's collection of writings by the Lowell mill girls contains a small number of poems by female factory workers. The best source for this poetry, however, is the World Wide Web (see the "Web Resources" section below).

3. Reference Guides

Scholarly apparatus for the study of nineteenth-century American poetry is still relatively thin. Especially when supplemented by encyclopedias devoted to single authors, discussed in the "Single-Author Studies" section of this guide, Eric Haralson's biographically oriented *Encyclopedia of American Poetry: The Nineteenth Century* is the best and most reliable reference work available. The encyclopedia's alphabetically ordered entries cover all poets included in Hollander's *American Poetry: The Nineteenth Century*. Each entry gives a detailed account of the poet's life and work as well as the current state of critical discussion; a selected list of the poet's works and a bibliography of critical works invite further research. Additional entries provide information on more general topics such as nineteenth-century versions of American Indian poetry and popular poetry.

Though not specifically focused on poetry or the nineteenth century, William L. Andrews, Frances Smith Foster, and Trudier Harris's *The Oxford Companion to African American Literature* is another important resource. Its more than four hundred entries on individual authors cover all the African American poets discussed in this volume and many more. Its eight-page entry on poetry and its five-page entry on periodicals should be read by anyone interested in nineteenth-century African American poetry.

Volume 4 of Sacvan Bercovitch's *The Cambridge History of American Literature*, prepared by Barbara Packer and Shira Wolosky, is devoted entirely to nineteenth-century poetry and is highly recommended. In addition, the relevant sections in the standard histories of American literature, especially Jay Parini's *Columbia History of American Poetry*, offer dependable if more limited resources.

The bibliographies devoted to nineteenth-century poetry are more restricted in scope. Gwen Davis and Beverly A. Joyce's *Poetry by Women to 1900* counts 1,609 American women poets who published books of poetry during the nineteenth century but cites only titles and authors' names. Denise D. Knight and Emmanuel S. Nelson's indispensable *Nineteenth-Century American Women Writers: A Bio-bibliographical Critical Sourcebook* covers seventy-seven individual writers ranging from Louisa May Alcott to Constance Fenimore Woolson and provides useful introductions and short surveys of the life and work of a good number of both famous and lesser-known (e.g., Lizette Woodworth Reese, Rose Hawthorne Lathrop) women poets.

What Knight and Nelson's volume does for female authors, Nelson's *African American Authors, 1745–1945: A Bio-bibliographical Critical Sourcebook* and Joyce Pettis's *African American Poets: Lives, Works, and Sources* do for often neglected African American writers. Although published back in 1991, Jean Fagan Yellin and Cynthia D. Bond's wonderfully useful *The Pen Is Ours* remains the most complete listing of nineteenth-century African American women's writing extant. Sherman's *Invisible Poets: Afro-Americans of the Nineteenth Century* fulfills a similar function. It includes female poets but is otherwise far more limited in scope.

Although conservative in its choices and dated, Philip K. Jason's *Nineteenth Century American Poetry* provides useful information on criticism of mostly famous poems by sixteen writers including Crane, Melville, and Thoreau.

Finally, teachers wishing to gain an impression of earlier criticism of nineteenth-century poetry can consult J. Albert Robbins's entries "Poe and Nineteenth-Century Poetry" and "Nineteenth-Century Poetry" in the *American Literary Scholarship* issues of 1966 and 1967.

4. Biographies

Legacy profiles have done much to put neglected nineteenth-century women writers back on the map of literary criticism. Haralson's *Encyclopedia of American Poetry* provides an excellent source of information on individual poets and their work. As always, the *Dictionary of Literary Biography* (*DLB*) is an additional reliable source. For our purposes, the three volumes of *American Poets, 1880–1945*, edited by Peter Quartermain, are at least partly relevant. Other *DLB* volumes list earlier poets but typically only with respect to other aspects of their careers or their identities as writers—for example, as novelists, journalists, or Native American writers. The biographies of women in Edward T. James's three-volume *Notable American Women, 1607–1950* and in Lina Maniero's four-volume *American Women Writers* need to be used with caution, since, in the absence of modern scholarship on their subjects, both these breakthrough works were heavily dependent on nineteenth-century sources, virtually all of which are unreliable.

Among book-length biographies of major authors, Eve Kornfeld's concise account of Margaret Fuller's life is particularly useful for its inclusion of various documents pertaining to this eminent nineteenth-century figure's life. For critical biographies of Whitman's life and work, David S. Reynolds's monumental *Walt Whitman's America* and Justin Kaplan's earlier *Walt Whitman: A Life*, winner of the National Book Award, are the authoritative sources. Among the many biographies of Dickinson, Judith Farr's *The Passion of Emily Dickinson*, Alfred Habegger's *My Wars Are Laid Away in Books*, and Richard B. Sewall's *The Life of Emily Dickinson* are particularly recommended. Of Poe biographies, Arthur Hobson Quinn's *Edgar Allan Poe: A Critical Biography* stands out as the best account. In addition, Kenneth Silverman's *Edgar A. Poe: Mournful and Never-Ending Remembrance* is still a good source despite its almost obsessive focus on the themes of loss and mourning. As part of Twayne's United States Authors series, Rayburn S. Moore gives a brief account of the life and works of the Southern poet Paul Hamilton Hayne.

The Fireside Poets Longfellow and Holmes are also the subjects of good new biographies. In Charles C. Calhoun's *Longfellow: A Rediscovered Life*, the poet emerges as a central cultural figure of his time. G. Edward White's two biographies of Holmes and Sheldon M. Novick's *Honorable Justice* focus much of their attention on Holmes's judicial career. Ralph M. Aderman and Wayne R. Kime's *Advocate for America* directs attention to the life of James Kirke Paulding, a poet who rivaled the Fireside Poets for public exposure and, like them, published an extensive body of verse. Other biographies of lesser-known male writers can be gleaned from the brief bibliographies accompanying the entries in Haralson's *Encyclopedia*.

New biographical treatments of a number of less well known women authors are harder to find. For an account of Larcom's life that sheds light on the intersections between her writing and her work as a mill girl, Shirley Marchalonis's *The Worlds of Lucy Larcom* is well worth reading, and for an account of Thaxter's life and work, Norma H. Mandel's *Beyond the Garden Gate* and Jane E. Vallier's literary biography *Poet on Demand*, available in a 1994 reprint edition, are useful. Mainly based on a close examination of over a hundred of Emma Lazarus's letters, Bette Roth Young's *Emma Lazarus in Her World* documents the poet's ambivalent sense of Jewish identity. Valarie H. Ziegler's *Diva Julia: The Public Romance and Private Agony of Julia Ward Howe* discusses the difficult dynamics of marriage in Howe's life, as does Gary Williams's *Hungry Heart: The Literary Emergence of Julia Ward Howe*. Renée Sentilles's *Performing Menken: Adah Isaacs Menken and the Birth of American Celebrity* is devoted to another highly public figure of the period and explores the actress-poet's multiple performances of identity.

No book-length biography of Sarah Piatt is available, but Bennett's introduction to *Palace-Burner* provides a good starting point for those interested in this exceptional and long-neglected poet's life. Further notable biographies of nineteenth-century women poets are Rita K. Gollin's *Annie Adams Fields: Woman of Letters*, Leigh Fought's *Southern Womanhood and Slavery: A Biography of Louisa S. McCord*, Rosemary Whitaker's *Helen Hunt Jackson*, and Sharon L. Dean's *Constance Fenimore Woolson: Homeward Bound*.

Biographical treatments are available for three important Native American poets of the period: Alexander Posey, the Canadian poet E. Pauline Johnson, and John Rollin Ridge. Daniel F. Littlefield's *Alex Posey: Creek Poet, Journalist, and Humorist* provides a good introduction to this lively figure. In addition to Carole Gerson and Veronica Strong-Boag's *Paddling Her Own Canoe*, A. LaVonne Brown Ruoff's introduction to *The Moccasin Maker* and Theodore Watts-Dunton's introduction to *Flint and Feather* give good accounts of Johnson's life and work. Sheila M. F. Johnston's *Buckskin and Broadcloth* traces the life of the Canadian poet and performer and contains forty of her poems not included in *Flint and Feather.* James W. Parins's *John Rollin Ridge: His Life and Works* is the first full-length biographical study of the controversial Cherokee poet.

The African American poet Paul Laurence Dunbar has been the subject of two book-length biographies—*Oak and Ivy*, by Addison Gayle, and *Crossing the Line*, by Felton O. Best—both of which are still in print. The circumstances of Dunbar's failed marriage to Alice Dunbar-Nelson have been explored by Eleanor Alexander in *Lyrics of Sunshine and Shadow*.

5. Critical Debates

Since the publication of Ann Douglas's *The Feminization of American Culture* (1977), scholarly studies of nineteenth-century poetry, as of nineteenth-century literature generally, have swirled around the question of sentimentality and, with it, the issue of women's role at home and in the public sphere. Jane P. Tompkins's *Sensational Designs* and Joanne Dobson's later "Reclaiming Sentimental Literature" have been instrumental in revalorizing sentimentality as an aesthetic *and* political strategy after Douglas's stigmatization of it in *Feminization.* Other significant contributions to the Douglas-Tompkins debate—which is ultimately a debate about the valence of sentimentalism as both political discourse and feminist aesthetic—are Shirley Samuels's essay collection *The Culture of Sentiment*; Karen Sánchez-Eppler's *Touching Liberty: Abolition, Feminism, and the Politics of the Body*; and Dobson's "The American Renaissance Reenvisioned," which provides a good overview of the debate. Although the twin topics of sentimentality and domesticity are deeply entwined in the scholarly literature as well as in nineteenth-century texts themselves, I think it important to separate them here. Succinctly, nineteenth-century domesticity, which set the parameters of the woman's sphere, is best approached through historiographical research, as it has historical underpinnings that limit it to a particular time and place. Sentimentality, on the other hand, though it has a history, is a question of aesthetics raised by a particular set of rhetorical conventions that writers can deploy at any time or place.

5.1. Domesticity

From the perspective of gender studies, a number of monographs and essay collections by historians as well as by literary scholars have analyzed the varied positions on domesticity and the ideology of separate spheres available to nineteenth-century writers. Some scholars emphasize domesticity's oppressiveness; others underscore its empowering potential. Among the most important works in this debate are Carl N. Degler's *At Odds: Women and the Family in America from the Revolution to the Present*, Mary Kelley's *Private Woman, Public Stage*, Barbara Epstein's *The Politics of Domesticity*, Lori D. Ginzberg's *Women and the Work of Benevolence*, Karen Halttunen's *Confidence Men and Painted Women*, Lora Romero's *Home Fronts*, Gillian Brown's *Domestic Individualism*, Lori Merish's *Sentimental Materialism*, Mary P. Ryan's *Women in Public*, and the essays in the *No More Separate Spheres!* issue of *American Literature*, edited by Cathy N. Davidson.

More-specialized studies look at the ways in which male and female writers use humor and irony to challenge codes of domesticity. Gregg Camfield's *Necessary Madness* is an example; so is James E. Rocks's "Whittier's 'Snow-Bound,' " which shifts our attention to a male poet's use of domestic imagery.

Writing at a more theoretical level in *From School to Salon*, Mary Loeffelholz applies Richard Brodhead's concept of the domestic-tutelary complex, outlined in his seminal article "Sparing the Rod: Discipline and Fiction in Antebellum America," to the evolution of women's poetry through the century as a whole, showing how women carried over the disciplinary model of the early-nineteenth-century domestic schoolroom into the more public lives they came to lead toward the century's end.

5.2. Sentimentality

Treatments of sentimentality after Douglas and Tompkins have increasingly challenged earlier critics' identification of sentimentality as a gender-specific discourse. In *Sentimental Collaborations*, Mary Louise Kete argues that we should disassociate the question of sentimentality from the gender divide and focus instead on its cohesive function in the face of human loss and separation. Drawing on psychoanalysis and the Habermasian notion of the public sphere, Glenn Hendler's *Public Sentiments* argues that, in the nineteenth century, sympathetic identification was a quintessentially public feeling, with the transformative power to reshape identities as well as institutions. In *Poets in the Public Sphere*, Bennett also argues against reductive analyses of sentimentality, noting that the rhetorical conventions of sentimentality that were in play in the nineteenth century had a complex genealogy in male eighteenth-century philosophical and literary texts. To get some idea of how pervasive sentimental writing actually is in male texts, readers will find the essays in Mary Chapman and Hendler's *Sentimental Men* most helpful; Longfellow and Whitman are among the poets considered. Fred Kaplan's *Sacred Tears* is also useful here.

Discussions of nineteenth-century attitudes toward death almost invariably focus on sentimentality. Laurence Lerner's *Angels and Absences* provides a full-length study of the infant death motif, among the most prominent poetic conventions of nineteenth-century sentimental writing. Readers can also consult Sánchez-Eppler's *Dependent States* in this context. In "Changing Attitudes to Death," Colin B. Atkinson and Jo B. Atkinson document how the nineteenth-century culture of death left its traces not only in sentimental literature but also in folk poetry, folk songs, and parlor songs—a genre on which Caroline Moseley's "The Young Women of Nineteenth-Century American Parlor Song" provides background information.

The role of death in nineteenth-century poetry has also been the subject of two notable single-author studies, J. Gerald Kennedy's on Poe (*Poe*) and Thomas W. Ford's on Dickinson. For a comparison of Dickinson's and Sigourney's treatment of the infant death motif, see Elizabeth A. Petrino's "Feet So Precious Charged." Marianne Noble's *The Masochistic Pleasures of Sentimental Literature* likewise brings Dickinson into a dialogue with sentimental writers and thus reestablishes her place in a tradition from which generations of critics have thought it necessary to rescue her.

If all these studies complicate our understanding of the nineteenth-century relation among sentimentalism, gender, and the private-public divide, Suzanne Clark's *Sentimental Modernism* and Kilcup's *Robert Frost and Feminine Literary Tradition* also problematize the place of sentimentalism in literary history. Both studies investigate the long-ignored ties between nineteenth-century authors and their modernist successors and thus challenge critics' often exclusive association of sentimentalism with nineteenth-century literary production. Finally, the 2003 special issue *The Transatlantic Poetess* of the online journal *Romanticism on the Net*, edited by Laura Mandell, provides a good selection of revisionist essays on the figure of the poetess.

6. General Studies: Books, Essays, and Collections of Essays

After a century of silence, full-length critical studies of nineteenth-century poetry are finally beginning to appear, and their publication is profoundly reshaping how we read this verse and what parameters we set for the field as a whole. Emily Stipes Watts's *The Poetry of American Women from 1632 to 1945* and Walker's *The Nightingale's Burden* broke ground for women's poetry in 1977 and 1982, respectively. After sixteen years, these studies were followed by Petrino's *Emily Dickinson and Her Contemporaries*; Bennett's *Poets in the Public Sphere*, the most comprehensive study of nineteenth-century American women poets to date; Janet Gray's *Race and Time*; Eliza Richards's study of Poe and his female contemporaries, *Gender and the Poetics of Reception in Poe's Circle*; Loeffelholz's *From School to Salon*; Angela Sorby's *Schoolroom Poets*; and, important for its theoretical approach, Virginia Jackson's *Dickinson's Misery: A Theory of Lyric Reading*. Years in the making and varying widely in approach and concerns, these later books have forced reconsideration of the work of male and female poets alike; they have raised questions about canonization, about poetry's status as both an aesthetic and a social discourse, and about how poetry circulated in the period. Taken together, they mark the completion of the second stage in nineteenth-century poetry's resurgence as an academic field, even while a third wave of critical studies is in preparation. Many of those studies are revised versions of dissertations, but also among them is Kilcup's potentially invaluable *Poems, Readers, and Reviewers*.

These books are supplemented by others that focus more narrowly on small groups of poets in dialogue with one another. Daneen Wardrop in *Word, Birth, and Culture in the Poetry of Poe, Whitman, and Dickinson* brings the three most famous poets of the period, often studied in isolation elsewhere, into a conversation centering on the poets' different negotiations of femininity and gender identity, as well as their language experiments. Edward S. Cutler in *Recovering the New* unsettles both the national and the temporal categories of literary criticism, arguing that the modernity of European and American nineteenth-century cultural production lies in its engagement with and embeddedness in processes of commodification. Robert M. Greenberg's *Splintered Worlds* studies the personal and poetic responses of Emerson, Melville, Whitman, and Dickinson to the increasing fragmentation of their world. Steven Olson's *The Prairie in Nineteenth-Century American Poetry* traces the social, cultural, and political significance of prairie imagery in the work of poets as different as Bryant, Melville, Dickinson, Whitman, Holmes, Lowell, and Longfellow. Robert H. Walker's discussion of the social context of nineteenth-century poetry in *The Poet and the Gilded Age* also remains useful.

Beside monographs on nineteenth-century poetry, a steadily growing number of essay collections with scholarly work on poetry are now available. These include Joyce W. Warren's *The (Other) American Traditions*, Kilcup's *Nineteenth-Century American Women Writers: A Critical Reader*, A. Robert Lee's *Nineteenth-Century American Poetry*, and Dale M. Bauer and Philip Gould's *Cambridge Companion to Nineteenth-Century American Women's Writing*.

As the following sampling indicates, critical articles covering a broad range of issues in nineteenth-century American poetry are now beginning to make significant contributions. Wolosky's "The Claims of Rhetoric" traces nineteenth-century women poets' explorations of the private and public spheres. Focusing on Sigourney and Harper, Tricia Lootens's "Hemans and Her American Heirs" follows the transatlantic trajectory of the British poet Felicia Dorothea Browne Hemans's negotiations of domesticity and nationality. Mary De Jong's "Nineteenth-Century Reflections on 'The Poet of Today' " takes a close look at contemporary debates about the nature and direction of poetic production. Her "With My Burden I Begin" analyzes constructions of identity in nineteenth-century Puritan hymns, a genre that has not received much attention in literary-critical circles so far. The epic, another often overlooked genre, is the subject of John McWilliams's "The Epic in the Nineteenth Century." Loeffelholz in "The Religion of Art in the City at War" discusses the public use of poetry in the Boston Music Hall. For a wide-ranging stylistic account of different forms of nineteenth-century poetry, Paul G. Arakelian's "Personality and Style" is also worth consulting.

Finally, some scholars have chosen to explore the material conditions of poetry publication, paying particular attention to the kinds of venues in which poetry appeared. Kenneth M. Price and Susan Belasco Smith's essay collection *Periodical Literature in Nineteenth-Century America* provides detailed analyses of nineteenth-century periodical culture. These essays are usefully supplemented with Isabelle Lehuu's account in *Carnival on the Page* and Meredith L. McGill's *American Literature and the Culture of Reprinting, 1834–1853.* Patricia Okker's "Sarah Josepha Hale, Lydia Sigourney, and the Poetic Tradition in Two Nineteenth-Century Women's Magazines" situates two important women poets in the periodical context. Okker's *Our Sister Editors: Sarah J. Hale and the Tradition of Nineteenth-Century Women Editors* contains an invaluable analysis of how Hale's editorial policies brought diversity of thought and content into *Godey's Lady's Book.* The most recent contributions to this field, the essays collected in Sharon Harris's *Blue Pencils and Hidden Hands*, examine the efforts of women editors working at the apogee of periodical publishing in the United States.

7. Single-Author Studies

The number of single-author studies of nineteenth-century poets, including minority poets (see below under "Other Poetries") and long-neglected women writers, is expanding right along with more general studies of the period.

7.1. Dickinson and Whitman

Dickinson and Whitman are by far the most discussed poets of the nineteenth century. Even a brief survey of the range of critical debates sparked off by their poetry would require an article (or, rather, a book) of its own. For that reason and because a number of good reference works on the poets already exist, readers are here referred merely to a few entry points to vast fields of critical activity. For Dickinson are recommended Jane Donahue Eberwein's *An Emily Dickinson Encyclopedia*; Gudrun Grabher, Roland Hagenbuchle, and Christanne Miller's *Emily Dickinson Handbook*; Jonathan Morse's bibliographic essay; and Karen Dandurand's and Joseph Duchac's annotated bibliographies. Useful for an overview of

Whitman criticism are J. R. LeMaster and Donald D. Kummings's *Walt Whitman: An Encyclopedia*; David S. Reynolds's bibliographic essay; and the bibliographic reference works by Scott Giantvalley, by Kummings, and by Brent Lee Gibson. Further discussion of Whitman and Dickinson scholarship can be found in the "Biographies" section and in the "Abolitionist and Civil War Poetry," "Erotic Poetry," and "Single-Author Web Sites" subsections of this guide.

7.2. Poe

Shunned by F. O. Matthiessen, Poe has once again become a critical darling. For a cross-section of the current debate on Poe, J. Gerald Kennedy's collection of essays *A Historical Guide to Edgar Allan Poe* provides a good starting point. Another recent collection, *Romancing the Shadow*, coedited by Kennedy and Liliane Weissberg, contains essays on Poe's problematic racial attitudes. Robert von Hallberg in "Edgar Allan Poe, Poet-Critic" reminds us that Poe was a critic as well as a poet. For scholars interested in the latest developments in Poe criticism, *New Directions in Poe Studies*, the special issue *Poe Studies / Dark Romanticism*, edited by McGill, could prove a treasure trove.

7.3. Women Poets: Sigourney, Osgood, Piatt, and Others

Unless one counts biographies such as those on Fuller, Howe, and Menken, there are as of this writing no book-length critical studies devoted to individual women poets other than Dickinson. But an increasing number of single-author essays help fill this gap.

Sigourney is perhaps the prime example of the sentimental woman poet who was killed off by the New Criticism and resuscitated by recent recovery work. Nina Baym's breakthrough essay "Reinventing Lydia Sigourney" not only makes a strong case for reading this important writer's poetry as profoundly historical in orientation but also has forced a reappraisal of nineteenth-century American women's poetry generally. Annie Finch's "The Sentimental Poetess in the World" discusses the emotional impact of Sigourney's sentimentalism on the reader and reads her as a nature poet. In "Nineteenth-Century American Women Poets Revisited," Cheryl Walker moves Sigourney's work fully into the public sphere and argues that her writings can be read as examples of early national poetry. Tricia Lootens in "Hemans and Her American Heirs" also reads Sigourney as a poet committed to national concerns. Essays on Dickinson and Sigourney by Petrino ("Feet") and by Dorothy Z. Baker ("Ars Poetica") invite readers to study one of the most popular women poets of the nineteenth century alongside the most critically acclaimed. For more on Sigourney, readers are referred to entries in encyclopedias and sourcebooks: Patricia Crain's in Haralson's *Encyclopedia of American Poetry*, Kilcup's in Knight and Nelson's *Nineteenth-Century American Women Writers* ("Lydia . . . Sigourney"), and De Jong's *Legacy* profile.

On the poetry of Osgood, who is Sigourney's only serious rival for the title of major woman poet in the antebellum period, Dobson's "Sex, Wit, and Sentiment" is particularly instructive. Dobson discusses Osgood's critique of the codes of sentimental love and the mechanics of nineteenth-century reception, a reception that nevertheless established her as a sentimental poet. De Jong has contributed two important articles on Osgood ("Her Fair Fame" and "Lines"); "Lines from a Partly Published Drama" explores the poet's personal and aesthetic relationships with Poe. For a lively debate on Osgood's "Life Voyage" as a possible source of Poe's "Annabel Lee," see Buford Jones and Kent P. Ljungquist's "Poe, Mrs. Osgood, and 'Annabel Lee' " and John E. Reilly's "Mrs. Osgood's 'Life Voyage' and 'Annabel Lee.' " Richards's chapter on Osgood in her *Gender and the Poetics of Reception in Poe's Circle* explores the fantasy elements in Poe's presumed dalliance with Osgood and the role nineteenth-century conventions of newspaper publication played in giving rise to this popular myth.

In "Who Killed Lucretia Davidson?" Loeffelholz traces the posthumous rise to fame of another pair of sisters, Lucretia and Margaret Davidson, in what Richard Brodhead has called "the domestic-tutelary complex" ("Sparing" 89). The very different and far more tumultuous apprentice years of Julia Ward Howe are the subject of Gary Williams's *Hungry Heart*. Williams gives a detailed account of Howe's daring literary explorations into androgynous sexuality.

Judith Fetterley's recovery work has done much to bring Alice Cary into the literary canon, even though Fetterley devotes little attention to Cary's poetry. The poetry of Alice's sister Phoebe Cary is discussed in Cheryl Walker's essay "Nineteenth-Century Women Poets and Realism."

Jonathan Hall's entry in Haralson's *Encyclopedia of American Poetry* offers a highly useful overview of the sisters' poetic output; his discussion of Phoebe Cary's parodies of Poe, Wordsworth, Longfellow, and others is particularly good.

In "Passing as Fact," Janet Gray reveals the ways in which critical discourse has conflated the works of the African American writer Mollie E. Lambert with those of the white Southerner Mary Eliza Tucker Lambert. Gray uses this finding as a springboard for an extensive discussion of the dynamics of recovery work. Since the reintroduction of Piatt's poetry in 1995, interest in this long-lost Southern poet has steadily increased, and at least two substantial articles on her are slated for publication in 2007: Susan Grove Hall's essay on Piatt's relation to Amelia Welby's lyric tradition in her early poetry and Mary Wearn's essay on Piatt's poetics of maternal bereavement.

For an appraisal of the Boston poet and literary scholar Louise Imogen Guiney, see the article by Sheila A. Tully and Watts's *The Poetry of American Women* (139–40). Considering the disparagement of nineteenth-century women poets by modernist poets and critics, T. J. Jackson Lears's argument in *No Place of Grace* that Guiney was a resolutely antimodernist poet is instructive. Famous for her short story "The Yellow Wall-Paper," Charlotte Perkins Gilman also wrote verse, which is discussed in Bendixen's essay in this volume as well as by a number of other critics, including, most prominently, Denise D. Knight, Gary Scharnhorst, Joanne B. Karpinski, and Carol Farley Kessler.

7.4. Fireside Poets: Longfellow, Bryant, Lowell, Holmes, and Whittier

For a general introduction to the Fireside Poets, Thomas Wortham's "William Cullen Bryant and the Fireside Poets" still provides a good start, particularly since in recent years few critical studies of the group as a whole have been published. Sorby's *Schoolroom Poets* provides a sustained account of the important pedagogical role these poets played in the history of American education and what this role reveals about how poetry's uses were understood in the period. Readers may also wish to consult Dana Gioia's "Longfellow in the Aftermath of Modernism," which provides a detailed case study of a Fireside Poet's fate at the hands of scholars versed in modernist poetics. In the same vein, F. Brett Cox's "What Need,

Then, for Poetry?" is an important reassessment of genteel literature that investigates the political and historical contexts that enabled its disparagement from George Santayana ("Genteel American Poetry" and "Genteel Tradition") to the New Critics and beyond.

Studies of the individual poets are fairly common but vary widely in quality. Robert L. Gale's *Henry Wadsworth Longfellow Companion* offers a highly useful introduction to the professor-poet's life and work. It contains a brief introduction, a chronology of the main events in his life, and an alphabetical list of entries on a host of issues relating to his long writing career. Although more limited in scope, Haralson's "Mars in Petticoats" is a fascinating study that deftly inscribes Longfellow in a tradition of writing largely thought of as feminine. In a similar vein, Matthew Gartner's "Becoming Longfellow" interrogates Longfellow's negotiations of gender identity.

Authorial constructions of masculinity are also the focus of a recent article by Bryce Traister on Holmes. Peter Gibian's *Oliver Wendell Holmes and the Culture of Conversation* offers a more sustained treatment of the lawyer-poet's life and work. For an absorbing account of Holmes's exchange of thoughts with William James and Charles Sanders Peirce on the social origin of ideas, readers should consult Louis Menand's *The Metaphysical Club.*

On Bryant, Albert F. McLean's Twayne Series book is still useful. More recently, Kinereth Meyer in "Landscape and Counter-landscape in the Poetry of William Cullen Bryant" has explored the social and political implications of Bryant's poetic treatment of landscape, and Eric Carl Link has scrutinized Bryant's and Longfellow's contributions to national mythmaking in "American Nationalism and the Defense of Poetry."

No literary-critical books have been published on Lowell in recent years, but there are two important articles. Michael J. Bell's "The Only True Folk Songs We Have in English" discusses the contribution Lowell's poems made to the formation of national identity. Kent P. Ljungquist's "Fellowship with Other Poets" brings Lowell into a dialogue not only with another Fireside Poet (Longfellow) but also with Poe and Abijah Metcalf Ide, Jr., a young admirer of Poe. As with all the Fireside Poets, recent critical work on Whittier is sparse, so Jayne K. Kribbs's 1980 *Critical Essays on John Greenleaf Whittier* provides a still useful overview. Critics are now beginning to bring Whittier's work into a dialogue with that of women poets with similar concerns. Articles by Shirley Marchalonis

("Model"), Wendy Dasler Johnson, and Beverly Peterson establish connections between Whittier and Howe, Stowe, and Larcom.

7.5. They Wrote Poetry? Crane, Harte, Howells, Fuller, Emerson, and Very

Like Harte, Howells, Fuller, and Emerson, Crane is one of those nineteenth-century poets whose poetry has attracted far less attention than their other writings. Stanley Wertheim's *Stephen Crane Encyclopedia* is an invaluable source of information on all of Crane's life and work, including his poetry. David Halliburton's *The Color of the Sky* represents a substantial contribution to Crane scholarship that also discusses the writer's verse. Keith Gandal approaches *The Black Riders* from a biographical angle in "A Spiritual Autopsy of Stephen Crane" and explores the mysticism of Crane's prose and poetry in "Stephen Crane's 'Mystic Places.' " Finally, while most of the essays collected in Harold Bloom's *Stephen Crane* focus on Crane's prose, several critics also discuss Crane's poetry collection *War Is Kind.*

Better known for his frontier tales and literary parodies than his poetry, Bret Harte published poetry that had large popular appeal. In "Ways That Are Dark," the leading Harte scholar Gary Scharnhorst discusses the poet's critique of anti-Chinese propaganda in California. Scharnhorst has also written the Twayne Series *Bret Harte.*

It may surprise some readers of our volume that Howells, the dean of realist fiction, wrote a large body of poetry that ranges from the sentimental to the realist and protomodernist. Julie Bates Dock and Bernard F. Engel have each written a noteworthy essay on Howells's poetry. Edwin H. Cady, editor of Howells's *"Pebbles," "Monochromes," and Other Modern Poems,* reads part of Howells's later poetic oeuvre, particularly his "Black Cross Farm," as anticipating modernist concerns.

Like Emerson, Margaret Fuller ranks among the most influential intellectuals of her time, but her poetry, much of which draws on private symbolism, has attracted surprisingly little attention. Two critical articles by Jeffrey Steele, one on the process of editing her poetry ("Editing"), the other on her changing poetics ("Freeing"), help fill this void. In addition, chapter 7 of Steele's *Transfiguring America* is devoted to Fuller's 1844 poetry.

While the vast majority of Emerson scholarship focuses on his life or his essays, one full-length treatment of his poetic oeuvre is now available. Robert K. Hudnut's *The Aesthetics of Ralph Waldo Emerson* achieves no mean feat as it situates Emerson's poetics in his thought as a whole. Also useful is "Frolic Architecture," Brian Harding's study of the intersections between music and poetry, architecture and wildness in Emerson's verse.

Though, like Emerson, embarked on a spiritual quest, Jones Very wrote poetry of a very different kind. Sarah T. Clayton's *The Angelic Sins of Jones Very* explores the ecstatic poetry of this transcendentalist mystic, and David Seed's "Alone with God and Nature" considers Very's work with that of Very's student Frederick Goddard Tuckerman.

8. Other Poetries

As the introduction to our volume notes, nineteenth-century American poets wrote in a variety of distinctive lyric subgenres whose conventions were laid out beforehand, in the same way that poetic forms (e.g., the elegy, the sonnet) are given. They willingly subordinated their individual expressivity to the expressivity available in and associated with the kind of poem they were writing or the kind of poet they wanted to be recognized as. These subgenres could (and did) evolve around occasional circumstances (the Civil War), the ethnicity of the author (Native American, African American), and the social function of the poem (abolitionism, eroticism). This section touches on some of the categories of poetry that nineteenth-century American writers produced.

8.1. African American Poetry: Harper, Dunbar, and Others

To date, only one monograph on African American literature has taken nineteenth-century poetry as a substantial focus: Sherman's *Invisible Poets.* It includes sketches of twenty-six poets, many of them little known. Sherman quotes liberally from the poets' work, giving readers a good first impression of the writers' concerns and styles. Fahamisha Patricia Brown's *Performing the Word* is considerably more current in its concern with poets' negotiations of oral and written culture, but aside from Dunbar, Brown focuses on twentieth-century African American poets. Brown and Sherman are usefully supplemented with the *Encarta Africana*, a splendid reference work on CD-ROM that has useful entries on individual poets ranging from Charlotte L. Forten Grimké to Harper as well as on more general topics like dialect poetry or spirituals.

Several important critical articles on nineteenth-century African

American poetry are available. Taken together, Gloria T. Hull's two essays, "Black Women Poets from Wheatley to Walker" and "Afro-American Women Poets," provide a good introduction to a number of nineteenth-century African American women poets. A more recent account of the genealogy of African American poetry from a feminist-psychoanalytic perspective appears in the fifth chapter of Barbara Johnson's *The Feminist Difference*, where Johnson discusses the work of Phillis Wheatley, among others. Marcellus Blount's "The Preacherly Text" deals mainly with the work of Dunbar but also discovers the sources of other antebellum black poetry in preachers' sermons. A. G. Ullyatt's "The Hum of Omissions / The Chant of Vacancies" is a significant contribution to the study of a number of neglected African American poems.

With the exceptions of Harper and Dunbar, there are very few single-author studies of nineteenth-century African American poets. Harper is best known for her feminist activism and for her life spent in service to her ethnic community—which for her meant massive literary production. Melba Joyce Boyd, herself a poet as well as an African studies scholar, has contributed an important critical study on Harper. Her *Discarded Legacy* is worth reading for its skillful negotiation of Harper's aesthetic and political perspectives. Maryemma Graham and Frances Smith Foster have both written highly informative biocritical introductions to their respective collections of Harper's poetry (*Complete Poems* and *Brighter Coming Day*). Essays that deal explicitly with the interface between Harper's life and art are Sarah Elizabeth Bennison's "The Poetry and Activism of Frances Ellen Watkins Harper" and Janna Knittel's "Songs for the People." Although not on Harper's poetry, Carla L. Peterson's chapter on Harper as part of the preacherly tradition in black women's writing in *Doers of the Word* provides invaluable context for any understanding of her verse. Other scholars who have written extensively on Harper are Lauren Berlant, Michael Bennett, Paul Lauter ("Is Frances . . . Harper"), Janet Gray (*Race*), and Loeffelholz (*From School*).

Dunbar is Harper's only rival as a nineteenth-century African American poet of interest today. Houston A. Baker's chapter on him in *Singers of Daybreak* and Peter Revell and David J. Nordloh's study in the Twayne Series remain useful. For more recent critical contributions, see Joanne M. Braxton's introduction to Dunbar's *Collected Poetry*, Pierre Damien Mvuyekure's entry on Dunbar in *African American Authors, 1745–1945*, and Felton O. Best's "Paul Laurence Dunbar's Protest Literature." Since

Howells first raised the issue in his introduction to the poet's *Lyrics of Lowly Life* (1895), Dunbar's use of dialect in his poetry has generated heated debate in the scholarly literature over the merits of his dialect versus his standard verse. Many notable black scholars have lined up on either side of the argument, including James Weldon Johnson, Henry Louis Gates, Jr., and Marcellus Blount.

Aside from Dunbar; his wife, Alice Dunbar-Nelson; and Harper, other nineteenth-century black poets—from Ann Plato and George Moses Horton to the many turn-of-the-century women poets collected by Sherman as part of the Schomburg series—have received markedly less attention. Todd Gernes has published a groundbreaking article on the lesser-known poet Sarah Louisa Forten. His "Poetic Justice" provides a profile of Forten's life and work, at the same time revealing that some poems previously attributed to Forten were actually written by the white Quaker Eliza Earle. Paula Bennett treats four of the Schomburg poets—Lizelia Augusta Jenkins Moorer, Maggie Pogue Johnson, and the poet sisters Priscilla Jane Thompson and Clara Ann Thompson—in "Re-writing Dunbar: Realism, Black Women Poets, and the Genteel." A nineteenth-century viewpoint on African American women's writing is available through the Schomburg reprint of N. F. Mossell's *The Work of the Afro-American Woman* (1894).

For discussions of African American spirituals, W. E. B. DuBois's *The Souls of Black Folk*—now available in a splendid Norton critical edition that includes five contemporary reviews and seven critical articles—is still a great place to begin. For a detailed account of famous nineteenth-century singers of spirituals, scholars may turn to Andrew Ward's *Dark Midnight When I Rise,* about the Fisk Jubilee Singers. For more on the Fisk singers, Nassim Balestrini, whose essay on Dunbar is in this volume, also recommends the Fisk University Web site (*Jubilee Singers*) as well as the *Audio Companion* to Gates and McKay's *Norton Anthology of African American Literature*, which features the group's performance of "Been in the Storm So Long" (track 2) and "Go Down, Moses" as performed by Paul Robeson (track 1). Katherine Clay Bassard's *Spiritual Interrogations: Culture, Gender, and Community in Early African American Women's Writing* stresses the community-building function of spirituals and their performative redefinition of racial boundaries.

Finally, no discussion of nineteenth-century African American writing can afford to pass over Elizabeth McHenry's excellent *Forgotten Readers,* which traces the history of African American literacy among free blacks in the North both before and after the Civil War.

8.2. *Native American Poetry: Johnson, Ridge, Posey, and Others*

Most criticism of Native American poetry focuses either on the oral poetry from before the European invasion or on poetry published since the beginning of the Native American Renaissance in the late 1960s. To date, substantial general treatments of nineteenth-century Native American verse are rare. A notable exception is the contemporary poet Linda Henderson Hogan's groundbreaking "Nineteenth-Century Native American Poets," published in 1980, reminding readers of the existence of a generation of writers active well before the 1960s. Hogan discusses poets writing at the turn of the century (E. Pauline Johnson, Alexander Posey, Zitkala-Ša) as well as the earlier writer John Rollin Ridge—author of the first Native American novel and one of the earliest volumes of poetry. In the third chapter of his *Native American Literature*, Andrew Wiget also discusses the poetic works of Johnson, Ridge, and Posey. Wiget's two indispensable reference works, *Dictionary of Native American Literature* and *Handbook of Native American Literature*, cover a variety of nineteenth-century poets as well as more general topics. In addition, Matthew Parr's entry "Nineteenth-Century Versions of American Indian Poetry" in Haralson's *Encyclopedia* serves as a valuable guide.

While most of the Native American poetry published and read during the nineteenth century consisted of Europeanized translations of traditional songs and prayers (collected, typically, by anthropologists but widely imitated and paraphrased by white writers), Native American writers such as Jane Johnston Schoolcraft, Johnson, Posey, Ridge, and Zitkala-Ša, who sought to build bridges between cultures, published poetry in the strictly literary sense. Because they received a European-style education, these poets mix conventions in their writing, sometimes speaking in an explicitly "Indian" voice, at other times writing in a European one.

Of this group of writers, Johnson, daughter of a Mohawk leader and his English wife, carried out this internalized divide most fully. Indeed, in her paid performances, she would dress for half of the evening in Native garb to recite her "Indian poetry," then change to European dress to recite her European-style verse. In *Paddling Her Own Canoe*, Gerson and

Strong-Boag trace Johnson's multifaceted roles as poet, performer, women's rights spokesperson, and negotiator between the worlds of Mohawk society and larger Canadian culture. Mary Elizabeth Leighton's "Performing Pauline Johnson" documents Johnson's self-stylization and its representation in periodical literature.

For information on the highly public (and controversial) Native American figure Posey and his writing, Alexia M. Kosmider's critical monograph *Tricky Tribal Discourse* offers a place to begin. Much work still has to be done on nineteenth-century Native American poetry.

8.3. Ethnic Poetries: Jewish, Irish, Chicano/Chicana, Chinese, and Others

With the influx of immigrant populations into the United States from all over the world, nineteenth-century American literary production became visibly split between books and periodicals addressed to the original English-speaking population and those that sprang up, sometimes overnight, to serve the needs of ethnic communities for whom English was a second language, if it was spoken at all. Driven by their editors' desire to maintain group identity and solidarity, these publications tried to acculturate newly arrived immigrants to the radically different society in which they now lived. They also tried to help these immigrants maintain their ties to the land they had abandoned—as, for example, Irish newspapers did when offering lessons in Gaelic and picture tours of the great monuments of Ireland's past. Today, interested scholars are canvassing these and similar sources for the poetry they contain. This section touches on some of the most important recoveries of nineteenth-century ethnic poetries.

Among ethnic poetries, Jewish poetry has received the most attention to date, with Emma Lazarus and Adah Isaacs Menken receiving the bulk of interest. Five lines of "The New Colossus," inscribed on the pedestal of the Statue of Liberty, made Lazarus the best-known Jewish American poet of the nineteenth century. Daniel Marom's source study "Who Is the 'Mother of Exiles'?" positions the sonnet firmly in Jewish culture. Additional important critical contributions by Gregory Eiselein, Wolosky ("American-Jewish Typology"), and Ranen Omer-Sherman discuss other poems in Lazarus's oeuvre and situate them in a variety of different contexts, ranging from Jewish history to United States immigration and the interplay of national and ethnic identity.

For an introduction to critical work on Menken—the chameleon-like actress and poet who converted to Judaism on marrying the first of her four husbands, Alexander Isaac Menken (she would add an *s* to *Isaac*)—Peter Dollard's "A Guide to Core Critical Studies of Adah Isaacs Menken" is highly useful. John Cofran's "The Identity of Adah Isaacs Menken" is also important because of its persuasive argument that Menken was the daughter of Richard McCord, an Irish merchant, and his wife, Catherine. If true, this parentage would put to rest the hotly debated question of the poet's racial identity. But see Sentilles's *Performing Menken* for a more complicated view of this vexed issue.

Diane Lichtenstein's more general *Writing Their Nations: The Tradition of Nineteenth-Century American Jewish Women Writers* takes us beyond Lazarus and Menken. Lichtenstein discusses Jewish American poets' complex negotiations of gender, ethnicity, and nationality against the background of divided national loyalties and a profound desire to assimilate to American society. Among the poets she discusses are Rebekah Hyneman, Penina Moïse, Octavia Harby Moses, Lazarus, and Menken. In the classroom, such texts are usefully supplemented with auditory material—for instance, the collection of Jewish labor songs *In Love and in Struggle* (Mlotek et al.). One can also learn a great deal about the political concerns of nineteenth-century Yiddish writers from their early twentieth-century successors, whom Amelia Glaser and David Weintraub have collected in *Proletpen: America's Rebel Yiddish Poets.*

Two books that provide helpful contextual information for reading early Jewish poetry are Hutchins Hapgood's anecdotal study *The Spirit of the Ghetto*, first published in 1902, which gives insight into the spiritual and cultural lives of Jews living on the Lower East Side of New York City at the turn of the century, and Susan A. Glenn's *Daughters of the Shtetl*, which deals with the daily lives and values of young Jewish women working in the sweatshops of the period.

Although a potentially rich field of inquiry, Irish American poetry has provoked less scholarly attention than has Jewish poetry, despite the fact that most Irish American poets wrote in English. Irish poetry abounds in the newspapers and magazines directed to the Irish communities in large urban centers (e.g., the *Boston Pilot* and New York City's *Irish World*), and, though significantly understudied, a number of Irish poets penned volumes of verse, including, most notably, John Boyle O'Reilly, editor of the *Pilot*, and Mary McMullen Ford ("Una"). The one ethnically Irish author of books of poetry who has commanded attention is Louise Imogen

Guiney. But since she largely confined her Irish poems to occasional publications in the *Pilot*, such criticism as there is of her work has overwhelmingly focused on her mainstream verse. Not without irony, among the largest bodies of American verse on the state of Ireland in the nineteenth century was penned by an American Protestant poet, Sarah Piatt, who spent eleven years in what she called exile on the Emerald Isle and wrote scathingly of the conditions she found there.

Among Irish American periodical poets, none commanded greater reverence than Fanny Parnell, the America-dwelling sister of Charles Stuart Parnell, Ireland's "uncrowned king." In *Fanny and Anna Parnell: Ireland's Patriot Sisters*, Jane McL. Côté offers a biographical account of Charles's two activist sisters. Although Fanny died young, her fiery poetry in Ireland's cause was reprinted in Irish communities across the world. Bennett discusses her work and that of other Irish American women poets in *Poets in the Public Sphere*.

Patrick Ward's *Exile, Emigration and Irish Writing* provides a general discussion of thematic issues in Irish diasporic writing, arguing that the overemphasis on the theme of exile has blinded readers to the complexity of many texts. In *'Twas Only an Irishman's Dream*, William H. A. Williams looks at changing attitudes toward the Irish embedded in American popular song. For historical contextualization, Noel Ignatiev's *How the Irish Became White*—a fascinating study of how Irish Americans defined their ethnic identity vis-à-vis and, more often, against African Americans—is useful, as is Hasia R. Diner's *Erin's Daughters in America*, which traces the lives of Irish immigrant women in nineteenth-century America, and Mary P. Ryan's *Women in Public: Between Banners and Ballots, 1825–1880.*

It should not be surprising, given how long it takes for criticism to develop around recovered writers, that there is virtually no criticism extant other than introductions to texts for the remaining ethnic poetries mentioned here. But the rate of recovery for these poets is clearly accelerating. Examples of minority poetry in translation are now available in the *Heath Anthology of American Literature* (Lauter et al.) and in more specialized anthologies such as Louis Torres's *The World of Early Chicano Poetry, 1846–1910* and Janet Gray's *She Wields a Pen*, which is especially rich in women minority writers and has a good sampling of poetry in translation by the Hawaiian queen Lili'uokalini. Poems of Chinese immigrants are available in *Songs of Gold Mountain: Cantonese Rhymes from San Francisco Chinatown*, edited and translated by Marlon K. Hom, and in *Island:*

Poetry and History of Chinese Immigrants on Angel Island, edited and translated by Him Mark Lai, Genny Lim, and Judy Yung. The collected writings in English of the Japanese immigrant poet Yone Noguchi have recently been reprinted; volume 1 is devoted entirely to his verse.

General scholarly literature on each of these immigrant groups and on nineteenth-century immigration as a whole is far too vast to summarize here, but Matthew Frye Jacobson's *Whiteness of a Different Color: European Immigrants and the Alchemy of Race* and Priscilla Wald's *Constituting Americans: Cultural Anxiety and Narrative Form* are good places to start. Although much more specialized and sketchy, the essays in *Print Culture in a Diverse America*, edited by James P. Danky and Wayne A. Wiegand, are also useful.

8.4. Abolitionist and Civil War Poetry

For abolitionists in general—but especially for female abolitionists, whose outlets for reaching the public were so much more limited than they were for men—poetry was a primary vehicle through which to register convictions and enlist others in their struggle. All the major abolitionist newspapers (the *Liberator*, the *National Enquirer*, the *Pennsylvania Freeman*, and the *Genius of Universal Emancipation*, to name a few) carried at least some verse, as did African American publications such as Douglass's *North Star*, the *Colored American*, and the *National Anti-slavery Standard*. A full-dress scholarly study of this poetry has yet to be written, but Jean Fagan Yellin's *Women and Sisters: The Antislavery Feminists in American Culture* discusses many of the controversies to which this literature addressed itself as well as those to which it gave rise. Julie Winch's essay "You Have Talents—Only Cultivate Them" contains a rare and valuable discussion of African American women's abolitionist verse. Lyde Cullen Sizer's *The Political Work of Northern Women Writers and the Civil War* is useful for background but has little to say of verse, whether written before, during, or after the Civil War.

As Tyler B. Hoffman argues in this volume, the Civil War poetry of established writers like Whitman, Dickinson, and Melville is fruitfully studied against the background of the often deeply partisan war poetry contained in the anthologies mentioned earlier. These anthologies provide a good starting point, especially if read in conjunction with Alice Fahs's *The Imagined Civil War*, one of the few book-length critical treatments of Civil War poetry available. Although making no claim to be a study of Civil War poetry per se, Janet Gray's *Race and Time*, which gives close attention to two important Civil War poets (Harper and Piatt), takes the war years as a watershed period for the emergence of racial modernity. Stanton Garner's *The Civil War World of Herman Melville* is also an exception and like Fahs's study is based on extensive archival research. Garner is usefully supplemented by Elizabeth Renker's "Melville the Poet," which documents signs of growing scholarly interest in Melville's poetic oeuvre.

The importance of Whitman's poetry on the Civil War has never been in dispute, but the recovery of Dickinson's Civil War poetry marks a major shift in how this reclusive woman poet is read today. Wolosky's *Emily Dickinson: A Voice of War* remains indispensable. In addition, Leigh Anne Marcellin's "Emily Dickinson's Civil War Poetry" and "Singing off the Charnel Steps," Maurice S. Lee's "Writing through the War: Melville and Dickinson after the Renaissance," and Paul R. Cappucci's "Depicting the Oblique: Emily Dickinson's Poetic Response to the American Civil War" are highly recommended.

Several essays deal with more than one Civil War poet. Of these, Carolyn L. Karcher's comparison of Melville and Lydia Maria Child ("Moderate") and Lawrence Buell's on Whitman and Melville are particularly instructive.

8.5. Erotic Poetry

While Poe's dark eroticism and Whitman's sexually charged imagery have been widely noted, many students of the period may be surprised by the abundance of erotic themes, images, and motifs in the poetry of Victorian America. Recent scholarship, much of it on women poets, has done much to challenge popular notions about the absence of sexuality from nineteenth-century literature and culture.

Women poets as different in their poetic sensibilities as Dickinson, E. Pauline Johnson, Sara Jane Lippincott, Alice Cary, Margaret Fuller, and Harriet Prescott Spofford produced a wide range of erotic poetry, much of it daring in its exploration of autoeroticism and lesbian sexuality. Yopie Prins, in *The Victorian Sappho*, and Watts, in *The Poetry of American Women* (72–81, 174–85), notice frequent allusions to Sappho in nineteenth-century women's poetry. Ruth A. Roman's *Annie Adams Fields: The Spirit of Charles Street* invites us to speculate about the nature of the intimate relationship between Fields and Sarah Orne Jewett and its possible influence on Fields's erotic poetry. Judy Grahn's *The Highest Apple* puts Dickinson squarely in a tradition of lesbian poetry, a reading that is complicated by Paula Bennett in "The Pea That Duty Locks" and, even more, in "Critical Clitoridectomy," which draws its examples of female sexual imagery not just from Dickinson but also from such unlikely poets as Sigourney and Hannah Gould. Kilcup's "Emily Dickinson's Pearls" places Dickinson's autoerotic discourse in conversation with Hawthorne's in *The Scarlet Letter*.

On Whitman, one of the most openly erotic of nineteenth-century poets, Vivian R. Pollak's *The Erotic Whitman*, which draws heavily on the poet's biography and engages with current critical debates on masculinity, sets the standard. The first extensive discussion of Whitman as a homosexual artist can be found in Robert K. Martin's 1979 book *The Homosexual Tradition in American Poetry*, recently reissued in an expanded edition. In 1992, Martin also edited a collection of essays that has a strong focus on the subject, *The Continuing Presence of Walt Whitman*. More recent contributions are Michael Moon's *Disseminating Whitman*, Byrne R. S. Fone's *Masculine Landscapes*, and M. Jimmie Killingsworth's *Whitman's Poetry of the Body*; we can add to these Jonathan Ned Katz's discussion of Whitman in the *Queer World* reader and Hershel Parker's "The Real 'Live Oak, with Moss': Straight Talk about Whitman's Gay Manifesto."

Dickinson has also been the subject of a number of queer rereadings. Ellen Louise Hart's "The Encoding of Homoerotic Desire" and Martha Nell Smith's *Rowing in Eden* discuss Dickinson's intimate letters to and relationship with her sister-in-law, Susan Gilbert Dickinson.

9. Web Resources

The World Wide Web has already revolutionized the teaching of American literature, at home and abroad, because access has always been a key issue for both teachers and students. In addition to the print resources listed above, viewers can visit a rapidly growing number of Web sites that provide access to an unprecedented wealth of primary and secondary material. A very useful metasite is the Research Society for American Periodicals' *RSAP: Resources for Research*, which has links to various databases as well as to individual publications.

9.1. Online Periodicals and Newspapers

Perhaps the most useful Internet resources for researchers as well as students are digitized nineteenth-century periodicals and newspapers. These allow for a study of not only the poetry but also the illustrations and advertising that surround them. As Kilcup has argued, such contextualization can entirely reorient our understanding of a poem and of the poet's as well as the editor's ambitions on the reader.

The *Making of America* database stands out as the largest treasure trove. Funded by the Andrew W. Mellon Foundation, it is a collaborative project of the University of Michigan and Cornell University that makes available in electronic form about 9,500 books and 2,457 journal issues (or 50,000 journal articles) from the antebellum period through Reconstruction. Students of nineteenth-century poetry will find ample examples of periodical verse by poets ranging from Longfellow to Alice Cary and Phoebe Cary in the full-text issues of over twenty years of journals, ranging from major literary journals like the *Atlantic* and *Galaxy* to more regional ones like the *Southern Literary Messenger* and the *Overland Monthly*. What once had to be unearthed by arduous archival work is now available at the click of a mouse.

Other periodicals and newspapers available online in whole or part are the *Lowell Offering*; the *Occident*, a Jewish American magazine edited by Isaac Leeser; the *A.M.E. Church Review*, house organ for the African Methodist Episcopal Church; and some of the *Cherokee Phoenix* issues from 1828–34, which are hosted by the University of Georgia's Galileo virtual library. In the 12 March 1831 issue of the *Cherokee Phoenix*, Sigourney first published her "Cherokee Mother."

9.2. Poetry Databases

One of the good things about teaching nineteenth-century literature is that most works of the era are no longer copyrighted and for that reason easily available, often in several versions, on the World Wide Web. The first stop should be the University of Pennsylvania's *Online Books Page*, a metasite that indexes over 20,000 free books, including many poetry collections. This site is supremely useful because it provides a one-stop access point to e-text archives as diverse and extensive as *Project Gutenberg*, the

University of Virginia's *Electronic Text Center*, *Making of America*, *BoondocksNet.com*, and many others.

The *American Verse Project*, an extensive electronic archive of volumes of poetry published before 1920 with a strong emphasis on the nineteenth century, is another invaluable Web-based resource. Among other gems, the collection holds volumes by Sigourney, Poe, Bryant, Larcom, John Hay, Albery Allson Whitman, and Whittier as well as Caroline May's 1853 *American Female Poets* anthology. The *American Verse Project* hosts over 170 volumes.

Bartleby.com is another excellent Internet source for nineteenth-century poetry, though its collection is by no means limited to either the period or the genre. Its collection of verse reproduces the full texts of anthologies such as Edmund Stedman's *An American Anthology, 1787–1900* (1900), which contains a surprisingly large number of poets subsequently forgotten under New Critical influence; Louis Untermeyer's *Modern American Poetry* (1919), which includes poems by, among many others, Dickinson, Gilman, Guiney, and Reese; and Thomas Lounsbury's *Yale Book of American Verse* (1912). Apart from these anthologies, *Bartleby.com* also hosts the so-called *Complete Poems* of Emily Dickinson of the 1924 edition (597 in number).

Chadwyck-Healey packages American poetry in a variety of ways—including *LION*, or *Literature Online*—with the same texts. *American Poetry, 1600–1900* has four extensive subcollections that are all immensely useful to students of nineteenth-century poetry: *Early Nineteenth Century, 1800–1829*; *Pre–Civil War Period, 1830–1860*; *The Civil War and Its Aftermath, 1861–1889*; and *Late Nineteenth Century and Pre-modernist Era, 1890–1914*. There is also a separate database for *African American Poetry*. Although the permutations (and different types of search engine) are potentially bewildering, this collection of nineteenth-century poetry is possibly the largest available on the World Wide Web today. For Sigourney alone, the full text of fourteen volumes and additional eighteen individual poems are included. The collection as a whole features the work of more than two hundred poets, and much of the material is unavailable in even large research libraries. Note that this Web site is proprietary; students and teachers need to check with their libraries whether they carry it.

The University of Virginia's *Electronic Text Center* has many text collections but only a few are useful to scholars of nineteenth-century poetry. Among these are the *Walt Whitman, 1819–1892* pages, which host nine different versions of *Leaves of Grass* that can easily be compared thanks to a so-called side-by-side comparator—basically a split screen. Other resources are electronic editions of poems by Harper, Longfellow, and Holmes.

Students of nineteenth-century poetry may also wish to visit the University of Toronto's beautiful and well-maintained *Representative Poetry Online* site, which provides access to selected poems, a short note on life and works, and a bibliography of primary and secondary materials of almost five hundred British and American poets from the seventh to the twenty-first century. Among nineteenth-century poets, Thaxter, Howe, Phoebe Cary, Helen Hunt Jackson, Whitman, and many others are represented. In addition, this site hosts a good glossary of poetic terms.

9.3. Multiple-Author Web Sites

Other Web sites focus on specific groups of writers. *African American Women Writers of the Nineteenth Century*, maintained by the Schomburg Center for Research in Black Culture, is a particularly beautiful site that provides access to the poetry volumes collected in the print version of the Schomburg series. The site also provides short biographical sketches of African American women poets. For visual background material, Schomburg's extensive *Images of African Americans from the Nineteenth Century* collection, containing mostly digitized engravings and photographs, is also strongly recommended.

There are no major sites that focus exclusively on nineteenth-century African American poetry. But there are a number of more general electronic resources on African American literature and culture, some of them metasites, that do provide valuable information on the poetry of the period. Particularly recommended are Elna L. Saxton and Jo McClamroch's "African American Culture," a bibliographic essay published in *College and Research Libraries News* and available via the Web site of the American Library Association; San Antonio College's *Brief Chronology of African American Literature*; and *African American Writers: Online E-texts*, hosted by the Internet School Library Media Center. For information about African American spirituals—poems in their own right but also the popular background against which much African American literary production of the nineteenth century must be understood—the PBS documentary *Jubilee Singers: Sacrifice and Glory* is a starting point that includes audio samples and a teacher's guide.

For the teaching of nineteenth-century poetry by and about Native Americans, Edward S. Curtis's controversial *The North American Indian* provides an important context. *American Memory* makes available the more than two thousand photogravure plates in its collection *Edward S. Curtis's* The North American Indian. Studying some of Curtis's pictures alongside poems by Johnson, Sigourney, or Bryant gives students and teachers a great opportunity to discuss the politics of representing American Indians, including the deeply problematic topos of the vanishing Indian, with which so many nineteenth-century poets engaged, as Paul Lauter's and Elizabeth Petrino's essays in this volume underscore. For information relating to individual Native American poets of the nineteenth century, readers are advised to consult the Internet Public Library's excellent *Native American Authors* project, which provides very brief biographical accounts and an annotated guide to online resources on writers ranging from Johnson to Ridge and Zitkala-Ša.

For scholars interested in nineteenth-century working-class poetry, little of which is available in print, Jim Zwick's *Bread and Roses* Web site is of great use since it makes accessible over a hundred labor poems and songs from the late nineteenth to the early twentieth century and has a rich collection of historical materials that help contextualize this verse. Catherine Lavender's Web page "Texts about Lowell Mill Girls" gives access to the lyrics of a number of strike songs by the Lowell mill girls, while Stephen Railton's Uncle Tom's Cabin *and American Culture* site provides access to the minstrelsy of *Christy's Nigga Songster*, including performances of minstrel songs.

For Jewish writers, *Judaic Treasures of the Library of Congress: Nineteenth-Century American Poets* has information about four women poets, with short biographies, a few textual images, and some brief selections of poetry. Brown University maintains a Web site for *The Harris Collection of American Poetry and Plays*, which includes details on Yiddish poets.

9.4. Single-Author Web Sites

Many Web sites are devoted entirely to one nineteenth-century author. As might be expected, the canonical authors usually are better represented, but the range of Web materials for even obscure poets has redemocratized the field of American poetry, facilitating its reconstruction as a set of interconnected voices in regular conversation rather than a small group of the excellent. Not all sites are equal in quality, but teachers can help students select those that have the most to offer. The following selection highlights some gems.

The single best Web resource on Whitman is Ed Folsom and Kenneth M. Price's *Walt Whitman Archive.* This site offers a very good biography, written by the editors; digital reproductions of Whitman's manuscripts; a large number of high-quality images of the poet; a good selection of contemporary reviews and current criticism; an extensive searchable bibliography; a wax-cylinder recording of "America" read by Whitman himself; and much more. For the other preeminent writer of nineteenth-century poetry, Dickinson, the *Emily Dickinson International Society* maintains links both to the Dickinson electronic archives (which addresses the needs of scholars and teachers) and to the *Virtual Emily* site, which is directed more to general-interest readers.

The Works of Ralph Waldo Emerson (Emerson) is a large, searchable database that includes biographical data, some contemporary criticism, and a concordance. For Poe scholars, the *Edgar Allan Poe Society of Baltimore* is an invaluable research tool that contains not only all the poems he published in a variety of versions, together with their original places and dates of publication, but also extensive biographical and bibliographic information; a generous selection of articles from *Poe Studies / Dark Romanticism*; and additional articles, reviews, and essays written between 1827 and today. *Life and Works of Herman Melville* has a page on Melville's *Battle-Pieces and Aspects of the War* that gives access not only to some of the better-known poems but also to a selection of contemporary reviews and criticism of the volume. Here we can read in an 1866 review that "Nature did not make him a poet."

Many women poets of the nineteenth century were subjected to similar criticism, though rather more in the twentieth than in the nineteenth century. The Web now provides ready access to many of their texts as well as contextual material, thus allowing researchers and students to reevaluate the achievements of these poets. *Poems of Lydia Howard Huntley Sigourney* (Sigourney) contains nineteen of her more famous poems. In the context of this volume's concerns, it is interesting to note that the page is part of the *Classic Poetry* site, which, according to its editor, is designed "for students who hate poetry." Another good resource is *Elizabeth Oakes Smith, 1806–1893*, which hosts a chronology of Smith's life; a gallery of images of the poet, her family, and her places of residence; bibliographies of primary works and criticism; an annotated list of links; and her essay "Woman and Her Needs," which helps researchers situate her work in a broader social and political context. In addition, the site reproduces an oddity: a portrait of the poet on a 1910 collectible Mogul cigarette packet card. This card, part of Mogul's Famous Authors series, is interesting because it testifies to the poet's continuing fame into the early twentieth century.

Emma Lazarus, the Jewish Women's Archive's beautifully maintained site, provides extensive information on Lazarus, including a section entitled "Poet or Poetess," which touches on issues at the heart of this volume. *Sarah Morgan Bryan Piatt* contains images of the poet; some poems; a brief biography and bibliography; and, most importantly, a complete finding list for her widely distributed and reprinted poems. SeacoastNH.com maintains *Celia Laighton Thaxter*, an elaborate site dedicated to Thaxter, whose many ties to the Isles of Shoals have made her a much-loved regional figure.

Several Native American poets of the nineteenth century also have Web sites dedicated to their life and works. *Poems of John Rollin Ridge* (Ridge), by the American Native Press Archives, has a concise biography, a short bibliography, and the complete text of an 1868 edition of Ridge's poems. *The Pauline Johnson Archive*, hosted by McMaster University, provides extensive biographical information, documentary evidence in the form of digitized pictures of the poet and her family, and posters announcing Johnson's recitals. The site also gives access to several of her poems.

Single-author sites on African American poets include the excellent *Paul Laurence Dunbar Digital Text Collection* at Wright State University, which offers easy access to more than two hundred of Dunbar's poems, his *Who Dat Say Chicken in Dis Crowd* libretto, biographical and bibliographic information, and audio versions of four poems. Frances Harper is only one of the women poets of the nineteenth century covered by the University of Minnesota's *Voices from the Gaps* (*VG*), which provides reliable biographical and bibliographic information as well as annotated lists of links to other electronic resources.

In addition to single-author sites, Houghton Mifflin's *Authors Listed by Name* pages, which make available free of charge the introductions of the *Heath Anthology* (Lauter et al.), considerably facilitate the gathering of information on the life and work of a substantial number of nineteenth-century poets.

9.5. Contextual Material

The final category of Web sites discussed here makes available contextual material for teaching nineteenth-century poetry. In this group, *American Memory* is of primary significance. Hosted by the Library of Congress, it provides access to a wealth of material in over a hundred collections. Individual collections relevant to the concerns of this volume include *America Singing*, a database of often highly popular songs that range from the turn of the nineteenth century to the 1880s. The immense popularity of song sheets, which printed lyrics but no music, rivaled that of nineteenth-century poetry, and their study enables students of the period to gain further insights into social, political, and economic affairs of the time, in particular the Civil War. *Civil War Treasures from the New-York Historical Society* is another highly useful collection; it includes electronic reproductions of recruiting posters, stereographic views, photographs, and soldiers' drawings and writings. Together with the 1,118 photographs in *Selected Civil War Photographs*, this collection provides invaluable help in contextualizing and visualizing Civil War poetry.

Although it is hard to find an online source of contextual material as wide-ranging as *American Memory*, there are hundreds of Web sites that serve similar purposes. The Washington State University's *Nineteenth Century American Literary, Historical, and Cultural Studies* site functions as a guide to many of them. Its annotated collection of links testifies to the World Wide Web's potential as a source of information that teachers of nineteenth-century poetry may harness to great effect.

Notes on Contributors

Nassim W. Balestrini teaches American literature and culture at Johannes Gutenberg University in Mainz, Germany. She has published on nineteenth- and twentieth-century American literature, on American-Russian literary relations, and on literature and the other arts. Her latest book is *From Fiction to Libretto: Irving, Hawthorne, and James as Opera* (2005).

Alfred Bendixen is professor of English at Texas A&M University, College Station. Known for his work on such writers as Harriet Prescott Spofford, Charlotte Perkins Gilman, and Mark Twain, he is also the founder and executive director of the American Literature Association.

Paula Bernat Bennett, now retired, was professor of English at Southern Illinois University, Carbondale. She has published widely in the field of American women's poetry. Her latest book is *Poets in the Public Sphere: The Emancipatory Project of American Women's Poetry, 1800–1900* (2004).

Edward Brunner is professor of English at Southern Illinois University, Carbondale. A specialist in twentieth-century American poetry, he is the author of *Splendid Failure: Hart Crane and the Making of "The Bridge"* (1985), *Poetry as Labor and Privilege: The Writings of W. S. Merwin* (1991), and *Cold War Poetry* (2001).

Gregory Byrd is professor of English at Saint Petersburg College, Clearwater. A published poet, he teaches American and British literature and composition and has published essays on composition pedagogy and poetry.

Betty Booth Donohue is a Cherokee scholar, writer, professor, and teacher. A member of the Blue Panther Clan, she is from the Cooweescoowee District, Cherokee Nation, West.

Jane Donahue Eberwein is Distinguished Professor of English at Oakland University. A scholar of Emily Dickinson, she has published numerous books and articles on early American literature, including *An Emily Dickinson Encyclopedia* (1998).

Gregory Eiselen is professor of English at Kansas State University. He is the author of *Literature and Humanitarian Reform in the Civil War Era* (1996) and the editor of *Emma Lazarus: Selected Writings* (2002).

Frances Smith Foster is Charles Howard Candler professor of English and Women's Studies at Emory University. Her publications in African American and American literature include *Written by Herself: Literary Production by African American Women, 1726–1892* (1993) and the Norton

Critical Edition of Harriet Jacobs's *Incidents in the Life of a Slave Girl* (2001).

Tyler Hoffman is associate professor of English at Rutgers University, Camden. He is the author of *Robert Frost and the Politics of Poetry* (2001) and *Teaching with the* Norton Anthology of Poetry (2005). He has written on subjects ranging from Emily Dickinson and nineteenth-century American poetry to Thom Gunn and current popular forms of poetry.

Karen L. Kilcup is professor of English at the University of North Carolina, Greensboro. Her books include *Robert Frost and Feminine Literary Tradition* (1998), *Soft Canons: American Women Writers and Masculine Tradition* (1999) and *A Cherokee Woman's America: Memoirs of Narcissa Owen, 1831–1907* (2005).

Paul Lauter is Allan K. and Gwendolyn Miles Smith Professor of Literature at Trinity College, Connecticut. The general editor of the groundbreaking *Heath Anthology of American Literature*, he has published widely on a range of topics in American literature.

Barbara McCaskill is associate professor of English and General Sandy Beaver Teaching Professor at the University of Georgia. With Caroline Gebhard of Tuskegee University she coedited *Post-bellum, Pre-Harlem: African American Literature and Culture, 1877–1919* (2006). She edited *Running a Thousand Miles for Freedom: The Escape of William and Ellen Craft from Slavery* (1999).

Nan Morelli-White teaches in the Department of Communications at Saint Petersburg College. Her courses include freshman composition, humanities, world literature, and literature by women.

Elizabeth Petrino is associate professor of English at Fairfield University. She has published a number of articles on Dickinson and other nineteenth-century American women poets. She is the author of *Emily Dickinson and Her Contemporaries: Women's Verse in America, 1820–1885* (1998).

Elizabeth Renker is associate professor of English at Ohio State University. She is the author of *Strike through the Mask: Herman Melville and the Scene of Writing* (1996), the introduction to the Signet Classic edition of *Moby-Dick*, and articles on American literary culture and the history of higher education. Her new book is entitled *The Origins of American Literature Studies: An Institutional History* (2007).

Eliza Richards is associate professor of English at the University of North Carolina, Chapel Hill. She is the author of *Gender and the Poetics of Reception in Poe's Circle* (2004), which has chapters on Poe, Frances Sargent Osgood, Sarah Helen Whitman, and Elizabeth Oakes Smith.

Katharine Rodier is professor of English at Marshall University. She has published on Emily Dickinson and other nineteenth-century American writers. With Monika Elbert and Julie E. Hall she coedited *Reinventing the Peabody Sisters* (2006); with Amy E. Hudock she coedited *American Women Prose Writers, 1820–1870* (2001).

Valerie L. Ruffin received degrees in African American studies and women's studies at the University of Cincinnati. Her work focuses on Chicana, African American, and Jewish American women's literature and United States social movements. She is completing her PhD at Emory University.

Judith P. Saunders teaches courses in American literature, contemporary poetry, creative writing, and composition. Professor of English at Marist College, she has published essays on a wide range of subjects in nineteenth- and twentieth-century American literature. She is the author of *The Poetry of Charles Tomlinson: Border Lines* (2003).

Elizabeth Savage is associate professor of English at Fairmont State University. She has published on nineteenth- and twentieth-century American poets, including Lorine Niedecker, Laura Riding, and Susan Howe.

Philipp Schweighauser teaches at the University of Berne. He is the author of *The Noises of American Literature, 1890–1985: Toward a History of Literary Acoustics* (2006). He has also published on Nabokov, DeLillo, American realism, the French philosopher Michel Serres, literary soundscapes from realism to postmodernism, the poetry of Ruth Benedict, and masculinities.

Angela Sorby is associate professor of English at Marquette University, where she teaches American poetry from 1800 to the present. She is the author of *Schoolroom Poets: Childhood, Performance, and the Place of American Poetry* (2005) and a volume of poems, *Distance Learning* (1998).

Jeffrey Steele is professor of English at the University of Wisconsin, Madison. Author of numerous publications on nineteenth-century American literature, he edited *The Essential Margaret Fuller* (1992) and is the author of *Transfiguring America: Myth, Ideology, and Mourning in Margaret Fuller's Writing* (2001).

Cheryl Lawson Walker is Richard Armour Professor of Modern Languages at Scripps College. She is the author of *The Nightingale's Burden: Women Poets and American Culture before 1900* (1982), *Masks Outrageous and Austere: Culture, Psyche, and Persona in Modern Women Poets* (1991), *Indian Nation: Native American Literature and Nineteenth-Century Nationalisms* (1997), and *God and Elizabeth Bishop: Meditations on Religion and Poetry* (2005).

Works Cited and Recommended

Adelaide. "The Heroine of Columbia." *Lowell Offering* 1 (1841): 58–60.

Aderman, Ralph M., and Wayne R. Kime. *Advocate for America: The Life of James Kirke Paulding*. Selinsgrove: Susquehanna UP, 2003.

African American Poetry. 1994. Chadwyck-Healey. 28 Sept. 2004 <http://collections.chadwyck.com/>.

African American Women Writers of the Nineteenth Century. Digital Schomburg, New York Public Lib. Digital Lib. Collections. 1999. 7 July 2004 <http://digital.nypl.org/schomburg/writers_aa19/>.

African American Writers: Online E-Texts. Ed. Inez Ramsey. Internet School Lib. Media Center. 16 Nov. 2006 <http://falcon.jmu.edu/~ramseyil/afroonline.htm>.

Aguilar, Grace. *The Women of Israel*. 1845. 2 vols. New York: Appleton, 1851.

Albanese, Catherine L. *America: Religions and Religion*. 2nd ed. Belmont: Wadsworth, 1992.

Alcott, Louisa May. "Thoreau's Flute." *About Thoreau's Life and Writings*. Thoreau Inst. at Walden Woods Lib. 20 Aug. 2003. 6 Dec. 2006 <http://www.walden.org/Institute/thoreau/about2/A/LouisaMayAlcott/Thoreau's Flute.htm>.

———. "Transcendental Wild Oats." *Alternative Alcott*. Ed. Elaine Showalter. New Brunswick: Rutgers UP, 1988. 364–80.

Alexander, Eleanor. *Lyrics of Sunshine and Shadow: The Tragic Courtship and Marriage of Paul Laurence Dunbar and Alice Ruth Moore*. New York: New York UP, 2002.

Alves, Susan. "Intruding upon the Poet's Art: Considering the Poetic Production of Nineteenth-Century Female Factory Workers." *Nineteenth-Century American Women's Culture*. Ed. Karen L. Kilcup. Spec. issue of *Over Here: A European Journal of American Culture* 18 (1998): 29–48.

———. "Lowell's Female Factory Workers, Poetic Voice, and the Periodical." *"The Only Efficient Instrument": American Women Writers and the Periodical, 1837–1916*. Ed. Aleta Feinsod Cans and Alves. Iowa City: U of Iowa P, 2001. 149–64.

A.M.E. Church Review. Ohio Historical Soc. 2006. 15 Nov. 2006 <http://dbs.ohiohistory.org/africanam/serial/aa_se01.cfm>.

American Memory: Historical Collections for the National Digital Library. Lib. of Congress. 28 Mar. 2004 <http://memory.loc.gov/>.

American Originals: Selections from Reynolda House Museum of American Art. New York: Abbeville; Amer. Federation of Arts, 1990.

American Poetry: The Nineteenth Century. CD-ROM. New York: Lib. of Amer.; Voyager, 1994.

American Poetry, 1600–1900. Chadwyck-Healey. 28 Sept. 2004 <http://collections.chadwyck.com/>.

American Verse Project. U of Michigan Humanities Text Initiative; U of Michigan P. 16 May 2001. 6 June 2004. <http://www.hti.umich.edu/a/amverse/>.

American Women's History: A Research Guide. Ed. Ken Middleton. Middle Tennessee State U. 3 Apr. 2006 <http://www.mtsu.edu/~kmiddlet/history/women.html>.

America Singing: Nineteenth-Century Song Sheets. American Memory. Rare Book and Special Collections Div., Lib. of Congress. 22 Oct. 1999. 24 Aug. 2006 <http://rs6.loc.gov/ammem/amsshtml/amsshome.html>.

A.M.S. "Home." *Lowell Offering* 5 (1845): 45.

Andrew, John. *From Revivals to Removal: Jeremiah Evarts, the Cherokee Nation, and the Search for the Soul of America.* Athens: U of Georgia P, 1992.

Andrews, William L., Frances Smith Foster, and Trudier Harris, eds. *The Oxford Companion to African American Literature.* New York: Oxford UP, 1997.

"Angelina Abigail." *New England Offering* 2 (1849): 82.

Angelou, Maya. *I Know Why the Caged Bird Sings.* New York: Bantam, 1983.

Apple, Michael. *Ideology and Curriculum.* New York: Routledge, 1990.

Arakelian, Paul G. "Personality and Style: Options in Nineteenth-Century American Poetry." *Language and Style* 24.2 (1991): 239–50.

Atkinson, Colin B., and Jo B. Atkinson. "Changing Attitudes to Death: Nineteenth-Century Parlour Songs as Consolation Literature." *Canadian Review of American Studies / Revue canadienne d'études américaines* 23.2 (1993): 79–100.

The Audio Companion to The Norton Anthology of African American Literature. Ed. Henry Louis Gates, Jr., and Nellie Y. McKay. CD. Norton, 1996.

Authors Listed by Name. Houghton Coll. Div. Online Study Center. 2005. 24 Aug. 2006 <http://college.hmco.com/english/lauter/heath/4e/students/author_name/author_indexab.html>.

Avallone, Charlene. "What American Renaissance? The Gendered Geneaology of Critical Discourse." *PMLA* 112 (1997): 1102–20.

Axelrod, Steven Gould, Camille Roman, and Thomas Travisano, eds. *Traditions and Revolutions, Beginnings to 1900.* New Brunswick: Rutgers UP, 2003. Vol. 1 of *The New Anthology of American Poetry.*

Bacon, Martha. *Puritan Promenade.* Boston: Houghton, 1964.

Bain, Robert, ed. *Whitman's and Dickinson's Contemporaries: An Anthology of Their Verse.* Carbondale: Southern Illinois UP, 1996.

Baker, Dorothy Z. "Ars Poetica / Ars Domestica: The Self-Reflexive Poetry of Lydia Sigourney and Emily Dickinson." D. Baker, *Poetics* 69–89.

———, ed. *Poetics in the Poem: Critical Essays on American Self-Reflexive Poetry.* New York: Lang, 1997.

Baker, Houston A., Jr. "Paul Laurence Dunbar: An Evaluation." *Singers of Daybreak: Studies in Black American Literature.* Washington: Howard UP, 1974. 33–41.

Balfe, Michael William. *The Bohemian Girl.* 1844. Opera Librettos, Translations, and Related Texts. Ed. Mark D. Lew. 23 Aug. 2001. 28 Mar. 2004 <http://home.Earthlink.net/~markdlew/lib/bohgirl/>.

Bamboozled. Dir. Spike Lee. Forty Acres; New Line, 2000. DVD. New Line Home Video, 2001.

Barrett, Faith, and Cristanne Miller, eds. *"Words for the Hour": A New Anthology of American Civil War Poetry.* Amherst: U of Massachusetts P, 2005.

Bartleby.com. Ed. Steven H. van Leeuwen. 13 May 2004 <http://www.bartleby.com/>.

Bassard, Katherine Clay. *Spiritual Interrogations: Culture, Gender, and Community in Early African American Women's Writing*. Princeton: Princeton UP, 1999.

Bates, Charlotte Fiske. *The Cambridge Book of Poetry and Song*. 1882. New York: Crowell, 1910.

Batker, Carol. " 'Overcoming All Obstacles': The Assimilation Debate in Native American Women's Journalism of the Dawes Era." Jaskoski 190–203.

Battle-Pieces and Aspects of the War. Life and Works of Herman Melville. Ed. J. Madden. 6 May 2004 <http://www.melville.org/hmbattle.htm>.

Bauer, Dale M., and Philip Gould, eds. *The Cambridge Companion to Nineteenth-Century American Women's Writing*. Cambridge: Cambridge UP, 2001.

Baym, Nina, ed. *The Norton Anthology of American Literature*. 5th ed. 5 vols. New York: Norton, 1998.

———. "Reinventing Lydia Sigourney." *American Literature* 62 (1990): 385–404.

———. *Woman's Fiction: A Guide to Novels by and about Women in America, 1820–1870*. Ithaca: Cornell UP, 1978.

Baym, Nina, et al., eds. *The Norton Anthology of American Literature*. 6th ed. Vol. B. New York: Norton, 2002.

Beecher, Catharine. "Circular Addressed to Benevolent Ladies of the U. States." *Christian Advocate and Journal and Zion's Herald* (New York) 25 Dec. 1829: 65.

Beers, Ethel Lynn. "The Picket; or, All Quiet along the Potomac Tonight." 1861. *Women's History*. About.com. 19 May 2006 <http://womenshistory.about.com/library/etext/bl_all_quiet_potomac.htm>.

Bell, James Madison. "Modern Moses; or, 'My Policy' Man." *The Poetical Works of James Madison Bell* (1901). *African American Poetry* 107–23.

Bell, Michael Davitt. *The Problem of American Realism: Studies in the Cultural History of a Literary Idea*. Chicago: U of Chicago P, 1993.

Bell, Michael J. " 'The Only True Folk Songs We Have in English': James Russell Lowell and the Politics of the Nation." *Journal of American Folklore* 108 (1995): 131–55.

Belnap, Jeffrey, and Raúl Fernández, eds. *José Martí's "Our America": From National to Hemispheric Cultural Studies*. Durham: Duke UP, 1998.

Bennett, Michael. "Frances Ellen Watkins Sings the Body Electric." *Recovering the Black Female Body: Self-Representations by African American Women*. Ed. Bennett and Vanessa D. Dickerson. New Brunswick: Rutgers UP, 2001. 19–40.

Bennett, Paula Bernat. "Critical Clitoridectomy: Female Sexual Imagery and Feminist Psychoanalytic Theory." *Signs* 18.2 (1993): 235–59.

———. " 'The Descent of the Angel': Interrogating Domestic Ideology in American Women's Poetry, 1858–1890." *American Literary History* 7 (1995): 591–610.

———. *Emily Dickinson: Woman Poet*. Iowa City: U of Iowa P, 1990.

———. "Late Nineteenth-Century American Women's Nature Poetry and the Evolution of the Imagist Poem." *Legacy* 9.2 (1992): 89–103.

———. *My Life a Loaded Gun: Female Creativity and Feminist Poetics*. Boston: Beacon, 1986.

———, ed. *Nineteenth-Century American Women Poets: An Anthology.* Oxford: Blackwell, 1998.

———. "Not Just Filler and Not Just Sentimental: Women's Poetry in American Victorian Periodicals, 1860–1900." Price and Smith 202–19.

———. "The Pea That Duty Locks: Lesbian and Feminist-Heterosexual Readings of Emily Dickinson's Poetry." *Lesbian Texts and Contexts: Radical Revisions.* Ed. Karla Jay, Joanne Glasgow, and Catharine R. Stimpson. New York: New York UP, 1990. 104–25.

———. *Poets in the Public Sphere: The Emancipatory Project of American Women's Poetry, 1800–1900.* Princeton: Princeton UP, 2003.

———. " 'Pomegranate-Flowers': The Phantasmic Productions of Late-Nineteenth-Century Anglo-American Women Poets." *Solitary Pleasures: The Historical, Literary, and Artistic Discourses of Autoeroticism.* Ed. Bennett and Vernon A. Rosario, II. New York: Routledge, 1995. 155–61.

———. "Re-writing Dunbar: Realism, Black Women Poets, and the Genteel." *Post-Bellum–Pre-Harlem: African American Literature and Culture, 1877–1919.* Ed. Barbara McCaskill and Caroline Gebhard. New York: New York UP, 2006.

Bennison, Sarah Elizabeth. "The Poetry and Activism of Frances Ellen Watkins Harper." *Journal x* 6.2 (2002): 203–23.

Bercovitch, Sacvan, gen. ed. *Nineteenth-Century Poetry, 1800–1910.* Cambridge: Cambridge UP, 2004. Vol. 4 of *The Cambridge History of American Literature.*

Bergon, Frank. *Stephen Crane's Artistry.* New York: Columbia UP, 1975.

Berlant, Lauren. "The Queen of America Goes to Washington City: Harriet Jacobs, Frances Harper, Anita Hill." *American Literature* 65 (1993): 549–74.

Berryman, John. *Stephen Crane: A Critical Biography.* New York: Cooper Square, 2001.

Best, Felton O. *Crossing the Line: A Biography of Paul Laurence Dunbar, 1872–1906.* Dubuque: Hunt, 1996.

———. "Paul Laurence Dunbar's Protest Literature: The Final Years." *Western Journal of Black Studies* 17.1 (1993): 54–63.

Bibb, Eloise A. *Poems.* Boston: Monthly Rev., 1895.

The Bible, King James Version. Electronic Text Center, U of Virginia Lib. 14 May 2006 <http://etext.lib.virginia.edu/kjv.browse.html>.

Bierce, Ambrose. "The Hesitating Veteran." *Poetry and Music of the War between the States.* 23 Aug. 2004. 19 May 2006 <http://www.civilwarpoetry.org>. Path: Union Poetry; Postwar Remembrances; The Hesitating Veteran.

Bloom, Harold, ed. *Stephen Crane.* Philadelphia: Chelsea, 2002.

Blount, Marcellus. "The Preacherly Text: African American Poetry and Vernacular Performance." *PMLA* 107 (1992): 582–93.

BoondocksNet.com. Ed. Jim Zwick. 26 Aug. 2005 <http://www.boondocksnet.com/>.

Boswell, Jeanetta, and Richard Tuerk, eds. *The American Renaissance and the Critics: The Best of a Century in Criticism.* Wakefield: Longwood Academic, 1990.

Boudinot, Elias. "An Address to the Whites." Lauter et al. 1: 1411–18.

Boyd, Melba Joyce. *Discarded Legacy: Politics and Poetics in the Life of Frances E. W. Harper*. Detroit: Wayne State UP, 1994.

Branch, Douglas. *The Sentimental Years, 1836–1860*. New York: Appleton, 1934.

Brandon, Stephen. "Sacred Fires and Sovereign Rhetorics: Cherokee Literacy, Nationalism, and the Emergence of Professional Authorship in America." Diss. U of North Carolina, Greensboro, 2003.

Brawley, Benjamin. *Early Negro American Writers: Selections with Biographical and Critical Introductions*. Freeport: Books for Libs., 1968.

———. *The Negro Genius*. New York: Biblo, 1969.

Bread and Roses: Poetry and History of the American Labor Movement. Ed. Jim Zwick. 28 Mar. 2004 <http://www.boondocksnet.com/labor/history/>.

A Brief Chronology of African American Literature. Ed. Roger Blackwell Bailey. 2004. San Antonio Coll. 16 Nov. 2006 <http://www.accd.edu/sac/english/bailey/aframlit.htm>.

Brodhead, Richard. *Cultures of Letters: Scenes of Reading and Writing in Nineteenth-Century America*. Chicago: U of Chicago P, 1993.

———. "Sparing the Rod: Discipline and Fiction in Antebellum America." *Representations* 21 (1988): 67–96.

Brooks, Christopher A. "The 'Musical' Souls of Black Folk: Can a Double Consciousness Be Heard?" *The Souls of Black Folk: One Hundred Years Later*. Ed. Dolan Hubbard. Columbia: U of Missouri P, 2003. 269–83.

Brooks, Maria Gowen. *"Judith," "Esther," and Other Poems*. Boston: Cummings, 1820.

Brown, Dee. *Bury My Heart at Wounded Knee: An Indian History of the American West*. New York: Bantam, 1971.

Brown, Fahamisha Patricia. *Performing the Word: African American Poetry as Vernacular Culture*. New Brunswick: Rutgers UP, 1999.

Brown, Gillian. *Domestic Individualism: Imagining Self in Nineteenth-Century America*. Berkeley: U of California P, 1990.

Brown, Sterling. Negro Poetry and Drama *and* The Negro in American Fiction. New York: Atheneum, 1969.

Bryant, William Cullen. "Lines to a Waterfowl." McGuffey, *Sixth Eclectic Reader* 434–35.

———. *Poetical Works of William Cullen Bryant*. Whitefish: Kessinger, 2003.

Buell, Lawrence. "American Civil War Poetry and the Meaning of Literary Commodification: Whitman, Melville, and Others." *Reciprocal Influences: Literary Production, Distribution, and Consumption in America*. Ed. Steven Fink and Susan S. Williams. Columbus: Ohio State UP, 1999. 123–38.

Butler, Judith. "Imitation and Gender Insubordination." Fuss, *Inside/Out* 25.

———. *The Psychic Life of Power: Theories in Subjection*. Stanford: Stanford UP, 1997.

Cady, Edwin H. "Howells in the Modern Tradition: 'Black Cross Farm.' " *Nineteenth-Century Literature* 45 (1991): 478–94.

———. Introduction. Howells, *"Pebbles"* xi–xlvi.

Cain, William E., ed. *American Literature*. 2 vols. New York: Penguin Academics; Longman, 2004.

Calhoun, Charles C. *Longfellow: A Rediscovered Life*. Boston: Beacon, 2004.

Camfield, Gregg. *Necessary Madness: The Humor of Domesticity in Nineteenth-Century American Literature.* Oxford: Oxford UP, 1997.

The Campaign to End Child Labor. Ed. Jim Zwick. 28 Mar. 2004 <http://www.boondocksnet.com/labor/cl_intro.html>.

Campbell, Alfred Gibbs. "Warning: Suggested by the Christiana (PA.) Treason Trials." 1883. *Poems* 65–66. *African American Poetry.*

Capps, Claudius Meade, ed. *The Blue and the Gray: The Best Poems of the Civil War.* 1943. Freeport: Books for Libs., 1969.

Cappucci, Paul R. "Depicting the Oblique: Emily Dickinson's Poetic Response to the American Civil War." *War, Literature, and the Arts* 10.1 (1998): 260–73.

Cary, Alice. Conclusion. *Clovernook; or, Recollections of Our Neighborhood in the West.* Vol. 2. New York: Redfield, 1853. 361–64.

Cary, Phoebe. "Dorothy's Dower: In Three Parts." Bennett, *Nineteenth-Century American Women Poets* 105–06.

Catlin, George. *Drawings of the North American Indians.* Garden City: Doubleday, 1984.

———. *Letters and Notes on the Manners, Customs, and Condition of the North American Indians.* New York: Wiley, 1842.

Celia Laighton Thaxter. SeacoastNH.com. 21 Oct. 2005 <http://seacoastnh.com/Famous_People/Celia_Laighton_Thaxter/>.

Chafe, William Henry. *Women and Equality: Changing Patterns in American Culture.* New York: Oxford UP, 1977.

Chametzky, Jules, et al., eds. *Jewish American Literature: A Norton Anthology*. New York: Norton, 2001.

Chapman, Mary, and Glenn Hendler, eds. *Sentimental Men: Masculinity and the Politics of Affect in American Culture.* Berkeley: U of California P, 1999.

Cheever, George B. *The Poets of America.* New York: World, 1875.

Cherokee Phoenix. 1828–34. Galileo. 15 July 2004 <http://www.galileo.usg.edu/>.

Chesnutt, Charles W. "The Goophered Grapevine." *Atlantic Monthly* August. 1887. *The Conjure Woman.* Boston: Houghton, 1899. 1–35. *Documenting the American South.* U Lib., U of North Carolina, Chapel Hill. 28 Mar. 2005. 30 Nov. 2006 <http://docsouth.unc.edu/chesnuttconjure/conjure.html>.

Child, Lydia Maria. *"Hobomok" and Other Writings on Indians.* Ed. Carolyn L. Karcher. New Brunswick: Rutgers UP, 1986.

———. *A Lydia Maria Child Reader.* Ed. Carolyn L. Karcher. Durham: Duke UP, 1997.

———. "The Quadroons." *Rediscoveries: Short Stories by American Women, 1832–1916.* Ed. Barbara H. Solomon. New York: Mentor, 1994. 88–98.

Chinese Exclusion Act. Ch. 126. 6 May 1882. Stat. 22.58–61.

Christy's Nigga Songster: As Sung by Christy's, Pierce's, White's, and Dumbleton's Minstrels. New York: Strong, c. 1850. Uncle Tom's Cabin.

City of Spindles: The Textiles Mills of Lowell: Chapter 12. Ed. Catherine Lavender. Norton Digital History. 28 Mar. 2004 <http://www.wwnorton.com/inventing/content/ch12/lowell.htm>.

Civil War Treasures from the New-York Historical Society. American Memory: Historical Collections for the Natl. Digital Lib. Lib. of Congress. 15 July 2001.

26 Aug. 2005 <http://memory.loc.gov/ammem/ndlpcoop/nhihtml/cwnyhshome.html>.

Clark, Suzanne. *Sentimental Modernism: Women Writers and the Revolution of the Word*. Bloomington: Indiana UP, 1991.

Clayton, Sarah T. *The Angelic Sins of Jones Very*. New York: Lang, 1999.

Cofran, John. "The Identity of Adah Isaacs Menken: A Theatrical Mystery Solved." *Theatre Survey* 31 (1990): 47–54.

Cole, Thomas. "The Complaint of the Forest." Thomas Cole Papers. Box 5, folder 14. New York State Lib., Albany, New York.

———. *Scene from* The Last of the Mohicans: *Cora Kneeling at the Feet of Tamenund*. 1827. Masters in Liberal Arts, U of Wisconsin, Milwaukee. 14 Aug. 2000. 17 May 2007 <http://www.uwm.edu/Dept/MLS/syllabi/images/70108.html>.

———. *Sketchbook*. 1827. New York State Lib., Albany, New York. N. pag.

Côté, Jane McL. *Fanny and Anna Parnell: Ireland's Patriot Sisters*. New York: St. Martin's, 1991.

Courtwright, David T. *Dark Paradise: A History of Opiate Addiction in America*. Cambridge: Harvard UP, 2001.

"Coverture." *Encyclopedia of Women's History*. Ed. Jone Johnson Lewis. About.com. 13 May 2004 <http://womenshistory.about.com/library/ency/blwh_coverture.htm>.

Cox, F. Brett. " 'What Need, Then, for Poetry?': The Genteel Tradition and the Continuity of American Literature." *New England Quarterly* 67 (1994): 229–33.

Cox, Samuel S. "Persecution of the Jews in Russia." Lazarus, *Selected Poems* 349–53.

Crain, Patricia. "Lydia Huntley Sigourney, 1791–1865." Haralson, *Encyclopedia* 381–84. *Literature Online*. 6 Apr. 2007 <http://lion.chadwyck.co.uk>. Path: Authors; Author Index; Browse an A-Z List; Sigourney, L. H.; Reference Works; Lydia Huntley Sigourney.

Crane, Stephen. *The Complete Poems of Stephen Crane*. Ed. Joseph Katz. Ithaca: Cornell UP, 1972.

———. *Prose and Poetry*. New York: Lib. of Amer., 1984.

Cronon, William. *Changes in the Land: Indians, Colonists, and the Ecology of New England*. New York: Hill, 1983.

Cronyn, George W. *American Indian Poetry: An Anthology of Songs and Chants*. New York: Ballantine, 1991.

Cutler, Edward S. *Recovering the New: Transatlantic Roots of Modernism*. Hanover: UP of New England, 2002.

Daly, John. "Confederate Daughters." 1998–2002. *Civil War Poetry*. 6 May 2004 <http://home.att.net/~lah-rbh/civilwar/poem58.html>.

Dandurand, Karen. *Dickinson Scholarship: An Annotated Bibliography, 1969–1985*. New York: Garland, 1988.

Danky, James P., and Wayne A. Wiegand, eds. *Print Culture in a Diverse America*. Urbana: U of Illinois P, 1998.

Davidson, Cathy N., ed. *No More Separate Spheres!* Spec. issue of *American Literature* 70 (1998): 443–668.

Davis, Gwen, and Beverly A. Joyce, comps. *Poetry by Women to 1900: A Bibliography of American and British Women Writers*. Toronto: U of Toronto P, 1991.

Davis, Rebecca Harding. *Life in the Iron Mills; or, The Korl Woman, with a Biographical Interpretation by Tillie Olsen.* New York: Feminist, 1972.

Dayan, Joan. "Amorous Bondage: Poe, Ladies, and Slaves." *The American Face of Edgar Allan Poe.* Ed. Shawn Rosenheim and Stephen Rachman. Baltimore: Johns Hopkins UP, 1995. 179–209.

Dean, Sharon L. *Constance Fenimore Woolson: Homeward Bound.* Knoxville: U of Tennessee P, 1995.

Dearborn, Mary V. *Pocahontas's Daughters: Gender and Ethnicity in American Culture.* New York: Oxford UP, 1986.

Degler, Carl N. *At Odds: Women and the Family in America from the Revolution to the Present.* Oxford: Oxford UP, 1980.

De Jong, Mary. "Her Fair Fame: The Reputation of Frances Sargent Osgood, Woman Poet." Myerson, *Studies* 265–83.

———. "Lines from a Partly Published Drama: The Romance of Frances Sargent Osgood and Edgar Allan Poe." Marchalonis, *Patrons* 31–58.

———. "Legacy Profile: Lydia Huntley Sigourney, 1791–1865." *Legacy* 5.1 (1988): 35–43.

———. "Nineteenth-Century Reflections on 'The Poet of Today.' " D. Baker, *Poetics* 46–68.

———. " 'With My Burden I Begin': The (Im)Personal 'I' of Nineteenth-Century Hymnody." *Puritanism in America: The Seventeenth through the Nineteenth Centuries.* Ed. Michael Schuldiner. Lewiston: Mellen, 1993. 185–223.

Delaney, Lucy. *From the Darkness Cometh the Light; or, Struggles of Freedom.* Saint Louis: Smith, 189?. *Documenting the American South.* University Lib., U of North Carolina, Chapel Hill. 2004. 15 May 2007 <http://docsouth.unc.edu/neh/delaney/menu.html>.

D'Emilio, John, and Estelle B. Freedman. *Intimate Matters: A History of Sexuality in America.* New York: Harper, 1988.

Dickinson, Emily. *The Letters of Emily Dickinson.* Ed. Thomas H. Johnson and Theodora Ward. 3 vols. Cambridge: Belknap-Harvard UP, 1958.

———. *The Manuscript Books of Emily Dickinson.* Ed. R. W. Franklin. 2 vols. Cambridge: Belknap-Harvard UP, 1981.

———. *The Poems of Emily Dickinson: Reading Edition.* Ed. R. W. Franklin. Cambridge: Belknap-Harvard UP, 1999.

———. *The Poems of Emily Dickinson: Variorum Edition.* 3 vols. Ed. R. W. Franklin. Cambridge: Belknap-Harvard UP, 1998.

Diner, Hasia R. *Erin's Daughters in America: Irish Immigrant Women in the Nineteenth Century.* Baltimore: Johns Hopkins UP, 1983.

DMX. *It's Dark and Hell Is Hot.* Audio CD. Def Jam, 1998.

Dobson, Joanne. "The American Renaissance Reenvisioned." J. Warren 164–82.

———. "Emily Dickinson and the 'Prickly Art' of Housekeeping." *Women's Studies* 16.1–2 (1989): 231–37.

———. "Reclaiming Sentimental Literature." *American Literature* 69 (1997): 263–88.

———. "Sex, Wit, and Sentiment: Frances Osgood and the Poetry of Love." *American Literature* 65 (1993): 631–50.

Dobyns, Henry F. "Estimating Aboriginal American Population: An Appraisal of

Techniques with a New Hemisphere Estimate." *Current Anthropology* 7 (1966): 395–416.

Dock, Julie Bates. "William Dean Howells." Haralson, *Encyclopedia* 224–30.

Dollard, Peter. "A Guide to Core Critical Studies of Adah Isaacs Menken." *Bulletin of Bibliography* 59.2 (2002): 77–83.

Donaldson, Scott. *Archibald MacLeish: An American Life.* Boston: Houghton, 1992.

Dooley, Patrick K. *The Pluralistic Philosophy of Stephen Crane.* Urbana: U of Illinois P, 1993.

Douglas, Ann. *The Feminization of American Culture.* New York: Doubleday, 1977.

Douglass, Frederick. *Narrative of the Life of Frederick Douglass, an American Slave.* Ed. Houston Baker, Jr. New York: Penguin, 1986.

Dray, Philip. *At the Hands of Persons Unknown: The Lynching of Black America.* New York: Random, 2002.

Duberman, Martin Bauml, Martha Vicinus, and George Chauncey, Jr., eds. *Hidden from History: Reclaiming the Gay and Lesbian Past.* New York: New Amer. Lib., 1989.

Dublin, Thomas. *Women at Work: The Transformation of Work and Community in Lowell, Massachusetts, 1826–1860.* 2nd ed. New York: Columbia UP, 1993.

DuBois, W. E. B. *The Souls of Black Folk.* Ed. Henry Louis Gates, Jr., and Terri Hume Oliver. New York: Norton, 1999.

Duchac, Joseph. *The Poems of Emily Dickinson: An Annotated Guide to Commentary Published in English, 1978–1989.* New York: Hall, 1993.

Dunbar, Paul Laurence. *The Collected Poetry of Paul Laurence Dunbar.* Ed. Joanne M. Braxton. Charlottesville: UP of Virginia, 1993.

Dunbar-Nelson, Alice. *The Works of Alice Dunbar-Nelson.* Ed. Gloria T. Hull. 3 vols. New York: Oxford UP, 1988.

Dwight, Timothy. *Greenfield Hill: A Poem, in Seven Parts.* New York: Childs, 1794. *Literature Online.*

Dylan, Bob. *A Hard Rain's a-Gonna Fall.* 1991. 1 Dec. 2006 <http://www.bobdylan.com/songs/hardrain.html>.

Eastman, Mary. *The American Aboriginal Portfolio, Illustrated by Seth Eastman.* Philadelphia: Lippincott, 1853.

Eberwein, Jane Donahue, ed. *An Emily Dickinson Encyclopedia.* Westport: Greenwood, 1998.

Edelshtadt, David. "My Testament." Chametzky et al. 139.

Edgar Allan Poe Society of Baltimore. Edgar Allan Poe Soc. of Baltimore. 1 May 1997. 2 May 2006 <http://www.eapoe.org/index.htm>.

Edward S. Curtis's The North American Indian*: Photographic Images.* American Memory: Historical Collections for the Natl. Digital Lib. Lib. of Congress. 25 Apr. 2001. 13 May 2004 <http://memory.loc.gov/ammem/award98/ienhtml/curthome.html>.

Eiselein, Gregory. "Emotion and the Jewish Historical Poems of Emma Lazarus." *Mosaic* 37.1 (2004): 33–48.

Eisler, Benita, ed. *The Lowell Offering: Writings by New England Mill Women, 1840–1845.* Philadelphia: Lippincott, 1977.

Electronic Text Center. U of Virginia Lib. 10 Aug. 2006. 24 Aug. 2006 <http://etext.lib.virginia.edu/>.

Eliot, George. *Daniel Deronda.* 1877. Oxford: Oxford UP, 1984.

Eliot, T. S. "The Metaphysical Poets." *Selected Essays, 1917–1932.* New York: Harcourt, 1932. 241–50.

Elizabeth Oakes Smith, 1806–1893. Ed. Timothy H. Scherman. Northeastern Illinois U. 23 Oct. 2003. 13 May 2004 <http://www.neiu.edu/~thscherm/eos/eospage.htm>.

Elliot, Jane. "O Is for the Other Things She Gave Me: Jonathan Franzen's *The Corrections* and Contemporary Women's Fiction." *Bitch* Feb. 2002: 70–74. 15 Nov. 2006 <http://www.bitchmagazine.com/archives/02_02franzen/franzen.shtml>.

Elliott, Emory, et al., eds. *American Literature.* Vol. 1. Englewood Cliffs: Prentice, 1991.

Ellison, Julie. "The Politics of Fancy in the Age of Sensibility." *Re-visioning Romanticism: British Women Writers, 1776–1837.* Philadelphia: U of Pennsylvania P, 1994. 228–55.

Ellmann, Richard, ed. *The Oxford Book of American Verse.* New York: Oxford UP, 1976.

Emerson, Ralph Waldo. *Collected Poems and Translations.* New York: Lib. of Amer., 1994.

———. *The Complete Works of Ralph Waldo Emerson.* 12 vols. Boston: Houghton, 1903.

———. "Hamatreya." *Emerson's Prose and Poetry.* Norton Critical Ed. Ed. Joel Porte and Saundra Morris. New York: Norton, 2001. 438–39.

———, ed. *Parnassus.* Boston: Houghton, 1880.

———. *Poems.* Boston: Houghton, 1900.

———, ed. *Songs of Three Centuries.* Boston: Houghton, 1890.

———. *Ralph Waldo Emerson.* Ed. Richard Poirier. New York: Oxford UP, 1990.

———. "The Transcendentalist." Emerson, *Ralph Waldo Emerson* 97–110.

———. *The Works of Ralph Waldo Emerson.* RWE Inst. 13 Oct. 2005 <http://www.rwe.org/comm/>.

Emily Dickinson International Society. Ed. Gary Lee Stonum. Case Western Reserve U. Aug. 2005. 21 Oct. 2005 <http://www.cwru.edu/affil/edis/edis index.html>.

Emma Lazarus. Exhibit: Women of Valor. Jewish Women's Archive. 26 July 2004 <http://www.jwa.org/exhibits/wov/lazarus/>.

Encarta Africana. Ed. Henry Louis Gates, Jr., and Kwame Anthony Appiah. CD-ROM. 3rd ed. Seattle: Microsoft, 2002.

Engel, Bernard F. "The Genteel Poetry of William Dean Howells." *Midamerica: The Yearbook of the Society for the Study of Midwestern Literature* 6 (1979): 44–61.

Epstein, Barbara. *The Politics of Domesticity: Women, Evangelism, and Temperance in Nineteenth-Century America.* Middletown: Wesleyan UP, 1981.

Erkkila, Betsy, and Jay Grossman, eds. *Breaking Bounds: Whitman and American Cultural Studies.* New York: Oxford UP, 1996.

Everett, Edward. *Orations and Speeches on Various Occasions.* 6th ed. Boston: Little, 1859–60.

Exercises for Authors' Days, for School and Evening Exercises. Boston: Educ. Pub., 1888.

Faderman, Lillian. *Surpassing the Love of Men: Romantic Friendships and Love between Women from the Renaissance to the Present.* New York: Morrow, 1981.

Fahs, Alice. *The Imagined Civil War: Popular Literature of the North and South, 1861–1865.* Chapel Hill: U of North Carolina P, 2003.

Farley, Harriet. "Factory Blossoms for Queen Victoria." *Lowell Offering* 3 (1842): 1–5.

Farr, Cecilia Konchar. *Reading Oprah: How Oprah's Book Club Changed the Way America Reads.* Albany: State U of New York P, 2004.

Farr, Judith. *The Passion of Emily Dickinson.* Cambridge: Harvard UP, 1992.

Fashion-Era. Ed. Pauline Weston Thomas and Guy Thomas. 13 May 2004 <http://www.fashion-era.com/>.

Felski, Rita. *The Gender of Modernity.* Cambridge: Harvard UP, 1995.

Fetterley, Judith. "Entitled to More than 'Peculiar Praise': The Extravagance of Alice Cary's *Clovernook.*" *Legacy* 10.2 (1993): 103–19.

Fiducia [Harriet Farley]. "Fancy." *Lowell Offering* 1 (1841): 117–18.

Finch, Annie. "The Sentimental Poetess in the World: Metaphor and Subjectivity in Lydia Sigourney's Nature Poetry." *Legacy* 5.2 (1988): 1–15.

Finch, Francis Miles. *The Blue and the Gray.* Bartleby.com. 2005. 19 May 2006 <http://www.bartleby.com/248/490.html>.

Finding List for Sarah Piatt's Poetry. Comp. Pamela J. Kincheloe. 25 Feb. 2003. 23 May 2006 <http://www.rit.edu/~pjknge/Piatt%20Page/find list.html>.

Fletcher, Angus. "James Russell Lowell." Haralson, *Encyclopedia* 271–76.

Folsom, Ed, ed. *Whitman and the Civil War.* Spec. issue of *Walt Whitman Quarterly Review* 15.2–3 (1997–98): 67–140.

Fone, Byrne R. S. *Masculine Landscapes: Walt Whitman and the Homoerotic Text.* Carbondale: Southern Illinois UP, 1992.

Foner, Philip S. *American Labor Songs of the Nineteenth Century.* Urbana: U of Illinois P, 1975.

Ford, Thomas W. *Heaven Beguiles the Tired: Death in the Poetry of Emily Dickinson.* Tuscaloosa: U of Alabama P, 1966.

Foucault, Michel. *The History of Sexuality.* London: Penguin, 1978.

Fought, Leigh. *Southern Womanhood and Slavery: A Biography of Louisa S. McCord, 1810–1879.* Columbia: U of Missouri P, 2003.

Franklin, John Hope, and Alfred A. Moss, Jr. *From Slavery to Freedom: A History of African Americans.* 8th ed. Boston: McGraw, 2000.

Freire, Paulo. *Pedagogy of the Oppressed.* Trans. Myra Ramos. New York: Continuum, 1970.

Fuchs, Kenneth. " 'That Music Always round Me': A Response to Helen Vendler." *Michigan Quarterly Review* 39 (2000): 19–24.

Fuller, Margaret. "Come!" bMS Am 1221 (198). Tappan papers. Houghton Lib., Harvard.

———. *The Essential Margaret Fuller.* Ed. Jeffrey Steele. New Brunswick: Rutgers UP, 1992.

———. "God of the Splendid Stars." MS Am 1450 (128). Fuller papers. Boston Public Lib.

———. *The Letters of Margaret Fuller*. Ed. Robert Hudspeth. 4 vols. Ithaca: Cornell UP, 1983.

———. "To E." bMS Am 1221 (197). Fuller papers. Houghton Lib., Harvard.

———. "To ___: Sunset, after Leaving New York, August 1835." MS Am 1450 (145). Fuller papers. Boston Public Lib.

———. "To the Fair Unknown:— F.H.H." bMS Am 1465 (920). Papers of Samuel Gray Ward and Anna Hazard Barker. Houghton Lib., Harvard.

———. "To the Same: Glen-Anna: August 1835." MS Am 1450 (145). Fuller papers. Boston Public Lib.

Fuss, Diana. "Inside/Out." Fuss, *Inside/Out* 6–7.

———, ed. *Inside/Out, Lesbian Theories, Gay Theories*. New York: Routledge, 1991.

Gale, Robert L. *Henry Wadsworth Longfellow Companion*. Westport: Greenwood, 2003.

Gandal, Keith. "A Spiritual Autopsy of Stephen Crane." *Nineteenth-Century Literature* 51 (1997): 500–30.

———. "Stephen Crane's 'Mystic Places.' " *Arizona Quarterly* 55.1 (1999): 97–126.

Garber, Marjorie. *Vice-Versa: Bisexuality and the Eroticism of Everyday Life*. New York: Simon, 1995.

Garner, Stanton. *The Civil War World of Herman Melville*. Lawrence: U of Kansas P, 1993.

Gartner, Matthew. "Becoming Longfellow: Work, Manhood, and Poetry." *American Literature* 72 (2000): 59–86.

Gates, Henry Louis, Jr. "Dis and Dat: Dialect and the Descent." *Figures in Black*. New York: Oxford UP, 1986. 167–95.

Gates, Henry Louis, Jr., and Nellie Y. McKay, eds. *The Norton Anthology of African American Literature*. 1997. 2nd ed. New York: Norton, 2004.

Gayle, Addison. *Oak and Ivy: A Biography of Paul Laurence Dunbar*. New York: Doubleday, 1971.

Gernes, Todd. "Poetic Justice: Sarah Forten, Eliza Earle, and the Paradox of Intellectual Property." *New England Quarterly* 71 (1998): 229–65.

Gerson, Carole, and Veronica Strong-Boag. *Paddling Her Own Canoe: The Time and Texts of E. Pauline Johnson (Tekahionwake)*. Toronto: U of Toronto P, 2000.

Giantvalley, Scott. *Walt Whitman, 1838–1939: A Reference Guide*. Boston: Hall, 1981.

Gibian, Peter. *Oliver Wendell Holmes and the Culture of Conversation*. Cambridge: Cambridge UP, 2001.

Gibson, Brent Lee. *An Annotated Walt Whitman Bibliography, 1976–1985*. Lewiston: Mellen, 2001.

Gilbert, Sandra M., and Susan Gubar. *The Madwoman in the Attic: The Woman Writer and the Nineteenth-Century Literary Imagination*. New Haven: Yale UP, 1979.

———. *No Man's Land: The Place of the Woman Writer in the Twentieth Century.* 3 vols. New Brunswick: Rutgers UP, 1995.

Gilman, Charlotte Perkins. Herland, *"The Yellow Wall-Paper," and Selected Writings.* Ed. Denise D. Knight. New York: Penguin, 1999.

———. In This Our World *and Other Poems.* San Francisco: Barry, 1898.

———. *The Later Poetry of Charlotte Perkins Gilman.* Ed. Denise D. Knight. Newark: U of Delaware P, 1996.

———. *The Living of Charlotte Perkins Gilman.* 1935. Madison: U of Wisconsin P, 1991.

Gilmore, Susan. " 'Ye May Not Wash It Out': Women Poets, Native Subjects, and Sentimental Resistance." Conf. on Race, Gender and Sentimentality in Nineteenth-Century American Literature. Cornell U. 29–31 Mar. 1990.

Ginzberg, Lori D. *Women and the Work of Benevolence: Morality, Politics, and Class in the Nineteenth-Century United States.* New Haven: Yale UP, 2002.

Gioia, Dana. "Longfellow in the Aftermath of Modernism." Parini 64–96.

Glaser, Amelia, and David Weintraub, eds. *Proletpen: America's Rebel Yiddish Poets.* Trans. Amelia Glaser. Madison: U of Wisconsin P, 2005.

Glazener, Nancy. *Reading for Realism: The History of a U.S. Literary Institution, 1850–1910.* Durham: Duke UP, 1997.

Glenn, Susan A. *Daughters of the Shtetl: Life and Labor in the Immigrant Generation.* Ithaca: Cornell UP, 1990.

Golding, Alan. *From Outlaw to Classic: Canons in American Poetry.* Madison: U of Wisconsin P, 1996.

Gollin, Rita K. *Annie Adams Fields: Woman of Letters.* Amherst: U of Massachusetts P, 2002.

Grabher, Gudrun, Roland Hagenbuchle, and Christanne Miller, eds. *The Emily Dickinson Handbook.* Amherst: U of Massachusetts P, 1998.

Graff, Gerald. *Beyond the Culture Wars: How Teaching the Conflicts Can Revitalize American Education.* New York: Norton, 1992.

Grahn, Judy. *The Highest Apple: Sappho and the Lesbian Poetic Tradition.* San Francisco: Spinsters Ink, 1985.

Gray, Charlotte. *Flint and Feather: The Life and Times of E. Pauline Johnson.* Toronto: Harper, 2002.

Gray, Janet. "Passing as Fact: Mollie E. Lambert and Mary Eliza Tucker Lambert Meet as Racial Modernity Dawns." *Representations* 64 (1998): 41–75.

———. *Race and Time: American Women's Poetics from Antislavery to Racial Modernity.* Iowa City: U of Iowa P, 2004.

———, ed. *She Wields a Pen: American Women Poets of the Nineteenth Century.* Iowa City: U of Iowa P, 1997.

Gray, Thomas. "The Progress of Poesy: A Pindaric Ode." *The Oxford Book of English Verse.* Ed. Arthur Thomas Quiller-Couch. Oxford: Clarendon, 1919. *Bartleby.com.* Jan. 1999. 5 Dec. 2006 <http://www.bartleby.com/101/455.html>.

Greenberg, Robert M. *Splintered Worlds: Fragmentation and the Ideal of Diversity in the Work of Emerson, Melville, Whitman, and Dickinson.* Boston: Northeastern UP, 1993.

Griffin, George, and Sigourney, Lydia Howard. George Griffin-Lydia H. Sigourney Papers, William L. Clements Lib., U of Michigan. 13 May 2004 <http://www.Clements.umich.edu/Webguides/S/Sigourney.html>.

Griswold, Rufus Wilmot, ed. *The Female Poets of America.* Philadelphia: Carey, 1849.

———, ed. *The Poets and Poetry of America.* Philadelphia: Carey, 1842.

Grossman, Jay. *Reconstituting the American Renaissance: Emerson, Whitman, and the Politics of Representation.* Durham: Duke UP, 2003.

Gurney, George, and Therese Thau Heyman, eds. *George Catlin and His Indian Gallery.* New York: Smithsonian Amer. Art Museum; Norton, 2002.

Habegger, Alfred. *My Wars Are Laid Away in Books: The Life of Emily Dickinson.* New York: Random, 2001.

Haight, Gordon S. *Mrs. Sigourney: The Sweet Singer of Hartford.* New Haven: Yale UP, 1930.

Halker, Clark D. *For Democracy, Workers, and God: American Labor Song-Poems and Labor Protest, 1865–95.* Urbana: U of Illinois P, 1991.

Hall, Jonathan. "Alice Cary (1820–1871) and Phoebe Cary (1824–1871)." Haralson, *Encyclopedia* 65–67.

Hall, Susan Grove. "From Voice to Persona: Amelia Welby's Lyric Tradition in Sarah M. B. Piatt's Early Poetry." *Tulsa Studies in Women's Literature*, forthcoming.

Hallberg, Robert von. "Edgar Allan Poe, Poet-Critic." A. Lee 80–99.

Halliburton, David. *The Color of the Sky: A Study of Stephen Crane.* Cambridge: Cambridge UP, 1989.

Halttunen, Karen. *Confidence Men and Painted Women: A Study of Middle-Class Culture in America, 1830–1870.* New Haven: Yale UP, 1986.

Hapgood, Hutchins. *The Spirit of the Ghetto.* Ed. Moses Rischin. Cambridge: Belknap-Harvard UP, 1967.

Haralson, Eric, ed. *Encyclopedia of American Poetry: The Nineteenth Century.* Chicago: Fitzroy, 1998.

———. "Mars in Petticoats: Longfellow and Sentimental Masculinity." *Nineteenth-Century Literature* 51.3 (1996): 327–56.

Harding, Brian. " 'Frolic Architecture': Music and Metamorphosis in Emerson's Poetry." A. Lee 100–17.

Harding, Walter, ed. *Thoreau: Man of Concord.* New York: Holt, Rinehart, 1960.

Harjo, Joy, and Gloria Bird, eds. *Reinventing the Enemy's Language: Contemporary Native Women's Writings of North America.* New York: Norton, 1997.

Harper, Frances Ellen Watkins. *A Brighter Coming Day: A Frances Ellen Watkins Harper Reader.* Ed. Frances Smith Foster. New York: Feminist, 1990.

———. *Complete Poems of Frances E. W. Harper.* Ed. Maryemma Graham. New York: Oxford UP, 1988.

———. *Iola Leroy; or, Shadows Uplifted.* Introd. Hazel Carby. Black Women Writers. Boston: Beacon, 1987.

The Harris Collection of American Poetry and Plays. Ed. Rosemary Cullen. John Hay Lib., Brown U. 7 Feb. 2003. 21 Oct. 2005 <http://www.brown.edu/Facilities/University_Library/collections/harris/Harris.Home.html>.

Harris, Sharon, ed. *Blue Pencils and Hidden Hands: Women Editing Periodicals, 1830–1910.* Boston: Northeastern UP, 2004.

———. *Rebecca Harding Davis and American Realism.* Philadelphia: U of Pennsylvania P, 1991.

Harris, Susan K. " 'But Is It Any *Good*?': Evaluating Nineteenth-Century American Women's Fiction." J. Warren 263–79.

Hart, Ellen Louise. "The Encoding of Homoerotic Desire: Emily Dickinson's Letters and Poems to Susan Dickinson, 1850–1886." *Tulsa Studies in Women's Literature* 9.2 (1990): 251–72.

Hawthorne, Nathaniel. *The Letters, 1853–1856.* Ed. Thomas Woodson et al. Columbus: Ohio State UP, 1987. Vol. 17 of *The Centenary Edition of the Works of Nathaniel Hawthorne.*

———. "Mrs. Hutchinson." *Hawthorne: Tales and Sketches.* New York: Lib. of Amer., 1996. 18–24.

———. *The Scarlet Letter.* New York: Penguin, 1983.

Hendler, Glenn. *Public Sentiments: Structures of Feeling in Nineteenth-Century American Literature.* Chapel Hill: U of North Carolina P, 2001.

Hershberger, Mary "Mobilizing Women, Anticipating Abolition: The Struggle against Indian Removal." *Journal of American History* 86 (1999): 15–40.

Higginson, Thomas Wentworth. *Army Life in a Black Regiment.* 1869. New York: Norton, 1984.

Hill, Mary A. *Charlotte Perkins Gilman: The Making of a Radical Feminist, 1860–1896.* Philadelphia: Temple UP, 1980.

Hilmes, Michele. *Radio Voices: American Broadcasting, 1922–1952.* Minneapolis: U of Minnesota P, 1997.

Hine, Darlene Clark, William C. Hine, and Stanley Harrold. *African Americans: A Concise History.* Upper Saddle River: Prentice, 2004.

"[Charles Fenno] Hoffman's Poems: A Review." *Southern Literary Messenger* Feb. 1848: 97–105.

Hogan, Linda Henderson. "The Nineteenth-Century Native American Poets." *Wassaja* 13 (1980): 24–29.

Holland, Jeanne. "Scraps, Stamps, and Cutouts: Emily Dickinson's Domestic Technologies of Publication." *Cultural Artifacts and the Production of Meaning: The Page, the Image, and the Body.* Ed. Margaret J. M. Ezell and Katherine O'Keeffe. Ann Arbor: U of Michigan P, 1994. 139–81.

Hollander, John, ed. *American Poetry: The Nineteenth Century.* 2 vols. New York: Lib. of Amer., 1993.

Holmes, Oliver Wendell. *The Complete Poetical Works of Oliver Wendell Holmes.* Cambridge: Houghton, 1895.

Rev. of Holmes. *North American Review* Jan. 1847: 208–13.

Hom, Marlon K., ed. and trans. *Songs of Gold Mountain: Cantonese Rhymes from San Francisco Chinatown.* Berkeley: U of California P, 1992.

Horowitz, Helen Lefkowitz. *Re-reading Sex: Battles over Sexual Knowledge and Suppression in Nineteenth-Century America.* New York: Knopf, 2002.

Horton, George Moses. *The Black Bard of North Carolina: George Moses Horton and His Poetry.* Ed. Joan R. Sherman. Chapel Hill: U of North Carolina P, 1997.

Howe, Julia Ward. *Battle-Hymn of the Republic.* 1862. Bartleby.com. 6 May 2004 <www.bartleby.com/102/137.html>.

Howells, William Dean. Introduction to *Lyrics of Lowly Life.* By Paul Laurence Dunbar. New York: Dodd, 1906. xiii–xx.

———. "Novel-Writing and Novel-Reading: An Impersonal Explanation." Baym, *Norton Anthology* 2: 241–57.

———. *"Pebbles," "Monochromes," and Other Modern Poems, 1891–1916.* Ed. Edwin H. Cady. Athens: Ohio UP, 2000.

Hudnut, Robert K. *The Aesthetics of Ralph Waldo Emerson: The Materials and Methods of His Poetry.* Lewiston: Mellen, 1996.

Hughes, Gertrude Reif. "Subverting the Cult of Domesticity: Emily Dickinson's Critique of Women's Work." *Legacy* 3.1 (1986): 17–28.

Hull, Gloria T. "Afro-American Women Poets: A Bio-critical Survey." *Shakespeare's Sisters: Feminist Essays on Women Poets.* Ed. Sandra M. Gilbert and Susan Gubar. Bloomington: Indiana UP, 1979. 165–82.

———. "Black Women Poets from Wheatley to Walker." *Sturdy Black Bridges: Visions of Black Women in Literature.* Ed. Roseann P. Bell, Betty J. Parker, and Beverly Guy-Sheftall. Garden City: Doubleday, 1979. 69–86.

Hull, Gloria T., et al., eds. *All the Women Are White, All the Blacks Are Men, but Some of Us Are Brave: Black Women's Studies.* Old Westbury: Feminist, 1982.

Hutchinson, George. "Race and the Family Romance: Whitman's Civil War." *Walt Whitman Quarterly Review* 20.3–4 (2003): 134–50.

Huyssen, Andreas. *After the Great Divide: Modernism, Mass Culture, Postmodernism.* Bloomington: Indiana UP, 1986.

Hyneman, Rebekah. *"The Leper" and Other Poems.* Philadelphia: Hart, 1853.

Ignatiev, Noel. *How the Irish Became White.* New York: Routledge, 1995.

Images of African Americans from the Nineteenth Century. Digital Schomburg, New York Public Lib. Digital Lib. Collections. 1999. 12 July 2004 <http://digital.nypl.org/schomburg/images_aa19/>.

"Infant Mortality." *Gale Encyclopedia of Childhood and Adolescence.* 13 May 2004 <http://www.findarticles.com/cf_dls/g2602/0003/2602000321/p1/article.jhtml>.

Isaacs, Abram S. "Will the Jews Return to Palestine?" Lazarus, *Selected Poems* 353–57.

Jackson, Helen Hunt. *A Century of Dishonor: A Sketch of the United States Government's Dealings with Some of the Indian Tribes.* 1881. New York: Indian Head, 1993.

Jackson, Virginia. *Dickinson's Misery: A Theory of Lyric Reading.* Princeton: Princeton UP, 2005.

Jacob, Betty. Personal interview. 15 May 1998.

Jacobs, Harriet. *Incidents in the Life of a Slave Girl.* Ed. L. Maria Child. 1861. Hypertexts, Amer. Studies at the U of Virginia. 14 Feb. 2004. 28 June 2006 <http://xroads.virginia.edu/~Hyper/JACOBS/hjhome.htm>.

Jacobson, Matthew Frye. *Whiteness of a Different Color: European Immigrants and the Alchemy of Race.* Cambridge: Harvard UP, 1998.

James, Edward T., ed. *Notable American Women, 1607–1950.* 3 vols. Cambridge: Belknap-Harvard UP, 1971.

James, Henry. *The Real Thing.* 1893. Project Gutenberg. July 2001. 23 May 2006 <http://www.gutenberg.org/dirs/etext01/rlthg10.txt>.

Jarrell, Randall. "The Age of Criticism." *No Other Book: Selected Essays.* Ed. Brad Leithauser. New York: Harper, 2000. 281–97.

Jaskoski, Helen, ed. *Early Native American Writing: New Critical Essays.* Cambridge: Cambridge UP, 1996.

Jason, Philip K. *Nineteenth Century American Poetry: An Annotated Bibliography.* Pasadena: Salem, 1989.

The Jazz Singer. Dir. Alan Crosland. Perf. Al Jolson. 1927. Videocassette. MGM, 1994.

Jennings, Francis. *The Invasion of America: Indians, Colonialism, and the Cant of Conquest.* New York: Norton, 1975.

Jim Crow Museum of Racist Memorabilia. Ferris State U. 15 May 2006 <http://www.ferris.edu/jimcrow/>.

Johnson, Barbara. "Euphemism, Understatement, and the Passive Voice: Genealogy of African-American Poetry." *The Feminist Difference.* Cambridge: Harvard UP, 1999. 91–100.

Johnson, E. Pauline. *E. Pauline Johnson, Tekahionwake: Collected Poems and Selected Prose.* Ed. Carole Gerson and Veronica Strong-Boag. Toronto: U of Toronto P, 2002.

———. *Flint and Feather: The Complete Poems of E. Pauline Johnson.* Ed. and introd. Theodore Watts-Dunton. Toronto: Musson, 1917.

———. *The Moccasin Maker.* Introd. A. LaVonne Brown Ruoff. Norman: U of Oklahoma P, 1998.

Johnson, James Weldon. Preface to *The Book of American Negro Poetry.* Gates and McKay 861–84.

Johnson, Thomas H., ed. *The Poems of Emily Dickinson.* Cambridge: Belknap-Harvard UP, 1955.

Johnson, Wendy Dasler. "Male Sentimentalists through the 'I-s' of Julia Ward Howe's Poetry." *South Atlantic Review* 64.4 (1999): 16–35.

Johnston, Sheila M. F. *Buckskin and Broadcloth: A Celebration of E. Pauline Johnson, Tekahionwake, 1861–1913.* Toronto: Natural Heritage, 1997.

Jones, Buford, and Kent P. Ljungquist. "Poe, Mrs. Osgood, and 'Annabel Lee.' " Myerson, *Studies* 275–80.

Jubilee Singers. Fisk U. 2001. 13 Oct. 2005 <http://www.fisk.edu/index.asp?cat=16>.

Jubilee Singers: Sacrifice and Glory. Public Broadcasting Service. 2000. 9 July 2004 <http://www.pbs.org/wgbh/amex/singers/>.

Judaic Treasures of the Library of Congress: Nineteenth-Century American Poets. Jewish Virtual Lib. 11 Oct. 2005 <http://www.jewishvirtuallibrary.org/jsource/loc/Poets.html>.

Julia A. Moore: The Sweet Singer of Michigan, 1847–1920. Dept. of English, Western Michigan U. 6 May 1996. 13 May 2004 <http://www.wmich.edu/english/txt/Moore/>.

Justus, James H. "The Fireside Poets: Hearthside Values and the Language of Care." A. Lee 146–65.

Kane, Paul, ed. *Poetry of the American Renaissance: A Diverse Anthology from the Romantic Period.* New York: Braziller, 1995.

Kaplan, Fred. *Sacred Tears: Sentimentality in Victorian Literature.* Princeton: Princeton UP, 1987.

Kaplan, Justin. *Walt Whitman: A Life.* New York: Harper, 2003.

Karcher, Carolyn L. *The First Woman of the Republic: A Cultural Biography of Lydia Maria Child.* Durham: Duke UP, 1994.

———. "The Moderate and the Radical: Melville and Child on the Civil War and Reconstruction." *ESQ* 45.3–4 (1999): 187–257.

Scharnharst Karpinski, Joanne B., ed. *Critical Essays on Charlotte Perkins Gilman.* New York: Hall, 1992.

———. "When the Marriage of True Minds Admits Impediments: Charlotte Perkins Gilman and William Dean Howells." Karpinski, *Critical Essays* 202–21.

Katz, Joseph. Introduction. Crane, *Complete Poems* xi–xxxvii.

Katz, Jonathan Ned. "Coming to Terms: Conceptualizing Men's Erotic and Affectional Relations with Men in the United States, 1820–1892." *A Queer World: The Center for Lesbian and Gay Studies Reader.* Ed. Martin Duberman. New York: New York UP, 1997. 216–35.

Keats, John. "Fancy." *The Oxford Book of English Verse.* Ed. Arthur Thomas Quiller-Couch. Oxford: Clarendon, 1919. *Bartleby.com.* Jan. 1999. 5 Dec. 2006 <http://www.bartleby.com/101/631.html>.

Kelley, Mary. *Private Woman, Public Stage: Literary Domesticity in Nineteenth-Century America.* Chapel Hill: U of North Carolina P, 2002.

Kelly, Franklin, et al., eds. *Frederic Edwin Church.* Washington: Natl. Gallery of Art, 1989.

Kendall, Stephen R. *Substance and Shadow: Women and Addiction in the United States.* Cambridge: Harvard UP, 1996.

Kennedy, J. Gerald, ed. *A Historical Guide to Edgar Allan Poe.* New York: Oxford UP, 2001.

———. *Poe, Death, and the Life of Writing.* New Haven: Yale UP, 1987.

———. "Poe, 'Ligeia,' and the Problem of Dying Women." *New Essays on Poe's Major Tales.* Ed. Kenneth Silverman. New York: Cambridge UP, 1993. 113–29.

Kennedy, J. Gerald, and Liliane Weissberg, eds. *Romancing the Shadow: Poe and Race.* New York: Oxford UP, 2001.

Kenschaft, Lori J. *Lydia Maria Child: A Quest for Racial Justice.* New York: Oxford UP, 2002.

Kessler, Carol Farley. "Brittle Jars and Bitter Jangles: Light Verse by Charlotte Perkins Gilman." *Charlotte Perkins Gilman: The Woman and her Work.* Ed. Sheryl L. Meyerling. Ann Arbor: UMI Research, 1989. 133–43.

Kete, Mary Louise. *Sentimental Collaborations: Mourning and Middle-Class Identity in Nineteenth-Century America.* Durham: Duke UP, 1999.

Kilcup, Karen L. "Anthologizing Matters: The Poetry and Prose of Recovery Work." *Symploke* 8.1 (2000): 36–56.

———. "Emily Dickinson's Pearls." *Hawthorne and Women: Engendering and Expanding the Hawthorne Tradition.* Ed. John L. Idol, Jr., and Melinda M. Ponder. Amherst: U of Massachusetts P, 1999. 237–49.

———. "Lydia Howard Huntley Sigourney (1791–1865)." Knight and Nelson 361–67.

———, ed. *Native American Women's Writing, c. 1800–1924: An Anthology.* Oxford: Blackwell, 2000.

———, ed. *Nineteenth-Century American Women's Writing: An Anthology.* Malden: Blackwell, 1998.

———, ed. *Nineteenth-Century American Women Writers: A Critical Reader.* Oxford: Blackwell, 1998.

———, ed. *Nineteenth-Century American Women Writers: An Anthology.* Malden: Blackwell, 1997.

———. *Robert Frost and Feminine Literary Tradition.* Ann Arbor: U of Michigan P, 1998.

———, ed. *Soft Canons: American Women Writers and Masculine Tradition.* Iowa City: U of Iowa P, 1999.

———. " 'Something of a Sentimental Sweet Singer': Robert Frost, Lucy Larcom, and 'Swinging Birches.' " *Roads Not Taken: Rereading Robert Frost.* Ed. Earl J. Wilcox and Jonathan N. Barron. Columbia: U of Missouri P, 2000. 11–31.

Killingsworth, M. Jimmie. *Whitman's Poetry of the Body: Sexuality, Politics, and the Text.* Chapel Hill: U of North Carolina P, 1989.

Kindilien, Carlin T. *American Poetry in the Eighteen Nineties.* Providence: Brown UP, 1956.

Kirkland, Caroline. *A New Home: Who'll Follow?; or, Glimpses of Western Life. Pioneering the Upper Midwest.* Amer. Memory. Lib. of Congress. 19 Oct. 1998. 23 May 2006 <http://memory.loc.gov/ammem/umhtml/umhome.html>. Path: Authors; Kirkland.

Kleeberg, Minna. *Gedichte.* Louisville: Knöfel, 1877.

Knight, Denise D., ed. *The Diaries of Charlotte Perkins Gilman.* 2 vols. Charlottesville: U of Virginia P, 1994.

———. " 'With the First Grass-Blade': Whitman's Influence on the Poetry of Charlotte Perkins Gilman." *Walt Whitman Quarterly Review* 11.1 (1993): 18–29.

Knight, Denise D., and Emmanuel S. Nelson, eds. *Nineteenth-Century American Women Writers: A Bio-bibliographical Critical Sourcebook.* Westport: Greenwood, 1997.

Knittel, Janna. " 'Songs for the People': Politics and Poetry in the Career of Frances Harper." *MAWA Review* 12.1 (1997): 30–43.

Kogen, Jay, and Wallace Wolodarsky. "Treehouse of Horror." *The Simpsons.* 25 Oct. 1990. Videocassette. 20th Century Fox, 1998.

Koller, Balint. "Response to L. H. Sigourney's Poem 'Indian Names.' " Amer. Studies Program, Trinity Coll. 3 Mar. 2004.

Kornfeld, Eve. *Margaret Fuller: A Brief Biography with Documents.* Boston: Bedford–St. Martin's, 1997.

Kosmider, Alexia M. *Tricky Tribal Discourse: The Poetry, Short Stories, and Fus Fixico Letters of Creek Writer Alex Posey.* Moscow: U of Idaho P, 1998.

Kribbs, Jayne K., ed. *Critical Essays on John Greenleaf Whittier.* Boston: Hall, 1980.

Kroeber, Karl, ed. *Traditional Literatures of the American Indian: Texts and Interpretations.* Lincoln: U of Nebraska P, 1997.

Kummings, Donald D. *Walt Whitman, 1940–1975: A Reference Guide.* Boston: Hall, 1982.

Lacey, Kate. "Radio in the Great Depression: Promotional Culture, Public Service, and Propaganda." *Radio Reader: Essays in the Cultural History of Radio.* Ed. Michele Hilmes and Jason Loviglio. New York: Routledge, 2002. 21–40.

Lai, Him Mark, Genny Lim, and Judy Yung, eds. and trans. *Island: Poetry and History of Chinese Immigrants on Angel Island.* Seattle: U of Washington P, 1999.

Lane, Ann J. *To* Herland *and Beyond: The Life and Work of Charlotte Perkins Gilman.* New York: Pantheon, 1980.

Lang, Amy Schrager. *Prophetic Woman: Anne Hutchinson and the Problem of Dissent in the Literature of New England.* Berkeley: U of California P, 1987.

Larcom, Lucy. [*See also* Nymphea.] "Among Lowell Mill-Girls: A Reminiscence." *Atlantic Monthly* Nov. 1881: 593–612. *Making.* Path: Browse; Atlantic Monthly; 1881; November; Among Lowell Mill Girls.

———. *The Poetical Works of Lucy Larcom.* Boston: Houghton, 1885.

Lauter, Paul. *Canons and Contexts.* New York: Oxford UP, 1991.

———. "Is Frances Ellen Watkins Harper Good Enough to Teach?" *Legacy* 5.1 (1988): 27–32.

———. "Teaching Nineteenth-Century Women Writers." J. Warren 280–301.

Lauter, Paul, et al., eds. *The Heath Anthology of American Literature.* 4th ed. 2 vols. New York: Houghton, 2002. 5th ed. 5 vols. New York: Houghton, 2005.

Lavender, Catherine, ed. "Texts about Lowell Mill Girls." 2004. *Liberty Rhetoric.* 28 Mar. 2004 <http://www.library.csi.cuny.edu/dept/americanstudies/lavender/lowetext.html#transcript>.

Lazarus, Emma. "The Persecution of the Jews in Russia." Lazarus, *Selected Poems* 349–53).

———. *The Poems of Emma Lazarus.* Boston: Houghton, 1895.

———. *Selected Poems and Other Writings.* Ed. Gregory Eiselein. Peterborough, ON: Broadview, 2002.

Lears, T. J. Jackson. *No Place of Grace: Antimodernism and the Transformation of American Culture, 1880–1920.* Chicago: U of Chicago P, 1994.

Lee, A. Robert, ed. *Nineteenth-Century American Poetry.* Totowa: Barnes, 1985.

Lee, Maurice S. "Writing through the War: Melville and Dickinson after the Renaissance." *PMLA* 115 (2000): 1124–28.

Lehuu, Isabelle. *Carnival on the Page: Popular Print Media in Antebellum America.* Chapel Hill: U of North Carolina P, 2000.

Leighton, Mary Elizabeth. "Performing Pauline Johnson: Representations of 'the Indian Poetess' in the Periodical." *Essays on Canadian Writing* 65 (1998): 141–64.

LeMaster, J. R., and Donald D. Kummings, eds. *Walt Whitman: An Encyclopedia.* New York: Garland, 1998.

Lerner, Laurence. *Angels and Absences: Child Deaths in the Nineteenth Century.* Nashville: Vanderbilt UP, 1997.

Leverenz, David. *Manhood and the American Renaissance.* Ithaca: Cornell UP, 1989.

Levertov, Denise. "What Were They Like?" *The Sorrow Dance.* New York: New Directions, 1967. 84.

Levine, Lawrence W. *Highbrow/Lowbrow: The Emergence of Cultural Hierarchy in America.* Cambridge: Harvard UP, 1988.

Lewis, David Rich. *Neither Wolf nor Dog: American Indians, Environment, and Agrarian Change.* New York: Oxford UP, 1994.

Lhamon, W. T., Jr. *Raising Cain: Blackface Performance from Jim Crow to Hip Hop.* Cambridge: Harvard UP, 1998.

Liberty Rhetoric. Ed. Catherine Lavender. Amer. Studies Program of the College of Staten Island; City U of New York. 19 Apr. 1999. 28 Mar. 2004 <http://www.library.csi.cuny.edu/dept/americanstudies/lavender/start.html>.

Lichtenstein, Diane. *Writing Their Nations: The Tradition of Nineteenth-Century American Jewish Women Writers.* Bloomington: Indiana UP, 1992.

"The Life and Genius of Goethe." Rev. of *The Works of Goethe*, by Johann Wolfgang von Goethe. *North American Review* Oct. 1824: 303–25.

Life and Works of Herman Melville. Ed. J. Madden. 6 May 2004 <http://www.melville.org>.

Lilienthal, [Max]. "The Festival of Chanuckah." Mar. 1847. *The Occident and American Jewish Advocate* 23 July 2003 <http://www.jewish-history.com/Occident/volume4/mar1847/chanucka.html>.

Lincoln, Kenneth. "Native American Literatures." *Smoothing the Ground: Essays on Native American Oral Literature.* Ed. Brian Swann. Berkeley: U of California P, 1983. 3–38.

———. *Sing with the Heart of a Bear: Fusions of Native and American Poetry, 1890–1999.* Berkeley: U of California P, 2000.

Link, Eric Carl. "American Nationalism and the Defense of Poetry." *Southern Quarterly* 41.2 (2003): 48–59.

"Literary Portraits: Miss H. F. Gould." *New-England Magazine* Apr. 1833: 309–12.

Literature Online. Chadwyck-Healey. 8 July 2004 <http://lion.chadwyck.co.uk/>. Path: Chadwyck-Healey Literature Collections; American Poetry.

Littlefield, Daniel F. *Alex Posey: Creek Poet, Journalist, and Humorist.* Lincoln: U of Nebraska P, 1992.

———. " 'They Ought to Enjoy the Home of Their Fathers': The Treaty of 1838, Seneca Intellectuals, and Literary Genesis." Jaskoski 83–103.

Litwack, Leon. *Been in the Storm So Long: The Aftermath of Slavery.* New York: Vintage, 1980.

Ljungquist, Kent P. " 'Fellowship with Other Poets': Lowell, Longfellow, and Poe Correspond with A. M. Ide Jr." *Resources for American Literary Study* 28 (2003): 27–51.

Loeffelholz, Mary. *From School to Salon: Reading Nineteenth-Century American Women's Poetry.* Princeton: Princeton UP, 2004.

———. "The Religion of Art in the City at War: Boston's Public Poetry and the Great Organ, 1863." *American Literary History* 13.2 (2001): 212–41.

———. "Who Killed Lucretia Davidson?; or, Poetry in the Domestic-Tutelary Complex." *Yale Journal of Criticism* 10.2 (1997): 271–93.

Loewen, James W. *Lies My Teacher Told Me: Everything Your American History Textbook Got Wrong.* New York: Touchstone, 1996.

Logan, Rayford W. *The Betrayal of the Negro, from Rutherford B. Hayes to Woodrow Wilson.* New York: Da Capo, 1997. Rpt. of *The Negro in American Life and Thought: The Nadir, 1877–1901.*

Longfellow, Henry Wadsworth. Evangeline *and Selected Tales and Poems.* Ed. Horace Gregory. New York: Penguin, 1964.

———. *The Midnight Ride of Paul Revere.* Illus. Christopher Bing. New York: Handprint, 2001.

———. *Poems and Other Writings.* Ed. J. D. McClatchy. New York: Lib. of Amer., 2000.

———. *The Poetical Works, 1886–1891.* Chadwyck-Healey. 28 Sept. 2004 <http://collections.chadwyck.com/>.

———. *The Poetical Works of Longfellow.* 1893. Boston: Houghton, 1975.

———. *Selected Poems.* Ed. Lawrence Buell. New York: Penguin, 1988.

———. *The Song of Hiawatha.* 1855. Poets' Corner–Bookshelf. 6 May 2004 <http://www.theotherpages.org/poems/hiawatha.html>.

Lootens, Tricia. "Hemans and Her American Heirs: Nineteenth-Century Women's Poetry and National Identity." *Women's Poetry, Late Romantic to Late Victorian: Gender and Genre, 1830–1900.* Ed. Isobel Armstrong and Virginia Blain. London: U of London P, 1999. 243–59.

Lott, Eric. *Love and Theft: Blackface Minstrelsy and the American Working Class.* New York: Oxford UP, 1993.

Lounsbury, Thomas Raynesford. *Yale Book of American Verse.* New Haven: Yale UP, 1912.

Lowell, Amy. "Patterns." *Selected Poems of Amy Lowell.* Ed. Melissa Bradshaw and Adrienne Munich. New Brunswick: Rutgers UP, 2002. 58–61.

Lowell, James Russell. "The Biglow Papers." Lowell, *Complete Poetical Works* 165–284.

———. *The Complete Poetical Works of James Russell Lowell.* Cambridge: Riverside, 1896.

———. "The Heritage." McGuffey, *Fifth Eclectic Reader* 228–30.

Lowell, Maria White. "The Slave-Mother." C. Walker, *American Women Poets* 193–94.

The Lowell Offering: Writings by New England Mill Women. Berwick Acad. Apr. 2001. 24 Aug. 2006 <http://www.berwickacademy.org/millgirls/offering.htm>.

Lystra, Karen. *Searching the Heart: Women, Men, and Romantic Love in Nineteenth-Century America.* New York: Oxford UP, 1989.

M. "The Admirer of Nature." *Lowell Offering* 3 (1943): 173–74.

MacLeish, Archibald. "The Young Dead Soldiers." *New and Collected Poems, 1917–1976.* Boston: Houghton, 1976. 381–82.

———. *The Young Dead Soldiers Do Not Speak.* Lyrical Legacy: Four Hundred Years of Amer. Song and Poetry. Lib. of Congress. 5 May 2006 <http://www.loc.gov/teachers/lyrical/poems/docs/young_trans.pdf>.

Maines, Rachel. *The Technology of Orgasm: "Hysteria," the Vibrator, and Women's Sexual Satisfaction.* Baltimore: Johns Hopkins UP, 1999.

Making of America. 1999. Cornell U Lib. 6 June 2004 <http://cdl.library.cornell.edu/moa>.

Mandel, Norma H. *Beyond the Garden Gate: The Life of Celia Laighton Thaxter.* Hanover: UP of New England, 2004.

Mandell, Laura, ed. *The Transatlantic Poetess.* Spec. issue of *Romanticism on the Net* 29–30 (2003). 28 Sept. 2004 <http://www.erudit.org/revue/ron/2003/v/n29/>.

Maniero, Lina, ed. *American Women Writers: A Critical Reference Guide from Colonial Times to the Present.* 4 vols. New York: Ungar, 1981.

Marcellin, Leigh Anne Urbanowicz. "Emily Dickinson's Civil War Poetry." *Emily Dickinson Journal* 5.2 (1996): 107–12.

———. " 'Singing off the Charnel Steps': Soldiers and Mourners in Emily Dickinson's War Poetry." *Emily Dickinson Journal* 9.2 (2000): 64–74.

Marchalonis, Shirley. "A Model for Mentors? Lucy Larcom and John Greenleaf Whittier." Marchalonis, *Patrons* 94–121.

———, ed. *Patrons and Protegees: Gender, Friendship, and Writing in Nineteenth-Century America.* New Brunswick: Rutgers UP, 1994.

———. *The Worlds of Lucy Larcom.* Athens: U of Georgia P, 1989.

Marinoni, Rosa Zagnoni. *Side Show.* Philadelphia: McKay, 1938.

Marius, Richard, et al., eds. *The Columbia Book of Civil War Poetry.* New York: Columbia UP, 1994.

Marom, Daniel. "Who Is the 'Mother of Exiles'? Jewish Aspects of Emma Lazarus's 'The New Colossus.' " *Prooftexts* 20.3 (2000): 231–61.

Martin, Robert K., ed. *The Continuing Presence of Walt Whitman: The Life after the Life.* Iowa City: U of Iowa P, 1992.

———. *The Homosexual Tradition in American Poetry.* Rev. ed. U of Iowa P, 1998.

Marx, Leo. *The Machine in the Garden: Technology and the Pastoral Ideal in America.* New York: Oxford UP, 1964.

Matthiessen, F. O. *The American Renaissance: Art and Expression in the Age of Emerson and Whitman.* New York: Oxford UP, 1962.

May, Caroline, ed. *The American Female Poets.* Philadelphia: Lindsay, 1848.

McClatchy, J. D., ed. *Poets of the Civil War.* New York: Lib. of Amer., 2005.

McCord, Louisa Susannah Cheves. *Poems, Drama, Biography, Letters.* Ed. Richard C. Lounsbury. Charlottesville: UP of Virginia, 1996.

McGill, Meredith L. *American Literature and the Culture of Reprinting, 1834–1853.* Philadelphia: U of Pennsylvania P, 2003.

———, ed. *New Directions in Poe Studies.* Spec. issue of *Poe Studies / Dark Romanticism* 33.1–2 (2000): 1–63.

McGuffey, William Holmes. *Eclectic Primer.* New York: Van Antwerp, 1879.

———. *Fifth Eclectic Reader.* New York: Van Antwerp, 1879.

———. *Fourth Eclectic Reader.* New York: Van Antwerp, 1879.

———. *Sixth Eclectic Reader.* New York: Van Antwerp, 1879.

McHenry, Elizabeth. " 'Dreaded Eloquence': The Origins and Rise of African American Literary Societies and Libraries." *Harvard Library Bulletin* 6.2 (1995): 32–56.

———. *Forgotten Readers: Recovering the Lost History of African American Literary Societies.* Durham: Duke UP, 2002.

McKenney, Thomas Loraine, and James Hall. *Catalogue of One Hundred and Seventeen Indian Portraits, Representing Eighteen Different Tribes, Accompanied by a Few Brief Remarks on the Character &c. of Most of Them.* Philadelphia, 1836.

———. *History of the Indian Tribes of North America with Biographical Sketches of the Principal Chiefs.* 3 vols. Philadelphia: Bowen, 1848.

McLean, Albert F. *William Cullen Bryant.* Boston: Twayne, 1989.

McWilliams, John. "The Epic in the Nineteenth Century." Parini 33–63.

Melville, Herman. *Battle-Pieces and Aspects of the War.* New York: Da Capo, 1995.

———. *Clarel: A Poem and Pilgrimage in the Holy Land.* Ed. Walter E. Bezanson. New York: Hendricks, 1960.

———. *Collected Poems.* 1947. Chadwyck-Healey. 28 Sept. 2004 <http://collections.chadwyck.com/>.

———. *The Poems of Herman Melville.* Ed. Douglas Robillard. 1976. Rev. ed. Albany: Kent State UP, 2000.

Menand, Louis. *The Metaphysical Club: A Story of Ideas in America.* New York: Farrar, 2002.

Menken, Adah Isaacs. Infelicia *and Other Writings.* Ed. Gregory Eiselein. Peterborough, ON: Broadview, 2002.

———. "To the Sons of Israel." *Israelite* 28 Jan. 1859: 236.

Merish, Lori. *Sentimental Materialism: Gender, Commodity Culture, and Nineteenth-Century American Literature.* Durham: Duke UP, 2000.

Merriam, Eve. *Emma Lazarus Rediscovered.* Introd. and afterword Morris U. Schappes. New York: Biblio, 1998.

Meyer, Kinereth. "Landscape and Counter-landscape in the Poetry of William Cullen Bryant." *Nineteenth-Century Literature* 48.2 (1993): 194–211.

Michaels, Walter Benn, and Donald E. Pease, eds. *The American Renaissance Reconsidered.* Baltimore: Johns Hopkins UP, 1985.

The "Mill Girls." Lowell Natl. Historical Park and Tsongas Industrial History Center. 2003. United States National Park Service. 28 Mar. 2004 <http://www.nps.gov/lowe/2002/loweweb/lowe_history/lowe_brochures/millgirls.htm>.

Milton, John. *Paradise Lost.* New York: Mentor, 1961.

Mlotek, Zalmen, et al. *In Love and in Struggle: The Musical Legacy of the Jewish Labor Bund.* New York: YIVO Inst. for Jewish Research, 1999.

Moïse, Penina. *Secular and Religious Works of Penina Moïse, with a Brief Sketch of Her Life.* Charleston: Charleston Section, Council of Jewish Women, 1911.

Moon, Michael. *Disseminating Whitman: Revision and Corporeality in* Leaves of Grass. Cambridge: Harvard UP, 1991.

"Moonward Gushings." *New England Offering* 2 (1849): 82.

Moore, Julia A. "Little Libbie." *Julia A. Moore: The Sweet Singer of Michigan, 1847–1920.* Dept. of English, Western Michigan U. 6 May 1996. 15 Aug. 2006 <http://www.wmich.edu/english/txt/Moore/Little.Libbie. html>.

Moore, Rayburn S. *Paul Hamilton Hayne.* New York: Twayne, 1972.

———. "Poetry of the Late Nineteenth Century." *The History of Southern Litera-*

ture. Ed. Louis D. Rubin., Jr., et al. Baton Rouge: Louisiana State UP, 1985. 189–98.

Morris, Timothy. *Becoming Canonical in American Poetry*. Urbana: U of Illinois P, 1995.

Morse, Jonathan. "Bibliographical Essay." *A Historical Guide to Emily Dickinson*. Ed. Vivian Pollak. Oxford: Oxford UP, 2004. 255–83.

Moseley, Caroline. "The Young Women of Nineteenth-Century American Parlor Song." *New Jersey Folklore* 7 (1982): 6–9.

Mosier, Richard. *Making the American Mind: Social and Moral Ideas in the McGuffey Readers*. New York: Russell, 1965.

Mossell, N. F. *The Work of the Afro-American Woman*. New York: Oxford UP, 1988.

Mulvey, Christopher. "George Catlin in Europe." *George Catlin and His Indian Gallery*. Ed. Therese Thau Heyman and George Gurney. Washington: Norton, 2003. 63–91.

The Multicultural Archive of Georgia. Ed. Timothy B. Powell and Barbara McCaskill. U of Georgia. 11 Apr. 2003. 14 May 2006 <http://www.mcgeorgia.uga.edu/>.

Mvuyekure, Pierre Damien. "Paul Laurence Dunbar, 1872–1906." E. Nelson 132–38.

Myerson, Joel, ed. *Studies in the American Renaissance*. Charlottesville: UP of Virginia, 1983.

———. *Walt Whitman: A Descriptive Bibliography*. Pittsburgh: U of Pittsburgh P, 1993.

Native American Authors. Internet Public Lib. U of Michigan. 1 May 2006. 26 July 2004 <http://www.ipl.org/div/natam/>.

Neely, Mark E., Jr. "Whitman and the Civil War: A Response to Helen Vendler." *Michigan Quarterly Review* 39.1 (2000): 25–35.

Nelson, Cary. "Martial Lyrics: The Vexed History of the Wartime Poem Card." *American Literary History* 16 (2004): 263–89.

———. *Repression and Recovery: Modern American Poetry and the Politics of Cultural Memory*. Madison: U of Wisconsin P, 1989.

Nelson, Emmanuel S., ed. *African American Authors, 1745–1945: A Bio-bibliographical Critical Sourcebook*. Westport: Greenwood, 2000.

Nineteenth Century American Literary, Historical, and Cultural Studies. 1998. Program in Amer. Studies, Washington State U. 26 July 2004 <http://www.wsu.edu/~amerstu/19th/19th.html>.

Nineteenth-Century Schoolbooks. Nietz Old Textbook Collection. U of Pittsburgh Digital Research Lib. Sept. 2003. 26 May 2006 <http://digital.library.pitt.edu/neitz/>.

Noble, Marianne. *The Masochistic Pleasures of Sentimental Literature*. Princeton: Princeton UP, 2000.

Noguchi, Yone. *Poetry*. Ed. Yoshinobu Hakutani. Madison: Fairleigh Dickinson UP, 1992. Vol. 1 of *Selected English Writings of Yone Noguchi: An East-West Literary Assimilation*.

Novick, Sheldon M. *Honorable Justice: The Life of Oliver Wendell Holmes*. Boston: Little, 1989.

Noyes, Alfred. "The Highwayman." *The Oxford Book of Narrative Verse.* Ed. Iona Opie and Peter Opie. Oxford: Oxford UP, 1983. 341–44.

Nye, David E. *American Technological Sublime.* Cambridge: MIT P, 1994.

Nymphea [Lucy Larcom]. "The Sorrows of Sensibility." *Lowell Offering* 5 (1845): 81.

The Occident and American Jewish Advocate [1843–1850]. Ed. Isaac Leeser. Jewish-Amer. History Documentation Foundation. 22 July 2003 <http://www.jewish-history.com/Occident/index.html>.

Okker, Patricia. *Our Sister Editors: Sarah J. Hale and the Tradition of Nineteenth-Century Women Editors.* Athens: U of Georgia P, 1995.

———. "Sarah Josepha Hale, Lydia Sigourney, and the Poetic Tradition in Two Nineteenth-Century Women's Magazines." *American Periodicals* 3 (1993): 32–42.

Older, Julia. "Fluttering Drapery and Controlled Panic: Celia Thaxter and Elizabeth Bishop, Parallel Poets a Century Later." *Worcester Review* 18.1–2 (1997): 96–100.

Olson, Steven. *The Prairie in Nineteenth-Century American Poetry.* Norman: U of Oklahoma P, 1995.

Omer-Sherman, Ranen. "Emma Lazarus, Jewish American Poetics, and the Challenge of Modernity." *Legacy* 19.2 (2002): 170–91.

The Online Books Page. Ed. John Mark Ockerbloom. U of Pennsylvania Lib. 7 July 2004 <http://onlinebooks.library.upenn.edu/>.

Osgood, Frances Sargent. *Poems.* Philadelphia: Carey, 1850.

Oskison, John Milton. *Tecumseh and His Times: The Story of a Great Indian.* New York: Putnam, 1938.

Ostriker, Alicia Suskin. *Stealing the Language: The Emergence of Women's Poetry in America.* Boston: Beacon, 1986.

Paredes, Américo. *"With a Pistol in His Hand": A Border Ballad and Its Hero.* Austin: U of Texas P, 1978.

Parini, Jay, ed. *The Columbia History of American Poetry.* New York: Columbia UP, 1993.

Parins, James W. *John Rollin Ridge: His Life and Works.* Lincoln: U of Nebraska P, 2004.

Parker, Hershel. "The Real 'Live Oak, with Moss': Straight Talk about Whitman's Gay Manifesto." *Nineteenth-Century Literature* 51.2 (1996): 145–60.

Parr, Matthew. "Nineteenth-Century Versions of American Indian Poetry." Haralson, *Encyclopedia* 314–20.

Paula Bernat Bennett's Research Materials for Her Collection of Sarah M. B. Piatt Poems: Palace-Burner: The Selected Poetry of Sarah Piatt *(2001).* Comp. Mary Manning, Amy Thompson, and Kyle Roberts. Ohio State U Libs. 2003. 23 May 2006 <http://library.osu.edu/sites/rarebooks/finding/piatt.html>.

The Pauline Johnson Archive. McMaster U. Sept. 1996. 7 July 2004 <http://www.humanities.mcmaster.ca/~pjohnson/emily.html>.

Paul Laurence Dunbar Digital Text Collection. 2004. Wright State U Libs. 17 Jan. 2006. 9 July 2004 <http://www.libraries.wright.edu/dunbar/>.

Paymer, Marvin E., ed. *Facts behind the Songs: A Handbook of American Popular Music from the Nineties to the '90s.* New York: Garland, 1993.

Person, Leland. *Aesthetic Headaches: Women and a Masculine Poetics in Poe, Melville, and Hawthorne.* Athens: U of Georgia P, 1988.

Peterson, Beverly. "Stowe and Whittier Respond in Poetry to the Fugitive Slave Law." *Resources for American Literary Study* 26.2 (2000): 184–99.

Peterson, Carla L. *Doers of the Word: African American Women Speakers and Writers in the North, 1830–1880.* New Brunswick: Rutgers UP, 1998.

Petrino, Elizabeth A. *Emily Dickinson and Her Contemporaries: Women's Verse in America, 1820–1885.* Hanover: UP of New England, 1998.

———. " 'Feet So Precious Charged': Dickinson, Sigourney, and the Child Elegy." *Tulsa Studies in Women's Literature* 13 (1994): 317–38.

———. "Nineteenth-Century American Women's Poetry." Bauer and Gould 122–42.

Pettis, Joyce. *African American Poets: Lives, Works, and Sources.* Westport: Greenwood, 2002.

Piatt, Sarah. *Palace-Burner: The Selected Poetry of Sarah Piatt.* Ed. Paula Bernat Bennett. Urbana: U of Illinois P, 2001.

Pizer, Donald, ed. *The Cambridge Companion to American Realism and Naturalism.* Cambridge: Cambridge UP, 1995.

———, ed. *Documents of American Realism and Naturalism.* Carbondale: Southern Illinois UP, 1998.

Plato, Ann. "Advice to Young Ladies." Sherman, *African-American Poetry* 51.

Poe, Edgar Allan. *Broadway Journal Prose.* Ed. Burton Pollin. New York: Gordian, 1986. Vol. 3, pt. 1, of *The Collected Writings of Edgar Allan Poe.*

———. *The Collected Works of Edgar Allan Poe.* Ed. Thomas Ollive Mabbott. Cambridge: Belknap-Harvard UP, 1969.

———. *The Complete Poems.* Ed. Thomas Ollive Mabbott. Urbana: U of Illinois P, 2000.

———. *Complete Poems and Selected Essays.* Ed. Richard Gray. London: Everyman, 1993.

———. *Essays and Reviews.* Ed. G. R. Thompson. New York: Lib. of Amer., 1984.

———. *"The Fall of the House of Usher" and Other Writings.* Ed. David Galloway. New York: Penguin, 1986.

———. "Mr. Griswold and the Poets." Poe, *Works.* Path: Literary Criticism; "Rufus W. Griswold and the Poets."

———. *Poetry and Tales.* Ed. Patrick F. Quinn. New York: Lib. of Amer., 1984.

———. *The Works of Edgar Allan Poe.* Edgar Allan Poe Soc. of Baltimore. 4 Apr. 1998. 24 Feb. 2006 <http://www.eapoe.org/works/index.htm>.

———. Rev. of *A Wreath of Wild Flowers from New England,* by Frances Sargent Osgood. Poe, *Works.* Path: Literary Criticism; Osgood; Review of "A Wreath."

Pollak, Vivian R. *Dickinson: The Anxiety of Gender.* Ithaca: Cornell UP, 1984.

———. *The Erotic Whitman.* Berkeley: U of California P, 2000.

———. "Poetic Value and Erotic Norms: A Response to Helen Vendler." *Walt Whitman Quarterly Review* 18 (2001): 134–46.

Posey, Alexander. *The Poems of Alexander Lawrence Posey.* Comp. Minnie H. Posey. Topeka: Crane, 1910.

Pound, Ezra. "A Retrospect." *Literary Essays of Ezra Pound.* Ed. T. S. Eliot. New York: New Directions, 1968. 3–14.

———. *Selected Poems of Ezra Pound.* New York: New Directions, 1957.

Price, Kenneth M., and Susan Belasco Smith, eds. *Periodical Literature in Nineteenth-Century America.* Charlottesville: UP of Virginia, 1995.

Prins, Yopie. *The Victorian Sappho.* Princeton: Princeton UP, 1999.

Project Gutenberg. Project Gutenberg Literary Archive Foundation. 3 Apr. 2006. 26 Aug. 2005 <http://www.gutenberg.org/>.

Quartermain, Peter, ed. *American Poets, 1880–1945. Dictionary of Literary Biography.* 1st ser.; vol. 45. Detroit: Gale, 1986. 2nd ser.; vol. 48 (1986). 3rd ser.; vol. 54 (1987).

Quinn, Arthur Hobson. *Edgar Allan Poe: A Critical Biography.* Baltimore: Johns Hopkins UP, 1997.

Reilly, John E. "Mrs. Osgood's 'Life Voyage' and 'Annabel Lee.' " *Poe Studies / Dark Romanticism* 17.1 (1984): 23.

Renker, Elizabeth. "Melville the Poet: Response to William Spengemann." *American Literary History* 12.1–2 (2000): 348–54.

Representative Poetry Online. Ed. Ian Lancashire. U of Toronto Libs. 24 July 2004 <http://rpo.library.utoronto.ca/display/indexpoet.html>.

Revell, Peter, and David J. Nordloh. *Paul Laurence Dunbar.* Boston: Twayne, 1979.

Reynolds, David S. *Beneath the American Renaissance: The Subversive Imagination in the Age of Emerson and Melville.* Cambridge: Harvard UP, 1989.

———. "Bibliographical Essay." *A Historical Guide to Walt Whitman.* Ed. Reynolds. New York: Oxford UP, 1999. 251–59.

———. *Walt Whitman's America: A Cultural Biography.* New York: Knopf, 1995.

Rich, Adrienne. "Compulsory Heterosexuality and Lesbian Existence." *Signs* 5 (1980): 631–60.

Richards, Eliza. *Gender and the Poetics of Reception in Poe's Circle.* Cambridge: Cambridge UP, 2004.

———. "Women's Place in Poe Studies," *Poe Studies / Dark Romanticism* 31.1–2 (2000): 10–14.

Ridge, John Rollin. *Poems of John Rollin Ridge.* Ed. Jeff Ward. Sequoyah Research Center. Amer. Native Press Archives. 2003. 26 July 2004 <http://anpa.ualr.edu/digital_library/jrr/jrr.htm>.

Riis, Jacob A. *How the Other Half Lives.* New York: Scribner's, 1890.

The Rise and Fall of Jim Crow. Public Broadcasting Service. 2002. 14 May 2006 <http://www.pbs.org/wnet/jimcrow/index.html>.

Robbins, J. Albert. "Nineteenth-Century Poetry." *American Literary Scholarship: An Annual, 1966.* Bloomington: Indiana UP, 1966. 129–46.

———. "Poe and Nineteenth-Century Poetry." *American Literary Scholarship: An Annual, 1967.* Bloomington: Indiana UP, 1967. 149–65.

Robinson, Harriet Hanson. *Loom and Spindle; or, Life among the Early Mill Girls, with a Sketch of "The Lowell Offering" and Some of Its Contributors* [chs. 1–5]. *The Industrial Revolution in America.* Ed. Gary J. Kornblith. Oberlin Coll. 28 Mar. 2004 <http://www.oberlin.edu/history/GJK/H258S2000/LoomSpindle.html>.

———. "The Lowell Offering." *New England Magazine* 7 (1889): 461–67. *Making*. Path: Browse; New England Magazine; 1889; December; Lowell Offering.

Robinson, William H., Jr. *Early Black American Poets: Selections with Biographical and Critical Introductions*. Dubuque: Brown, 1969.

Rocks, James E. "Whittier's 'Snow-Bound': 'The Circle of Our Hearth' and the Discourse on Domesticity." *Studies in the American Renaissance* 17 (1993): 339–53.

Rodier, Katharine. Syllabus for American Literature, 1830–1860. Marshall U.

Roemer, Kenneth M., ed. *Native American Writers of the U.S.* Detroit: Gale Research, 1997. Vol. 175 of *Dictionary of Literary Biography*.

Roman, Ruth A. *Annie Adams Fields: The Spirit of Charles Street*. Bloomington: Indiana UP, 1990.

Romero, Lora. *Home Fronts: Domesticity and Its Critics in the Antebellum United States*. Durham: Duke UP, 1997.

Rosenfeld, Morris. *Songs from the Ghetto*. Trans. Leo Wiener. New York: Irvington, 1976.

Ross, Marlon B. *The Contours of Masculine Desire: Romanticism and the Rise of Women's Poetry*. New York: Oxford UP, 1989.

Rotundo, E. Anthony. *American Manhood: Transformations in Masculinity from the Revolution to the Modern Era*. New York: Basic, 1993.

RSAP: Resources for Research: Periodicals. Ed. Ellen Gruber Garvey. Research Soc. for Amer. Periodicals. 9 Oct. 2005 <http://home.earthlink.net/%7Eellengarvey/rsapresource1.html>.

Rubin, Gayle, "Thinking Sex: Notes for a Radical Theory of the Politics of Sexuality." *The Lesbian and Gay Studies Reader*. Ed. Henry Abelove, Michele Aina Barale, and David M. Halperin. New York: Routledge, 1993. 3–44.

Ruoff, A. LaVonne Brown. "Early Native American Women Authors: Jane Johnston Schoolcraft, Sarah Winnemucca, S. Alice Callahan, E. Pauline Johnson, and Zitkala-Ša." Kilcup, *Nineteenth-Century American Women Writers: A Critical Reader* 81–111.

Ryan, Mary P. *Women in Public: Between Banners and Ballots, 1825–1880*. Baltimore: Johns Hopkins UP, 1990.

Samuels, Shirley, ed. *The Culture of Sentiment: Race, Gender, and Sentimentality in Nineteenth-Century America*. New York: Oxford UP, 1992.

Sánchez-Eppler, Karen. *Dependent States: The Child's Part in Nineteenth-Century American Culture*. Chicago: U of Chicago P, 2005.

———. *Touching Liberty: Abolition, Feminism, and the Politics of the Body*. Berkeley: U of California P, 1993.

Santayana, George. "Genteel American Poetry." *The Genteel Tradition: Nine Essays*. Ed. Douglas L. Wilson. Cambridge: Harvard UP, 1967. 25–35.

———. "The Genteel Tradition in American Philosophy." *Winds of Doctrine: Studies in Contemporary Opinion*. London: Dent, 1940. 186–215.

Sarah Morgan Bryan Piatt. Ed. Pamela Kincheloe. Rochester Inst. of Technology. 25 Feb. 2003. 21 Oct. 2005 <http://www.rit.edu/~pjknge/Piattindex2.html>.

Sarna, Jonathan D., ed. *The American Jewish Experience.* New York: Holmes, 1997.

Savage, Barbara Dianne. *Broadcasting Freedom: Radio, War, and the Politics of Race, 1938–1948.* Chapel Hill: U of North Carolina P, 1999.

Saxton, Elna L., and Jo McClamroch. "African American Culture: Some Sites You Should Bookmark." *College and Research Libraries News* 60.1 (1999). 7 Feb. 2006. 15 Nov. 2006. <http://www.ala.org/ala/acrl/acrlpubs/crlnews/backissues1999/january1/africanamerican.htm>.

Scarberry-Garcia, Susan. *Landmarks of Healing: A Study of* House Made of Dawn. Albuquerque: U of New Mexico P, 1990.

Scharnhorst, Gary. *Bret Harte.* New York: Twayne, 1992.

———. *Charlotte Perkins Gilman.* Boston: Twayne, 1985.

———, comp. *Charlotte Perkins Gilman: A Bibliography.* Metuchan: Scarecrow, 1985.

———. "Reconstructing Here Also: On the Later Poetry of Charlotte Perkins Gilman." Karpinski, *Critical Essays* 249–68.

———. " 'Ways That Are Dark': Appropriations of Bret Harte's 'Plain Language from Truthful James.' " *Nineteenth-Century Literature* 51 (1996): 377–99.

Schomburg Center for Research in Black Culture. *Standing in the Need of Prayer: A Celebration of Black Prayer.* New York: Free, 2003.

Schoolcraft, Henry Rowe. *The Literary Voyager; or, Muzzeniegun.* Ed. Philip P. Mason. East Lansing: U of Michigan P, 1962.

Scott, Joan C. "Deconstructing Equality-versus-Difference; or, The Uses of Poststructuralist Theory for Feminists." *Theorizing Feminism: Parallel Trends in the Humanities and Social Sciences.* Ed. Anne C. Herrmann and Abigail J. Stewart. Boulder: Westview, 2001. 254–70.

Search for Specific Artworks. Smithsonian Amer. Art Museum. 7 Aug. 2006 <http://americanart.si.edu/search/search_artworks.cfm#search>.

Sears, Stephen W. *Landscape Turned Red: The Battle of Antietam.* New Haven: Ticknor, 1983.

Sedgwick, Catharine Maria. *Hope Leslie; or, Early Times in the Massachusetts.* Ed. Carolyn L. Karcher. New York: Penguin, 1998.

Seed, David. "Alone with God and Nature: The Poetry of Jones Very and Frederick Goddard Tuckerman." A. Lee 166–93.

Selected Civil War Photographs. American Memory: Historical Collections for the Natl. Digital Lib. Lib. of Congress. 15 Jan. 2000. 6 May 2004 <http://memory.loc.gov/ammem/cwphtml/cwphome.html>.

Sentilles, Renée. *Performing Menken: Adah Isaacs Menken and the Birth of American Celebrity.* Cambridge: Cambridge UP, 2003.

Sewall, Richard B. *The Life of Emily Dickinson.* Cambridge: Harvard UP, 1994.

Shakur, Tupac. *Me against the World.* Audio CD. Jive, 1995.

Shelley, Percy Bysshe. *Shelley's Poetry and Prose.* Norton Critical Ed. Ed. Donald H. Reiman and Sharon B. Powers. New York: Norton, 1977.

Sherman, Joan R., ed. *African-American Poetry of the Nineteenth Century: An Anthology.* Urbana: U of Illinois P, 1992.

———. "Afro-American Women Poets of the Nineteenth Century: A Guide to Research and Bio-bibliographies of the Poets." Hull et al. 245–60.

———, ed. *Collected Black Women's Poetry.* 4 vols. New York: Oxford UP, 1988.

———. *Invisible Poets: Afro-Americans of the Nineteenth Century.* 2nd ed. Urbana: U of Illinois P, 1989.

Show Boat. Dir. George Sidney. 1951. DVD. Warner Home Video, 2000.

Sigourney, Lydia Huntley. "The Cherokee Mother." 1831. *The Poem Book.* 6 May 2004 <http://poetrybook.freeservers.com/Page3.html>.

———. *Illustrated Poems.* Philadelphia: Carey, 1849.

———. "The Indian Summer." *The Western Home.* New York: Cary, 1854. 252–53. *Literature Online.*

———. "Last Words of an Indian Chief." Sigourney, *"Pocahontas"* 181–82.

———. *Letters of Life.* New York: Appleton, 1866.

———. "Oriska." *The Words of a Woman.* 20 Aug. 2003. 6 Dec. 2006 <http://www.photoaspects.com/lilip/poets/sigourney.html#1>.

———. "Pocahontas." Sigourney, *"Pocahontas"* 13–38.

———. *"Pocahontas" and Other Poems.* New York: Harper, 1841. *Making.* Path: Other Searches; Title: Pocahontas.

———. *Poems.* Philadelphia: Key, 1834.

———. *Poems of Lydia Howard Huntley Sigourney.* 2003. *Classic Poetry for Students Who Hate Poetry!* Ed. Linda Sue Grimes. 6 May 2004 <http://www.geocities.com/classicpoetry/lydiasigourneypoems.html>.

———. *Traits of the Aborigines of America: A Poem.* Cambridge: Cambridge UP, 1822.

Silverman, Kenneth. *Edgar A. Poe: Mournful and Never-Ending Remembrance.* London: Weidenfeld, 1993.

Simms, William Gilmore. *Selected Poems of William Gilmore Simms.* Ed. James Everett Kibler, Jr. Athens: U of Georgia P, 1990.

Sizer, Lyde Cullen. *The Political Work of Northern Women Writers and the Civil War, 1850–1871.* Chapel Hill: U of North Carolina P, 2000.

Slotkin, Richard. *Regeneration through Violence: The Mythology of the American Frontier, 1600–1860.* Middletown: Wesleyan UP, 1973.

Smith, Henry Nash. *Virgin Land: The American West as Symbol and Myth.* Cambridge: Harvard UP, 1950.

Smith, Martha Nell. "The Belle of the Belle of Amherst." *Harvard Gay and Lesbian Review* 3.1 (1996): 25–27.

———. *Rowing in Eden: Rereading Emily Dickinson.* Austin: U of Texas P, 1992.

Sorby, Angela. *Schoolroom Poets: Childhood and the Place of American Poetry, 1865–1917.* Durham: U of New Hampshire P, 2005.

"The Southern Mother's Charge." *Poetry and Music of the War between the States.* 16 Apr. 2001. 11 Dec. 2006 <http://www.civilwarpoetry.org/confederate/homefront/mother_charge.html>.

Rev. of *The Southern Poets of the War*, *War Poetry of the South*, *Beechenbrook: A Rhyme of the War. Southern Review* Apr. 1867: 273–85.

Spengemann, William C., and Jessica F. Roberts, eds. *Nineteenth-Century American Poetry.* New York: Penguin, 1996.

Stange, C. Robert. "1887 and the Making of the Victorian Canon." *Victorian Poetry* 25 (1987): 151–68.

Stannard, David E. *American Holocaust: The Conquest of the New World.* New York: Oxford UP, 1992.

Stedman, Edmund Clarence, ed. *An American Anthology, 1787–1900: Selections Illustrating the Editor's Critical Review of American Poetry in the Nineteenth Century.* New York: Greenwood, 1968.

———. *The Poetical Works of Edmund Clarence Stedman.* Boston: Houghton, 1884.

Steele, Jeffrey. "Editing Margaret Fuller's Poetry." *Margaret Fuller's Cultural Critique: Her Age and Legacy.* Ed. Fritz Fleischmann. New York: Lang, 2000. 265–74.

———. "Freeing the 'Prisoned Queen': The Development of Margaret Fuller's Poetry." *Studies in the American Renaissance* 16 (1992): 137–75.

———. *Transfiguring America: Myth, Ideology, and Mourning in Margaret Fuller's Writing.* Columbia: U of Missouri P, 2001.

Steinmetz, Lee, ed. *The Poetry of the American Civil War.* East Lansing: Michigan State UP, 1991.

Stevens, Wallace. *Collected Poetry and Prose.* Ed. Frank Kermode and Joan Richardson. New York: Lib. of Amer., 1997.

Still, William. *The Underground Rail Road.* Philadelphia: Porter, 1872.

Storey, John, ed. *Cultural Theory and Popular Culture: A Reader.* Athens: U of Georgia P, 1998.

Stowe, Harriet Beecher. *Uncle Tom's Cabin; or, Life among the Lowly.* 1852. Electronic Text Center, U of Virginia Lib. 1999. 3 Aug. 2006 <http://etext.lib.virginia.edu/toc/modeng/public/StoCabi.html>.

———. *Woman in Sacred History.* New York: Ford, 1874.

Sullivan, A. M. *A Day in Manhattan.* New York: Dutton, 1941.

Sullivan, Dolores P. *William Holmes McGuffey, Schoolmaster to the Nation.* Rutherford: Farleigh Dickinson UP, 1994.

Sundquist, Eric J., ed. *American Realism: New Essays.* Baltimore: Johns Hopkins UP, 1982.

Tangled Roots: A Project Exploring the Histories of Americans of Irish Heritage and Americans of African Heritage. Gilder Lehrman Center for the Study of Slavery, Resistance, and Abolition. 28 Mar. 2004 <http://www.yale.edu/glc/tangledroots>.

Textbook Site for The Heath Anthology of American Literature, *Fifth Edition.* Houghton Mifflin Online Study Center. 24 July 2004 <http://college.hmco.com/english/lauter/heath/4e/students/toc/index.html>.

Thaxter, Celia Laighton. *Poems of Celia Thaxter.* Ed. Sarah Orne Jewett. 2nd ed. Introd. Jane E. Vallier. Portsmouth: Randall, 1996.

Thomas, M. Wynn. "Fratricide and Brotherly Love: Whitman and the Civil War." *The Cambridge Companion to Walt Whitman.* Ed. Ezra Greenspan. Cambridge: Cambridge UP, 1995. 37–44.

Thoreau, Henry David. *Collected Essays and Poems.* New York: Lib. of Amer., 2001.

———. *Collected Poems.* Ed. Carl Bode. Baltimore: Johns Hopkins UP, 1964.

Thurston, Michael. *Making Something Happen: American Political Poetry between the World Wars.* Chapel Hill: U of North Carolina P, 2001.

Todd, Janet. *Sensibility: An Introduction.* London: Metheun, 1986.

Toll, Robert C. *Blacking Up: The Minstrel Show in Nineteenth-Century America.* London: Oxford UP, 1974.

Tompkins, Jane P. "The Other American Renaissance." Michaels and Pease 34–57.

———. *Sensational Designs: The Cultural Work of American Fiction, 1790–1860.* New York: Oxford UP, 1985.

Torres, Louis. *The World of Early Chicano Poetry, 1846–1910.* Encino: Floricanto, 1994.

Trachtenberg, Alan. *Reading American Photographs: Images as History: Matthew Brady to Walker Evans.* New York: Hill, 1989.

Traister, Bryce. "Sentimental Medicine: Oliver Wendell Holmes and the Construction of Masculinity." *Studies in American Fiction* 27.2 (1999): 205–27.

Truettner, William H. *The Natural Man Observed: A Study of Catlin's Indian Portraits.* Washington: Smithsonian, 1979.

Truettner, William H., and Nancy K. Anderson, eds. *The West as America: Reinterpreting Images of the Frontier, 1820–1920.* Washington: Smithsonian, 1991.

Tully, Sheila A. "Heroic Failures and the Literary Career of Louise Imogen Guiney." *American Transcendental Quarterly* 47–48 (1982): 171–86.

Twain, Mark. *Ode to Stephen Dowling Bots, Dec'd.* 1885. Representative Poetry Online. 1998. Ed. Ian Lancashire. 5 May 2006 <http://rpo.library.utoronto.ca/poem/2225.html>.

Ullyatt, A. G. "The Hum of Omissions / The Chant of Vacancies: Prologue to a Study of the American Long Poem Tradition and the Contribution of Some Nineteenth-Century Afro-American Poets." *American Studies International* 34.1 (1996): 43–54.

Uncle Tom's Cabin *and American Culture.* 2005. Ed. Stephen Railton. Inst. for Advanced Technology in the Humanities, U of Virginia. 28 Mar. 2004 <http://www.iath.virginia.edu/utc/sitemap.html>.

Untermeyer, Louis. *Modern American Poetry.* New York: Harcourt, 1919. *Bartleby.com.* 1999. 16 Aug. 2006 <http://www.bartleby.com/104/>. 6th rev. ed. 1942.

Vallier, Jane E. *Poet on Demand: The Life, Letters, and Works of Celia Thaxter.* Camden: Down East, 1994.

Vanderlyn, John. "The Murder of Jane McCrea." 1804. *Women of the Wild West.* 13 May 2004 <http://69.69.245.68/gallery/women/wwfron04.htm>.

Van Wienen, Mark. *Partisans and Poets: The Political Work of American Poetry in the Great War.* Cambridge: Cambridge UP, 1997.

———, ed. *Rendezvous with Death: American Poems of the Great War.* Urbana: U of Illinois P, 2002.

Vendler, Helen. "Poetry and the Mediation of Value: Whitman on Lincoln." *Michigan Quarterly Review* 39:1 (2000): 1–18.

Vergil [P. Vergili Maronis]. *Aeneidos, Liber Primus.* Ed. G. Austin. Oxford: Clarendon, 1971.

Very, Jones. *The Complete Poems.* Ed. Helen R. Deese. Athens: U of Georgia P, 1993.

VG: Voices from the Gaps: Women Artists and Writers of Color: An International Website. U of Minnesota. 2006. 26 July 2004 <http://voices.cla.umn.edu/vg/>.

Vicinus, Martha. "The Study of Nineteenth-Century Working-Class Poetry." *The Politics of Literature*. Ed. Louis Kampf and Paul Lauter. New York: Pantheon, 1972. 322–55.

Virtual Emily. U of Massachusetts. 1996. Apr. 1997. 6 June 2004 <http://www.unix.oit.umass.edu/~emilypg/index1.html>.

Wald, Alan. *Exiles from a Future Time: The Forging of the Mid-Twentieth-Century Literary Left*. Chapel Hill: U of North Carolina P, 2002.

Wald, Priscilla. *Constituting Americans: Cultural Anxiety and Narrative Form*. Durham: Duke UP, 1995.

Walker, Cheryl, ed. *American Women Poets of the Nineteenth Century*. New Brunswick: Rutgers UP, 1992.

———. "Dickinson in Context: Nineteenth-Century American Women Poets." *A Historical Guide to Emily Dickinson*. Ed. Vivian Pollak. Oxford: Oxford UP, 2004. 175–200.

———. "In Bluebeard's Closet: Women Who Write with the Wolves." *LIT: Literature Interpretation Theory* 7 (1996). 13–25.

———. *The Nightingale's Burden: Women Poets and American Culture before 1900*. Bloomington: Indiana UP, 1982.

———. "Nineteenth-Century American Women Poets Revisited." Kilcup, *Nineteenth-Century American Women Writers: A Critical Reader* 231–44.

———. "Nineteenth-Century Women Poets and Realism." *American Literary Realism* 23.3 (1991): 25–41.

Walker, Robert H. *The Poet and the Gilded Age: Social Themes in Late Nineteenth Century American Verse*. Philadelphia: U of Pennsylvania P, 1963.

The Walt Whitman Archive. Ed. Ed Folsom and Kenneth M. Price. 13 July 2004 <http://www.whitmanarchive.org/>.

Ward, Andrew. *Dark Midnight When I Rise: The Story of the Jubilee Singers Who Introduced the World to the Music of Black America*. New York: Farrar, 2000.

Ward, Patrick. *Exile, Emigration and Irish Writing*. Dublin: Irish Academic, 2001.

Wardrop, Daneen. *Word, Birth, and Culture in the Poetry of Poe, Whitman, and Dickinson*. Westport: Greenwood, 2002.

Warren, Gwendolin Sims. *Ev'ry Time I Feel the Spirit: A Hundred and One Best-Loved Psalms, Gospel Hymns, and Spiritual Songs of the African-American Church*. New York: Henry Holt, 1997.

Warren, Joyce W., ed. *The (Other) American Traditions: Nineteenth-Century Women Writers*. New Brunswick: Rutgers UP, 1993.

Warren, Joyce W., and Margaret Dickie, eds. *Challenging Boundaries: Gender and Periodization*. Athens: U of Georgia P, 2000.

Washington, Booker T. Preface. *Twenty-Four Negro Melodies* By Samuel Coleridge-Taylor. New York: Ditson, 1905. *The Booker T. Washington Papers*. U of Illinois P. Vol. 8. 112–17. History Cooperative. 2000. 14 May 2006 <http://www.historycooperative.org/btw/>.

Watts, Emily Stipes. *The Poetry of American Women from 1632 to 1945*. Austin: U of Texas P, 1977.

Wearn, Mary. "Subversive Motherhood: The Maternal Poetics of Sarah Piatt." *Legacy*, forthcoming.

Wells-Barnett, Ida B. *A Red Record. On Lynchings*. Introd. Patricia Hill Collins. New York: Humanity, 2002. 55–151.

Welter, Barbara. *Dimity Convictions: The American Woman in the Nineteenth Century*. Athens: Ohio UP, 1976.

Wertheim, Stanley. *A Stephen Crane Encyclopedia*. Westport: Greenwood, 1997.

Wexler, Laura. "Tender Violence: Literary Eavesdropping, Domestic Fiction, and Educational Reform." Samuels 9–38.

Wharton, Edith. *The House of Mirth*. Introd. Anna Quindlen. New York: Signet, 2000.

What the Hell Happened to Me? Dir. Keith Truesdell. Perf. Adam Sandler. Warner Brothers, 1996.

Whitaker, Rosemary. *Helen Hunt Jackson*. Boise: Boise State UP, 1987.

White, G. Edward. *Justice Oliver Wendell Holmes: Law and the Inner Self*. Oxford: Oxford UP, 1995.

———. *Oliver Wendell Holmes: Sage of the Supreme Court*. Oxford: Oxford UP, 2000.

Whitman, Albery Allson. *Not a Man and Yet a Man*. 1877. *African American Poetry* 17–213.

Whitman, Walt. *The Complete Poems*. Ed. Francis Murphy. New York: Penguin, 2004.

———. *"Democratic Vistas" and Other Papers*. Amsterdam: Fredonia, 2002.

———. Leaves of Grass *and Other Writings*. Norton Critical Ed. Ed. Michael Moon. New York: Norton, 2002.

———. *Poetry and Prose*. New York: Lib. of Amer., 1982.

———. "Vigil Strange I Kept on the Field One Night." 1865. Baym et al. 100–11.

———. *Walt Whitman: Selected Poems*. Ed. and introd. Harold Bloom. New York: Lib. of Amer., 2003.

———. "The Wound-Dresser." 1865. Baym et al. 113–15.

Whittier, John Greenleaf. *The Complete Poetical Works of John Greenleaf Whittier*. Boston: Houghton, 1892.

———. *Selected Poems*. New York: Lib. of Amer., 2004.

Wiebe, Robert H. *The Search for Order, 1877–1920*. New York: Hill, 1967.

Wiget, Andrew, ed. *Dictionary of Native American Literature*. New York: Garland, 1994.

———, ed. *Handbook of Native American Literature*. New York: Garland, 1996.

———. *Native American Literature*. Boston: Twayne, 1985.

Wilcox, Ella Wheeler. *Poems of Passion*. Chicago: Belford, 1883. *Ella Wheeler Wilcox*. Ella Wheeler Wilcox Soc. Ed. Richard A. Edwards. 1 July 2001. 29 Nov. 2006 <http://books.ellawheelerwilcox.org/books/passion1.htm>.

Williams, Gary. *Hungry Heart: The Literary Emergence of Julia Ward Howe*. Amherst: U of Massachusetts P, 1999.

Williams, Juan, and Quinton Dixie. *This Far by Faith: Stories from the African American Religious Experience*. New York: Morrow, 2003.

Williams, William H. A. *'Twas Only an Irishman's Dream: The Image of Ireland and the Irish in American Popular Song*. Urbana: U of Illinois P, 1996.

Wilson, Edmund. *Patriotic Gore: Studies in the Literature of the American Civil War*. New York: Norton, 1994.

Winch, Julie " 'You Have Talents—Only Cultivate Them': Philadelphia's Black Female Literary Societies and the Abolitionist Crusade." *The Abolitionist Sisterhood: Women's Political Culture in Antebellum America*. Ed. Jean Fagan Yellin and John C. Van Horne. Ithaca: Cornell UP, 1994. 101–18.

Without Sanctuary: Photographs and Postcards of Lynching in America. Comp. James Allen and John Littlefield. 2000–05. 14 May 2006 <http://www.withoutsanctuary.org/main.html>.

Wolford, Chester L. *The Anger of Stephen Crane: Fiction and the Epic Tradition*. Lincoln: U of Nebraska P, 1983.

Wolosky, Shira. "An American-Jewish Typology: Emma Lazarus and the Figure of Christ." *Prooftexts* 16.2 (1996): 113–25.

———. "The Claims of Rhetoric: Toward a Historical Poetics, 1820–1900." *American Literary History* 15.1 (2003): 14–21.

———. *Emily Dickinson: A Voice of War*. New Haven: Yale UP, 1984.

———, ed. *Major Voices: Nineteenth-Century American Women's Poetry*. New Milford: Toby, 2003.

Wordsworth, William. "Perfect Woman." *The Oxford Book of English Verse*. Ed. Arthur Thomas Quiller-Couch. Oxford: Clarendon, 1919. *Bartleby.com*. Jan. 1999. 5 Dec. 2006 <http://www.bartleby.com/101/529.html>.

Rev. of Wordsworth's poems. *Boston Quarterly Review* Apr. 1839: 139–68.

Wortham, Thomas. "William Cullen Bryant and the Fireside Poets." *Columbia Literary History of the United States*. Ed. Emory Elliott. New York: Columbia UP, 1987. 278–88.

Yellin, Jean Fagan. *Women and Sisters: The Antislavery Feminists in American Culture*. New Haven: Yale UP, 1989.

Yellin, Jean Fagan, and Cynthia D. Bond, comps. *The Pen Is Ours: A Listing of Writings by and about African-American Women before 1910 with Secondary Bibliography to the Present*. New York: Oxford UP, 1991.

Young, Bette Roth. *Emma Lazarus in Her World: Life and Letters*. Philadelphia: Jewish Pub. Soc., 1995.

Zagarell, Sandra. "Expanding 'America': Lydia Sigourney's *Sketch of Connecticut*, Catharine Sedgwick's *Hope Leslie*." *Redefining the Political Novel: American Women Writers, 1797–1901*. Ed. Sharon M. Harris. Knoxville: U of Tennessee P, 1995. 43–65.

Ziegler, Valarie H. *Diva Julia: The Public Romance and Private Agony of Julia Ward Howe*. Harrisburg: Trinity, 2003.

Zwarg, Christina. *Feminist Conversations: Fuller, Emerson, and the Play of Reading*. Ithaca: Cornell UP, 1995.

Index

Modern Language Association of America
Options for Teaching
Joseph Gibaldi, series editor

Teaching Nineteenth-Century American Poetry. Ed. Paula Bernat Bennett, Karen L. Kilcup, and Philipp Schweighauser. 2007.

Teaching Representations of the Spanish Civil War. Ed. Noël Valis. 2007.

Teaching the Representation of the Holocaust. Ed. Marianne Hirsch and Irene Kacandes. 2004.

Teaching Tudor and Stuart Women Writers. Ed. Susanne Woods and Margaret P. Hannay. 2000.

Teaching Literature and Medicine. Ed. Anne Hunsaker Hawkins and Marilyn Chandler McEntyre. 1999.

Teaching Shakespeare through Performance. Ed. Milla Cozart Riggio. 1999.

Teaching the Literatures of Early America. Ed. Carla Mulford. 1999.

Teaching Oral Traditions. Ed. John Miles Foley. 1998.

Teaching Contemporary Theory to Undergraduates. Ed. Dianne F. Sadoff and William E. Cain. 1994.

Teaching Children's Literature: Issues, Pedagogy, Resources. Ed. Glenn Edward Sadler. 1992.

Teaching Literature and Other Arts. Ed. Jean-Pierre Barricelli, Joseph Gibaldi, and Estella Lauter. 1990.

New Methods in College Writing Programs: Theories in Practice. Ed. Paul Connolly and Teresa Vilardi. 1986.

School-College Collaborative Programs in English. Ed. Ron Fortune. 1986.

Teaching Environmental Literature: Materials, Methods, Resources. Ed. Frederick O. Waage. 1985.

Part-Time Academic Employment in the Humanities: A Sourcebook for Just Policy. Ed. Elizabeth M. Wallace. 1984.

Film Study in the Undergraduate Curriculum. Ed. Barry K. Grant. 1983.

The Teaching Apprentice Program in Language and Literature. Ed. Joseph Gibaldi and James V. Mirollo. 1981.

Options for Undergraduate Language Programs: Four-Year and Two-Year Colleges. Ed. Renate A. Schulz. 1979.

Options for the Teaching of English: Freshman Composition. Ed. Jasper P. Neel. 1978.

Options for the Teaching of English: The Undergraduate Curriculum. Ed. Elizabeth Wooten Cowan. 1975.